THE AFRICA CUP
OF NATIONS 1957-2010

A Statistical Record

Romeo Ionescu

British Library Cataloguing in Publication Data
A catalogue record for this book is available from the British Library

ISBN: 978-1-86223-206-8

Copyright © 2010, SOCCER BOOKS LIMITED (01472 696226)
72 St. Peter's Avenue, Cleethorpes, N.E. Lincolnshire, DN35 8HU, England
Web site   www.soccer-books.co.uk
e-mail   info@soccer-books.co.uk

Printed in the UK by QNS Printing, Newcastle-upon-Tyne

The Africa Cup of Nations

In June 1956, during the third FIFA Congress which was held in Lisbon, the Egyptian representative Abdel Aziz Abdallah Salem, proposed that a Confederation of African Football should be created. However, his proposal was rejected by the Congress on the grounds that there were, at the time, only four African members of FIFA. Salem walked out of the Congress alongside Mohamed Abdel Halim, the Sudanese representative, an action which put pressure on FIFA and led to an agreement to form a body representing African countries.

The representatives of the four African members subsequently agreed to meet in Khartoum in February 1957 to create the Confederation of African Football with plans to organise an immediate international competition to commence after the statutes and regulations of the new body had been drawn up.

The Constitutional Assembly of the CAF took place on 8th February 1957 at the Grand Hotel in Khartoum with the four African FIFA members – Egypt, Ethiopia, Sudan and South Africa – as the founder members. Since then, the CAF has become a body of increasing importance in world football and membership has now grown to no fewer than 55 countries (including two associate members).

As planned, the first match in the new Africa Cup of Nations competition was played on 10th February 1957, two days after the formation of the CAF, but only three of the four founder members took part in this tournament, South Africa being excluded due to their refusal to field a multi-racial team under their apartheid policy. Therefore, the 1957 series consisted of just two games.

Scheduled as a bi-annual competition and held early in the year to avoid excessive heat and rainy seasons, the format has changed considerably over the years in line with the enormous increase in numbers of participating African countries.

During the period covered by this book, no fewer than 27 separate tournaments have taken place and, with the increasing globalisation of football and footballing events, press and television coverage is now spreading far beyond the shores of Africa.

This book concentrates on the statistical history of the Finals series of the competition, containing full statistics for the vast majority of these games. Regrettably, full statistics were not recorded for a handful of games from the earlier tournaments and, where this is the case, we have included the most complete information we have available. As full statistics are not available for the majority of the games played in qualification tournaments in earlier years, I have decided to include just the dates and results of qualification games.

The Author.

Finals/top scorers

	Hosts	Final	Topscorer	Gls
1957	Sudan	EGYPT – Ethiopia 4-0	Abd El-Diba (Egypt)	5
1959	Egypt	EGYPT – Sudan 2-1	Mahmoud El-Gohary (Egypt)	3
			Esam Baheeg (Egypt)	2
1962	Ethiopia	ETHIOPIA – Egypt 4-2	Abdelfattah Badawi (Egypt)	3
			Menguistou Worku (Ethiopia)	3
1963	Ghana	GHANA – Sudan 3-0	Hassan El-Shazly (Egypt)	6
			Mohamed Morsi Hussein "Reda"	4
1965	Tunisia	GHANA – Tunisia 3-2	Osei Kofi (Ghana)	3
			Ben Acheampong (Ghana)	3
			Eustache Mangle (Ivory Coast)	3
1968	Ethiopia	ZAIRE – Ghana 1-0	Laurent Pokou (Ivory Coast)	6
			Wilberforce Mfum (Ghana)	5
1970	Sudan	SUDAN – Ghana 1-0	Laurent Pokou (Ivory Coast)	8
			Hassan El-Shazly (Egypt)	5
1972	Cameroon	CONGO – Mali 3-2	Fantamady Keita (Mali)	5
			Jean-Michel M'bono (Congo)	4
			Edmond Apety "Kaolo" (Togo)	4
1974	Egypt	ZAIRE – Zambia 2-2, 2-0	Mulamba N'Daye (Zaire)	9
			Ali Abougreisha (Egypt)	4
1976	Ethiopia	MOROCCO – Guinea 1-1 (group	William N'Jo Lea (Guinea)	4
		format)	Baba Out (Nigeria), Ahmed Abdullah Faras (Morocco), Ali Gagarine (Sudan)	3
1978	Ghana	GHANA – Uganda 2-0	Phillip Omondi (Uganda)	4
			Opoku Afriye (Ghana), Segun Odegbami (Nigeria)	3
1980	Nigeria	NIGERIA – Algeria 3-0	Segun Odegbami (Nigeria)	3
			Khaled Labied (Morocco)	3
1982	Lybia	GHANA – Libya 1-1, 7-6 pen	George Alhassan (Ghana)	4
			Mohammed El Beshari (Libya), Peter Kaumba (Zambia)	3
1984	Ivory Coast	CAMEROON – Nigeria 3-1	Taher Abou Zaid (Egypt)	4
			Théophile Abéga (Cameroon)	3
1986	Egypt	EGYPT – Cameroon 0-0, 5-4 pen	Roger Milla (Cameroon)	4
			Abdoulaye Traoré (Ivory Coast)	3
			Taher Abou Zaid (Egypt)	3
1988	Morocco	CAMEROON – Nigeria 1-0	Roger Milla (Cameroon), Gamal Abdelhamid (Egypt), Lakhdar Belloumi (Algeria), Abdoulaye Traoré (Ivory Coast)	2
1990	Algeria	ALGERIA – Nigeria 1-0	Djamel Menad (Algeria)	4
			Djamel Amani (Algeria), Rashidi Yekini (Nigeria)	3
1992	Senegal	IVORY COAST – Ghana 0-0, 11-10 pen	Rashidi Yekini (Nigeria)	4
			Abedi Pelé (Ghana)	3
1994	Tunisia	NIGERIA – Zambia 2-1	Rashidi Yekini (Nigeria)	5
			Joël Tiéhi (Ivory Coast)	4

1996	South Africa	SOUTH AFRICA – Tunisia 2-0	Kalusha Bwalya (Zambia)	5
			Mark Williams, John Moshoeu (South Africa)	4
1998	Burkina Faso	EGYPT – South Africa 2-0	Benedict McCarthy (South Africa)	7
			Hossam Hassan (Egypt)	7
2000	Nigeria & Ghana	CAMEROON – Nigeria 2-2, 6-5 pen	Shaun Barlett (South Africa)	5
			Patrick Mboma, Samuel Eto'o (Cameroon)	4
2002	Mali	CAMEROON – Senegal 0-0, 3-2 pen	Patrick Mboma, Salomon Olembé (Cameroon), Julius Aghahowa (Nigeria)	3
2004	Tunisia	TUNISIA – Morocco 2-1	Francileudo dos Santos (Tunisia), Frédéric Kanouté (Mali), Patrick Mboma (Cameroon)	4
2006	Egypt	EGYPT – Ivory Coast 0-0, 4-2 pen	Samuel Eto'o (Cameroon)	5
			Ahmed Hassan (Egypt), Francileudo dos Santos (Tunisia), Pascal Feindouno (Guinea)	4
2008	Ghana	EGYPT – Cameroon 1-0	Samuel Eto'o (Cameroon)	5
			Manucho (Angola), Mohamed Aboutraika, Amr Zaky, Hosni Abd Rabbou (Egypt)	4
2010	Angola	EGYPT – GHANA 1-0	Mohamed Nagui 'Geddo'	5
			Flávio da Silva Amado (Angola), Ahmed Hassan (Egypt), Asamoah Gyan (Ghana), Seydou Keita (Mali)	3

Egypt have won the trophy 7 times (1957, 1959, 1986, 1998, 2006, 2008, 2010), Cameroon (1984, 1988, 2000, 2002) and Ghana (1963, 1965, 1978, 1982) 4 times, DR Congo (1968, 1974) and Nigeria (1980, 1994) twice, Algeria (1990), South Africa (1996), Congo (1972), Ivory Coast (1992), Ethiopia (1962), Morocco (1976), Sudan (1970) and Tunisia (2004) once.

The hosts have won the tournament on 11 occasions: Egypt (1959, 1986 and 2006), Ethiopia (1962), Ghana (1963 and 1978), Sudan (1970), Nigeria (1980), Algeria (1990), South Africa (1996), Tunisia (2004). Egypt is the only country to have won the trophy 3 consecutive times (2006, 2008, 2010). Egypt have also won 2 consecutive editions of the tournament in the past (in 1957 and 1959) as have Ghana (1963, 1965) and Cameroon (2000, 2002).

Egypt have played in the most final tournaments (21), followed by Ivory Coast (17) and Ghana (16). Ghana have played in 4 consecutive finals, between 1963 and 1970. Three players have won the trophy 3 times, all of them Egyptians: Essam El-Hadary, Ahmed Hassan, Hossam Hassan. The Cameroonian Rigobert Song has played most matches (36) spread over 8 editions (1996-2010) and Samuel Eto'o is the competition's top scorer with 18 goals.

Final places

	1957	1959	1962	1963	1965	1968	1970	1972	1974	1976	1978	1980	1982	1984
Algeria						G						2	4	3
Cameroon							G	3					G	1
DR Congo					G	1	G	4	1	G				
Congo						G		1	4		G			
Egypt	1	1	2	3			3		3	4		4		4
Ethiopia	2	3	1	4	G	4	G			G			G	
Ghana				1	1	2	2				1	G	1	G
Guinea							G	G		2		G		
Ivory Coast				3	3	4			G			G		G
Kenya								G						
Libya													2	
Malawi														G
Mali								2						
Mauritius										G				
Morocco								G		1	G	3		
Mozambique														
Nigeria				G						3	3	1	G	2
Senegal					4	G								
Sudan	3	2		2			1	G		G				
Tanzania												G		
Togo								G						G
Tunisia			3	G	2						4		G	
Uganda			4			G			G	G	2			
Upper Volta											G			
Zambia									2		G		3	

Cameroon and Nigeria have met in the final on 3 occasions with Cameroon lifting the trophy each time. Egypt have met Cameroon twice, winning both games. Egypt and Ethiopia have met in the final twice, each lifting the trophy once, as have Ghana and Sudan and also Nigeria and Algeria.

	1986	1988	1990	1992	1994	1996	1998	2000	2002	2004	2006	2008	2010
Algeria	G	3	1	G		Q	G	Q	G	Q			4
Angola						G	G				G	Q	Q
Benin										G		G	G
Burkina Faso						G	4	G	G	G			G
Cameroon	2	1	G	4		G	Q	1	1	Q	Q	2	Q
DR Congo		G		Q	Q	Q	3	G	Q	G	Q		
Congo				Q				G					
Egypt	1	G	G	D	Q	Q	1	Q	Q	G	1	1	1
Gabon						G	Q	G					G
Ghana				2	Q	4	G	Q	G		G	3	2
Guinea					G		G			Q	Q	Q	
Ivory C.	3	G	G	1	3	G	Q	G	G		2	4	Q
Kenya		G	G	G						G			
Liberia						G			G				
Libya											G		
Malawi													G
Mali					4				4	4		G	G
Morocco	4	4		G			Q	G	G	2	G	G	
Mozambique	G					G	G						G
Namibia							G					G	
Nigeria		2	2	3	1			2	3	3	3	Q	3
Rwanda										G			
Senegal	G		4	Q	Q			Q	2	Q	4	G	
Sierra Leone				G	G								
South Africa						1	2	3	Q	G	G	G	
Sudan												G	
Togo						G	G	G			G		R
Tunisia					G	2	Q	4	G	1	Q	Q	G
Zambia	G		3	Q	2	3	G	G	G		G	G	Q
Zimbabwe										G	G		

Up to and including the 2010 edition, 53 countries have participated in the Africa Cup of Nations, with 34 nations reaching the finals tournament itself. Thirteen of these nations have gone on to win the trophy and 6 others have lost in the final.

First Edition - 1957
Final Tournament (Sudan)

In February 1957 the first edition of the African Cup, inaugurated by the Sudanese Prime Minister Sayed Ismail El Azhari, took place in Khartoum following the construction of a new stadium with a capacity of 30,000 seats. This first edition took place without any qualification stage as just the four founding nations of CAF – Sudan, Egypt, Ethiopia and South Africa – were eligible to play. However, South Africa were disqualified from the tournament before it commenced when they refused to send a multi-racial team to the competition (the South African delegate, Fred W. Fell proposed to send a team comprising solely white or solely black players). The resulting disqualification gave Ethiopia a bye into the final which meant that just two matches were played in this inaugural tournament, a semi-final between the hosts Sudan and Egypt (won by the latter by the score of 2-1), then the final itself between Ethiopia and Egypt. The Egyptian team won this game convincingly with a 4-0 scoreline to win the "Abdelaziz Abdallah Salem Trophy" and be crowned as first African Champions. One interesting fact to note is that the regulations of the competition stated that all players selected must play in their own country which excluded some of the more talented footballers playing as professionals overseas.

Semi-finals

10.02.1957

SUDAN - EGYPT 1-2 (0-1)
Stade Municipal, Khartoum
Referee: Guebeyehu Doubé (Ethiopia), Attendance: 30 000
SUDAN: Faysal, Osman Dim, Boraî Selim, Ibrahim Kabir, Hedi Syam, Sayed Mostafa, Cheri, Boraî Bashir, Abu Aîla, Seddik Manzul, Hajjaj Agab.
EGYPT: Brascos, Nour El-Dali, Mosaad Daoud, Rifaat El-Fanageely, Rafaat Ateya, Samir Qotb, Ibrahim Tawfik, Abd El-Diba, Bidho, Alaa El-Hamouly, Hamdi Abdel Fattah. Trainer: Mourad Fahmy (Egypt)
Goals: Seddik Manzul (58) / Raafat Ateya (21 penalty), Abd El-Diba (72)

10.02.1957

ETHIOPIA - bye
(South Africa disqualified because of apartheid)

Final

16.02.1957

EGYPT - ETHIOPIA 4-0
Stade Municipal, Khartoum,
Referee: Mohammed Youssef (Sudan), Attendance: 30 000
EGYPT: Brascos, Nour El-Dali, Mossaad Daoud, Rifaat El-Fanageely, Hanafi Bastan, Rifaat Ateya, Samir Qotb, Ibrahim Tawfik, Abd El-Diba, Rafaat Attia, Alaa El-Homouli, Hamdi Abdel Fattah. Trainer: Mourad Fahmy (Egypt)
ETHIOPIA: Mikael Bahta Gila, Ayele, Adale, Adamu, Asefaw, Asmelash Berhe, Metaferia Kebede, Zewode, Abreha, Abde Selassie Netsere, Berhane.
Goals: Abd El-Diba (4 goals)

Second edition - 1959
Final Tournament (Egypt)

A year after the first tournament, in 1958, Egypt and Syria merged to form the United Arab Republic. The following year, when the second edition of the Africa Cup of Nations was held in Cairo, the three participating teams were the same as those who competed in 1957, Egypt, Ethiopia and Sudan. Led by Mahmoud Al-Gohary, Egypt again won the title following a round-robin tournament between the three nations this being in spite of strong protests from Sudan due to the hostility of the crowds and of the poor quality of the refereeing.

22.05.1959

EGYPT - ETHIOPIA 4-0 (2-0)
Al Ahly Stadium, Cairo
Refeere: Zivko Bajić (Yugoslavia), Attendance: 50 000
EGYPT: Adel Hekal, Tarek Selim, Yakan Hussein, Rifaat El-Fanageely, Taha Ismail, El-Shaghby, Mimi El-Sherbini, Mahmoud El-Gohary, Mohei Sharshar, Gomaa Farag, Esam Baheeg. Trainer: Pal Titkos (Hungary)
ETHIOPIA: Mikael Bahta Gila, Fisseha Wolde Amanuel, Mohammed Awad, Mekouria Tadesse, Guermaye I, Omer, Araya Kiflom, Menguistou Worku, Gebre Medhin Tesfayé, Tessema, Haile Mariam. Coach: Jiri Starosta (Czechoslovakia)
Goals: Mahmoud El-Gohary (29, 42, 73), Mimi El-Sherbini (64)

25.05.1959

SUDAN - ETHIOPIA 1-0 (1-0)
Al Ahly Stadium, Cairo
Refeere: Tsissis (Greece), Attendance: 40 000
SUDAN: Sabbit, Mutawakil, Mansour Romdane, Moutaz Ibrahim Kabir, Hedi Syam, Osman Babakr, Wahaga, Boraî Bashir, Drissa, Ettoum, Abd Zoubeir. Trainer: Josef Hada (Czechoslovakia)
ETHIOPIA: Mikael Bahta Gila, Mohammed Awad, Abdulkader, Mekouria Tadesse, Guermaye I, Nassir Berhe, Araya Kiflom, Menguistou Worku, Gebre Medhin Tesfayé, Guermaye II, Haile Mariam. Trainer: Jiri Starosta (Czechoslovakia)
Goal: Drissa (40)

29.05.1959

EGYPT - SUDAN 2-1 (1-0)
Al Ahly Stadium, Cairo
Referee: Zivko Bajić (Yugoslavia), Attendance: 60 000
EGYPT: Adel Hekal, Tarek Selim, Yakan Hussein, Rifaat El-Fanageely, Taha Ismail, Mimi El-Sherbini, Mahmoud El-Gohary, Sherif El-Far, Saleh Selim, Esam Baheeg, Alaa El-Hamouly. Trainer: Pal Titkos (Hungary)
SUDAN: Samir, Mutawakil, Hassan Abd, Moutaz Ibrahim Kabir, Hedi Syam, Mahina, Abd Zoubeir, Boraî Bashir, Drissa, Seddik Manzul, Wahaga. Trainer: Jozef Hada (Czechoslovakia)
Goals: Esam Baheeg (12, 89) / Seddik Manzul (65)

1.	EGYPT	2	2	0	0	6	1	4
2.	Sudan	2	1	0	1	2	2	2
3.	Ethiopia	2	0	0	2	0	5	0

Third edition - 1962
Qualifying Tournament

The third edition of the African Cup, originally scheduled to be held in Ethiopia in 1961 was delayed by a year following a failed coup d'état in the country in December 1960. By this time, the number of entrants had increased to nine, so knock-out qualification stages were played to decide two places in the finals tournament taking place in Addis Ababa, the other two finalists being the hosts, Ethiopia and the defending champions, Egypt. Uganda and Tunisia progressed through the qualifiers but to no avail as Egypt reached a third consecutive final where they played Ethiopia following a victory for the hosts over Tunisia in the semi-final. Ethiopia duly lifted the trophy after beating Egypt in the final although extra-time was required. From this tournament onwards, the defending champions and hosts both automatically qualified for the finals tournament without needing to progress through any qualifying matches.

Round 1
Tunisia - Morocco [Morocco withdrew]

08.04.1961 Nigeria – Ghana 0-0
30.04.1961 Ghana - Nigeria 2-2 [Nigeria won on lots]

Zanzibar – Uganda 1-2
Uganda – Zanzibar 2-0

Ethiopia – Kenya 6-1
Kenya – Ethiopia 5-4

Round 2
25.11.1961 Nigeria – Tunisia 2-1
10.12.1961 Tunisia - Nigeria [awarded 2-0 after Nigeria walked off following Chetali's equaliser after 65 minutes]
Tunisia qualified

Kenya - Uganda 0-1
Uganda - Kenya 0-1
Uganda won on lots
Kenya replaced Sudan who withdrew

Final Tournament (Ethiopia)

Semi-finals

14.01.1962

ETHIOPIA - TUNISIA 4-2 (2-1)
Haile-Selaisse stadium, Addis Abeba
Referee: Brooks (Uganda)
ETHIOPIA: Mikael Bahta Gila, Araya Kiflom, Asmelash, Berhe, Mohammed Awad, Gebre Medhin Tesfaye, Luciano Vassalo, Girma Tekle, Menguistou Worku, Italo Vassalo, Wolde Guetacheou.
TUNISIA: Ghalem, A. Azaiez, M. Sghaier, Ridha Routabi, Taoufik, Hadj Ali, Rached Meddeb, Chedli Laaouini, Moncef Chérif, Ammar Merrichko, Mohamed Salah Jedidi. Trainer: Matosic (Yugoslavia)
Goals: Luciano Vassalo (2), Girma, Menguistou Worku / Ammar Merrichko, Moncef Chérif

18.01.1962

EGYPT - UGANDA 2-1 (0-1)
Haile-Selaisse stadium, Addis Abeba
Referee: Belkhouas (Tunisia)
EGYPT: Adel Heykal, Ahmed Mostafa, Raafat, Tarek Selim, Samir Kotb, Mohamed Badawi, Mostafa Riadh, Abdelfattah Badawi, Salah Selim, Taha, Cherbini.
UGANDA: Akarad, Simabayo, Otey, Fariax, Simo, Kabeyo, Dank, Boninzi, Eosa, Jonathan, Alowo.
Goals: Abdelfattah Badawi (50), Salah Selim (57) / Jonathan (16)

Third Place Match

20.01.1962

TUNISIA – UGANDA 3-0 (1-0)
Haile-Selaisse stadium, Addis Abeba
TUNISIA: Ghalem (Kechiche), A. Azaiez, Ridha Rouatbi, M. Sghaier, T. Ben Othmane, Hadj Ali, Rached Meddeb, Mohamed Salah Jedidi, Moncef Chérif, Chedli Laaouini, Mongi Haddad.
UGANDA: Akarad, Simabayo, Otey, Fariax, Simo, Kabeyo, Dank, Boninzi, Atema, Banar, Alowa.
Goals: Mohamed Salah Jedidi, Moncef Chérif, Rached Meddeb

Final

21.01.1962

ETHIOPIA - EGYPT 4-2 (0-1, 2-2)
Haile-Selaisse stadium, Addis Abeba
Referee: Brooks (Uganda)
ETHIOPIA: Mikael Bahta Gila, Araya Kiflom, Asmelash, Berhe, Mohammed Awad, Gebre Medhin Tesfaye, Luciano Vassalo, Girma Tekle, Menguistou Worku, Italo Vassalo, Wolde Guetacheou.
EGYPT: Adel Heykal, Ahmed Mostafa, Raafat, Tarek Selim, Fanaguili, Mohamed Badawi, Chehta, Abdelfattah Badawi, Salah Selim, Taha, Cherbini.
Goals: Girma Tekle (74), Menguistou Worku (84, 117), Italo Vassalo (101) / Abdelfattah Badawi (35, 79)

Fourth edition - 1963
Qualifying Tournament

In 1963, Ghana made a first appearance in the competition as the country was selected to host the tournament. Ten countries in total entered the competition and six teams progressed to the finals held in Accra as two countries were eliminated in the qualifiers and two others withdrew. Ghana, as hosts, won their first title, comfortably beating Sudan in the final.

16.06.1963 Tunisia – Morocco 4-1
02.07.1963 Morocco – Tunisia 4-2

Egypt - Uganda w/o
Sudan - Kenya w/o

27.07.1963 Nigeria – Guinea 2-2
06.10.1963 Guinea – Nigeria 1-0

11

Guinea were disqualified for breach of the rules (for not providing neutral officials for the 2nd leg), Nigeria took their place in the finals.

Final Tournament (Ghana)
GROUP A

24.11.1963

GHANA - TUNISIA 1-1 (1-1)
Accra stadium
Referee: Hussein Imam (Egypt)
GHANA: Dodo Ankrah, Franklin Crentsil, Edward Aggrey-Fynn, Charles Addo Odametey, Ben Simmons, Oblitey, Kwame Adarkwa, Ofei Dodo, Wilberforce Awadwao Mfum, Edward Acquah, Mohamadu Salisu.
TUNISIA: Attouga, Benzerti, M. Sghaier, Mohsen Habacha, Douiri, Taoufik, Abdelmajid Chetali, Alaya Sassi, Mohamed Salah Jedidi, Ben Amor, Hamadi Henia.
Goals: Wilberforce Awadwao Mfum (9) / Mohamed Salah Jedidi (36)

26.11.1963

GHANA – ETHIOPIA 2-0
Accra stadium
Goals: Edward Acquah 2

28.11.1963

ETHIOPIA – TUNISIA 4-2
Accra stadium
Goals: Menguistou Worku 2, Girma, Gebre Medhin Tesfaye / Abdelmajid Chetali, Mohamed Salah Jedidi

1.	GHANA	2	1	1	0	3	1	3
2.	Ethiopia	2	1	0	1	4	4	2
3.	Tunisia	2	0	1	1	3	5	1

GROUP B

24.11.1963

EGYPT - NIGERIA 6-3 (4-0)
Kumasi stadium
EGYPT: Fathi Khorshid, Khalaf, Sayed El-Tabbakh, Ayman El-Esnawi, Rifaat El-Fanageely, Mimi El-Sherbini, Mohamed Morsi Hussein "Reda", Taha Ismail, Hassan El-Shazly, Mahmoud Hassan, Moustafa Reyadh
Goals: Hassan El-Shazly (42, 44, 81, 87), Mohamed Morsi Hussein "Reda" (30, 32) / Okepe (78), Bassey (82), Onya (89)

26.11.1963

EGYPT - SUDAN 2-2 (2-0)
Kumasi stadium
Referee: Miller (Ghana)

EGYPT: Fathi Khorshid (Reda), Mimi Darwish, Sayed El-Tabbakh, Ayman El-Esnawi, Rifaat El-Fanageely, Mimi El-Sherbini, Mohamed Morsi Hussein "Reda", Taha Ismail, Hassan El-Shazly, Mahmoud Hassan, Moustafa Reyadh.
SUDAN: Sabbit, Samir, Moutaz Ibrahim Kabir, Amin, Omar, Zarzour, Magid, Ibrahima, Abas Nasreldin Gaksa, Nagy, Jagdoul.
Goals: Hassan El-Shazly (5), Mohamed Morsi Hussein "Reda" (7) / Abas Nasreldin Gaksa (60, 75)

28.11.1963

SUDAN - NIGERIA 4-0
Kumasi stadium
Goals: Abas Nasreldin Gaksa 2, El-Kawarti, Jakdoul

1.	SUDAN	2	1	1	0	6	2	3
2.	Egypt	2	1	1	0	8	5	3
3.	Nigeria	2	0	0	2	3	10	0

Third Place Match

30.11.1963

EGYPT – ETHIOPIA 3-0 (0-0)
Accra stadium
EGYPT: Fathi Khorshid, Mimi Darwish, Sayed El-Tabbakh, Ayman El-Esnawi, Rifaat El-Fanageely, Mimi El-Sherbini, Mohamed Morsi Hussein "Reda", Taha Ismail, Hassan El-Shazly, Mahmoud Hassan, Moustafa Reyadh.
Goals: Mohamed Morsi Hussein "Reda", Hassan El-Shazly, Taha Ismail

Final

1.12.1963

GHANA – SUDAN 3-0 (0-0)
Accra stadium
Referee: Abdelkader (Tunisia)
GHANA: Dodo Ankrah, Franklin Crentsil, Edward Aggrey-Fynn, Charles Addo Odametey, Ben Simmons, Oblitey, Kwame Adarkwa, Ofei Dodo, Wilberforce Awadwao Mfum, Edward Acquah, Mohamadu Salisu.
SUDAN: Sabbit, Samir, Moutaz Ibrahim Kabir, Amin, Omar, Zarzour, Magid, Ibrahima, Abas Nasreldin Gaksa, Nagy, Jagdoul.
Goals: Edward Aggrey-Finn (62 penalty), Wilberforce Awadwao Mfum (72, 82)

Fifth edition - 1965
Qualifying Tournament

The finals tournament for the 1965 competition was to be held in Tunisia but, following a speech in March 1965 by the Tunisian President, Habib Bourguiba, which advocated dialogue between Palestine and Israel, a number of Islamic nations refused to participate. Egypt (then still known as the United Arab Republic) had qualified for the finals but withdrew and Congo-Leopoldville took their place. Two years after winning their first title, Ghana showed the strength of their football as they again lifted the Africa Cup of Nations by beating the hosts 3-2, this being despite the fact that their squad contained just two returning members from the 1963 team.

13

28.02.1965 Senegal – Guinea 2-0
31.03.1965 Guinea – Senegal 3-0
25.04.1965 Senegal – Mali 2-0
Senegal qualified

28.02.1965 Ethiopia – Uganda 2-0
28.03.1965 Sudan – Ethiopia 2-1
04.04.1965 Uganda – Egypt 5-1
07.04.1965 Sudan – Kenya 4-2
25.04.1965 Ethiopia – Sudan 2-1
Ethiopia qualified

Egypt and Ivory Coast also qualified.

Final Tournament (Tunisia)

GROUP A

12.11.1965

TUNISIA - ETHIOPIA 4-0 (1-0)
Stade Zouiten, Tunis
Referee: Fula (Congo)
TUNISIA: Attouga, Benzerti, Douiri, Mohsen Habacha, Ahmed Lamine, Abdelmajid Chetali, Tahar Chaibi, Alaya Sassi, Gribba (A. Lahmar), Mongi Dalhoum, Mohamed Salah Jedidi.
ETHIOPIA: Abebe Guetacheou, Negassie, Araya Kiflom, Yehedego, Mohammed Awad, Feseha, Luciano Vassalo, Ismael, Menguistou Worku, Italo Vassalo, Shewangezaw.
Goals: Tahar Chaibi (32), Mohamed Salah Jedidi (62), Mongi Dalhoum (80), A. Lahmar (84)

14.11.1965

SENEGAL - TUNISIA 0-0
Stade Zouiten, Tunis
Referee: Djira (Ivory Coast)
TUNISIA: Attouga, Benzerti, Douiri, Mohsen Habacha, Ahmed Lamine, Abdelmajid Chetali, Tahar Chaibi, Alaya Sassi, Gribba, Mongi Dalhoum, Mohamed Salah Jedidi.
SENEGAL: Toumani, Y. Diagne, Amadou Mustapha Dieng, Issa M'Baye, Ousmane Camara, Louis Gomis, Louis Camara, Omar Gueye, Matar Niang, A. Diop, Demba Thioye.

19.11.1965

SENEGAL - ETHIOPIA 5-1 (1-1)
Stade Zouiten, Tunis
Referee: Wontumi (Ghana)
SENEGAL: Toumani, Y. Diagne, Issa M'Baye, Abdoulaye Diallo, Ousmane Camara, Louis Gomis, Louis Camara, Omar Gueye, Moussa Baye, Matar Niang, Demba Thiaye.
ETHIOPIA: Abebe Guetacheou, Gebrehiwot Bekurtsion, Negassie, Yehedego, Mohammed Awad, Feseha, Luciano Vassalo, Ismael, Menguistou Worku, Nuer, Shewangezaw.
Goals: Louis Camara (3, 52), Matar Niang (48, 53), Omar Guèye (37) / Luciano Vassalo (12 penalty)

1.	TUNISIA	2	1	1	0	4	0	3
2.	Senegal	2	1	1	0	5	1	3
3.	Ethiopia	2	0	0	2	1	9	0

Tunisia qualified on the toss of a coin.

14

GROUP B

12.11.1965

GHANA - CONGO-LÉOPOLDVILLE 5-2 (2-1)
Stade Maarouf, Sousse
Referee: Seyoum (Ethiopia)
GHANA: John Naawu, Ben Kusi, Willy Evans, Addo Odametey, Edward Acquah, Kwame Nti, Ben Acheampong, Osei Kofi, Jones Attuquayefio, Kofi Pare, Frank Odoi.
CONGO: Makiadi, Katumba, Antoine Lessa, Mabela, Mbuli, Mafu Kibonge, Diantela, Kalala, Kabala, Kabeya, Albert Mwila.
Goals: Osei Kofi (13), Ben Acheampong (18, 59), Jones Attuquayefio (84, 89) / Kalala (43 penalty, 45)

14.11.1965

IVORY COAST – CONGO LEOPOLDVILLE 3-0 (1-0)
Stade Mehiri, Sfax
Referee: Zarrouk (Tunisia)
IVORY COAST: Keita, Niankoury, Wawa, Konan, Diagou, Zadi, Yaboue, Gnaore, Ernest Kallet Bially, Eustache Mangle, Sylla.
CONGO: Ngoie, Katumba, Mabela, Albert Mwila, Antoine Lessa, Diantela, Mawa Mokili, Kalala, Mbula, Kabeya.
Goals: Eustache Mangle (14, 59, 80)

19.11.1965

GHANA - IVORY COAST 4-1 (2-0)
Stade Municipal, Bizerte
Referee: Ngom (Senegal)
GHANA: John Naawu, Edward Acquah, Willy Evans, Addo Odametey, Ludrot, Kwame Nti, Agyeman Gyau, Osei Kofi, Ben Acheampong, Kofi Pare, Salami.
IVORY COAST: Keita (Dossou), Niankoury, Wawa, Konan, Diagou, Zadi, Yaboue, Joseph Bleziri, Ernest Kallet Bially, Eustache Mangle, Tahi.
Goals: Ben Acheampong (20), Kwame Nti (43), Ludrot (52), Osei Kofi (70) / Joseph Bleziri (66)

1.	GHANA	2	2	0	0	9	3	4
2.	Ivory Coast	2	1	0	1	4	4	2
3.	Congo	2	0	0	2	2	8	0

Third Place Match

21.11.1965

IVORY COAST – SENEGAL 1-0 (1-0)
Stade Zouiten, Tunis
Referee: Meziah (Algeria)
IVORY COAST: Dossou, Idrissa, Wawa, Konan, Diagou, Zadi, Bazo, Joseph Bleziri, Eustache Mangle, Yaboue, Tahi.
SENEGAL: Massata, Y. Diagne, Issa M'Baye, Abdoulaye Diallo, Ousmane Camara, Louis Gomis, Louis Camara, Omar Gueye, Moussa Baye, A. Diop, Fall.
Goal: Yoboue (35)

Final

21.11.1965

GHANA - TUNISIA 3-2 (1-0, 2-2)
Stade Zouiten, Tunis
Referee: Chekaimi (Algeria)
GHANA: John Naawu, Ben Kusi, Edward Acquah, Willy Evans, Addo Odametey, Kwame Nti, Mensah, Osei Kofi, Jones Attuquaeyefio, Kofi Pare, Frank Odoi.
TUNISIA: Attouga, Benzerti, Douiri, Mohsen Habacha, Ahmed Lamine, Abdelmajid Chetali, Tahar Chaibi, Alaya Sassi, Gribba (Lahmar), Mongi Dalhoum, Mohamed Salah Jedidi. Trainer: Mokhtar Ben Nacef
Goals: Frank Odoi (37, 96), Osei Kofi (79) / Abdelmajid Chetali (47), Tahar Chaibi (67)

Sixth edition - 1968
Qualifying Tournament

The sixth edition of the competition was not held until 1968 when Ethiopia hosted the finals tournament. A change in the regulations of the competition in May 1967 allowed each team to select up to two players who were playing outside their own country. No fewer than twenty nations participated in the qualifying round of this competition and the eight countries who reached the finals were split into two groups, each playing a round-robin of three games. At the end of these games, the first two teams from each group progressed to the semi-finals and this system remained in place for finals tournaments until 1992. In 1968, Congo-Kinshasa (previously Congo-Leopoldville and later known as Zaire), won its first continental title after beating Ghana in the final, notably with assistance from two professional players who were now eligible to play. From 1968 onwards, the tournament has been held biennially.

Group 1

29.07.1967 Guinea - Senegal 3-0
02.08.1967 Senegal - Liberia 4-1
16.08.1967 Liberia – Guinea 2-2
11.10.1967 Senegal - Guinea 4-1
01.11.1967 Guinea – Liberia 3-0
15.11.1967 Liberia – Senegal 1-1

1.	Senegal	4	2	1	1	9	6	5
2.	Guinea	4	2	1	1	9	6	5
3.	Liberia	4	0	2	2	4	10	2

Playoff
22.11.1967 Senegal - Guinea 2-1

Group 2

Algeria - Mali 1-0
Mali - Upper Volta 4-0
Upper Volta - Algeria 1-2
Mali - Algeria 0-3
Upper Volta - Mali 0-1
Algeria - Upper Volta 3-1

1.	ALGERIA	4	4	0	0	9	2	8
2.	Mali	4	2	0	2	5	4	4
3.	Upper Volta	4	0	0	4	2	10	0

Group 3

Ivory Coast - Nigeria 2-0
Nigeria - Togo 4-2
Togo - Ivory Coast 0-2
Nigeria - Ivory Coast 0-0
Togo – Nigeria 1-0
Ivory Coast - Togo 3-0

1.	IVORY COAST	4	3	1	0	7	0	7
2.	Nigeria	4	1	1	2	4	5	3
3.	Togo	4	1	0	3	3	9	2

Group 4

First Round
Egypt - Libya3-2
Libya - Egypt 2-2

Uganda - Kenya 2-1
Kenya - Uganda 3-3

Second Round
Uganda - Egypt 0-1
Egypt - Uganda [Egypt withdrew]

Group 5

05.02.1967 Tunisia – Cameroon 4-0
19.02.1967 Tunisia - Congo-Brazzaville 1-1
02.08.1967 Congo-Brazzaville - Cameroon 2-1
16.08.1967 Cameroon - Tunisia 2-0
Congo-Brazzaville - Tunisia [Tunisia withdrew]
Cameroon - Congo-Brazzaville not played

1.	CONGO-BRAZZAVILLE	3	2	1	0	3	2	5
2.	Tunisia	4	1	1	2	5	3	3
3.	Cameroon	3	1	0	2	3	6	2

Group 6

First Round
Congo Kinshasa - Sudan 3-2
Sudan - Congo Kinshasa 1-0
Sudan - Congo Kinshasa 1-2

Tanzania - Mauritius 1-0
Mauritius - Tanzania 1-1

17

Second Round
Congo Kinshasa - Tanzania [Tanzania withdrew]

Final Tournament (Ethiopia)

GROUP A

12.01.1968

ETHIOPIA - UGANDA 2-1 (1-0)
Haile Selassie stadium, Addis Abeba
Referee: Kandil (Egypt), Attendance: 20.000
ETHIOPIA: Abebe Guetacheou, Gebrehiwot Bekurtsion, Abraha Araya, Mohammed Awad, Araya Kiflom, Feseha, Luciano Vassalo, Girma, Shewangezaw, Menguistou Worku, Wolde Guetacheou.
UGANDA: Joseph Masajjage, Lokwago, Ezaga, Ibrahim Dafala, Parry Okech, David Otti, Baraza, Diabya, Waswr, Philip 'Polly' Ouma, Denis Obua.
Goals: Girma, Luciano Vassalo (pen) / Philip 'Polly' Ouma

12.01.1968

IVORY COAST – ALGERIA 3-0 (2-0)
Haile Selassie stadium, Addis Abeba
Referee: Gueye (Senegal), Attendance: 20.000
IVORY COAST: Keita, Nankoury, Zadi, Konan, Diagou, Bozon, Wawa, Joseph Bleziri, Eustache Mangle, Laurent Pokou, Tahi.
ALGERIA: Mohammed Abrouk, Messaoud Belloucif, Lemoui, Bouden, Ali Attoui, Hacene Djemaa, Seridi, Beroudji, Nourredine Hachouf (Hassen Lalmas), Mokhtar Khalem, Boualem Amirouche.
Goals: Bozon (15), Laurent Pokou (25, 65)

14.01.1968

ETHIOPIA - IVORY COAST 1-0 (0-0)
Haile Selassie stadium, Addis Abeba
Referee: Saleh (Sudan)
Goal: Gebrehiwot Bekurtsion (86)

14.01.1968

ALGERIA – UGANDA 4-0 (2-0)
Haile Selassie stadium, Addis Abeba
Referee: Mahombe (Congo Kinshasa)
ALGERIA: Laribi Krimo, Messaoud Belloucif, Belbekri, Lemoui, Ali Attoui, Abdi, Bechra, Selmi, Hassen Lalmas, Mokhtar Khalem, Achour.
UGANDA: Joseph Masajjage, Lokwago, Ezaga, Ibrahim Dafala, Parry Okech, David Otti, Baraza, Diabya, Waswr, Philip 'Polly' Ouma, Denis Obua.
Goals: Hassen Lalmas (15, 25, 70), Khalem (60)

16.01.1968

IVORY COAST – UGANDA 2-1 (1-0)
Haile Selassie stadium, Addis Abeba
Referee: George Lamptey (Ghana), Attendance: 15.000
Goals: Laurent Pokou, Eustache Mangle / Denis Obua

16.01.1968

ETHIOPIA – ALGERIA 3-1 (3-0)
Haile Selassie stadium, Addis Abeba
Referee: Angaud (Congo Brazaville), Attendance: 15.000
ETHIOPIA: Abebe Guetacheou, Gebrehiwot Bekurtsion, Abraha Araya, Mohammed Awad, Araya Kiflom, Feseha, Luciano Vassalo, Girma, Shewangezaw, Menguistou Worku, Wolde Guetacheou.
ALGERIA: Laribi Krirno, Bouyahi, Lemoui, Belbekri, Ali Attoui, Hacene Djemaa, Abdi, Selmi, Hassen Lalmas, Nourredine Hachouf (Boualem Amirouche), Achour.
Goals: Menguistou Worku (16), Shewangezaw (19), Luciano Vassalo (27 penalty) / Boualem Amirouche (68)

1.	ETHIOPIA	3	3	0	0	6	2	3
2.	IVORY COAST	3	2	0	1	5	2	2
3.	Algeria	3	1	0	2	5	6	1
4.	Uganda	3	0	0	3	2	8	1

GROUP B

12.01.1968

GHANA - SENEGAL 2-2 (0-1)
Saba stadium, Asmara
Referee: Attar "El Diba" (Egypt)
GHANA: Robert Mensah, Franklin Crentsil, John Eshun, Addo Odametey, Ben Kusi, Ibrahim Sunday, Edward Acquah, Osei Kofi, Frank Odoi, Wilberforce Awadwao Mfum, Stephens.
SENEGAL: Amady Thiam, Yerim, Amadou Mustapha Dieng, Issa M'Baye, Alioune Djibrill 'Petit' Gueye, Louis Gomis Diop, Louis Camara, Ndiaye, Moussa Baye, Doudou Diongue, Yatma Diop.
Goals: Osei Kofi (63), Wilberforce Awadwao Mfum (87) / Doudou Diongue (10), Yatma Diop (65)

12.01.1968

CONGO KINSHASA - CONGO-BRAZZAVILLE 3-0 (2-0)
Saba stadium, Asmara
Referee: Khlifi (Algeria)
CONGO KINSHASA: Robert M'wamba Kazadi, Bilengi, Tshimanga, Kutumba, Mange, Kabamba, Muwawa, Mokili, Kasongo, Mafu Kibonge, Mungamuni.
CONGO BRAZAVILLE: Maxime Matsima, Boukaka, Bilanzoulou, Koko, Alphonse Niangou, Ondiole, Nzabana, Bikouri, Foundou, Jean-Michele M'Bono, Foutika.
Goals: Muwawa (19), Kabamba (27 penalty, 51)

14.01.1968

SENEGAL - CONGO-BRAZZAVILLE 2-1 (1-1)
Saba stadium, Asmara
Referee: M.A. Rajab (Uganda)
Goals: Yatma Diop (27), Yatma Diouck (86) / Foutika (31)

14.01.1968

GHANA - CONGO KINSHASA 2-1 (1-1)
Saba stadium, Asmara
Referee: Boua (Ivory Coast)

GHANA: John Naawu, Franklin Crentsil, John Eshun, Addo Odametey, Ben Kusi, Ibrahim Sunday, Frank Odoi, Osei Kofi, Jones Attuquayefio, Wilberforce Awadwao Mfum, Malik.
CONGO KINSHASA: Robert M'wamba Kazadi, Albert M'wanza Mukombo, Tshimanga, Katumba, Mange, Kabamba, Muwawa, Mokili, Kasongo, Kalala, Mungamuni.
Goals: Osei Kofi (17 penalty), Wilberforce Awadwao Mfum (84) / Mohili (42)

16.01.1968

CONGO KINSHASA – SENEGAL 2-1
Saba stadium, Asmara
Referee: Terckgen (Ethiopia)
CONGO KINSHASA: Robert M'wamba Kazadi, Bilengi, Tshimanga, Katumba, Albert M'wanza Mukombo, Kabamba, Muwawa, Raoul Mantanu Kidumu, Kasongo, Kembo, Mungamuni.
SENEGAL: Amady Thiam, Yerim, Amadou Mustapha Dieng, Issa M'Baye, Alioune Djibrill 'Petit' Gueye, Louis Gomis Diop, Louis Camara, Moussa Baye, Doudou Diongue, Yatma Diouck, Yatma Diop.
Goals: Raoul Mantanu Kidumu, Tshimanga / Yatma Diouck

16.01.1968

GHANA - CONGO-BRAZZAVILLE 3-1 (2-1)
Saba stadium, Asmara
Referee: Awanda (Kenya)
Goals: Osei Kofi 2, Wilberforce Awadwao Mfum / Jean-Michel M'bono

1.	GHANA	3	2	1	0	7	4	5
2.	CONGO KINSHASA	3	2	0	1	6	3	4
3.	Senegal	3	1	1	1	5	5	3
4.	Congo-Brazzaville	3	0	0	3	2	8	0

Semi-finals

19.01.1968

ETHIOPIA - CONGO KINSHASA 2-3 (1-2,2-2)
Haile Selassie stadium, Addis Abeba
Referee: Kandil (Egypt), Attendance: 25.000
ETHIOPIA: Abebe Guetacheou, Gebrehiwot Bekurtsion, Araya Kiflom, Abraha Araya, Mohammed Awad, Feseha, Luciano Vassalo, Girma, Menguistou Worku, Wolde Guetacheou, Berhe.
CONGO KINSHASA: Robert M'wamba Kazadi, Mange, Tshimanga, Katumba, Albert M'wanza Mukombo, Muwawa, Kasongo, Kalala, Raoul Mantanu Kidumu, Kemba, Mungamuni.
Goals: Luciano Vassalo (25), Menguistou Worku (65) / Raoul Mantanu Kidumu (3), Mungamuni (16, 100)

19.01.1968

GHANA - IVORY COAST 4-3 (2-1)
Saba stadium, Asmara
Referee: Attar El-Diba (Egypt)
GHANA: Robert Mensah, Franklin Crentsil, John Eshun, Addo Odametey, Ben Kusi, Ibrahim Sunday, Edward Acquah, Osei Kofi, Frank Odoi, Wilberforce Awadwao Mfum, Stephens.
IVORY COAST: Keita, Niankoury, Zadi, Konan, Diagou, Bozon, Wawa, Joseph Bleziri, Eustache Mangle, Pokou, Tahi.
Goals: Wilberforce Awadwao Mfum 2, Ibrahim Sunday, Frank Odoi / Laurent Pokou 2, Konan Henri (penalty)

Third Place Match

21.01.1968

IVORY COAST – ETHIOPIA 1-0 (1-0)
Haile Selassie stadium, Addis Abeba
IVORY COAST: Keita, Niankoury, Zadi, Konan, Yapobi, Bozon, Baza, Joseph Bleziri, Laurent Pokou, Yovan, Tahi.
Goal: Laurent Pokou (28)

Final

21.01.1968

CONGO KINSHASA - GHANA 1-0 (0-0)
Haile Selassie stadium, Addis Abeba
Referee: Attar El-Diba (Egypt)
CONGO KINSHASA: Robert M'wamba Kazadi, Mange, Tshimanga, Katumba, Albert M'wanza Mukombo, Mafu Kibonge, Kasongo, Kalala, Raoul Mantanu Kidumu, Kembo, Mungamuni. Trainer: Csanadi (Hungary)
GHANA: John Naawu, Franklin Crentsil, John Eshun, Addo Odametey, Ben Kusi, Ibrahim Sunday, Frank Odoi, Osei Kofi, Jones Attuquayefio, Wilberforce Awadwao Mfum, Malik. Trainer: Marotzke (Germany)
Goal: Kalala (66)

Seventh edition - 1970
Qualifying Tournament

The finals tournament of the 7th edition of the Africa Cup of Nations was held in Sudan in 1970 and the hosts themselves lifted the trophy for the first and, so far, only time in their history beating Ghana who had reached their fourth consecutive final. Twenty-three countries entered the qualifiers although 4 of them withdrew in the first round without playing.

First Round

09.03.1969 Algeria – Morocco 2-0
22.03.1969 Morocco – Algeria 1-0

10.08.1969 Guinea - Togo 4-0
24.08.1969 Togo – Guinea 1-1

16.02.1969 Kenya – Tanzania 0-1
01.03.1969 Tanzania – Kenya 1-1

17.11.1968 Zambia – Mauritius 2-2
08.12.1968 Mauritius – Zambia 2-3

10.08.1969 Uganda - Cameroon 1-1
24.08.1969 Cameroon - Uganda 2-0

Egypt – Somalia w/o
Mali - Upper Volta w/o
Niger - Nigeria w/o
Senegal - Sierra Leone w/o

Second Round

19.09.1969 Egypt - Algeria 1-0
28.09.1969 Algeria - Egypt 1-1

08.10.1969 Ethiopia - Tanzania 7-0
22.10.1969 Tanzania - Ethiopia 1-2

17.08.1969 Ghana - Niger 6-0
21.09.1969 Niger - Ghana 1-9

08.10.1969 Mali - Ivory Coast 0-0
22.10.1969 Ivory Coast – Mali 4-0

08.10.1969 Senegal - Guinea 1-1
22.10.1969 Guinea - Senegal 4-3

08.10.1969 Zambia - Cameroon 2-2
22.10.1969 Cameroon - Zambia 2-1

Final Tournament (Sudan)

GROUP A

06.02.1970

CAMEROON - IVORY COAST 3-2 (0-2)
Municipal, Khartoum
Referee: Mostafa Kamel (Egypt), Attendance: 20.000
CAMEROON: Jean Atangana Ottou, Evou, Pascal Owona, Essomba, Jean Moukoko, Jean-Marie Tsébo, Gabriel Abossolo, Jean Moutassié, Emmanuel Koum, Dieudonné Bassanguen, Jean-Baptiste Ndoga. Trainer: Raymond Fobété
IVORY COAST: Fanny, Wawa, Denis Gnegnery, Jean-Baptiste Akassou Akran, Diagou, Kallet, Bazo, Gnaore, Laurent Pokou, Lorougnon, Tahi.
Goals: Emmanuel Koum (57, 66), Jean-Baptiste Ndoga (60) / Laurent Pokou (25, 45)

6.02.1970

SUDAN - ETHIOPIA 3-0 (1-0)
Municipal, Khartoum
Referee: Faber (Guinea), Attendance: 20.000
SUDAN: Abraham Abdel Aziz, Mahmoud Said Salim James, Nasr Awad Musa 'Koka', Amin, Salih Samir, Bushra, Dahish, El-Issed, Ali Gagarine, Abas Nasreldin Gaksa, Hasabou El Rasoul Omer.
ETHIOPIA: Abebe Guetacheou, Gebrehiwot Bekurtsion, Berehe, Araya, Afework, Feseha, Luciano Vassalo, Schwangezaw, Menguistou Worku, Italo Vassalo, Tariku Engdework.
Goals: Ali Gagarine (43), Hasabou El Rasoul Omer (47), Abas Nasreldin Gaksa (85)

8.02.1970

CAMEROON - ETHIOPIA 3-2 (2-1)
Municipal, Khartoum
Referee: Robert Quarshie (Ghana), Attendance: 20.000

CAMEROON: Jean Atangana Ottou, Evou, Pascal Owona, Essomba, Jean Moukoko, Jean-Marie Tsébo, Dieudonné Bassanguen, Gabriel Abossolo, Jean Moutassié, Jean Manga-Onguené, Jean-Baptiste Ndoga.
ETHIOPIA: Mikael, Afework, Gebrehiwot Bekurtsion, Berehe, Gezahane, Wolde Guetacheou (H. Gaber), Gueremou, Menguistou Worku, Schewangezaw, Feseha, Tariku Engdework.
Goals: Tsebo (21), Jean Manga-Onguené (43), Jean-Baptiste Ndoga (70) / Menguistou Worku (12, 75)

8.02.1970

IVORY COAST - SUDAN 1-0 (0-0)
Municipal, Khartoum
Referee: A. Muhombe (Congo), Attendance: 20.000
IVORY COAST: Fanny, Andre Obrou, Denis Gnegnery, Jean-Baptiste Akassou Akran, Diagou, Kallet, Bazo, Gnaore, Laurent Pokou, Yoro (Losseni), Tahi.
SUDAN: Abraham Abdel Aziz, Mahmoud Said Salim James, Nasr Awad Musa 'Koka', Zaki, Salih Samir, Bushra, Dahish, El-Issed, Ali Gagarine, Abas Nasreldin Gaksa, Hasabou El Rasoul Omer.
Goal: Tahi (89)

10.02.1970

IVORY COAST - ETHIOPIA 6-1 (2-1)
Municipal, Khartoum
Referee: George Lamptey (Ghana)
IVORY COAST: Fanny, Andre Obrou, Denis Gnegnery, Jean-Baptiste Akassou Akran, Diagou, Kallet, Bazo, Gnaore, Laurent Pokou, Losseni, Tahi.
ETHIOPIA: Mikael, Afework, Gebrehiwot Bekurtsion, Berehe, Gezahane, Wolde Guetacheou, Gueremou, Menguistou Worku, Schewangezaw, Feseha, Tariku Engdework.
Goals: Losseni (16), Laurent Pokou (21, 60, 71, 80, 87) / Menguistou Worku (33)

10.02.1970

SUDAN - CAMEROON 2-1 (1-1)
Municipal, Khartoum
Referee: N'Gom (Senegal)
SUDAN: Abraham Abdel Aziz, El Sir Abdalla 'Kaunda' Mohammed, Suliman, Amin, Mahmoud Said Salim James, Negmeldeen, Bushra, El-Issed, Dahish, Abas Nasreldin Gaksa, Hasabou El Rasoul Omer.
CAMEROON: Jean Atangana Ottou, Evou, Pascal Owona, Essomba, Jean Moukoko, Jean-Marie Tsébo, Dieudonné Bassanguen, Gabriel Abossolo, Mouthe, Emmanuel Koum, Jean Manga-Onguené.
Goals: Abas Nasreldin Gaksa (20), Hasabou El Rasoul Omer (60) / Jean-Marie Tsébo (34)

1.	IVORY COAST	3	2	0	1	9	4	4
2.	SUDAN	3	2	0	1	5	2	4
3.	Cameroon	3	2	0	1	7	6	4
4.	Ethiopia	3	0	0	3	3	12	0

GROUP B

7.02.1970

GHANA - ZAIRE 2-0 (2-0)
Municipal, Wad Medani
Referee: Gindil (Sudan), Attendance: 18.000

23

GHANA: Robert Mensah, Edward Boye, Alex Mingle (Mango), John Eshun, Edward Acquah, Joe Ghartey, Ibrahim Sunday, Robert Foley, Jones Attuquayefio, Kwasi Owusu, Malik.
ZAIRE: Robert M'wamba Kazadi, Likimba, Raymond Tshimen Bwanga, Katumba, Albert M'wanza Mukombo, Mafu Kibonge, Raoul Mantanu Kidumu, Mokili, Kalonzo (Leonard Saidi), Kembo, Emmanuel Etepe Kakoko (Adelard Maku Mayanga).
Goals: Kwasi Owusu (29, 32)

7.02.1970

EGYPT - GUINEA 4-1 (2-1)
Municipal, Wad Medani
Referee: Tesfaye (Ethiopia), Attendance: 18.000
EGYPT: Hassan Mokhtar, Mahmoud El-Seyagui, Bobbo, Mimi Darwish, Hany Moustafa, Shehta, Hassan El-Shazly, Reda, Taha Basry, Ali Abougreisha, Farouk El-Sayed.
GUINEA: Sano, Pierre Bangoura, Edente, Ali Ibrahim 'Kolev' Keita, Sekou Conde, Blinky, Chérif Souleymane, Ousmane Thiam Tollo, Ali Ibrahim 'Petit Sory' Keita, Kandia, Mamadou Maxime Camara.
Goals: Ali Abougreisha (5, 10), Taha Basri (66), Hassan El-Shazly (73 penalty) / Edenté (25 penalty)

9.02.1970

ZAIRE - GUINEA 2-2 (0-1)
Municipal, Wad Medani
Referee: Koudou Poll (Ivory Coast)
ZAIRE: Robert M'wamba Kazadi, Mange, Mamuya, Katumba, Albert M'wanza Mukombo, Leonard Saidi, Mafu Kibonge, Tshibangu, Wamunda Tshianbu, Kalonzo, Mungamuni.
GUINEA: Morlaye, Campbell, Ali Ibrahim 'Kolev' Keita, Jacob Bangoura, Sekou Conde, Blinky, Edente, Ali Ibrahim 'Petit Sory' Keita, Kandia, Chérif Souleymane, Mamadou Maxime Camara.
Goals: Kalonzo (70), Mungamuni (72) / Ali Ibrahim 'Petit Sory' Keita (5), Edente (55 penalty)

9.02.1970

EGYPT - GHANA 1-1 (0-0)
Municipal, Wad Medani
Referee: Kandem (Cameroon)
EGYPT: Hassan Mokhtar, Mahmoud El-Seyagui, Bobbo, Mimi Darwish, Hany Moustafa, Shawki Hussein, Hassan El-Shazly, Sayed Abdel Razek, Taha Basry, Ali Abougreisha, Farouk El-Sayed.
GHANA: Robert Mensah, Edward Boye, Alex Mingle, John Eshun, Edward Acquah, Joe Ghartey, Ibrahim Sunday, Robert Foley, Jones Attuquayefio, Kwasi Owusu, Malik.
Goals: Sayed Abdel Razek (70) / Ibrahim Sunday (60)

11.02.1970

GUINEA - GHANA 1-1 (1-0)
Municipal, Wad Medani
Referee: Khelifi Ahmed (Algeria)
GUINEA: Morlaye, Jacob Bangoura, Campell, Ali Ibrahim 'Kolev' Keita, Sekou Conde, Blinky, Chérif Souleymane, Ousmane Thiam Tollo, Ali Ibrahim 'Petit Sory' Keita, Mama Douba N'Dongo Camara, Mamadou Maxime Camara.
GHANA: Robert Mensah, Edward Boye, Alex Mingle, John Eshun, Edward Acquah, Joe Ghartey, Ibrahim Sunday, Robert Foley, Jones Attuquayefio, Kwasi Owusu, Ankrah.
Goals: Ousmane Thiam Tollo (10) / Kwasi Owusu (50)

11.02.1970

EGYPT - ZAIRE 1-0 (0-0)
Municipal, Wad Medani
Referee: Simfukwe (Zambia)
EGYPT: Hassan Mokhtar, Mahmoud El-Seyagui, Bobbo, Mimi Darwish, Hany Moustafa, Shawki Hussein, Hassan El-Shazly, Sayed Abdel Razek, Taha Basry, Ali Abougreisha, Farouk El-Sayed.
ZAIRE: Robert M'wamba Kazadi, Mange, Raymond Tshimen Bwanga, Katumba, Albert M'wanza Mukombo, Raoul Mantanu Kidumu, Leonard Saidi, Mungamuni, Kalonzo, Emmanuel Etepe Kakoko, Wamunda Tshianbu.
Goal: Ali Abougreisha (71)

1.	EGYPT	3	2	1	0	6	2	5
2.	GHANA	3	1	2	0	4	2	4
3.	Guinea	3	0	2	1	4	7	2
4.	Zaire	3	0	1	2	2	5	1

Semi-finals

14.02.1970

IVORY COAST - GHANA 1-2 (0-1,1-1)
Municipal, Khartoum
Referee: N'Gom (Senegal), Attendance: 30.000
IVORY COAST: Fanny, Andre Obrou, Denis Gnegnery, Jean-Baptiste Akassou Akran, Diagou, Kailet, Bazo, Yoro, Pokou, Losseni, Tahi.
GHANA: Robert Mensah, Edward Boye, Alex Mingle, John Eshun, Edward Acquah, Joe Ghartey, Ibrahim Sunday, Robert Foley, Jones Attuquayefio, Kwasi Owusu, Malik.
Goals: Losseni (78) / Ibrahim Sunday (21), Malik (100)

14.02.1970

EGYPT - SUDAN 1-2 (0-0,1-1)
Municipal, Khartoum
Referee: Khlifi (Algeria), Attendance: 30.000
SUDAN: Abraham Abdel Aziz, El Sir Abdalla 'Kaunda' Mohammed, Suliman, Mahmoud Said Salim James, Salih Samir, Negmeldeen, Bushra, El-Issed, Hahish, Abas Nasreldin Gaksa, Hasabou El Rasoul Omer.
EGYPT: Hassan Mokhtar, Mahmoud El-Seyagui, Bobbo, Mimi Darwish, Hany Moustafa, Shawki Hussein, Shehta, Reda, Taha Basry, Hassan El-Shazly, Ali Abougreisha, Farouk El-Sayed.
Goals: Hassan El-Shazly (84) / El-Issed (83, 102)

Third Place Match

16.02.1970

EGYPT - IVORY COAST 3-1 (2-0)
Municipal, Khartoum
Referee: Boukili (Morocco), Attendance: 35.000
EGYPT: Hassan Mokhtar, Mahmoud El-Seyagui, Bobbo, Mimi Darwish, Hany Moustafa, Mohamed Aboul Ezz, Abdel Karim El-Gohary, Hassan El-Shazly, Sayed Abdel Razek, Taha Basry, Farouk El-Sayed.
IVORY COAST: Keita, Andre Obrou, Denis Gnegnery, Jean-Baptiste Akassou Akran, Diagou, Kailet, Bazo, Yoro, Lorougnon, Djike, Pokou.
Goals: Hassan El-Shazly (3, 14, 50) / Laurent Pokou (72)

25

Final

16.02.1970

SUDAN - GHANA 1-0 (1-0)
Municipal, Khartoum
Referee: Tesfaye (Ethiopia), Attendance: 35.000
SUDAN: Abraham Abdel Aziz, El Sir Abdalla 'Kaunda' Mohammed, Suliman, Amin, Salih Samir, Bushra, Bushara, El-Issed, Dahish, Abas Nasreldin Gaksa, Hasabou El Rasoul Omer.
GHANA: Robert Mensah, Edward Boye, Alex Mingle, John Eshun, Edward Acquah, Joe Ghartey, Ibrahim Sunday, Robert Foley, Jones Attuquayefio, Kwasi Owusu, Malik.
Goal: El-Issed (12)

Eighth edition - 1972
Qualifying Tournament

The 8th edition of the Africa Cup of Nations, held in Cameroon, retained the same system for both qualifiers and final tournament as the previous edition but the number of participants grew to 26 countries. Mali, in their first finals tournament, progressed to the final where they were defeated by the Republic of the Congo (formerly known as Congo-Brazzaville) who lifted the trophy for the first and, so far, only time.

First Round
10.12.1970 Algeria - Morocco 3-1
27.12.1970 Morocco - Algeria 3-0

03.01.1971 Egypt - Libya 2-1
13.07.1971 Libya - Egypt 0-1

29.11.1970 Ethiopia - Kenya 0-1
15.12.1970 Kenya - Ethiopia 2-0

08.11.1970 Gabon - Ivory Coast 1-2
22.11.1970 Ivory Coast - Gabon 1-0

Ghana - Upper Volta w/o

18.08.1971 Guinea - Senegal 1-0
01.09.1971 Senegal – Guinea 0-0

15.11.1970 Madagascar - Mauritius 2-1
29.11.1970 Mauritius - Madagascar 4-1

12.12.1970 Niger - Mali 0-1
27.12.1970 Mali - Niger 3-1

08.11.1970 Nigeria - Congo 0-0
22.11.1970 Congo - Nigeria 2-1

15.10.1970 Tanzania - Zambia 1-1
01.11.1970 Zambia - Tanzania 5-1

08.11.1970 Togo - Dahomey 2-1
22.11.1970 Dahomey - Togo 0-0
08.11.1970 Uganda - Zaire 1-4
24.11.1970 Zaire – Uganda 1-0

Second Round
13.10.1971 Guinea - Mali 0-0
27.10.1971 Mali - Guinea 3-1

13.10.1971 Ivory Coast - Congo 3-2
27.10.1971 Congo - Ivory Coast 2-0

04.07.1971 Kenya - Mauritius 2-1
18.07.1971 Mauritius - Kenya 0-0

13.10.1971 Morocco - Egypt 3-0
27.10.1971 Egypt - Morocco 3-2

13.10.1971 Togo - Ghana 0-0
27.10.1971 Ghana - Togo 0-1

13.10.1971 Zambia - Zaire 2-1
27.10.1971 Zaire - Zambia 3-0

Final Tournament (Cameroon)

GROUP A

23.02.1972

CAMEROON - KENYA 2-1 (2-1)
Omnisports, Yaoundé
Referee: Benjelloun (Morocco)
CAMEROON: M'Bengalack, Michel Kaham, Paul N'Lend, Jean-Paul Akono, Simo, Emmanuel Mvé, Gaston Ngondo, François Doumbe "Léa", Joseph Maya, Jean-Pierre Tokoto, Gaston Paul N'Doga.
KENYA: James Sianga, Makunda, Daniel Anyanzwa, Odore, Jonathan Niva, Allen Thigo, Jackson Aluko, Peter Ouma, Madegwa Nicodemus, Chege, John Nyawanga.
Goals: Gaston Paul N'Doga (7), Gaston Ngondo (20) / Jonathan Niva (44)

24.02.1972

MALI - TOGO 3-3 (1-1)
Omnisports, Yaoundé
Referee: Ickias (Congo)]
MALI: Séydou Traoré, Idrissa Coulibaly, Cheick Sangaré, Kidian Diallo, Cheikna Traoré, Bakary Traoré, Ousmane Traoré, Gigla, Bako Touré, Salif Keita, Fantamady Keita.
TOGO: Tommy Sylvestre, Sanvi Kponton, Anyaku Ohin, da Silveira Adjévi, Hermann Hunkpati, Arnold Fiaty Nyémébuéo, Luc Agbala Watékou, Michael Sokpo, Sadji, Edmond Apety "Kaolo", Clément Mébounou Kpadé. Trainer: Gottlieb Goeller,
Goals: Bakary Traoré (10), Fantamady Keita (46), Bako Traoré (49) / Edmond Apety "Kaolo" (45 penalty, 60, 81)

26.02.1972

MALI - KENYA 1-1 (1-0)
Omnisports, Yaoundé
Referee: Mutombo (Zaire), Attendance: 45.000
MALI: Mamadou Keita, Idrissa Coulibaly, Kidian Diallo, Idrissa Maiga (Cheik Diallo), Moktar Maiga, Bakary Traoré, Ousmane Traoré, Idrissa Kante, Bako Touré, Salif Keita, Fantamady Keita.
KENYA: James Sianga, Makunda, Daniel Anyanzwa, Odore, Jonathan Niva (Oduor), Allen Thigo, Peter Ouma, Jackson Aluko, Daniel Nicodémus, Chege, John Nyawanga.
Goals: Fantamady Keita (45) / Nicodemus (60)

26.02.1972

CAMEROON - TOGO 2-0 (0-0)
Omnisports, Yaoundé
Referee: Babiker Issa (Sudan)
CAMEROON: M'Bengalack, Michel Kaham, Paul N'Lend, Jean-Paul Akono, Simo, Emmanuel Mvé, Gaston Ngondo, François Doumbe "Léa" (Etame), Joseph Maya, Jean-Pierre Tokoto, Gaston Paul N'Doga (Mouthe). Trainer: Peter Schnittger
TOGO: Tommy Sylvestre, Sanvi Kponton, da Silveira Adjévi, Hermann Hunkpati, Anyaku Ohin, Arnold Fiaty Nyémébuéo, Agbala, Michael Sokpo, Sadji (Ayitégan), Edmond Apety "Kaolo", Covi (Clément Mébounou Kpadé). Trainer: Gottlieb Goeller,
Goals: Joseph Maya (64), Emmanuel Mvé (79)

28.02.1972

TOGO - KENYA 1-1 (0-1)
Omnisports, Yaoundé
Referee: Abdelkader Aouissi (Algeria), Attendance: 45.000
TOGO: Tommy Sylvestre, Anyaku Ohin, Hermann Hunkpati, da Silveira Adjévi, Ayitégan, Arnold Fiaty Nyémébuéo, Atsou, Michael Sokpo, Edmond Apety "Kaolo", Akakpo, Clément Mébounou Kpadé. Trainer: Gottlieb Goeller,
KENYA: James Sianga, Makunda, Daniel Anyanzwa, Odore, Jonathan Niva, Allen Thigo, Jackson Aluko, Peter Ouma, Daniel Nicodémus, Chege, Niawan.
Goals: Edmond Apety "Kaolo" (60) / Peter Ouma (30)

28.02.1972

CAMEROON - MALI 1-1 (0-1)
Omnisports, Yaoundé
Referee: Mostafa amel (Egypt)
CAMEROON: M'Bengalack, Michel Kaham, Paul N'Lend, Jean-Paul Akono, Evou, Jean-Pierre Tokoto, Emmanuel Mvé, François Doumbe "Léa", Joseph Maya, Manga (Etame), Mouthe. Trainer: Peter Schnittger
MALI: Mamadou Keita, Idrissa Coulibaly, Moktar Maiga, Kidian Diallo, Djane (Bakary Traoré), Sadio Cisse, Ousmane Traoré, Bako Touré, Cheikh Diallo, Fantamady Keita, Moussa Diakité.
Goals: François Doumbe 'Léa' (67) / Fantamady Keita (43)

1.	CAMEROON	3	2	1	0	5	2	5
2.	MALI	3	0	3	0	5	5	3
3.	Kenya	3	0	2	1	3	4	2
4.	Togo	3	0	2	1	4	6	2

GROUP B

25.02.1972

CONGO - MOROCCO 1-1 (1-1)
Omnisports, Douala
Referee: Olimba (Kenya), Attendance: 40.000
CONGO: Maxime Matsima, Gabriel Alphonse N'Dengati, Joseph N'gassati, Jacques N'dolou, Alphonse Niangou, Noel Birindi Minga, François M'Pelé, Jonas Bahamboula-M'Bemba (Joseph Matongo), Mayanda, Paul Moukila, Jean Balekita.
MOROCCO: Ben Allal Kassou, Boujemaa Benkrif, Khalifa, Abdallah Lamrani, Larbi Ihardane, Mohamed El Filali (Larbi Chabbak), Maaroufi, Mustapha Choukri, Abdelkader El Khayati, Ahmed Abdullah Faras, Dgazouani (Bouali).
Goals: Paul Moukila (45) / Ahmed Abdullah Faras (34)

25.02.1972

ZAIRE - SUDAN 1-1 (0-0)
Omnisports, Douala
Referee: Diallo (Mali), Attendance: 40.000
ZAIRE: Robert M'wamba Kazadi, Joseph N'dongala Lungwila, Raymond Tshimen Bwanga, Kialunda, Albert M'wanza Mukombo, Mutombo, Jean Kalala N'tumba, Raoul Mantanu Kidumu (Leonard Saidi), Adelard Maku Mayanga, Ngassebe, Emmanuel Etepe Kakoko (Wamunda Tshianbu).
SUDAN: Mohammed Ali Zughbeir, El Sir Abdalla 'Kaunda' Mohammed, Gadura, Mahmoud Said Salim James, Nasr Awad Musa 'Koka', Negmeldeen, Bushra (Kafi), Hamori, Mohammed El Basheir (Kamal Abdel Wahab), Bushara Abdel Nadif, Hasabou El Rasoul Omer.
Goals: Adelard Maku Mayanga (53) / Hasabou El Rasoul Omer (55)

27.02.1972

MOROCCO - SUDAN 1-1 (1-0)
Omnisports, Douala
Referee: Wacka (Cameroon)
MOROCCO: Ben Allal Kassou, Boujemaa Benkrif, Najah, Abdallah Lamrani, Larbi Ihardane, Khalifa, Maaroufi, Mustapha Choukri (Larbi Chabbak), Abdellah Tazi, Bouali (Ayache), Ahmed Abdullah Faras.
SUDAN: El Masri, El Sir Abdalla 'Kaunda' Mohammed, Gadura, Mahmoud Said Salim James, Nasr Awad Musa 'Koka', Negmeldeen, Bushra, Hamouri, Bushara Abdel Nadif, Kamal Abdel Wahab, Hasabou El Rasoul Omer (Kassala El Gadi).
Goals: Ahmed Abdullah Faras (32) / Bushara (49)

27.02.1972

ZAIRE - CONGO 2-0 (1-0)
Omnisports, Douala
Referee: Lacle Theodore (Togo)
ZAIRE: Robert M'wamba Kazadi, Joseph N'dongala Lungwila, Albert M'wanza Mukombo, Raymond Tshimen Bwanga, Kialunda, Mutombo, Massamba Kilasu, Adelard Maku Mayanga, Tshamala (Ngassebe), Jean Kalala N'tumba, Emmanuel Etepe Kakoko.
CONGO: Maxime Matsima, Gabriel Alphonse N'Dengati, Alphonse Niangou, Joseph N'gassati, Jacques N'dolou, Noel Birindi Minga (Fotou), Ongania, Paul Moukila, Mayanda, François M'Pelé, Jean Balekita (Ndouli).
Goals: Jean Kalala N'tumba (16, 59)

29.02.1972

MOROCCO - ZAIRE 1-1 (1-1)
Omnisports, Douala
Referee: Foiret (Mauritius), Attendance: 20.000
MOROCCO: Ben Allal Kassou, Boujemaa Benkrif, Abdallah Lamrani, Khalifa, Wazir (Maouhoub Ghazouani), Najah, Maaroufi, Mustapha Choukri, Ahmed Abdullah Faras, Bouali (Abdelkader El Khayati), Abdellah Tazi.
ZAIRE: Robert M'wamba Kazadi, Joseph N'dongala Lungwila, Albert M'wanza Mukombo, Raymond Tshimen Bwanga, Kialunda, Mutombo, Jean Kalala N'tumba, Massamba Kilasu (Leonard Saidi), Adelard Maku Mayanga (Wamunda Tshianbu), Ngassebe, Emmanuel Etepe Kakoko.
Goals: Ahmed Abdullah Faras (3) / Adelard Maku Mayanga (36)

29.02.1972

CONGO - SUDAN 4-2 (2-2)
Omnisports, Douala
Referee: George Lamptey (Ghana), Attendance: 20.000
CONGO: Maxime Matsima, Gabriel Alphonse N'Dengati, Joseph N'gassati, Jacques N'dolou, Fotou (Alphonse Niangou), Noel Birindi Minga, Jean Balekita, François M'Pelé, Jonas Bahamboula-M'Bemba, Joseph Matongo (Mayanda), Jean-Michel M'bono.
SUDAN: El Masri, El Sir Abdalla 'Kaunda' Mohammed, Gadura, Mahmoud Said Salim James, Nasr Awad Musa 'Koka', Negmeldeen, Bushra, Hamouri, Mohammed El Basheir (Kassala El Gadi), Bushara Abdel Nadif (El Ata), Kamal Abdel Wahab.
Goals: Jean-Michel M'bono (8, 55), François M'Pelé (32), Bahamboula (46) / Kamal Abdel Wahab (37), Bushara (44)

1.	ZAIRE	3	1	2	0	4	2	4
2.	CONGO	3	1	1	1	5	5	3
	Morocco	3	0	3	0	3	3	3
4.	Sudan	3	0	2	1	4	6	2

Congo qualified after the drawing of lots.

Semi-finals

02.03.1972

CONGO - CAMEROON 1-0 (1-0)
Omnisports, Yaoundé
Referee: Moustafa Kamel (Egypt), Attendance: 40.000
CONGO: Maxime Matsima, Gabriel Alphonse N'Dengati, Joseph N'gassati, Jacques N'dolou, Alphonse Niangou, Noel Birindi Minga (Fotou), Jean Balekita Balekita, Jonas Bahamboula-M'Bemba, Jean-Michel M'bono, François M'Pelé, Joseph Matongo.
CAMEROON: M'Bengalack, Michel Kaham, Paul N'Lend, Jean-Paul Akono, Evou, Ndongo, Emmanuel Mvé (Pascal Owona), François Doumbe "Léa" (Moutaisse), Joseph Maya, Jean-Pierre Tokoto, Ndoga. Trainer: Peter Schnittger
Goal: Noel Birindi Minga (31)

02.03.1972

ZAIRE - MALI 3-4 (1-1, 3-3)
Omnisports, Douala
Referee: George Lamptey (Ghana)

MALI: M. Keita, Moktar Maiga, Sangaré, Kidian Diallo, Cheik Traoré (Bakary Traoré), Sadio Cisse (Idrissa Maiga), Ousmane Traoré, Bako Touré, Adama Traoré, Fantamady Keita, Moussa Diakité.
ZAIRE: Robert M'wamba Kazadi, Joseph N'dongala Lungwila, Raymond Tshimen Bwanga, Kialunda, Albert M'wanza Mukombo, Mutombo, Leonard Saidi, Adelard Maku Mayanga, Tshamala (Ngassebe), Jean Kalala N'tumba (Wamunda Tshianbu), Emmanuel Etepe Kakoko.
Goals: Jean Kalala N'tumba (6), Emmanuel Etepe Kakoko (61), Ngassebe (78) / A.Traoré (17), Bako Touré (68), Fantamady Keita (48, 92)

Third Place Match

04.03.1972

CAMEROON - ZAIRE 5-2 (5-2)
Omnisports, Yaoundé
Referee: George Lamptey (Ghana)
CAMEROON: M'Bengalack, Michel Kaham, Paul N'Lend, Jean-Paul Akono, Simo (Bell), Ndongo, Jean-Pierre Tokoto, Mouthe, François Doumbe "Léa" (Manga), Owana, Ndoga. Trainer: Peter Schnittger
ZAIRE: Pombi, Kafula N'Goie, Raymond Tshimen Bwanga, Kialunda, Joseph N'dongala Lungwila, Mutombo (Kapata), Massamba Kilasu, Adelard Maku Mayanga, Tshamala, Jean Kalala N'tumba, Emmanuel Etepe Kakoko.
Goals: Akono (4 penalty), Ndongo (31), Pascal Owona (32), Mouthé (34), N'Doga (42) / Emmanuel Etepe Kakoko (13), Adelard Maku Mayanga (17)

Final

05.03.1972

CONGO - MALI 3-2 (0-1)
Omnisports, Yaoundé
Referee: Abdelkader Aouissi (Algeria)
CONGO: Maxime Matsima, Gabriel Alphonse N'Dengati, Joseph N'gassati, Jacques N'dolou, Alphonse Niangou, Noel Birindi Minga, Jean Balekita, Jonas Bahamboula-M'Bemba, François M'Pelé, Joseph Matongo (Ongania), Paul Moukila (Jean-Michel M'bono).
MALI: M. Keita, Moktar Maiga, Sangaré, Kidian Diallo, Cheik Traoré, Bakary Traoré, Ousmane Traoré, Bako Touré (Moussa Traoré), Salif Keita (Adama Traoré), Fantamady Keita, Moussa Diakité.
Goals: Jean-Michel M'bono (57, 59), François M'Pelé (63) / Moussa Diakhité (42), Moussa Traoré (75)

Ninth edition - 1974
Qualifying Tournament

No fewer than 29 countries entered the 9th edition of the competition, so a preliminary round before the qualifiers was required. However, five teams subsequently withdrew. Zambia reached the finals tournament (held in Egypt) for the first time and won through to the final where they faced Zaire, a team on a high as they had become the first African country to qualify for the FIFA World Cup finals just a few months earlier. Zaire eventually proved too strong for Zambia and lifted the trophy although a replay was required after the first game was drawn 2-2. This replay was the first and only final that was replayed in the competition, with Mulamba Ndaye scoring twice to win the game 2-0. Notably, Ndaye scored all 4 of Zaire's goals in the final and the replay and netted nine goals in total in the finals tournament – a record which stands to this day.

Preliminary Round

Central African Republic – Gabon w/o
Sierra Leone - Benin w/o

12.08.1973 Somalia - Uganda 2-0
26.08.1973 Uganda - Somalia 5-0

First Round

16.09.1973 Central African Republic - Ivory Coast 4-2
30.09.1973 Ivory Coast - Central African Republic 2-1
Central African Republic were disqualified

16.09.1973 Ethiopia - Tanzania 2-1
30.09.1973 Tanzania – Ethiopia 3-0

16.09.1973 Ghana - Senegal 3-2
30.09.1973 Senegal - Ghana 1-0, 3-5 on penalties

16.09.1973 Lesotho - Mauritius 0-0
30.09.1973 Mauritius - Lesotho 5-1

16.09.1973 Sierra Leone - Mali 1-1
30.09.1973 Mali - Sierra Leone 4-2

16.09.1973 Sudan - Nigeria 1-1
30.09.1973 Nigeria - Sudan 2-1

16.09.1973 Uganda - Kenya 1-0
30.09.1973 Kenya - Uganda 1-2

16.09.1973 Upper Volta - Zaire 0-5
30.09.1973 Zaire - Upper Volta 4-1

16.09.1973 Zambia - Madagascar 3-1
30.09.1973 Madagascar - Zambia 2-1

Algeria - Libya w/o
Cameroon - Niger w/o
Guinea - Togo w/o

Second Round

28.10.1973 Cameroon - Zaire 2-1
11.11.1973 Zaire - Cameroon 2-0

28.10.1973 Ghana - Ivory Coast 0-3
11.11.1973 Ivory Coast - Ghana 1-0

28.10.1973 Mali - Guinea 2-2
11.11.1973 Guinea - Mali 1-1
Guinea qualified on penalties

28.10.1973 Tanzania - Mauritius 1-1
11.11.1973 Mauritius - Tanzania 0-0
Mauritius qualified on penalties

28.10.1973 Uganda - Algeria 2-1
11.11.1973 Algeria – Uganda 1-1

28.10.1973 Zambia - Nigeria 5-1
11.11.1973 Nigeria – Zambia 3-2

Final Tournament (Egypt)

GROUP A

01.03.1974

EGYPT - UGANDA 2-1 (1-1)
Nasser, Cairo
Referee: Youssou N'Diaye (Senegal)
EGYPT: Hassan Ali, Mohamed Abou Amin, Mohamed Aboul Ezz, Hany Moustafa, Abdel Karim El-Gohary, Farouk Gaafar, Hassan Shehata, Taha Basry, Sayed Abdel Razek, Ali Abougreisha, Ali Khalil.
UGANDA: Natan, Edward Ssemwanga, Ashe Mukasa, Jimmy Kirunda, Ahmed Doka, Kula, Phillip Omondi, Timothy Ayieko, Stanley Mubiru, Denis Obua, Kirumira.
Goals: Ali Abougreisha (6), Ali Khalil (52) / Stanley Mubiru (28)

02.03.1974

ZAMBIA - IVORY COAST 1-0 (1-0)
Mehalla, Al-Qubra
Referee: Abdelkader Aouissi (Algeria), Attendance: 4000
ZAMBIA: Emmanuel M'wape, Mbaso, Dickson Chama, Dickson Makwaza, Ackim Musenge, Brighton Sinyangwe (Godfrey Chitalu), Boniface Simutowe, Nkole, Willie Phiri, Simeon Kaushi, Bernard Chanda.
IVORY COAST: Marc Gohi Bi, Andre Obrou, Soma Sagnaba, Denis Gnegnery, Doumbia Adama, Ouattara Mama, Emmanuel Moh, Yoro, Noel Kouame (Gohi), Kouman Kobinam, Tahi.
Goal: Simeon Kaushi (2)

04.03.1974

EGYPT - ZAMBIA 3-1 (2-1)
Nasser, Cairo
Referee: Waghiren (Nigeria), Attendance: 40.000
EGYPT: Hassan Ali, Mohamed Abou Amin, Mohamed Aboul Ezz, Hany Moustafa, Abdel Karim El-Gohary, Farouk Gaafar, Raafat Mekki, Taha Basry, Sayed Abdel Razek, Ali Abougreisha, Gamal Abdel Azim.
ZAMBIA: Emmanuel M'wape, Dickson Makwaza, Ackim Musenge, Dickson Chama, Mbaso, Boniface Simutowe, Jani Simulambo, Godfrey Chitalu, Brighton Sinyangwe, Bernard Chanda, Willie Phiri.
Goals: Gamal Abdel Azim (4), Ali Abougreisha (18), Taha Basry (52) / Godfrey Chitalu (10)

04.03.1974

IVORY COAST - UGANDA 2-2 (1-0)
Mehalla, Al-Qubra
Referee: El Ghoul (Libya), Attendance: 3000
IVORY COAST: Marc Gohi Bi, Laurent N'Dri Pokou, Yoro, Ouattara Mama, Emmanuel Moh, Doumbia, Kouman Kobinam, Ouelle, Soma Sagnaba, Denis Gnegnery, Tahi (Valentin Loue Bouazo).

UGANDA: Joseph Masajjage (Natan), Edward Ssemwanga, Ashe Mukasa, Jimmy Kirunda, Ahmed Doka, Francis Kulabigwo, Stanley Mubiru, Nsobya, Kirumira, Timothy Ayieko, Denis Obua (Phillip Omondi).
Goals: Kouman Kobinan 2 / Stanley Mubiru 2

06.03.1974

EGYPT - IVORY COAST 2-0 (2-0)
Nasser, Cairo
Referee: Deneke Menguistou (Ethiopia)
EGYPT: Hassan Orabi, Mohamed Tawfik, Mohamed El-Seyagui, Hassan Darwish, Mohamed Abou Amin, Raafat Mekki, Hassan Shehata, Mahmoud El-Khateeb, Moustafa Abdou, Hassan El-Shazly, Ali Khalil.
IVORY COAST: Marc Gohi Bi, Andre Obrou, Jean-Baptiste Akassou Akran, Denis Gnegnery, Doumbia Adama, Ouattara Mama, Emmanuel Moh, Yoro, Laurent N'Dri Pokou, Kouman Kobinam, Bernard N'Guessan.
Goals: Hassan El-Shazly (1), Ali Khalil (44)

06.03.1974

ZAMBIA - UGANDA 1-0 (1-0)
Mehalla, Al-Qubra
Referee: George Lamptey (Ghana), Attendance: 2000
ZAMBIA: Emmanuel M'wape, Mbaso, Kalambo, Dickson Chama, Dickson Makwaza, Boniface Simutowe, Obi Kapita, Mwila, Simeon Kaushi, Bernard Chanda, Brighton Sinyangwe.
UGANDA: Natan, Edward Ssemwanga, Ashe Mukasa, Jimmy Kirunda, Ahmed Doka, Francis Kulabigwo, Stanley Mubiru, Phillip Omondi, Kirumira, Timothy Ayieko, Nasur.
Goal: Obi Kapita

1.	EGYPT	3	3	0	0	7	2	6
2.	ZAMBIA	3	2	0	1	3	3	4
3.	Uganda	3	0	1	2	3	5	1
4.	Ivory Coast	3	0	1	2	2	5	1

GROUP B

03.03.1974

ZAIRE - GUINEA 2-1 (1-1)
Damanhour, Alexamdria
Referee: Gamar (Libya)
ZAIRE: Robert M'wamba Kazadi, Ilunga M'Wepu, Albert M'wanza Mukombo, Raymond Tshimen Bwanga, Boba Lobilo (Kafula N'Goie), Mabwene Mana, Mafu Kibonge, Adelard Maku Mayanga (Kembo Uba Kembo), Mulamba N'Daie, Raoul Mantanu Kidumu, Etepe Kakoko.
GUINEA: Abdoulaye Keita Sylla, Ali Badara Bangoura, Badara Keita, Sekou Conde, Soryba Soumah, Thiam, Ibrahima 'Petit Sory' Keita (Chérif Souleymane), Mamadou Keita, Nabi Laye Camara, Bengaly Sylla, Maxime Camara.
Goals: Mulamba N'Daye (18, 65) / Bangaly Sylla (25)

03.03.1974

CONGO - MAURITIUS 2-0 (1-0)
Municipal, Alexandria
Referee: Tesfaye (Ethiopia), Attendance: 5000

34

CONGO: Tandou, Gabriel Alphonse N'Dengaki, Mouiri, N'Ganga, Joseph N'gassati, Jacques N'dolou, Jonas Bahamboula-M'Bemba, Poaty, Paul Moukila, Jacques Ndomba, Lakou (Jean-Michel M'bono).
MAURITIUS: Lucien Edouard Leste, Noel, Jean Florine, Maurel, Premeswar Ramzan Ramchurn, Louis Roland Augustin, Godunt (Perdrau), Bathfield, Chowchinsung (France Michel Moutou), Marie Serge René Munso, Daniel Jean Robert Imbert.
Goals: Paul Moukila, Lakou

05.03.1974

GUINEA - MAURITIUS 2-1 (1-0)
Damanhour, Alexandria
Referee: Farah Addo (Somalia), Attendance: 1500
GUINEA: Bernard, Ali Badara Bangoura, Badara Keita, Ibrahim Fofana, Sekou Conde (Sandi), Ismail Sylla, Soryba Soumah, Maxime Camara, Bengaly Sylla, Morcire Sylla, Aliou Keita (Y. Camara).
MAURITIUS: Lucien Edouard Leste, Jean Sylvio Jatha, Jean Florine, Maurel, Jackaria (Bathfield), Louis Roland Augustin, Moniaruth, France Michel Moutou, Daniel Jean Robert Imbert, Perdrau (Mungly), Chowchinsung.
Goals: Morciré Sylla 2 / Daniel Jean Robert Imbert

05.03.1974

CONGO - ZAIRE 2-1 (0-1)
Municipal, Alexandria
Referee: Benghazal (Algeria), Attendance: 8000
CONGO: Tandou, Gabriel Alphonse N'Dengaki, Joseph N'gassati, Mbouta, Jacques N'dolou, Ondana, Noel Birindi Minga, Paul Moukila, François M'Pelé, Jonas Bahamboula-M'Bemba, Jean-Michel M'bono.
ZAIRE: Robert M'wamba Kazadi, Ilunga M'Wepu, Raymond Tshimen Bwanga, Boba Lobilo, Albert M'wanza Mukombo, Mabwene Mana, Mafu Kibonge, Adelard Maku Mayanga, Mulamba N'Daie, Raoul Mantanu Kidumu, Etepe Kakoko.
Goals: Jean-Michel M'bono (70), Noel Birindi Minga (81) / Adelard Maku Mayanga (25)

07.03.1974

GUINEA - CONGO 1-1 (0-0)
Municipal, Alexandria
Referee: Ahmed Gindeel (Sudan), Attendance: 7000
GUINEA: Abdoulaye Keita Sylla, Ali Badara Bangoura, Ali Keita, Sandipe, Soryba Soumah, Thiam, Ali Ibrahim 'Petit Sory' Keita (Aliou Keita), Morcine Sylla, Ismail Sylla, Bengaly Sylla (Maxime Camara), Chérif Souleymane.
CONGO: Maxime Matsima, Gabriel Alphonse N'Dengaki, Joseph N'gassati, Jacques N'dolou, Ondana, Noel Birindi Minga, Mbouta, Jonas Bahamboula-M'Bemba (Jacques Ndomba), François M'Pelé, Paul Moukila, Jean-Michel M'bono.
Goals: Edenté (60 penalty) / Jacques Ndomba (65)

07.03.1974

ZAIRE - MAURITIUS 4-1 (3-0)
Damanhour, Alexandria
Referee: Wallace Johnson (Sierra Leone)
ZAIRE: Dimbi Tubilandu, Ilunga M'Wepu, Albert M'wanza Mukombo, Boba Lobilo, Kafula N'Goie, Mabwene Mana, Adelard Maku Mayanga, Mavuba, Mulamba N'Daie, Kembo Uba Kembo (Ekofa M'bungu), Emmanuel Etepe Kakoko (Wamunda Tshianbu).

MAURITIUS: Lucien Edouard Leste, Jean Sylvio Jatha, Jean Florine, Maurel, Bathfield, Louis Roland Augustin, Dinally (Jackaria), Moniaruth, Daniel Jean Robert Imbert, Marie Serge René Munso, Chowchinsung (Noel).
Goals: Adelard Maku Mayanga 2, Mulamba N'Daye, Emmanuel Etepe Kakoko / Daniel Jean Robert Imbert

1.	CONGO	3	2	1	0	5	2	5
2.	ZAIRE	3	2	0	1	7	4	4
3.	Guinea	3	1	1	1	4	4	3
4.	Mauritius	3	0	0	3	2	8	0

Semi-finals

09.03.1974

EGYPT - ZAIRE 2-3 (1-0)
Nasser, Cairo
Referee: Abdelkader Aouissi (Algeria), Attendance: 50.000
EGYPT: Hassan Orabi, Mohamed Tawfik (Abdel Karim El-Gohary), Mohamed Abou Amin, Hany Moustafa, Mohamed Aboul Ezz, Hassan Darwish, Farouk Gaafar, Hassan Shehata, Sayed Abdel Razek, Ali Abougreisha, Ali Khalil.
ZAIRE: Robert M'wamba Kazadi, Ilunga M'Wepu, Raymond Tshimen Bwanga, Boba Lobilo, Kafula N'Goie, Mavuba, Mabwene Mana, Adelard Maku Mayanga, Mulamba N'Daie, Raoul Mantanu Kidumu (Ekofa M'bungu), Etepe Kakoko.
Goals: Ilunga M'Wepu (41 owngoal), Ali Abougreisha (54) / Mulamba N'Daye (55, 72), Kigumu (61)

09.03.1974

CONGO - ZAMBIA 2-4 aet
Municipal, Alexandria
Referee: Matovu (Tanzania), Attendance: 2000
ZAMBIA: Emmanuel Mwape, Dickson Makwaza, Ackim Musenge, Dickson Chama, Mbaso, Boniface Simutowe, Jani Simulambo, Kauchi, Bernard Chanda, Mapulanga, Willie Phiri (Brighton Sinyangwe).
CONGO: Maxime Matsima, Gabriel Alphonse N'Dengaki, Joseph N'gassati, Koko (Mbouta), Ondana, Noel Birindi Minga, Jacques N'dolou, Jonas Bahamboula-M'Bemba Jean-Michel M'bono (Jacques Ndomba), François M'Pelé, Paul Moukila.
Goals: Jacques Ndomba, François M'Pelé / Bernard Chanda (3), Mapulanga

Third Place Match

11.03.1974

EGYPT - CONGO 4-0 (2-0)
Nasser, Cairo
EGYPT: Ahmed Ikramy, Raafat Mekki, Mohamed aboul Ezz, Hassan Darwish, Hany Moustafa, Taha Basry, Farouk Gaafar, Hassan Shehata, Moustafa Abdou, Ali Abougreisha, Ali Khalil.
CONGO: Tandou, Gabriel Alphonse N'Dengaki, Mbouta, Joseph N'gassati, François Yamba, Nganga, Mouivi, Poaty, Jean-Michel M'bono, Ndouli, Paul Moukila, Lakou.
Goals: Moustafa Abdou (5), Hassan Shehata (18, 80), Ali Abougreisha (62)

Final

12.03.1974

ZAIRE - ZAMBIA 2-2 (0-1, 2-2)
Nasser, Cairo
Referee: Gamar (Libya)
ZAIRE: Robert M'wamba Kazadi, Ilunga M'Wepu, Raymond Tshimen Bwanga, Boba Lobilo, Kafula N'Goie, Mavuba, Mabwene Mana, Adelard Maku Mayanga, Mulamba N'Daie, Raoul Mantanu Kidumu, Etepe Kakoko.
ZAMBIA: Emmanuel Mwape, Ackim Musenge, Dickson Chama, Dickson Makwaza, Mbaso, Boniface Simutowe, Jani Simulambo, Bernard Chanda, Mapulanga, Simeon Kaushi, Brighton Sinyangwe.
Goals: Mulamba N'Daye (65, 117) / Simeon Kaushi (40), Brighton Sinyangwe (120)

Final Replay

14.03.1974

ZAIRE - ZAMBIA 2-0 (1-0)
Nasser, Cairo
Referee: Gamar (Libya), Attendance: 1000
ZAIRE: Robert M'wamba Kazadi, Ilunga M'Wepu, Albert M'wanza Mukombo, Raymond Tshimen Bwanga, Lobila, Mabwene Mana, Adelard Maku Mayanga, Mavuba, Mulamba N'Daie, Raoul Mantanu Kidumu, Etepe Kakoko.
ZAMBIA: Emmanuel Mwape, Ackim Musenge, Dickson Chama, Dickson Makwaza, Mbaso, Boniface Simutowe, Mapulanga, Jani Simulambo, Bernard Chanda, Brighton Sinyangwe, Simeon Kaushi.
Goals: Mulamba N'Daye (30, 76)

Tenth edition - 1976
Qualifying Tournament

Thirty-two countries entered the 10th edition of the competition, but four withdrew without playing a game. The finals tournament was held in Ethiopia and, in a change of format from previous years, the two winners of each finals group qualified for a further round-robin tournament to decide the champions. Morocco duly earned two victories and a draw to finish top of the table and lift the trophy for the first time.

Preliminary Round

Mali - Lesotho w/o
Niger - Benin w/o

10.08.1975 Morocco - Gambia 3-0
24.08.1975 Gambia - Morocco 0-3

10.08.1975 Somalia - Burundi 0-2
24.08.1975 Burundi - Somalia 0-1

10.08.1975 Togo - Liberia 1-0
24.08.1975 Liberia - Togo 0-2

10.11.1974 Tunisia - Libya 1-0
22.11.1974 Libya - Tunisia 1-0
Tunisia qualified on penalties

First Round

14.09.1975 Burundi - Egypt 0-3
28.09.1975 Egypt - Burundi 2-0

14.09.1975 Cameroon - Togo 3-0
28.09.1975 Togo - Cameroon 4-0

14.09.1975 Congo - Ivory Coast 1-0
28.09.1975 Ivory Coast - Congo 2-1

14.09.1975 Mali - Ghana 3-1
28.09.1975 Ghana - Mali 4-0

14.09.1975 Morocco - Senegal 4-0
28.09.1975 Senegal - Morocco 2-1

14.09.1975 Niger - Guinea 2-4
28.09.1975 Guinea - Niger 3-0

14.09.1975 Sudan - Kenya 1-0
28.09.1975 Kenya - Sudan 0-2

23.03.1975 Tunisia - Algeria 1-1
06.05.1975 Algeria - Tunisia 1-2

14.09.1975 Uganda - Mauritius 4-0
28.09.1975 Mauritius - Uganda 1-1

14.09.1975 Zambia - Malawi 3-3
28.09.1975 Malawi - Zambia 1-6

Nigeria - Central African Republic w/o
Tanzania - Madagascar w/o

Second Round

26.10.1975 Congo - Nigeria 0-1
09.11.1975 Nigeria - Congo 2-1

26.10.1975 Ghana - Morocco 2-0
09.11.1975 Morocco - Ghana 2-0
Morocco qualified on penalties

26.10.1975 Tanzania - Egypt 1-1
09.11.1975 Egypt - Tanzania 5-2

26.10.1975 Togo - Guinea 2-2
09.11.1975 Guinea - Togo 2-0

06.07.1975 Tunisia - Sudan 3-2
16.08.1975 Sudan - Tunisia 2-1

26.10.1975 Zambia - Uganda 2-1
09.11.1975 Uganda - Zambia 3-0

Final Tournament (Ethiopia)

GROUP A

29.02.1976

ETHIOPIA - UGANDA 2-0 (1-0)
National, Addis Abeba
Referee: Abdelkader Aouissi (Algeria).
ETHIOPIA: Abebe Guetacheou, Alemayehu Haile Selassie, Asfaw Bayu, Gezahgne, Ahmed Buker, Kibrom, Kassahum Tekalinge, Berhane Mulugeta, Tesfaye Seyoum, Hailu Goshu (Nigousse), Solomon Sheferaw.
UGANDA: Matovu, Edward Ssemwanga, Ashe Mukasa, Tom Lwanga, Jimmy Kirunda, Francis Kulabigwo, Moses Nsereko, Stanley Mubiru (Mike Kiganda), Okindi (Philip 'Polly' Ouma), Abra, Denis Obua.
Goals: Solomon Sheferaw (2), Tesfaye Seyoum (83)

29.02.1976

EGYPT - GUINEA 1-1 (1-1)
National, Addis Abeba
Referee: Youssou N'Diaye (Senegal).
EGYPT: Hassan Ali, Ahmed Abdel Baguy, Moustafa Younis, Ghanem Sultan (Mahmoud El-Seyagui), Mohamed Salah El-Din, Farouk Gaafar, Hassan Shehata, Taha Basry, Moustafa Abdou, Mahmoud El-Khateeb (Osama Khalil), Mahmoud Abdel Dayem.
GUINEA: Abdoulaye Keita Sylla, Ali Badara Bangoura, Morcire Sylla (Calva), Chérif Souleymane, Djibrill Diarra, Bengaly Conde, Naby Laye 'Papa' Camara, Jansky, Ali Ibrahim 'Petit Sory' Keita, Ali Sylla (Mamadou Aliou 'N'Jo Lea' Keita), Bengaly Sylla.
Goals: Taha Basri (43) / Seydouba Sylla (44 penalty)

03.03.1976

EGYPT - UGANDA 2-1 (2-1)
National, Addis Abeba
Referee: Lawson (Togo).
EGYPT: Hassan Ali, Mohamed Salah El-Din, Moustafa Younis, Ghanem Sultan, Abdelkarim El-Gohary, Farouk Gaafar, Taha Basry, Hassan Shehata (Mohamed El-Seyagui), Moustafa Abdou, Mahmoud El-Khateeb, Osama Khalil.
UGANDA: Sendegeya, Edward Ssemwanga, Francis Kulabigwo, Jimmy Kirunda, Ashe Mukasa, Moses Nsereko, Phillip Omondi (Philip 'Polly' Ouma), Stanley Mubiru, Tom Lwanga, Mike Kiganda, Jimmy Muguwa (Denis Obua).
Goals: Moustafa Abdou (26), Taha Basry (32) / Denis Obua (21)

03.03.1976

GUINEA - ETHIOPIA 2-1 (1-1)
National, Addis Abeba
Referee: Gamar (Libya)
GUINEA: Abdoulaye Keita Sylla, Ali Badara Bangoura, Ibrahim Fofana, Chérif Souleymane, Djibrill Diarra, Bengaly Conde, Naby Laye 'Papa' Camara, Jansky, Ali Ibrahim 'Petit Sory' Keita, Mamadou Aliou 'N'Jo Lea' Keita, Bengaly Sylla.
ETHIOPIA: Abebe Guetacheou, Alemayehu Haile Selassie, Asfaw Bayu, Gezahgne, Ahmed Buker, Kibrom, Kassahum Tekalinge, Berhane Mulugeta (Fekade), Tesfaye Seyoum, Solomon Sheferaw, Engeda (Asrat Haile).
Goals: Mamadou Aliou 'N'Jo Lea' Keita (15), Ali Ibrahim 'Petit Sory' Keita (85) / Solomon Sheferaw (40)

05.03.1976
GUINEA - UGANDA 2-1 (2-0)
National, Addis Abeba
Referee: Amengor (Ghana).
GUINEA: Abdoulaye Keita Sylla, Ali Badara Bangoura, Ibrahim Fofana, Chérif Souleymane, Djibrill Diarra, Bengaly Conde (Ismael Sylla), Naby Laye 'Papa' Camara, Jansky, Ali Ibrahim 'Petit Sory' Keita, Mamadou Aliou 'N'Jo Lea' Keita, Bengaly Sylla (Mory Koné).
UGANDA: Sendegeya, Mindrea, Francis Kulabigwo, Jimmy Kirunda, Ashe Mukasa, Edward Ssemwanga, Mike Kiganda, Moses Nsereko, Abraa (Godfrey Kisitu), Philip 'Polly' Ouma (Stanley Mubiru), Jimmy Muguwa.
Goals: Mamadou Aliou 'N'Jo Léa' Keita (2), Bengally Sylla (20) / Jimmy Muguwa (85)

05.03.1976
ETHIOPIA - EGYPT 1-1 (0-1)
National, Addis Abeba
Referee: Abdelkader Aouissi (Algeria).
ETHIOPIA: Abebe Guetacheou, Alemayehu Haile Selassie, Asrat Haile, Gezahgne, Ahmed Buker, Kibrom, Kassahum Tekalinge, Berhane Mulugeta (Mohamed Ali), Tesfaye Seyoum, Solomon Sheferaw, Bekeri (Neguse).
EGYPT: Ahmed Ikramy (Thabet El-Batal), Ibrahim Youssef, Moustafa Younis, Hassan Hamdi, Ghanem Sultan, Taha Basry, Hassan Shehata, Farouk Gaafar, Mokhtar Mokhtar, Omasha, Moustafa Abdou.
Goals: Mohamed Ali (46) / Hassan Shehata (26)

1.	GUINEA	3	2	1	0	5	3	5
2.	EGYPT	3	1	2	0	4	3	4
3.	Ethiopia	3	1	1	1	4	3	3
4.	Uganda	3	0	0	3	2	6	0

GROUP B

01.03.1976
NIGERIA - ZAIRE 4-2 (3-0)
Dire-Dawa
Referee: Seoudi (Tunisia).
NIGERIA: Joseph Erico, Sanni Mohammed, Samuel Ojebode, Godwin Odiye (Idowu Otubusen), Mudashiru Lawal, Kelechi Emeteole, Alloysius Atuegbu, Haruna Ilerika, Baba Otu, Thompson Usiyen, Adekunle Awesu.
ZAIRE: Sambi, Binda, Boba Lobilo, Raymond Tshimen Bwanga, Massamba Kilasu, Raoul Mantanu Kidumu, Babayilla (Kabasu), Ekofa M'bungu, Masengo (Mwanza), Mulamba N'Daie, Emmanuel Etepe Kakoko.
Goals: Baba Otu (28, 44), Samuel Ojebode (37 penalty), Thompson Usiyen (88) / Kabasu Balanganayi (51), M'Bungu Tathy (58)

01.03.1976
MOROCCO - SUDAN 2-2 (1-1)
Dire-Dawa
Referee: Gration Hemans Matovu (Tanzania).
MOROCCO: Mohamed Hazzaz, Moustapha 'Chérif' El-Fetoui, Ahmed 'Baba' Meghrouh, Mehdi Belmejdoub, Abdellah Semmat, Abdelmajid Dolmy, Ahmed Moujahid (Abdellah Tazi), Ahmed Abdullah Faras, Abouali, Hassan 'Acila' Amcharrat, Ahmed Larbi.
SUDAN: Tayeb, Ibid, Sharfeldin, Fawzi, El Kori, Mussa, Awad (El Gally), Bushara, Santo, Ali Gagarine, Mutassim.
Goals: Moustapha 'Chérif' El-Fetoui (1), Abouali (58) / Ali Gagarine (9, 79)

04.03.1976

NIGERIA - SUDAN 1-0 (1-0)
Dire-Dawa
Referee: Chayu (Zambia).
NIGERIA: Joseph Erico, Sanni Mohammed (Ike Edezinma), Samuel Ojebode, Godwin Odiye, Mudashiru Lawal, Kelechi Emeteole, Alloysius Atuegbu, Haruna Ilerika, Baba Otu, Thompson Usiyen (Sunday Oyarekhua), Adekunle Awesu.
SUDAN: Tayeb, Ibid, Fawzi (Abdelmonem), El Kori, Mussa, El Gally, Sharfeldin, Bushara, Santo, Ali Gagarine, Mutassim.
Goal: Thompson Usiyen (8)

04.03.1976

MOROCCO - ZAIRE 1-0 (0-0)
Dire-Dawa
Referee: El-Ghoul (Libya).
MOROCCO: Mohamed Hazzaz, Moustapha 'Chérif' El-Fetoui, Ahmed 'Baba' Meghrouh, Mehdi Belmejdoub, Ahmed Larbi, Abdellah Semmat (Kamal Smiri), Abdel Ali Zahraoui, Abdellah Tazi, Ahmed Abdullah Faras, Abouali, Hassan 'Acila' Amcharrat (Abdelmajid Dolmy).
ZAIRE: Sambi, Binda, Raymond Tshimen Bwanga, Boba Lobilo, Massamba Kilasu (Mwape), Raoul Mantanu Kidumu, Kabasu, Kasamba, Kembo Uba Kembo (M'Wanza Mukombo), Mulamba N'Daie, Emmanuel Etepe Kakoko.
Goal: Abdel Ali Zahraoui (80)

06.03.1976

MOROCCO - NIGERIA 3-1 (2-1)
Dire-Dawa
Referee: Grah (Ivory Coast).
MOROCCO: Mohamed Hazzaz, Moustaph 'Chérif' El-Fetoui, Ahmed 'Baba' Meghrouh, Abbad Jawad El-Andaloussi, Ahmed Larbi, Ahmed Moujahid (Kamal Smiri), Abdel Ali Zahraoui, Abdellah Tazi, Ahmed Abdullah Faras, Abouali (Driss Haddadi), Abdelmajid Dolmy.
NIGERIA: Joseph Erico, Ike Edezinma, Samuel Ojebode, Godwin Odiye, Mudashiru Lawal, Kelechi Emeteole, Alloysius Atuegbu, Haruna Ilerika (Kenneth Olayombo), Baba Otu, Sunday Oyarekhua (Idowu Otubusin), Adekunle Awesu.
Goals: Ahmed Abdullah Faras (8), Abdellah Tazi (19), Ahmed Larbi (81) / Samuel Ojebode (5 penalty)

06.03.1976

ZAIRE - SUDAN 1-1 (1-1)
Dire-Dawa
Referee: Foiret (Mauritius)
ZAIRE: Mbuya, Binda, Raymond Tshimen Bwanga, Boba Lobilo, Mwape, Raoul Mantanu Kidumu, Kabasu, Kasamba, Mwanza (Kembo Uba Kembo), Mulamba N'Daie, Emmanuel Etepe Kakoko (Massengo)
SUDAN: Tayeb, Ibid, Mahgoub, El Kori, Mussa, Sharfeldin, Bushara, Khalid (Eddaw), Ali Gagarine, Mutassim, Hassan.
Goals: Mulamba N'Diaye (41) / Ali Gagarine (14)

1.	MOROCCO	3	2	1	0	6	3	5
2.	NIGERIA	3	2	0	1	6	5	4
3.	Sudan	3	0	2	1	3	4	2
4.	Zaire	3	0	1	2	3	6	1

Final round

09.03.1976

GUINEA - NIGERIA 1-1 (0-0)
National, Addis Abeba
Referee: Seoudi (Tunisia).
GUINEA: Abdoulaye Keita Sylla, Ali Badara Bangoura, Ibrahim Fofana, Chérif Souleymane, Djibrill Diarra, Bengaly Conde, Naby Laye 'Papa' Camara, Jansky, Ali Ibrahim 'Petit Sory' Keita, Mamadou Aliou 'N'Jo Lea' Keita, Bengaly Sylla (Aly Sylla).
NIGERIA: Joseph Erico, Godwin Odiye, Samuel Ojebode (Francis Okorie), Christian Chukwu, Mudashiru Lawal, Kelechi Emeteole, Alloysius Atuegbu, Haruna Ilerika, Baba Otu, Kenneth Olayombo, Adekunle Awesu.
Goals: Naby Laye 'Papa' Camara (88) / Mudashiru Lawal (55)

09.03.1976

MOROCCO - EGYPT 2-1 (1-1)
National, Addis Abeba
Referee: Y. El-Ghoul (Libya).
MOROCCO: Mohamed Hazzaz, Moustapha 'Chérif' El-Fetoui, Ahmed 'Baba' Meghrouh, Abbad Jawad El-Andaloussi, Ahmed Larbi, Abdellah Semmat (Abdelmajid Dolmy), Abdel Ali Zahraoui, Abdellah Tazi, Ahmed Abdullah Faras, Kamal Smiri, Hassan 'Acila' Amcharrat (Guezzar Redouane).
EGYPT: Ahmed Ikramy, Ibrahim Youssef, Moustafa Younis, Hassan Hamdi, Ghanem Sultan, Taha Basry, Farouk Gaafar, Mokhtar Mokhtar, Moustafa Abdou, Omar Abdallah (Ahmed Abou Rehab), Osama Khalil.
Goals: Ahmed Abdullah Faras (23), Abdel Ali Zahraoui (88) / Ahmed Abou Rehab (34)

11.03.1976

MOROCCO - NIGERIA 2-1 (0-0)
National, Addis Abeba
Referee: Youssou N'Diaye (Senegal).
MOROCCO: Mohamed Hazzaz, Moustapha 'Chérif' El-Fetoui, Ahmed 'Baba' Meghrouh, Mehdi Belmejdoub, Ahmed Larbi, Abdallah Semmat, Abdel Ali Zahraoui, Abdellah Tazi, Ahmed Abdullah Faras, Kamal Smiri (Abdelmajid Dolmy), Hassan 'Acila' Amcharrat (Guezzar Redouane).
NIGERIA: Joseph Erico, Godwin Odiye (Idowu Otubusin), Samuel Ojebode, Christian Chukwu, Francis Okorie, Mudashiru Lawal, Alloysius Atuegbu, Haruna Ilerika, Baba Otu, Kenneth Olayombo, Adekunle Awesu (Ogidinma Ibeabuchi).
Goals: Ahmed Abdullah Faras (82), Guezzar Redouane (87) / Baba Otu (57)

11.03.1976

GUINEA - EGYPT 4-2 (1-1)
National, Addis Abeba
Referee: Lawson (Togo).
GUINEA: Abdoulaye Keita Sylla, Ali Badara Bangoura, Morcire Sylla, Chérif Souleymane, Doarra, Ismael Sylla, Naby Laye 'Papa' Camara, Jansky, Ali Ibrahim 'Petit Sory' Keita, Mamadou Aliou 'N'Jo Lea' Keita, Bengaly Sylla.
EGYPT: Thabet El-Batal, Mohamed Salah El-Din, Mohamed El-Seyagui, Ghanem Sultan, Fathi Mabrouk, Hassan Shehata, Taha Basry, Farouk Gaafar, Omar Abdallah (Osama Khalil), Moustafa Abdou, Ahmed Abou Rehab.
Goals: Mamadou Aliou 'N'Jo Léa' Keita (24, 65), Ghamen Sultan (53 owngoal), Morciré Sylla (62) / Moustafa Abdou (33), Mohamed El-Sayagui (86)

42

14.03.1976

NIGERIA - EGYPT 3-2 (1-2)
National, Addis Abeba
Referee: Grah (Ivory Coast).
NIGERIA: Joseph Erico, Sanni Mohammed, Christian Chukwu, Godwin Odiye, Samuel Ojebode, Mudashiru Lawal, Haruna Ilerika, Alex Nwosu, Alloysius Atuegbu, Thompson Usiyen (46.Kenneth Olayombo), Ogidinma Ibeabuchi.
EGYPT: Ahmed Ikramy, Ibrahim Youssef, Hassan Hamdi, Ghanem Sultan, Mohamed Salah El-Din, Mokhtar Mokhtar, Hassan Shehata, Osama Khalil, Ahmed Abou Rehab, Mahmoud El-Khateeb (Taha Basry), Moustafa Abdou.
Goals: Haruna Ilerika (35, 62), Mudashiru Lawal (82) / Mahmoud El-Khateeb (7), Osama Khalil (41)

14.03.1976

MOROCCO - GUINEA 1-1 (0-1)
National, Addis Abeba
Referee: Chayu (Zambia).
MOROCCO: Mohamed Hazzaz, Moustapha 'Chérif' El-Fetoui, Ahmed 'Baba' Meghrouh, Jlaoua, Mehdi Belmejdoub (Guezzar Redouane), Ahmed Larbi, Abdallah Semmat, Abdel Ali Zahraoui, Abdellah Tazi, Ahmed Abdullah Faras, Abouali (Abdelmajid Dolmy).
GUINEA: Abdoulaye Keita Sylla, Ali Badara Bangoura, Morcire Sylla, Chérif Souleymane, Djibrill Diarra, Ismael Sylla, Naby Laye 'Papa' Camara, Jansky, Ali Ibrahim 'Petit Sory' Keita, Mamadou Aliou 'N'Jo Lea' Keita, Bengaly Sylla (Mory Koné).
Goals: Ahmed 'Baba' Meghrouh (86) / Chérif Souleymane (35)

1.	MOROCCO	3	2	1	0	5	3	5
2.	Guinea	3	1	2	0	6	4	4
3.	Nigeria	3	1	1	1	5	5	3
4.	Egypt	3	0	0	3	5	9	0

Eleventh edition - 1978
Qualifying Tournament

Just 27 teams entered the 11th edition of the competition and Ghana hosted the finals tournament for the second time. The finals tournament format reverted to semi-finals and a final replacing the round-robin group stage which had decided the winners of the previous edition. The hosts, Ghana, defeated Uganda in the final to win their third title and retain the trophy outright.

Preliminary Round

24.10.1976 Malawi - Mauritius 1-1
28.01.1977 Mauritius - Malawi 3-2

First Round

18.09.1977 Algeria - Kenya 4-1
02.10.1977 Kenya - Algeria 2-1

18.09.1977 Cameroon - Congo 2-0
02.10.1977 Congo - Cameroon 4-0

13.03.1977 Egypt - Tunisia 2-2
27.04.1977 Tunisia - Egypt 3-2

18.09.1977 Guinea - Libya 3-0
02.10.1977 Libya - Guinea 0-2

28.09.1977 Mauritius - Ethiopia 2-3
12.10.1977 Ethiopia - Mauritius 1-0

18.09.1977 Senegal - Togo 2-1
02.10.1977 Togo - Senegal 0-1

18.09.1977 Sierra Leone - Nigeria 1-1
02.10.1977 Nigeria - Sierra Leone 2-0

18.09.1977 Upper Volta - Ivory Coast 0-1
02.10.1977 Ivory Coast - Upper Volta 4-1

Mali - Niger w/o
Uganda - Tanzania w/o
Zambia – Sudan w/o

Second Round:
30.10.1977 Algeria - Zambia 2-0
13.11.1977 Zambia - Algeria 2-0, 6-5 on penalties

30.10.1977 Congo - Gabon 3-2
13.11.1977 Gabon - Congo 3-3

30.10.1977 Ethiopia - Uganda 0-0
13.11.1977 Uganda - Ethiopia 2-1

30.10.1977 Senegal - Nigeria 3-1
13.11.1977 Nigeria - Senegal 3-0

30.10.1977 Tunisia - Guinea 3-0
13.11.1977 Guinea - Tunisia 3-2

Ivory Coast - Mali
Both teams were disqualified, and Upper Volta, losers to Ivory Coast in the previous round, were given a place in the finals

Final Tournament (Ghana)

GROUP A

05.03.1978

GHANA - ZAMBIA 2-1 (1-1)
Municipal, Accra
Referee: El Naim Soulayman (Sudan), Attendance: 50.000
GHANA: Joseph Carr, Isaac Paha, Ofei Ansah (Awuley Quaye), Isaac Acquaye, James Kuuka Dadzie, Adolph Armah, Anas Seidu Nketiah Yawson, Kayede, Opoku Afriye, Karim Abdul Razak, Blankson.

ZAMBIA: Vincent Chileshe, Mutale, Kaiser Kalombo, Robert Lutoba, Ackim Musenge, Katebe, Moses Simwala, Jani Simulambo, Alex Chola, Godfrey Chitalu (Brighton Sinyangwe), Obi Kapita (Willie Phiri).
Goals: Opoku Afriye (21), Karim Abdul Razak (55) / Obi Kapita (8)

05.03.1978

NIGERIA - UPPER VOLTA 4-2 (3-0)
Referee: Sylla (Guinea), Attendance: 50.000
Municipal, Accra
NIGERIA: Emmanuel Okala, Annas Ahmed, Anyafo, Muda, Christian Chukwu, Godwin Odiye, Segun Odegbami, Alloysius Atuegbu, Adeleke, Mohammed, Adokie Amesiamaka.
UPPER VOLTA: Sidiki Diarra, Bah, Zakaria Sanou, René Nikiema, Badou, Compaore, Hubert Hien, Keita, Ouédraogo, Tewinde Compaore, Cisse (A. Compaore).
Goals: Christian Chukwu (17), Adekiye (31), Segun Odegbami (44, 82) / Hubert Hien (50), Koita (52)

08.03.1978

ZAMBIA - UPPER VOLTA 2-0 (1-0)
Municipal, Accra
Referee: C. Monty (Mauritius), Attendance: 60.000
ZAMBIA: Vincent Chileshe, Bernard Mutale, Kaiser Kalombo, Robert Lutoba, Ackim Musenge, Katebe (Willie Phiri), Moses Simwala, Jani Simulambo, Alex Chola, Patrick Phiri, Obi Kapita (Bizwell Phiri).
UPPER VOLTA: Sidiki Diarra, Banadi, Zakaria Sanou, René Nikiema, Badou, Compaore, Hubert Hien (Traoré), Keita, Corneille Nignan, Tewinde Compaore, Cisse (Ouédraogo).
Goals: Patrick Phiri (20), Bizwell Phiri (88)

08.03.1978

NIGERIA - GHANA 1-1 (1-0)
Municipal, Accra
Referee: Hawary (Egypt), Attendance: 60.000
NIGERIA: Emmanuel Okala, Annas Ahmed, Awolaby, Muda, Christian Chukwu, Godwin Odiye, Ogu, Alloysius Atuegbu, Dina, Adokie Amesiamaka (Segun Odegbami), Kadiri.
GHANA: Salifu, Isaac Paha, Awuley Quaye, Isaac Acquaye, James Kuuka Dadzie, Adolph Armah, Anas Seidu Nketiah Yawson, Emmanuel Quarshie, Opoku Afriye, Karim Abdul Razak, Ahmed (Klutse).
Goals: Segun Odegbami (33) / Kluste (76)

10.03.1978

ZAMBIA - NIGERIA 0-0
Municipal, Accra
Referee: Benghanif (Algeria), Attendance: 25.000
ZAMBIA: Vincent Chileshe, Bernard Mutale, Kaiser Kalombo (Mwaba), Robert Lutoba, Ackim Musenge, Willie Phiri, Moses Simwala, Jani Simulambo, Godfrey Chitalu (Brighton Sinyangwe), Bizwell Phiri, Obi Kapita.
NIGERIA: Emmanuel Okala, Annas Ahmed, Awolaby, Muda (Baba Otu), Christian Chukwu, Godwin Odiye, Segun Odegbami, Alloysius Atuegbu, Adeleke (Ohnaubunwa), Ogu, Adokie Amesiamaka.

10.03.1978

GHANA - UPPER VOLTA 3-0 (1-0)
Municipal, Accra
Referee: Mutombo (Zaire), Attendance: 25.000
GHANA: Salifu, Isaac Paha, Awuley Quaye, Isaac Acquaye, James Kuuka Dadzie, Kyenkyehene, Klutse, Kayede, Alhassan, Karim Abdul Razak, Blankson (Mohamed Polo).
UPPER VOLTA: Sidiki Diarra, Bah, Zakaria Sanou, René Nikiema, Adama Oeudraogo, Compaore, Hubert Hien, Cisse, T. Ouédraogo, A. Ouédraogo, Corneille Nignan.
Goals: Alhassan (3, 59), Mohammed Polo (52)

1.	GHANA	3	2	1	0	6	2	5
2.	NIGERIA	3	1	2	0	5	3	4
3.	Zambia	3	1	1	1	3	2	3
4.	Upper Volta	3	0	0	3	2	9	0

GROUP B

06.03.1978

MOROCCO - TUNISIA 1-1 (1-0)
Municipal, Kumasi
Referee: Gebreysus Tesfaye (Ethiopia)
MOROCCO: Mohammed Hazzaz, Moustapha 'Chérif' El-Fetoui, Abbad Jawad, Larbi Ihardane, Sheita, Mohou, Mohammed Boussati, Abdallah Semmat, Ahmed Abdullah Faras, Abdelmajid Dolmy, Acila Amcharrat.
TUNISIA: Sadouk 'Attouga' Sassi, Mokhtar Dhouib, Chebli Kamel, Ali Kaabi, Mohsen Jendoubi, Ghommid, Khemais Labidi, Tarak Dhiab, Temine Lahzami, Ali Akid, Abderraouf Ben Aziza.
Goals: Acila Amcharrat (29) / Ali El Kaabi (63)

06.03.1978

UGANDA - CONGO 3-1 (2-0)
Municipal, Kumasi
Referee: Fahmy (Egypt)
UGANDA: Paul Ssali, Edward Ssemwanga, Sam Musenze, Tom Lwanga, Jimmy Kirunda, Timothy Ayieko, Mike Kiganda, Moses Nsereko, Philip 'Polly' Ouma, Phillip Omondi, Mwejiga (Godfrey Kisitu).
CONGO: Maboundou, Martial Lasiz, Gaston N'Ganga-Mouivi, Dimonekene, Joseph Mounoundzi, Dominique M'Bama, Jonas Bahamboula-M'Bemba, Jacques Ndomba, Paul Moukila, François M'Pelé, Sebastian Lakou (Mamounoubala).
Goals: Phillip Omondi (1), Edward Ssemwanga (31), Godfrey Kisitu (81) / Mamounoubala (80)

09.03.1978

TUNISIA - UGANDA 3-1 (2-0)
Municipal, Kumasi
Referee: Aouissi (Algeria), Attendance: 50.000
TUNISIA: Sadouk 'Attouga' Sassi, Mokhtar Dhouib, Mohsen Jendoubi, Chebli Kamel, Gouchi, Ghommid, Khemais Labidi, Tarak Dhiab, Lemmay Liman, Ali Akid, Abderraouf Ben Aziza.
UGANDA: Paul Ssali, Edward Ssemwanga, Sam Musenze, Tom Lwanga, Jimmy Kirunda, Moses Nsereko, Timothy Ayieko, Mike Kiganda, Phillip Omondi, Godfrey Kisitu, Barnabas Mwesiga.
Goals: Khermais Labidi (36), Abderraouf Ben Aziza (38, 83) / Sam Musenze (71)

09.03.1978

MOROCCO - CONGO 1-0 (1-0)
Municipal, Kumasi
Referee: Ndiaye (Senegal), Attendance: 50.000
MOROCCO: Mohammed Hazzaz, Moustapha 'Chérif' El-Fetoui, Abbad Jawad, Larbi Ihardane,
Anafal, Moustafa Megrouh, Mohammed Boussati, Yaghcha, Ahmed Abdullah Faras, Sheita, Acila
Amcharrat.
CONGO: Nkombou, Dimonekene, Gaston N'Ganga-Mouivi, Endzanga, Joseph Mounoundzi,
Tselantsiene, Jonas Bahamboula-M'Bemba, Dominique M'Bama, François M'Pelé, Paul Moukila,
Mamounoubala.
Goal: Acila Amcharrat (28)

11.03.1978

CONGO - TUNISIA 0-0
Municipal, Kumasi
Referee: Salem (Libya), Attendance: 20.000
CONGO: Nkombou, Dimonekene, Gaston N'Ganga-Mouivi, Endzanga, Joseph Mounoundzi,
Tselantsiene, Bouanga, Poaty, Dominique M'Bama, Daniel Ebomoa, François M'Pelé, Mamounoubala.
TUNISIA: Sadouk 'Attouga' Sassi, Ellouze, Jebali, Mohsen Jendoubi, Ali Kaabi, Gasmi (Oman
Chehaibi), Khemais Labidi (Chebli Kamel), Tarak Dhiab, Majri, Ali Akid, Abderraouf Ben Aziza.

11.03.1978

UGANDA - MOROCCO 3-0 (3-0)
Municipal, Kumasi
Referee: Lawson Tevi (Togo)
MOROCCO: Mohammed Hazzaz, Moustapha 'Chérif' El-Fetoui, Abbad Jawad, Larbi Ihardane,
Moustafa Megrouh, Sheita, Abdallah Semmat, Yaghcha, Ahmed Abdullah Faras, Abdelmajid Dolmy,
Acila Amcharrat.
UGANDA: Paul Ssali, Edward Ssemwanga, Sam Musenze (Ashe Mukasa), Tom Lwanga, Jimmy
Kirunda, Mike Kiganda, Nasur, Moses Nsereko, Phillip Omondi, Godfrey Kisitu, Isabirye.
Goals: Godfrey Kisitu (13), Moses Nsereko (32), Phillip Omondi (36)

1.	UGANDA	3	2	0	1	7	4	4
2.	TUNISIA	3	1	2	0	4	2	4
3.	Morocco	3	1	1	1	2	4	3
4.	Congo	3	0	1	2	1	4	1

Semi-finals

14.03.1978

GHANA - TUNISIA 1-0 (0-0)
Municipal, Accra
Referee: Youssef El Ghoul (Libya), Attendance: 10.000
GHANA: Joseph Carr, Isaac Paha, Awuley Quaye, Isaac Acquaye, James Kuuka Dadzie,
Kyenkyehene, Anas Seidu Nketiah Yawson, Anas, Opoku Afriye, Karim Abdul Razak, Mohamed Polo.
TUNISIA: Sadouk 'Attouga' Sassi, Mokhtar Dhouib, Mohsen Jendoubi, Ali Kaabi, Chebli Kamel,
Ghommid, Khemais Labidi, Tarak Dhiab, Lemmay Liman, Ali Akid, Abderraouf Ben Aziza (Oman
Chehaibi, Lamine Ben Aziza).
Goals: Karim Abdul Razak (57)

47

14.03.1978

UGANDA - NIGERIA 2-1 (1-0)
Municipal, Kumasi
Referee: Aouissi (Algeria)
UGANDA: Paul Ssali, Edward Ssemwanga, Musenze, Tom Lwanga, Jimmy Kirunda, Mike Kiganda, Nasur, Moses Nsereko, Phillip Omondi, Godfrey Kisitu, Isabirye.
NIGERIA: Emmanuel Okala, Annas Ahmed, Awolaby, Mudashiru Lawal, Christian Chukwu, Godwin Odiye, Ogu (Martin Eyo), Alloysius Atuegbu, Segun Odegbami, Eyele, Adokie Amesiamaka (Baba Otu).
Goals: Nasur (11), Phillip Omondi (58) / Martin Eyo (54)

Third Place Match

16.03.1978

NIGERIA - TUNISIA 1-1, awarded 2-0
Municipal, Kumasi
Refere: Lawson (Togo)
TUNISIA: Lamine Ben Aziza, Mokhtar Dhouib, Chebli Kamel, Mohsen Jendoubi, Ali Kaabi, Omar Jebali, Oman Chehaibi, Majri, Lemmay Liman, Ali Akid, Abderraouf Ben Aziza. Trainer: Chetali
NIGERIA: Emmanuel Okala, Ikhala, Christian Chukwu, Ilechukwu (Bamidele), Owolabi, Annas Ahmed, Alloysius Atuegbu, Baba Otu, Segun Odegbami, Eyo, Eyele.
Goals: Ali Akid (19) / Baba Out (42)
Match stopped at 42th minute, Tunisia withdrew

Final

16.03.1978

GHANA - UGANDA 2-0 (1-0)
Municipal, Accra
Referee: El Ghoul (Livya), Attendance: 40.000
GHANA: Joseph Carr, Isaac Paha, Awuley Quaye, Isaac Acquaye, James Kuuka Dadzie, Kyenkyehene, Anas Seidu Nketiah Yawson, Seidi, Opoku Afriye, Karim Abdul Razak, Ahmed.
UGANDA: Paul Ssali, Edward Ssemwanga, Musenze, Tom Lwanga, Jimmy Kirunda, Mike Kiganda, Nasur, Moses Nsereko, Phillip Omondi, Godfrey Kisitu, Isabirye (Lubega).
Goals: Opoku Afriye (38, 64)

Twelfth edition - 1980
Qualifying Tournament

Twenty-nine teams initially entered the competition for the 12th edition, but five of them withdrew. Nigeria, who was hosting the event, defeated Algeria by a 3-0 scoreline to win the competition for the first time and lift the new trophy.

Preliminary Round

Benin - Niger w/o

03.12.1978 Madagascar - Malawi 2-1
17.12.1978 Malawi - Madagascar 5-1

12.08.1979 Mauritius - Lesotho 0-1
26.08.1979 Lesotho - Mauritius 1-2

First Round

16.09.1979 Benin - Ivory Coast 1-0
30.09.1979 Ivory Coast - Benin 4-1

16.09.1979 Congo - Zaire 4-2
30.09.1979 Zaire - Congo 4-1

16.09.1979 Guinea - Cameroon 3-0
30.09.1979 Cameroon - Guinea 3-0
Guinea qualified on penalties

16.09.1979 Libya - Ethiopia 2-1
30.09.1979 Ethiopia - Libya 1-1

15.04.1979 Malawi - Zambia 0-2
29.04.1979 Zambia - Malawi 2-0

16.09.1979 Mauritania - Morocco 2-2
30.09.1979 Morocco - Mauritania 4-1

16.09.1979 Mauritius - Tanzania 3-2
30.09.1979 Tanzania - Mauritius 4-0

16.09.1979 Togo - Gambia 2-0
30.09.1979 Gambia - Togo 1-0

Algeria - Burundi w/o
Egypt - Somalia w/o
Kenya - Tunisia w/o
Sudan - Uganda w/o

Second Round

24.10.1979 Algeria - Libya 3-1
06.11.1979 Libya - Algeria 1-0

24.10.1979 Kenya - Egypt 3-1
06.11.1979 Egypt - Kenya 3-0

28.10.1979 Morocco - Togo 7-0
11.11.1979 Togo - Morocco 2-1

28.10.1979 Sudan - Ivory Coast 2-0
11.11.1979 Ivory Coast - Sudan 4-0

28.10.1979 Tanzania - Zambia 1-0
11.11.1979 Zambia - Tanzania 1-1

28.10.1979 Zaire - Guinea 3-2
11.11.1979 Guinea - Zaire 3-1

Final Tournament (Nigeria)

GROUP A

08.03.1980

NIGERIA - TANZANIA 3-1 (2-0)
Surulere, Lagos
Referee: El-Naim Suliman (Sudan), Attendance: 80.000
NIGERIA: Best Ogedegbe, David Adiele, Okey Isima, Tunde Bamidele, Christian Chukwu, Alloysius Atuegbu (Sylvanus Okpalla), Mudashiru Lawal, Henry Nwosu, Segun Odegbami, Ifeanyi Onyedika (Felix Owolabi), Adokie Amiesiamaka.
TANZANIA: Mambosasa, Leopold Tasso, Leodgar Tenga, Jella Matagwa, Mohammed Kajole, Hussein N'gulungo, M'temi Ramadhan, Juma M'Kambi, Omar Hussein, Massewa, Waziri (Peter Tino).
Goals: Mudashiru Lawal (13), Ifeanyi Onyedika (36), Segun Odegbami (85) / Juma M'Kambi (54)

8.03.1980

EGYPT - IVORY COAST 2-1 (2-1)
Surulere, Lagos
Referee: J.D. Mondoka (Zambia), Referee: 80.000
EGYPT: Adel El-Maamour (Ahmed Ikramy), Mohamed Salah El-Din, Maher Hammam, Mohamed Bedair, Fathi Mabrouk, Shawki Gareeb, Hassan Shehata (Mohamed Amer), Ahmed Abdel Halim, Moustafa Abdou, Mokhtar Mokhtar, Mosaad Nour.
IVORY COAST: Ettoukan (Konate), Die Foneye, Bouabre, Kuyo, Gaston Adjoukoua, François Zahoui, Kobenan, Pascal Miézan, Ani Gome, Laurent N'Dri Pokou, Traoré.
Goals: Maher Hammam (8), Mokhtar Mokhtar (20) / Ani Gomé (7)

12.03.1980

EGYPT - TANZANIA 2-1 (2-0)
Surulere, Lagos
Referee: R. Sohan (Mauritius), Attendance: 55.000
EGYPT: Ahmed Ikramy Ahmed El-Shahat, Mohamed Salah El-Din, Maher Hammam, Mahmoud Saad (Moustafa Younis), Fathi Mabrouk, Shawki Ghareeb, Hassan Shehata, Saad Selait, Moustafa Abdou, Mokhtar Mokhtar (Mohamed Amer), Mosaad Nour.
TANZANIA: Juma Pondamali, Mohammed Rishard, Leodgar Tenga, Jella Matagwa, Ahmed Thabit, Hussein N'gulungo, M'temi Ramadhan, Juma M'Kambi (Charles Alberto), Omar Hussein, Massewa (Peter Tino), Waziri.
Goals: Hassan Shehata (32), Mosaad Nour (38) / Wazir (86)

12.03.1980

NIGERIA - IVORY COAST 0-0
Surulere, Lagos
Referee: T. Lawson-Hetcheli (Togo), Attendance: 55.000
NIGERIA: Best Ogedegbe, David Adiele, Okey Isima, Tunde Bamidele, Christian Chukwu, Sylvanus Okpalla, Mudashiru Lawal, Henry Nwosu (Martin Eyo), Segun Odegbami, Ifeanyi Onyedika (Shefiu Mohammed), Adokie Amiesiamaka.
IVORY COAST: Konate, Zogbo, Cisse, Kuyo, Depie, François Zahoui, Kobenan, Pascal Miézan, Ani Gome, Bohe (Laurent N'Dri Pokou), Lebri.

15.03.1980

IVORY COAST - TANZANIA 1-1 (1-0)
Surulere, Lagos
Referee: M. Diallo Bakai (Cameroon), Attendance: 70.000
TANZANIA: Juma Pondamali, Salim Amir, Jella Matagwa (Leopold Tasso), Leodgar Tenga, Ahmed Thabit, Mohamed Rishard, M'temi Ramadhan, Wazir, Omar Hussein, Charles Alberto, Peter Tino (Massewa)
IVORY COAST: Konate, Zogbo, Cisse (Boaubre), Kuyo, Emile Gnahoré, François Zahoui, Kobenan, Pascal Miézan, Ani Gome, Michael Goba Michel, Lebri.
Goals: Kobenan (7) / Wazir (59)

15.03.1980

NIGERIA - EGYPT 1-0 (1-0)
Surulere, Lagos
Referee: Gebreysus Tesfaye (Ethiopia), Attendance: 70.000
NIGERIA: Best Ogedegbe, David Adiele, Okey Isima, Tunde Bamidele, Christian Chukwu, Alloysius Atuegbu, Mudashiru Lawal, Felix Owalabi (Sylvanus Okpalla), Segun Odegbami, Ifeanyi Onyedika (Godwin Odiye), Adokie Amiesiamaka.
EGYPT: Ahmed Ikramy Ahmed El-Shahat, Moahmed Omar, Moustafa Younis (Mohamed Bedair), Maher Hammam, Sami Mansour, Shawki Ghareeb, Ramadan El-Sayed, Ahmed Abdel Halim, Mohamed Amer, Moustafa Abdou, Yasser Mohamadi (Mahmoud El-Khateeb).
Goal: Okey Isima (15)

1.	NIGERIA	3	2	1	0	4	1	5
2.	EGYPT	3	2	0	1	4	3	4
3.	Ivory Coast	3	0	2	1	2	3	2
4.	Tanzania	3	0	1	2	3	6	1

GROUP B

09.03.1980

GHANA - ALGERIA 0-0
Liberty, Ibadan
Referee: Mohamed El-Ghoul (Libya), Attendance: 40.000
GHANA: Joseph Carr, Ofei Ansah, Isaac Acquaye, Charles Dadzie, Hesse Odamtten, Adolf Armah, Dan Kayede (Papa Arko), Emmanuel Quarshie, Anas Seidu Nketiah Yawson, Opoku Afriyie, Francis Kumi (Willie Klutse).
ALGERIA: Mehdi Cerbah, Chaabane Merzekane, Mahmoud Guendouz, Mohamed Kheddis, Mustapha Kouici, Bouzid Mahyouz, Ali Fergani, Lakhdar Belloumi, Rabah Madjer, Tadj Bensaoula, Salah Assad (Hocine Benmiloudi).

09.03.1980

MOROCCO - GUINEA 1-1 (1-1)
Liberty, Ibadan
Referee: P. Preira (Senegal), Attendance: 40.000
MOROCCO: Laalou, M'barek El Filali, Ahmed Limane, Mouhou, Tahir Mustapha, Timoumi, Abdelaziz Daidi, Fatmi Houmma, Khaled Labied, Jamel Jebbran, Aziz Bouderbala.
GUINEA: Abdoulaye Keita, Fode Fofana, Diaby Alseny, Ibrahima Touré, Ibrahima Sory, Moussa Camara, Naby Laye Camara (Ibrahima Diawara), Cheikh Keita, Mory Koné, Amara Touré, Seydouba Bangoura (S. Traoré), Bengaly Sylla.
Goals: Moustafa Tahiri (7) / Moussa Camara (8)

51

13.03.1980

ALGERIA - MOROCCO 1-0 (0-0)
Liberty, Ibadan
Referee: Ali Dridi (Tunisia).
ALGERIA: Mehdi Cerbah, Chaabane Merzekane, Mahmoud Guendouz, Mohamed Kheddis, Mustapha Kouici (Salah Larbès), Bouzid Mahyouz, Ali Fergani, Lakhdar Belloumi, Rabah Madjer, Tadj Bensaoula, Salah Assad (Hocine Benmiloudi).
MOROCCO: Badou Zaki, Hocine Bouchkhachekh, Ahmed Limane, Essedik Hannoun, M'barek El-Filali, Said Benzemmouri, Fatmi Houmma, Abdelaziz Daidi, Aziz Bouderbala (Mohamed Loukhaïli), Jamel Jebran, Khaled Labied.
Goal: Lakhdar Belloumi (90)

13.03.1980

GHANA - GUINEA 1-0 (0-0)
Liberty, Ibadan
Referee: G. Odengo (Kenya)
GHANA: Joseph Carr, Ofei Ansah, Isaac Acquaye, Charles Dadzie, Hesse Odamtten, Adolf Armah, Emmanuel Quarshie, Dan Kayede, Anas Seidu Nketiah Yawson, Opoku Afriyie (Willie Klutse), Francis Kumi.
GUINEA: Abdoulaye Keita, Fode Fofana, Diaby Alseny, Ibrahima Touré, Moussa Camara, Naby Laye Camara (Cheikh Keita), Djibril Diarra, Mory Koné, Amara Touré, Seydouba Bangoura, Bengaly Sylla.
Goals: Willie Klutse (69)

16.03.1980

ALGERIA - GUINEA 3-2 (2-0)
Liberty, Ibadan
Referee: Idrissa Traoré (Mali).
ALGERIA: Mehdi Cerbah, Chaabane Merzekane (Abderahmane Derouaz), Mahmoud Guendouz, Mohamed Kheddis, Salah Larbès, Rabah Madjer (Smaïn Slimani), Ali Fergani, Lakhdar Belloumi, Tadj Bensaoula, Hocine Benmiloudi, Salah Assad.
GUINEA: Abdoulaye Keïta, Djibril Diarra, Ibrahima Sory, Alseni Diaby, Moussa Camara, Sekou Sylla (Salifou Keita), Cheikh Mohamed Keita (Ibrahima Diawara), Mory Koné, Amara Toure, Seydouba Bangoura, Bengaly Sylla.
Goals: Tadj Bensaoula (12, 49), Hocine Benmiloudi (37) / Ibrahima Diawara (82), Seydoura Bangoura (90)

16.03.1980

MOROCCO - GHANA 1-0 (1-0)
Liberty, Ibadan
Referee: Dodou N'Jie (Gambia)
MOROCCO: Badou Zaki, M'barek El-Filali, Essedik Hannoun, Ahmed Limane, Said Benzemmouri, Timoumi, Fatmi Houmma, Abdelaziz Daidi, Khaled Labied, Jamel Jebran, Aziz Bouderbala.
GHANA: Joseph Carr, Ofei Ansah, Isaac Acquaye, Charles Dadzie, Hesse Odamtten (Isaac Paha), Adolf Armah, Emmanuel Quarshie, Kingston Asabir (Papa Arko), Anas Seidu Nketiah Yawson, Willie Klutse, Francis Kumi.
Goal: Khaled Labied (44)

1.	ALGERIA	3	2	1	0	4	2	5
2.	MOROCCO	3	1	1	1	2	2	3
3.	Ghana	3	1	1	1	1	1	3
4.	Guinea	3	0	1	2	3	5	1

Semi-finals

19.03.1980

NIGERIA - MOROCCO 1-0 (1-0)
Surulere, Lagos
Referee: El-Naim Suliman (Sudan), Attendance: 70.000
NIGERIA: Best Ogedegbe, David Adiele, Okey Isima, Tunde Bamidele, Felix Owolabi (Sylvanus Okpalla), Mudashiru Lawal, Christian Chukwu, Alloysius Atuegbu, Segun Odegbami, Ifeanyi Onyedika (Godwin Odiye), Adokie Amiesiamaka.
MOROCCO: Badou Zaki, Said Benzemmouri (Loukhaili), Ahmed Limane, Essedik Hannoun, M'barek El-Filali, Timoumi, Abdelaziz Daidi, Fatmi Houmma, Khaled Labied (Bentaibi), Jamel Jebran, Aziz Bouderbala.
Goal: Felix Owolabi (8)

19.03.1980

ALGERIA - EGYPT 2-2 (0-1, 2-2), 4-2 penalties
Liberty, Ibadan
Referee: Tevi Lawson-Hetcheli (Togo), Attendance: 5000
ALGERIA: Mehdi Cerbah, Abderahmane Derouaz, Mohamed Kheddis, Chaabane Merzekane, Salah Larbès, Smaïn Slimani (Bouzid Mahyouz), Ali Fergani, Lakhdar Belloumi, Rabah Madjer (Hocine Benmiloudi), Tadj Bensaoula, Salah Assad.
EGYPT: Ahmed Ikramy, Mohamed Salah El-Din, Maher Hammam (Mahmoud Saad), Mahmoud Bedair, Fathi Mabrouk, Shawki Ghareeb, Hassan Shehata, Ramadhan El-Sayed (Mohamed Amer), Moustafa Abdou, Mokhtar Mokhtar, Mahmoud El-Khateeb.
Derouaz sent off
Goals: Salah Assad (55 penalty), Hocine Benmiloudi (62) / Mahmoud El-Khateeb (32), Ramadan El-Sayed (47)

Third Place Match

21.03.1980

MOROCCO - EGYPT 2-0 (1-0)
Surulere, Lagos
Referee: Gabriel Odengo (Kenya), Attendance: 5000
MOROCCO: Badou Zaki, Bouchkhachekh, Ahmed Limane, Mohou, M'barek El-Filali, Timoumi, Abdelaziz Daidi, Fatmi Houmma (Essedik Hannoun), Khaled Labied, Jamel Jebran, Aziz Bouderbala.
Trainer: Just Fontaine (France)
EGYPT: Adel El-Maamour, Mohamed Omar, Moustafa Younis, Mahmoud Saad, Fathi Mabrouk, Shawki Ghareeb (Saad Selait), Hassan Shehata, Mokhtar Mokhtar, Mohamed Amer, Mahmoud El-Khateeb (Ahmed Abdel Halim), Mosaad Nour.
Goals: Khaled Labied (9, 78)

Final

22.03.1980

NIGERIA - ALGERIA 3-0 (2-0)
Surulere, Lagos
Referee: Gebreyesus Tesfaye (Ethiopia), Attendance: 80.000
NIGERIA: Best Ogedengbe, David Adiele, Christian Chukwu, Babatunde Bamidele, Alloysius Atuegbu, Godwin Odiye (Ikhana Kadiri), Felix Owolabi, Okey Isima, Segun Odegbami, Mudashiru Lawal, Adokie Amiesemeka. Trainer: Otto Gloria (Brazil)
ALGERIA: Mehdi Cerbah, Chaabane Merzekane, Abdelkader Horr, Mohammed Khedis, Mustapha Kouici, Bouzid Mahyouz, Ali Fergani, Lakhdar Belloumi (Guemri), Salah Assad, Tadj Bensaoula (Rabah Madjer), Benmiloudi. Trainer: Mahieddine Khalef
Goals: Segun Odegbami (2, 42), Mudashiru Lawal (50)

Thirteen edition - 1982
Qualifying Tournament

Thirty five teams entered the 13th edition, but once again five of them withdrew. Libya was host of the finals tournament and the regulations of the competitions were adjusted to run in accordance with those of FIFA, which state that any player who is a citizen of a country, is qualified to play for the national team. This removed the Cup's previous limitation on the number of players who were signed to overseas clubs and allowed teams to field their strongest teams featuring all of their most talented professionals. Libya, the hosts, reached the final of the competition where they were beaten by Ghana following a penalty shoot-out, despite an intimidating projectile-throwing partisan crowd who invaded the pitch following the game! This was the fourth time the Ghanaians had won their continental title and they have not managed the same feat since.

Preliminary Round

17.11.80 Angola - Congo 1-1
30.11.80 Congo - Angola 0-0

09.11.80 Liberia - Gambia 0-0
23.11.80 Gambia - Liberia 1-1

14.09.80 Madagascar - Mauritius 0-0
28.09.80 Mauritius - Madagascar 1-1

26.10.80 Malawi - Zimbabwe 0-1
09.11.80 Zimbabwe - Malawi 1-1

28.09.80 Mali - Mauritania 2-0
12.10.80 Mauritania - Mali 2-1

10.08.80 Mozambique - Lesotho 6-1
24.08.80 Lesotho - Mozambique 2-1

17.11.80 Senegal - Sierra Leone 2-0
30.11.80 Sierra Leone - Senegal 1-2

Equatorial Guinea - Benin w/o
Rwanda - Uganda w/o
Upper Volta - Gabon w/o

First Round

10.04.81 Algeria - Mali 5-1
19.04.81 Mali - Algeria 3-0

05.04.81 Cameroon - Togo 4-0
19.04.81 Togo - Cameroon 2-2

26.04.81 Ethiopia - Rwanda 1-0
10.05.81 Rwanda - Ethiopia 1-0, 3-4 on penalties

11.04.81 Ghana - Congo 1-1
26.04.81 Congo - Ghana 0-1

04.04.81 Kenya – Egypt 3-5
18.04.81 Egypt - Kenya 2-0

25.03.81 Morocco - Liberia 3-1
04.04.81 Liberia - Morocco 0-5

12.04.81 Tunisia - Senegal 1-0
26.04.81 Senegal - Tunisia 0-0

05.04.81 Zaire - Mozambique 2-1
19.04.81 Mozambique - Zaire 3-3

11.04.81 Zimbabwe - Zambia 0-1
25.04.81 Zambia - Zimbabwe 2-0

Madagascar - Tanzania w/o
Guinea - Equatorial Guinea w/o

Second Round

30.08.81 Algeria - Upper Volta 7-0
20.09.81 Upper Volta - Algeria 1-1

16.08.81 Cameroon - Madagascar 5-1
30.08.81 Madagascar - Cameroon 2-1

22.07.81 Ghana - Zaire 2-2
02.08.81 Zaire - Ghana 1-2

28.06.81 Guinea - Ethiopia 2-2
04.10.81 Ethiopia - Guinea 1-1

16.08.81 Morocco - Zambia 2-1
30.08.81 Zambia - Morocco 2-0

Tunisia - Egypt w/o

Final Tournament (Libya)

GROUP A

05.03.1982

LIBYA - GHANA 2-2 (0-1)
11th June stadium, Tripoli
Referee: Ramlochun (Mauritius), Attendance: 40.000
LIBYA: Kouafi, Sasi El Ajaili, Kareif, Salah Sola, Mohammed El Beshari, Majdoub (Ferjani), Abdel Razik Salem Garana, Mansour Mohammed Omar, Suliman (Zeiw), Fawzi El Issawi, El Fergani.
GHANA: Owusu Mensah, Haruna Yusif, Sampson Lamptey, Isaac Paha, Kwame Sampson, Albert Asase, Kofi Badu, Emmanuel Quarshie (Abedi Pelé), Koffi Abbrey, George Alhassan, Samuel Opoku Nti.
Goals: Abdel Razik Salem Garana (58), Fawzi El Isswai (76) / George Alhassan (28), Samuel Opoku N'ti (89)

05.03.1982

CAMEROON - TUNISIA 1-1 (0-0)
11th June stadium, Tripoli
Referee: Bakary Sarr (Senegal), Attendance: 40.000
CAMEROON: Thomas N'Kono, René N'Djeya, Ibrahim Aoudou, François N'doumbé, Ephrem M'Bom, Theophile Abéga, Emmanuel Kundé, Gregoire Mbida, Ernest Ebongué, Roger Milla, Jacques N'Guea.
TUNISIA: Kamel, Ouachi, Kanzari, Khaled Ben Yahia, Ali Kaabi, Djebali, Tarak Dhiab, Seddik, Hsoumi, Fahem (Kamel Gabsi), Abdelli.
Goals: Gregoire Mbida (50) / Kamel Gabsi (49)

09.03.1982

CAMEROON - GHANA 0-0
11th June stadium, Tripoli
Referee: Mohamed Larache (Morocco), Attendance: 40.000
CAMEROON: Thomas N'Kono, Edmond Enoka, Ibrahim Aoudou, Jean Bosco Onana, Ephrem M'Bom, Theophile Abéga, Emmanuel Kundé, Gregoire Mbida, Bonaventure D'Jonkep, Roger Milla, Jacques N'Guea (Ekoule).
GHANA: Owusu Mensah, Haruna Yusif, Sampson Lamptey, Isaac Paha, Kwame Sampson, Albert Asase, Kofi Badu (Abedi Pelé), Emmanuel Quarshie, Koffi Abbrey, George Alhassan, Samuel Opoku Nti.

09.03.1982

LIBYA - TUNISIA 2-0 (1-0)
11th June stadium, Tripoli
Referee: Kambaji Kabongo (Zaire), Attendance: 40.000
LIBYA: Kouafi, Sasi El Ajaili, Kareif, Salah Sola, Mohammed El Beshari, Majdoub, Abdel Razik Salem Garana, El Fergami, Mansour Mohammed Omar, Fawzi El Issawi, Suliman (El Borosi).
TUNISIA: Kamel, Ouachi, Djebali, Kanzari, Chebbi, Ali Kaabi, Khaled Ben Yahia, Tarak Dhiab, Abdelli, Hsoumi (Ben Massaoud), Kamel Gabsi (Fahem).
Goals: Kamel (42 own goal), El Borosi (83)

12.03.1982

GHANA - TUNISIA 1-0 (1-0)
11th June stadium, Tripoli
Referee: Idrissa Traoré (Mali), Attendance: 40.000
GHANA: Owusu Mensah, Haruna Yusif, Sampson Lamptey, Isaac Paha, Kwame Sampson, Albert Asase, Abedi Pelé, Emmanuel Quarshie (Kofi Badu), John Essien, Opoku Afriyie (George Alhassan), Koffi Abbrey.
TUNISIA: Naili, Ouachi, Chergui, Chebbi, Ali Kaabi, Djebali, Khaled Ben Yahia, Tarak Dhiab, Seddik, Gomri (Hsoumi), Fahem (Kamel Gabsi).
Goal: John Essien (28)

12.03.1982

LIBYA - CAMEROON 0-0
11th June stadium, Tripoli
Referee: Babacar Fall (Mauritania), Attendance: 40.000
CAMEROON: Thomas N'Kono, Charles Toubé, Ibrahim Aoudou, Jean Bosco Onana, Ephrem M'Bom, Theophile Abéga, Emmanuel Kundé, Gregoire Mbida, Ekoule, Roger Milla, Bonaventure D'Jonkep (Ernest Ebongué).
LIBYA: Kouafi, Sasi El Ajaili, Salah Sola, Zeiw, Mohammed El Beshari, Majdoub, Karef, Abdel Razik Salem Garana (Suliman), Suliman Mansour Mohammed Omar (Ferjani), El Fergani, Fawzi El Issawi.

1.	LIBYA	3	1	2	0	4	2	4
2.	GHANA	3	1	2	0	3	2	4
3.	Cameroon	3	0	3	0	1	1	3
4.	Tunisia	3	0	1	2	1	4	1

GROUP B

07.03.1982

NIGERIA - ETHIOPIA 3-0 (2-0)
28th March stadium, Benghazi
Referee: Bester Kalombo (Malawi), Attendance: 5000
NIGERIA: Fregene, Charles Yanchio, Stephen Keshi, Tunde Bamidele, Okey Isima, Sylvanus Okpala, Mudashiru Lawal, Henry Nwosu, Ademola Adeshina (Orgi), Osigwe, Felix Owolabi.
ETHIOPIA: Tesfaye Gebru, Mulualem, Tamerat, Tesfaye Kebede, Ayele, Hailu (Ermias), Dagnachew, Tesfamical, Solomon, Nigussie, Kassahun.
Goals: Stephen Keshi (27, 82), Ademola Adeshina (40)

07.03.1982

ALGERIA - ZAMBIA 1-0 (0-0)
28th March stadium, Benghazi
Referee: Dodou N'Jie (Gambia), Attendance: 5000
ALGERIA: Mehdi Cerbah, Salah Larbes, Chaabane Merzekane, Abdelkader Horr, Moustapha Kouici, Ali Bencheikh, Ali Fergani, Salah Assad, Rabah Madjer, Ahmed Ait Hocine (Amokrane), Hocine Yahi (Khaloufi).
ZAMBIA: Michael Bwalya, Milton Muke (Mwaba), Emmy Musonda, Michael Musonda, John Kalusa, Shinde, Alex Chola, Willie Phiri, Geoffrey Munshya (Jack Chanda), Hangunyu, Peter Kaumba.
Goal: Chaabane Merzekane (85)

10.03.1982

ZAMBIA - ETHIOPIA 1-0 (0-0)
28th March stadium, Benghazi
Referee: Mohamed Jama (Somalia), Attendance: 5000
ZAMBIA: Mulenga, Milton Muke, Emmy Musonda, Michael Musonda, John Kalusa, Willie Phiri, Alex Chola, Shinde (Kaoma), Patrick Phiri, Geoffrey Munshya, Peter Kaumba.
ETHIOPIA: Lemma, Mulualem, Tamerat, Tesfaye Kebede, Ayele, Ermias, Tesfamical, Hailu, Tefera, Nigussie (Girma), Haddish.
Goal: Geoffrey Munshya (68)

10.03.1982

ALGERIA - NIGERIA 2-1 (1-1)
28th March stadium, Benghazi
Referee: Cheikh Mbaye (Senegal), Attendance: 5000
ALGERIA: Mehdi Cerbah, Salah Larbes, Chaabane Merzekane, Abdelkader Horr, Moustapha Kouici, Ali Bencheikh, Ali Fergani, Salah Assad, Rabah Madjer, Amokrane (Ahmed Ait Hocine), Hocine Yahi.
NIGERIA: Fregene, Charles Yanchio (Orgi), Stephen Keshi, Tunde Bamidele, Okey Isima, Fatai, Mudashiru Lawal, Henry Nwosu, Ademola Adeshina, Osigwe, Felix Owolabi.
Goals: Rabah Madjer (45), Salah Assad (65) / Okey Isima (44)

13.03.1982

ALGERIA - ETHIOPIA 0-0
28th March stadium, Benghazi
Referee: Hugue Opangault (Congo), Attendance: 5000
ALGERIA: Mehdi Cerbah, Salah Larbes, Chaabane Merzekane, Abdelkader Horr, Moustapha Kouici, Ali Bencheikh, Ali Fergani, Salah Assad, Rabah Madjer, Amokrane (Lakhdar Belloumi), Hocine Yahi (Khaloufi).
ETHIOPIA: Lemma, Mulualem, Nigussie, Tamerat, Tesfaye Kebede, Zaid, Tefera, Dagnachew, Ermias, Tesfamical, Solomon.

13.03.1982

ZAMBIA - NIGERIA 3-0 (1-0)
28th March stadium, Benghazi
Referee: Sydney Picon (Mauritius), Attendance: 5000
ZAMBIA: Mulenga, Milton Muke, Emmy Musonda, Michael Musonda, John Kalusa, Aron Njovu, Alex Chola, Willie Phiri, Patrick Phiri, Hangunyu, Peter Kaumba.
NIGERIA: Fregene, Okey Isima, Stephen Keshi, Tunde Bamidele, Felix Owolabi, Boateng, Mudashiru Lawal, Henry Nwosu (Orgi), Ademola Adeshina, Owokoribi, Adelabu.
Goals: Peter Kaumba (25), Aron Njovu (80), Fregence (81 own goal)

1.	ALGERIA	3	2	1	0	3	1	5
2.	ZAMBIA	3	2	0	1	4	1	4
3.	Nigeria	3	1	0	2	4	5	2
4.	Ethiopia	3	0	1	2	0	4	1

Semi-finals

16.03.1982

ALGERIA - GHANA 2-3 (1-1, 2-2)
28th March stadium, Benghazi
Referee: Bester Kalombo (Malawi), Attendance: 5000
GHANA: Owusu Mensah, Haruna Yusif, Sampson Lamptey, Isaac Paha, Kwame Sampson, Albert Asase, Emmanuel Quarshie, Kofi Badu, John Essien, George Alhassan, Koffi Abbrey (Samuel Opoku Nti).
ALGERIA: Mehdi Cerbah, Salah Larbes, Chaabane Merzekane (Rabah Djennadi), Abdelkader Horr, Moustapha Kouici, Ali Bencheikh, Ali Fergani, Lakhdar Belloumi, Rabah Madjer (Hocine Yahi), Djamel Zidane, Salah Assad.
Goals: Djamel Zidane (29), Asaad (62) / George Alhassan (4, 103), Samuel Opoku N'ti (90)

16.03.1982

LIBYA - ZAMBIA 2-1 (1-1)
11th June stadium, Tripoli
Referee: Bakary Sarr (Senegal), Attendance: 50.000
LIBYA: Kouafi, Sasi El Ajaili, Salah Sola, Zeiw, Mohammed El Beshari, Majdoub, Abdel Razik Salem Garana, Ferjani, El Fergani (Gonaim), Fawzi El Issawi, El Borosi (Kareif).
ZAMBIA: Mulenga (Michael Bwalya), Milton Muke, Emmy Musonda, Michael Musonda, John Kalusa, Aron Njovu, Alex Chola, Willie Phiri, Patrick Phiri (Kamana), Hangunyu, Peter Kaumba.
Goals: Mohammed El Beshari (38, 84) / Peter Kaumba (29)

Third Place Match

18.03.1982

ZAMBIA - ALGERIA 2-0 (2-0)
11th June stadium, Tripoli
Referee: Cheikh Mbaye (Senegal), Attendance: 2000
ZAMBIA: Michael Bwalya, Milton Muke, Emmy Musonda, Michael Musonda, John Kalusa, Kalombo, Jack Chanda, Aron Njovu, Geoffrey Munshya (Alex Chola), Ashios Melu, Peter Kaumba. Trainer: Ante Buselić (Yugoslavia)
ALGERIA: Mourad Sadek Amara, Rabah Djennadi, Abdelkader Horr, Meziane Ighil, Moustapha Kouici, Mohamed Kaci-Said, Ali Bencheikh, Lakhdar Belloumi, Rabah Madjer, Ahmed Ait Hocine (Hocine Yahi), Salah Assad. Trainer: Mahieddine Khalef / Rachid Mekloufi
Goals: Peter Kaumba (2), Geoffrey Munshya (25)

Final

19.03.1982

GHANA - LIBYA 1-1 (1-0, 1-1), 7-6 on penalties
11th June stadium, Tripoli
Referee: Sohan Ramlochun (Mauritius), Attendance: 50.000
GHANA: Owusu Mensah, Haruna Yusif, L. Sampson, Isaac Paha, Kwame Sampson, Albert Asase, Emmanuel Quarshie, Kofi Badu (Abedi Pelé), John Essien (Samuel Opoku Nti), George Alhassan, Kofi Abbrey. Trainer: Charles Kumi Gyamfi
LIBYA: Kouafi, Sasi El Ajaili, Salah Sola, Zeiw, Mohammed El Beshari, Majdoub (El Borosi), Abdel Razik Salem Garana, Ferjani, El Fergani (Suliman Abubaker), Fawzi El Issawi, Gonaim. Trainer: Bela Goltl (Hungary)
Goals: George Alhassan (35) / Mohammed El Beshari (70)

Fourteenth edition - 1984
Qualifying Tournament

Thirty-six countries entered the 14th edition of the competition though, due to various reasons, three of them withdrew. The finals tournament was held in the Ivory Coast and Cameroon beat Nigeria in the final to win their first-ever Africa Cup of Nations title.

Preliminary Round

18.11.82 Gabon - Angola 2-2
28.11.82 Angola - Gabon 4-0

12.09.82 Malawi - Zimbabwe 2-0
03.10.82 Zimbabwe - Malawi 0-2

14.11.82 Mali - Gambia 3-1
28.11.82 Gambia - Mali 1-0

14.11.82 Niger - Senegal 0-0
28.11.82 Senegal - Niger 1-0

19.09.82 Somalia - Rwanda 0-1

12.09.82 Tanzania - Uganda 1-1
26.09.82 Uganda - Tanzania 3-2

14.11.82 Togo - Sierra Leone 3-0
28.11.82 Sierra Leone - Togo 0-1

Benin - Liberia w/o
Mauritius - Lesotho w/o
Mozambique - Swaziland w/o

First Round

08.04.83 Algeria - Benin 6-2
24.04.83 Benin - Algeria 1-1

10.04.83 Congo - Egypt 2-0
22.04.83 Egypt - Congo 2-0
Egypt qualified on penalties

10.04.83 Ethiopia - Mauritius 1-0
24.04.83 Mauritius - Ethiopia 1-0
Ethiopia qualified on penalties

10.04.83 Guinea - Togo 0-1
24.04.83 Togo - Guinea 2-0

08.04.83 Libya - Senegal 2-1
24.04.83 Senegal - Libya 1-0

10.04.83 Madagascar - Uganda 1-0
24.04.83 Uganda - Madagascar 2-1

10.04.83 Morocco - Mali 4-0
24.04.83 Mali - Morocco 2-0

03.04.83 Mozambique - Cameroon 3-0
24.04.83 Cameroon - Mozambique 4-0

10.04.83 Nigeria - Angola 2-0
24.04.83 Angola - Nigeria 1-0

10.04.83 Sudan - Zambia 2-1
24.04.83 Zambia - Sudan 0-0

10.04.83 Tunisia - Rwanda 5-0
24.04.83 Rwanda - Tunisia 0-1

Malawi - Zaire w/o

Second Round

14.08.83 Cameroon - Sudan 5-0
28.08.83 Sudan - Cameroon 2-0

14.08.83 Egypt - Tunisia 1-0
28.08.83 Tunisia - Egypt 0-0

03.07.83 Ethiopia - Togo 2-1
28.08.83 Togo - Ethiopia 3-0

14.08.83 Madagascar - Malawi 0-1
28.08.83 Malawi - Madagascar 1-1

14.08.83 Nigeria - Morocco 0-0
28.08.83 Morocco - Nigeria 0-0, 3-4 on penalties

14.08.83 Senegal - Algeria 1-1
28.08.83 Algeria - Senegal 2-0

Final Tournament (Ivory Coast)

GROUP A

04.03.1984

IVORY COAST - TOGO 3-0 (1-0)
Félix Houphouet-Boigny, Abidjan
Referee: Benacceur (Tunisia), Attendance: 50.000
IVORY COAST: Koffi Kouadio, Emile Gnahoré, François Monguéhi, Aime Tchéchté, Gaston Adjoukoua, Pascal Miézan, Jean-Michel Akenon (71 Ignace Guédé-Gba), Joseph Gadji-Celi, Désiré Sikely, Tia Koffi (46 Michael Goba), Youssouf Fofana. Trainer: David Ferreira
TOGO: Assogba Yaovi, Sanunu Essoazina, Denké Wazo, Mawuéna Kodjovi, Alassane Nassirou, Koami Dos Reis, Djogou Tao Akoulassi, Efoé Mensah, Sunu Mawuli (Boukari Saadou), Messan Modjro (Da Silvéira Adjé), Moutairou Rafiou. Trainer: Gottlieb Goller
Goals: Tia Koffi (27), Yussuf Fofana (62), Michael Goba (75)

04.03.1984

EGYPT - CAMEROON 1-0 (0-0)
Félix Houphouet-Boigny, Abidjan
Referee: Gebreysus Tesfaye (Ethiopia), Attendance: 50,000
EGYPT: Thabet El-Batal, Ali Shehata, Hamada Sedki, Ibrahim Youssef, Rabei Yassin, Shawki
Ghareeb, Magdi Abdel Ghani, Taher Abou Zaid, Emad Soliman (82 Mahmoud Hassan), Mahmoud El-
Khateeb (60 Nasser Mohamed Ali), Zakaria Nasef. Trainer: Salah El-Wahsh
CAMEROON: Thomas N'Kono, Charles Toubé, René N'Djeya, François Ndoumbé, Ibrahim Aoudou,
Théophile Abéga, Emmanuel Kundé, Gregoire Gregoire Mbida (67 Dagobert Dang), Ernest Ebongué,
Roger Milla, Bonaventure D'Jonkep. Trainer: Reda Ognanović
Goal: Taher Abou Zaid (75)

07.03.1984

CAMEROON - TOGO 4-1 (3-0)
Félix Houphouet-Boigny, Abidjan
Referee: Mulenga (Zambia), Attendance: 40.000
CAMEROON: Thomas N'Kono, Charles Toubé, René N'Djeya, François Ndoumbé, Luc Mbassi,
Théophile Abéga (74 Dagobert Dang), Emmanuel Kundé, Ibrahim Aoudou, Ernest Ebongué, Roger
Milla (46 Nicolas Makon), Bonaventure D'Jonkep.
TOGO: Assogba Yaovi, Sanunu Essoazina, Denké Wazo, Mawuéna Kodjovi, Koami Dos Reis,
Moutairou Rafiou, Efoé Mensah, Djogou Tao Akoulassi, Abdoul Fayé, Boukari Saadou (25 Da Silvéira
Adjé), Quashie Ayivon (46 Sunu Mawuli).
Goals: Bonaventure D'Jonkep (6), Théophile Abéga (21, 60), Ibrahim Aoudou (45) / Rafiou Moutairou
(54)

07.03.1984

EGYPT - IVORY COAST 2-1 (0-0)
Félix Houphouet-Boigny, Abidjan
Referee: Picon (Mauritius), Attendance: 40.000
EGYPT: Thabet El-Batal, Ali Shehata, Hamada Sedki, Ibrahim Youssef, Rabei Yassin, Shawki
Ghareeb, Magdi Abdel Ghani, Taher Abou Zaid, Mohamed Radwan (46 Mahmoud Hassan), Zakaria
Nasef (67 Naser Mohamed Ali), Emad Soliman
IVORY COAST: Koffi Kouadio, Emile Gnahoré (7 Ignace Guédé-Gba), François Monguéhi, Aime
Tchéchté, Gaston Adjoukoua, Pascal Miézan, Joseph Gadji-Celi, Kablan Miézan, Désiré Sikely, Tia
Koffi (70 Michael Goba), Youssouf Fofana.
Goals: Taher Abou Zaid (66, 72) / Kablan Miézan (53)

10.03.1984

EGYPT – TOGO 0-0
Félix Houphouet-Boigny, Abidjan
EGYPT: Ahmed Ikramy, Ali Shehata, Hamada Sedki, Ibrahim Youssef, Rabei Yassin, Shawki
Ghareeb, Magdi Abdel Ghani, Taher Abou Zaid (70 Hamdi Nouh), Mohamed Radwan, Zakaria Nasef
(30 Naser Mohamed Ali), Emad Soliman
TOGO: Assogba Yaovi, Sanunu Essoazina, Mawuéna Kodjovi, Denké Wazo, Koami Dos Reis, Djogou
Tao Akoulassi, Efoé Mensah, Da Silvéira Adjé, Moutairou Rafiou, Boukari Saadou (72 Ali Mamane),
Gamal Abdel (75 Sunu Mawuli).

10.03.1984

CAMEROON - IVORY COAST 2-0 (1-0)
Félix Houphouet-Boigny, Abidjan
Referee: Larrache (Morocco), Attendance: 40.000
CAMEROON: Joseph-Antoine Bell, Charles Toubé, René N'Djeya, François Ndoumbé, Isaac Sinkot, Théophile Abéga, Ibrahim Aoudou (85 Emmanuel Kundé), Gregoire Mbida, Ernest Ebongué, Roger Milla, Bonaventure D'Jonkep.
IVORY COAST: Koffi Kouadio, Emile Gnahoré, Patrice Lago, François Monguéhi, Gbala Gnato, Miézan (64 Dré Moize), Jean-Michel Akenon, François Zahoui, Ignace Guédé-Gba, Michael Goba (35 Tia Koffi), Youssouf Fofana.
Goals: Roger Milla (42), Bonaventure D'Jonkep (61)

1.	EGYPT	3	2	1	0	3	1	5
2.	CAMEROON	3	2	0	1	6	2	4
3.	Ivory Coast	3	1	0	2	4	4	2
4.	Togo	3	0	1	2	1	7	1

GROUP B

05.03.1984

NIGERIA - GHANA 2-1 (2-1)
Municipal, Bouaké
Referee: Dodou N'Jie (Gambia), Attendance: 10.000
NIGERIA: Patrick Okala, Paul Kingsley, Stephen Keshi, Sunday Eboigbe, Yisa Sofoluwe (67 Ibrahim Mohamed), Mudashiru Lawal, Chibuzor Ehilegbu, Humphrey Edobor, Clement Temile, Rashidi Yekini, Henry Nwosu. Trainer: Adegboye Onigbinde
GHANA: Joseph Carr, Ernest Appau, Isaac Acquaye (61 Seth Ampadu), Isaac Paha, Joseph Odoi, Mohamed Polo (34 Papa Arko), Karim Abdul Razak, Samuel Opoku Nti, Francis Kumi, George Alhassan, Koffi Abbrey.
Goals: Henry Nwosu (13), Chibuzor Ehilegbu (31) / Samuel Opoku N'ti (19)

05.03.1984

ALGERIA - MALAWI 3-0 (3-0)
Municipal, Bouaké
Referee: Bakary Sarr (Senegal), Attendance: 10.000
ALGERIA: Mehdi Cerbah, Mohamed Chaïb, Mahmoud Guendouz, Nourredine Kourichi, Fawzi Mansouri, Mohamed Kaci-Said, Ali Fergani, Lakhdar Belloumi, Nasser Bouiche (75 Djamel Djefdjef), Djamel Menad, Hocine Yahi. Trainer: Mahieddine Khalef
MALAWI: Clement Mkwalula, Harry Waya, Young Chimodzi, Chamangwana, Dixon Mbetewa, Patson Nyengo, Jonathan Billie, Sito Mfarinya (46 Ricky Phuka), Moses Majiga (75 Pater Amosi), Henry Chikunje, Clifton Msiya. Trainer: Danny MacLennan
Goals: Nasser Bouiche (29), Lakhdar Belloumi (36), Ali Fergani (38)

08.03.1984

MALAWI - NIGERIA 2-2 (2-2)
Municipal, Bouaké
Referee: Abdel Hafiz (Sudan), Attendance: 15.000
MALAWI: Clement Mkwalula, Harry Waya, Young Chimodzi, Jack Chamangwana, Dixon Mbetewa, Patson Nyengo, Collins Thewe, Jonathan Billie, Moses Majiga, Pater Amosi, Clifton Msiya (51 Ricky Phuka, 79 Holman Malunga).
NIGERIA: Patrick Okala, John Benson (55 Ibrahim Mohamed), Stephen Keshi, Sunday Eboigbe, Yisa Sofoluwe, Mudashiru Lawal, Chibuzor Ehilegbu, Humphrey Edobor, Clement Temile, Rashidi Yekini (69 Ademola Adeshina), Henry Nwosu.
Goals: Harry Waya (7 penalty), Clifton Msiya (35) / Clement Temile (39, 41)

08.03.1984

ALGERIA - GHANA 2-0 (2-0)
Municipal, Bouaké
Referee: Bahhou (Morocco), Attendance: 15.000
ALGERIA: Mehdi Cerbah, Mohamed Chaïb, Mahmoud Guendouz, Nourredine Kourichi, Fawzi Mansouri, Mohamed Kaci-Said, Ali Fergani, Lakhdar Belloumi, Nasser Bouiche (82 Rabah Madjer), Djamel Menad, Hocine Yahi (62 Tadj Bensaoula).
GHANA: Michael Owusu Mensah, Joseph Odoi, Seth Ampadu, Isaac Paha, Kwasi Appiah (37 Ernest Appau), Albert Asase, Karim Abdul Razak, Papa Arko, John Bannerman, Dan Kayede (61 Francis Kumi), Koffi Abbrey.
Goals: Djamel Menad (75), Tadj Bensaoula (85)

11.03.1984

ALGERIA - NIGERIA 0-0
Municipal, Bouaké
Referee: Camara (Guinea), Attendance: 3000
ALGERIA: Mehdi Cerbah, Mohamed Chaïb (46 Abdelhamid Sadmi), Mahmoud Guendouz, Nourredine Kourichi, Hamid Bouras, Djamel Djefdjef, Rabah Madjer, Lakhdar Belloumi (46 Djamel Menad), Hocine Yahi, Nasser Bouiche, Tadj Bensaoula.
NIGERIA: Peter Rufai, Paul Kingsley, Stephen Keshi, Sunday Eboigbe, Yisa Sofoluwe, Mudashiru Lawal, Chibuzor Ehilegu, Humphrey Edobor, Clement Temile (89 Tarila Okorowanta), Rashidi Yekini, Henry Nwosu (52 Ali Bala).

11.03.1984

GHANA - MALAWI 1-0 (1-0)
Municipal, Bouaké
Referee: Salem Adal (Libya), Attendance: 3000
GHANA: Michael Owusu Mensah, Joseph Odoi, Seth Ampadu, Isaac Paha, Hesse Odamten, Albert Asase (58 Mohamed Polo), Karim Abdul Razak, Papa Arko, John Bannerman (74 Sampson Lamptey), Francis Kumi, Koffi Abbrey.
MALAWI: Clement Mkwalula, Gilbert Chirwa, Young Chimodzi, Jack Chamangwana, Dixon Mbetewa, Patson Nyengo, Collins Thewe, Jonathan Billie, Moses Majiga, Pater Amosi (74 Holman Malunga), Clifton Msiya.
Goal: Seth Amphadu (32)

1.	ALGERIA	3	2	1	0	5	0	5
2.	NIGERIA	3	1	2	0	4	3	4
3.	Ghana	3	1	0	2	2	4	2
4.	Malawi	3	0	1	2	2	6	1

Semi-finals

14.03.1984

EGYPT - NIGERIA 2-2 (2-1, 2-2), 7-8 on penalties
Félix Houphouet-Boigny, Abidjan
Referee: Dodou N'Jie (Gambia), Attendance: 15.000
NIGERIA: Peter Rufai, Paul Kingsley, Stephen Keshi, Sunday Eboigbe, Yisa Sofoluwe, Mudashiru Lawal, Chibuzor Ehilegu (46 Ademola Adeshina), Humphrey Edobor, Clement Temile, Tarila Okorowanta (85 Rashidi Yekini), Ali Bala.
EGYPT: Thabet El-Batal, Ali Shehata, Hamada Sedki, Ibrahim Youssef, Rabei Yassin, Shawki Ghareeb, Magdi Abdel Ghani, Taher Abou Zaid, Mahmoud Hassan, Naser Mohamed Ali (67 Zakaria Nasef), Emad Soliman (85 Mahmoud El-Khateeb)
Goals: Emad Soliman (25), Taher Abou Zaid (38) / Stephen Keshi (43 penalty), Ahli Bala (75)
Penalties: Magdi Abdel Ghani (Scored), Ali Shehata (Scored), Shawki Ghareeb (Scored), Mahmoud El-Khateeb (Scored), Taher Abouzaid (Scored), Zakaria Nasef (Scored), Rabei Yasin (Scored), Mahmoud Hassan (Missed), Ibrahim Youssef (Missed)

14.03.1984

ALGERIA - CAMEROON 0-0, 4-5 on penalties
Municipal, Bouaké
Referee: Picon (Mauritius), Attendance: 15.000
CAMEROON: Joseph-Antoine Bell, Charles Toubé, François N'doumbé, Ibrahim Aoudou, Isaac Sinkot, Hermann Kingué (94 Emmanuel Kundé), Theophile Abéga, Gregoire Mbida, Ernest Ebongué, Roger Milla, Bonaventure D'Jonkep (67 Jacques Enongué)
ALGERIA: Mehdi Cerbah, Abdelhamid Sadmi, Mahmoud Guendouz, Nourredine Kourichi, Mohamed Chaïb, Mohamed Kaci-Said, Ali Fergani, Lakhdar Belloumi, Rabah Madjer, Tadj Bensaoula (111 Nasser Bouiche), Djamel Menad (68 Hocine Yahi).

Third Place Match

17.03.1984

ALGERIA - EGYPT 3-1 (0-0)
Félix Houphouet-Boigny, Abidjan
Referee: Gebreysus Tesfaye (Ethiopia), Attendance: 5.000
ALGERIA: Mehdi Cerbah, Abdelhamid Sadmi, Mahmoud Guendouz, Boualem Laroum, Mohamed Chaïb, Djamel Djefdjef, Ali Fergani, Lakhdar Belloumi, Nasser Bouiche, Tadj Bensaoula (Hocine Yahi), Rabah Madjer. Trainer: Mahieddine Khalef
EGYPT: Ahmed Ikramy, Ali Shehata, Mahmoud Hassan, Hamada Sedki, Rabei Yassin, Shawki Ghareeb, Magdi Abdel Ghani, Taher Abou Zaid (Mohamed Radwan), Adel Abdel Wahed, Hamdi Nouh (Zakaria Nasef), Emad Soliman. Trainer: Salah El Wahsh
Goals: Rabah Madjer (67), Lakhdar Belloumi (70), Hocine Yahi (88) / Magdi Abdel Ghani (74 penalty)

Final

18.03.1984

CAMEROON - NIGERIA 3-1 (1-1)
Félix Houphouet-Boigny, Abidjan
Referee: Ali Bennaceur (Tunisia), Attendance: 50,000
CAMEROON: Joseph-Antoine Bell, Charles Toubé, René N'Djeya, François Ndoumbé, Isaac Sinkot, Théophile Abéga, Gregoire Mbida, Ibrahim Aoudou, Ernest Ebongué, Roger Milla, Bonaventure D'Jonkep (84 Emmanuel Kundé), Trainer: Radivoje Ognjanović (Yugoslavia)
NIGERIA: Patrick Okala, Paul Kingsley, Stephen Keshi, Sunday Eboigbe, Yisa Sofoluwe, Mudashiru Lawal, Ademola Adeshina (83 Paul Okoku), Humphrey Edobor, Bala Ali (46 Clement Temile), Henry Nwosu, James Etokebe. Trainer: Adegboye Onigbinde
Goals: René N'Djeya (32), Théophile Abéga (79), Ernest Ebongué (84) / Mudashiru Lawal (10)

Fifteenth edition - 1986
Qualifying Tournament

Thirty-four teams entered the 15th edition of the Africa Cup of Nations but four of them withdrew. The finals tournament was held in Egypt and the hosts once again reached the final. This was Egypt's first final since 1962 but they won the title for the third time after beating Cameroon in a penalty shoot-out following a goalless draw.

Preliminary Round

18.11.84 Gambia - Sierra Leone 3-2
02.12.84 Sierra Leone - Gambia 2-0

11.11.84 Liberia - Mauritania 3-1
23.11.84 Mauritania - Liberia 3-0

18.11.84 Mali - Benin 1-0
02.12.84 Benin - Mali 2-2

16.09.84 Mauritius - Mozambique 0-0
30.09.84 Mozambique - Mauritius 3-0

09.11.84 Somalia - Kenya 1-0
24.11.84 Kenya - Somalia 1-0, 4-3 on penalties

04.08.84 Tanzania - Uganda 0-1
18.08.84 Uganda - Tanzania 1-3

11.11.84 Zaire - Gabon 2-0
25.11.84 Gabon - Zaire 1-1

14.10.84 Zimbabwe - Swaziland 3-0
04.11.84 Swaziland - Zimbabwe 1-5

First Round

08.03.85 Algeria - Mauritania 4-0
22.03.85 Mauritania - Algeria 1-1

31.03.85 Congo - Zaire 2-5
14.04.85 Zaire - Congo 0-0

31.03.85 Ivory Coast - Mali 6-0
14.04.85 Mali - Ivory Coast 1-1

31.03.85 Ghana - Guinea 1-1
14.04.85 Guinea - Ghana 1-4

29.03.85 Libya - Tunisia 2-0
14.04.85 Tunisia - Libya 1-0

03.03.85 Madagascar - Zimbabwe 0-1
23.03.85 Zimbabwe - Madagascar 5-2

31.03.85 Malawi - Mozambique 1-1
16.04.85 Mozambique - Malawi 1-1, 6-5 on penalties

31.03.85 Togo - Senegal 0-1
14.04.85 Senegal - Togo 1-1

Kenya - Sudan w/o
Morocco - Sierra Leone w/o
Nigeria - Tanzania w/o
Zambia - Ethiopia w/o

Second Round

18.08.85 Ivory Coast - Ghana 2-0
01.09.85 Ghana - Ivory Coast 0-0

04.08.85 Kenya - Algeria 0-0
18.08.85 Algeria - Kenya 3-0

23.08.85 Libya - Mozambique 2-1
15.09.85 Mozambique - Libya 2-1, 4-3 on penalties

25.08.85 Morocco - Zaire 1-0
08.09.85 Zaire - Morocco 0-0

10.08.85 Nigeria - Zambia 0-0
18.08.85 Zambia - Nigeria 1-0

18.08.85 Zimbabwe - Senegal 1-0
01.09.85 Senegal - Zimbabwe 3-0

Final Tournament (Egypt)

GROUP A

07.03.1986

SENEGAL - EGYPT 1-0 (0-0)
International, Cairo
Referee: S. Picon (Mauritius), Attendance: 45.000
SENEGAL: Cheick Seck, Pape Abdourahmane Fall, Oumar Touré, Racine Kane, Roger Mendy, Amadou Diop, Oumar Sène, Boubacar Sarr Locotte, Mamadou Teuw, Jules François Bocandé, Thierno Youm.
EGYPT: Thabet El-Batal, Ali Shehata, Ashraf Quasem, Mohamed Omar, Rabei Yassin, Alaa Mayhoub, Magdi Abdel Ghani, Taher Abou Zaid (Hossam Hassan), Nasser El-Tallees, Gamal Abdel Hamid, Mahmoud El-Khateeb. Trainer: John Michael Smith (Scotland)
Goal: Thierno Youm (67)

07.03.1986

IVORY COAST - MOZAMBIQUE 3-0 (1-0)
International, Cairo
Referee: Gebreysus Tesfaye (Ethiopia), Attendance: 45.000
IVORY COAST: Marcel Zagouli, Emile Gnahoré, Abialy, Kouhon, François Monguéhi, Joseph Gadji-Celi, Oumar Ben Salah, François Zahoui, Kouassi N'Dri, Abdoulaye Traoré, Youssouf Fofana (89 Patrice Lago).
MOZAMBIQUE: Filipe, Ubisse (71 Cossa), Elcido Conde, Faruk Ali, Joaquim João, Matonse, Amade, Joaquim Lucas (66 Nicolao), Mabote, Ciquinho Conde, Geraldo Conde.
Goals: Abdoulaye Traoré (25, 74), Kouassy N'dri (86)

10.03.1986

SENEGAL - MOZAMBIQUE 2-0 (1-0)
International, Cairo
Referee: Okubule (Nigeria), Attendance: 50.000
SENEGAL: Cheick Seck, Pape Abdourahmane Fall, Racine Kane, Roger Mendy, Oumar Touré, Mamadou Teuw, Christophe Sagna (71 Joseph Koto), Oumar Sène, Amadou Diop, Jules François Bocandé, Thierno Youm (71 M. Diop).
MOZAMBIQUE: Filipe, Elcido Conde, Jeromino, Faruk Ali, Joaquim João, Mabote, Calton Banze, Amade, Cossa, Geraldo Conde, Ciquinho Conde.
Goals: Pape Abdourahmane Fall (28), Jules François Bocandé (83)

10.03.1986

EGYPT - IVORY COAST 2-0 (0-0)
International, Cairo
Referee: Kalombo (Malawi), Attendance: 50.000
EGYPT: Thabet El-Batal, Ali Shehata, Hamada Sedki, Mohamed Omar (Shawki Ghareeb), Rabei Yassin, Ashraf Quasem, Magdi Abdel Ghani, Gamal Abdel Hamid, Mahmoud El-Khateeb, Moustafa Abdou, Tarek Yehia (46 Taher Abou Zaid).
IVORY COAST: Marcel Zagouli, Emile Gnahoré, Sacre, Patrice Lago, François Monguéhi, Kouassi N'Dri (Miézan), Joseph Gadji-Celi, François Zahoui, Diecket, Abdoulaye Traoré (57 N'Diaye), Youssouf Fofana.
Goals: Shawki Ghareeb (73), Gamal Abdel Hamid (83)

13.03.1986

IVORY COAST - SENEGAL 1-0 (0-0)
International, Cairo
Referee: J. Diramba (Gabon), Attendance: 55.000
IVORY COAST: Marcel Zagouli, Emile Gnahoré, Sacre, Patrice Lago, François Monguéhi, Joseph Gadji-Celi, Oumar Ben Salah, François Zahoui, Kouassi N'Dri (Diecket), Abdoulaye Traoré, Youssouf Fofana.
SENEGAL: Cheick Seck, Pape Abdourahmane Fall, Oumar Touré (C. Tidiane Fall), Racine Kane, Roger Mendy, Boubacar Sarr Locotte, Amadou Diop, Oumar Sène, Mamadou Teuw, Jules François Bocandé, Joseph Koto.
Goal: Abdoulaye Traoré (71)

13.03.1986

EGYPT - MOZAMBIQUE 2-0 (2-0)
International, Cairo
Referee: Hafiz Ali (Tanzania), Attendance: 55.000
EGYPT: Thabet El-Batal, Ali Shehata, Mohamed Omar, Hamada Sedki, Ashraf Quasem, Rabei Yassin, Magdi Abdel Ghani, Taher Abou Zaid (Tarek Yehia), Gamal Abdel Hamid, Mahmoud El-Khateeb, Moustafa Abdou
MOZAMBIQUE: Filipe, Elcido Conde, Nhanombe, Faruk Ali, Machava, Calton Banze (40 Geraldo Conde), Mabote (66 Ubisse), Chababe, Cossa, Ciquinho Conde, Nicolau.
Goals: Taher Abou Zaid (13, 15)

1.	EGYPT	3	2	0	1	4	1	4
2.	IVORY COAST	3	2	0	1	4	2	4
3.	Senegal	3	2	0	1	3	1	4
4.	Mozambique	3	0	0	3	0	7	0

GROUP B

08.03.1986

ALGERIA - MOROCCO 0-0
Municipal, Alexandria
Referee: Ali Bennaceur (Tunisia), Attendance: 20.000
ALGERIA: Nassereddine Drid, Abdelhamid Sadmi, Fawzi Mansouri, Fodil Megharia, Mahmoud Guendouz (67 Mohamed Chaïb), Mohamed Kaci-Said, Bouiche (66 Medane), Ali Fergani, Djamel Menad, Karim Maroc, Nacer Bouiche.
MOROCCO: Badou Zaki, Labd Khalifa, Abdelmajid Lemriss, Mustapha El Biaz, Noureddine Bouyahyaoui, Abdelmajid Dolmy, Mustapha El Haddaoui (85 Labied), Fadili, Aziz Bouderbala, Abdelrazzak Khairi (81 Abdul Fatah Rhiati), Abdelaziz Souleymani.

08.03.1986

CAMEROON - ZAMBIA 3-2 (0-0)
Municipal, Alexandria
Referee: Traoré (Mali), Attendance: 20.000
CAMEROON: Thomas N'Kono, Ndip, Isaac Sinkot, Emmanuel Kundé, Ibrahim Aoudou, Mbouh, André Kana Biyik, Theophile Abéga (61 Gregoire Mbida), Ernest Ebongué (84 Oumarou), Roger Milla, Louis-Paul Mfédé.
ZAMBIA: David Efford Chabala, Mulenga, Jones Chilengi, Jerry Shinde, Chishala, Jack Chanda, Kalusha Bwalya, Ashios Melu, Muba, Charles Musonda, Mwenya (55 Michael Chabala).
Goals: Roger Milla (46), Louis-Paul Mfédé (67 penalties, 82) / Michael Chabala (65), Kalusha Bwalya (77 penalty)

11.03.1986

ALGERIA - ZAMBIA 0-0
Municipal, Alexandria
Referee: Karini Camara (Guinea), Attendance: 10.000
ZAMBIA: David Efford Chabala, Chishala, Ashios Melu, Jones Chilengi, Mulenga, Jerry Shinde, Makinka, Jack Chanda (77 B. Chanda), Mumba, Michael Chabala, Kalusha Bwalya.
ALGERIA: Nassereddine Drid, Kechamli, Fawzi Mansouri, Fodil Megharia, Mahmoud Guendouz, Mohamed Kaci-Said, Ali Fergani, Karim Maroc (67 Hocine Yahi), Rabah Madjer, Djamel Menad, Tadj Bensaoula.

11.03.1986

CAMEROON - MOROCCO 1-1 (0-0)
Municipal, Alexandria
Referee: Valdemarca (Zimbabwe), Attendance: 10.000
MOROCCO: Badou Zaki, Labd Khalifa, Abdelmajid Lemriss, Mustapha El Biaz, Noureddine
Bouyahyaoui, Abdelmajid Dolmy, Mustapha El Haddaoui (70 Lahcen Ouadani "Hçina"), Fadili, Aziz
Bouderbala, Abdelkrim Merry 'Krimau', Abdelaziz Souleymani.
CAMEROON: Thomas N'Kono, Ndip, Isaac Sinkot, Emmanuel Kundé, Ibrahim Aoudou, Mbouh,
André Kana Biyik, Gregoire Mbida, Roger Milla, Ernest Ebongué, Louis-Paul Mfédé.
Goals: Roger Milla (89) / Abdelkarim Merry 'Krimau' (63)

14.03.1986

MOROCCO - ZAMBIA 1-0 (1-0)
Municipal, Alexandria
Referee: Bantsimba (Congo), Atttendance: 10.000
MOROCCO: Badou Zaki, Labd Khalifa, Mustapha El Biaz, Noureddine Bouyahyaoui, Lahcen
Ouadani "Hçina", Abdelmajid Dolmy, Abdelrazzak Khairi, Fadili, Aziz Bouderbala, Abdelkrim Merry
"Krimau", Labied (84 Abdul Fatah Rhiati).
ZAMBIA: David Efford Chabala, Chishala, Ashios Melu, Jones Chilengi, Mulenga, Jerry Shinde,
Mwenya (B. Chanda), Makinka, N. Chabala (47 Jack Chanda), Mumba, Kalusha Bwalya.
Goal: Jones Chilengi (18 own goal)

14.03.1986

CAMEROON - ALGERIA 3-2 (0-0)
Municipal, Alexandria
Referee: Badou Jasseh (Gambia), Attendance: 15.000
CAMEROON: Thomas N'Kono, Ndip, Isaac Sinkot, Emmanuel Kundé, Ibrahim Aoudou, Mbouh,
André Kana Biyik, Gregoire Mbida, Roger Milla, Ernest Ebongué, Louis-Paul Mfédé.
ALGERIA: Nassereddine Drid, Abdelhamid Sadmi, Chaabane Merzekane, Mohamed Chaïb,
Mahmoud Guendouz, Ali Fergani, Karim Maroc, Rabah Madjer, Djamel Menad, Medane (74 Hocine
Yahi), Tadj Bensaoula (46 Ben Khalidi).
Goals: André Kana Biyik (66, 70), Roger Milla (72) / Rabah Madjer (61), Karim Maroc (73)

1.	CAMEROON	3	2	1	0	7	5	5
2.	MOROCCO	3	1	2	0	2	1	4
3.	Algeria	3	0	2	1	2	3	2
4.	Zambia	3	0	1	2	2	4	1

Semi-finals

17.03.1986

CAMEROON - IVORY COAST 1-0 (0-0)
Municipal, Alexandria
Referee: Picon (Mauritius), Attendance: 10.000
CAMEROON: Thomas N'Kono, Ndip, Isaac Sinkot, Emmanuel Kundé, Ibrahim Aoudou, Mbouh,
André Kana Biyik, Gregoire Mbida, Roger Milla, Ernest Ebongué (82 Oumarou), Louis-Paul Mfédé (63
Dagobert Dang).

IVORY COAST: Marcel Zagouli, Emile Gnahoré, Abialy, Patrice Lago, François Monguéhi, Joseph Gadji-Celi, Oumar Ben Salah, Kouassi N'Dri (59 Diecket), François Zahoui, Abdoulaye Traoré, Youssouf Fofana.
Goal: Roger Milla (46)

17.03.1986

EGYPT - MOROCCO 1-0 (0-0)
International, Cairo
Referee: Resfaye (Ethiopia), Attendance: 90.000
EGYPT: Thabet El-Batal, Ali Shehata, Mohamed Omar, Hamada Sedki, Ashraf Quasem, Rabei Yassin, Magdi Abdel Ghani, Taher Abou Zaid, Gamal Abdel Hamid, Mahmoud El-Khateeb (46 Tarek Yehia), Moustafa Abdou.
MOROCCO: Badou Zaki, Labd Khalifa, Abdelmajid Lemriss, Mustapha El Biaz, Noureddine Bouyahyaoui, Abdelmajid Dolmy, Fadili, Abdelrazzak Khairi (46 Abdul Fatah Rhiati), Aziz Bouderbala, Abdelkrim Merry "Krimau", Abdelaziz Souleymani.
Goal: Taher Abou Zaid (79)

Third Place Match

20.03.1986

IVORY COAST - MOROCCO 3-2 (2-1)
International, Cairo
Referee: Valdemarca (Zimbabwe), Attendance: 1000
IVORY COAST: Marcel Zagouli (73 Kouhon), Emile Gnahoré, Victor Miézan, Lue, François Monguéhi, Joseph Gadji-Celi, Oumar Ben Salah, Pascal Miézan, Abdoulaye Traoré, Youssouf Fofana (46 Patrice Lago), Kouassi Kouadio. Trainer: Pancho Gonzalez (France)
MOROCCO: Salahedine Hmied, Labd Khalifa, Noureddine Bouyahyaoui, Lahcen Ouadani "Hçina", Abdellah Bidar, Yakdani (72 Fadili), Mustapha El Haddaoui, Mohammed Sadil, Mourad Jabrane, Abdul Fatah Rhiati, Abdelaziz Souleymani. Trainer: José Faria (Brazil)
Goals: Oumar Ben Salah (8), Kouassi Kouadio (38 penalty, 68) / Abdul Fatah Rhiati (44), Mohammed Sadil (85)

Final

21.03.1986
EGYPT - CAMEROON 0-0 aet, 5-4 on penalties
International, Cairo
Referee: Ali Bennaceur (Tunisia), Attendance: 100.000
EGYPT: Thabet El-Batal, Ali Shehata, Mohamed Omar (53 Alaa Mayhoub), Hamada Sedki, Ashraf Quasem, Rabei Yassin, Magdi Abdel Ghani, Taher Abou Zaid (109 Tarek Yehia), Gamal Abdel Hamid, Mahmoud El-Khateeb, Moustafa Abdou. Trainer: John Michael Smith (Scotland)
CAMEROON: Thomas N'Kono, Ndip, Isaac Sinkot, Emmanuel Kundé, Ibrahim Aoudou, Mbouh, André Kana Biyik, Gregoire Mbida, Roger Milla, Ernest Ebongué (81 Oumarou), Louis-Paul Mfédé. Trainer: Claude Le Roy (France)
Penalties: 1-0 Tarek Yehia, 1-1 Louis-Paul Mfédé, 2-1 Magdi Abdel Ghani, 2-2 Emmanuel Kundé, Moustafa Abdou, Mbide, 3-2 Alaa Mayhoub, 3-3 Roger Milla, 4-3 Ali Shehata, 4-4 Ibrahim Aoudou, 5-4 Asharf Quasem, Kana Biyik.

Sixteenth edition - 1988
Qualifying Tournament

Thirty-six countries entered the 16th edition of the competition but eight subsequently withdrew. Morocco hosted the finals tournament but went out at the semi-final stage following a 9-8 penalty shoot-out defeat against Nigeria. Cameroon won through to what was their third consecutive final and faced Nigeria in a repeat of the 1984 final. A narrow 1-0 victory saw Cameroon lift the Africa Cup of Nations for the second time.

Preliminary Round

05.10.86 Angola - Gabon 1-0
19.10.86 Gabon - Angola 1-0, 3-5 penalties

05.10.86 Central African Republic – Congo 1-2
19.10.86 Congo - Central African Republic 5-1

05.10.86 Ethiopia - Tanzania 4-2
Tanzania - Ethiopia [Ethiopia withdrew]

16.08.86 Guinea - Gambia 2-1
30.08.86 Gambia - Guinea 0-1

05.10.86 Sierra Leone - Liberia 2-1
19.10.86 Liberia - Sierra Leone 1-1

05.10.86 Uganda - Somalia 5-0
19.10.86 Somalia - Uganda 0-0

Madagascar - Mauritius w/o
Rwanda - Lesotho w/o
Togo - Equatorial Guinea w/o
Tunisia - Mali w/o

First Round

27.03.87 Algeria - Tunisia 1-0
12.04.87 Tunisia - Algeria 1-1

29.03.87 Cameroon - Uganda 5-1
11.04.87 Uganda - Cameroon 3-1

29.03.87 Ivory Coast - Congo 2-0
05.04.87 Congo - Ivory Coast 1-1

30.03.87 Ghana - Sierra Leone 1-2
11.04.87 Sierra Leone - Ghana 0-0

28.03.87 Kenya - Madagascar 2-0
12.04.87 Madagascar - Kenya 2-1

29.03.87 Mozambique - Zimbabwe 1-1
12.04.87 Zimbabwe - Mozambique 3-2

28.03.87 Nigeria - Togo 2-0
12.04.87 Togo - Nigeria 1-1

29.03.87 Senegal - Guinea 4-0
12.04.87 Guinea - Senegal 0-0

29.03.87 Sudan - Tanzania 1-0
11.04.87 Tanzania - Sudan 1-1

29.03.87 Zaire - Angola 3-0
11.04.87 Angola - Zaire 1-0

Libya - Zambia w/o
Malawi - Rwanda w/o

Second Round

Algeria - Libya w/o

05.07.87 Cameroon - Sudan 2-0
18.07.87 Sudan - Cameroon 1-0

03.07.87 Malawi - Ivory Coast 1-2
18.07.87 Ivory Coast - Malawi 2-0

04.07.87 Nigeria - Sierra Leone 3-0
18.07.87 Sierra Leone - Nigeria 2-0

05.07.87 Senegal - Zaire 0-0
18.07.87 Zaire - Senegal 0-0, 4-2 on penalties

05.07.87 Zimbabwe - Kenya 1-1
18.07.87 Kenya - Zimbabwe 0-0

Final Tournament (Morocco)

GROUP A

13.03.1988

MOROCCO - ZAIRE 1-1 (1-0)
Stade Mohamed V, Casablanca
Referee: Gebreyesus Tesfaye (Ethiopia), Attendance: 70.000
MOROCCO: Khalid Azmi, Tijani El Maatoui, Mustapha El Biaz, Hassan Mouhaid, Abdelmajid Lemriss (62 Lahcen Ouadani "Hçina"), Mohammed Timoumi, Abdelrazzak Khairi, Mustapha El Haddaoui, Aziz Bouderbala, Hassan Fadel (53 Moulay El Gharef), Abdelkrim Merry "Krimau". Trainer: José Faria (Brazil)
ZAIRE: Pangi Merikani, Mbai Kalau, John Buana, Kalombo N'Kongolo, Danny Ngombo, Menayamé Tueba, Jacques Kigambo, Mboté Ndinga, Lemba Basaula (51 Ngolé Kana), Santos Muntubila (61 Vita Lutonadio), Eugène Kabongo. Trainer: Otto Pfister (West Germany)
Khairi sent off (61)
Goals: Abdelkarim Krimau (42 penalty) / Vita Lutonadio (87)

13.03.1988

IVORY COAST - ALGERIA 1-1 (0-1)
Stade Mohamed V, Casablanca
Referee: Eganaden Cadressen (Mauritius), Attendance: 70.000
IVORY COAST: Marcel Zagouli, Basile Kouamé Aka, Diaby Sekana, Lué Ruffin, Laurent Zahoui, Joseph Gadji-Celi, Pascal Miézan (79 Jean-Michel Guédé), François Zahoui, Serge-Alain Magui, Abdoulaye Traoré, Youssouf Fofana. Trainer: Yéo Martial
ALGERIA: Nassereddine Drid, Chaabane Merzekane, Abdelrrazak Belgherbi, Fodil Megharia, Mohammed Chaïb, Rachid Maatar, Mohammed Kaci-Said, Lakhdar Belloumi, Ali Bouafia (72 Djamel Menad), Hocine Yahi, Hakim Medane (85 Kamel Djahmoun). Trainer: Yevgeniy Rogov (USSR)
Goals: Abdoulaye Traoré (48) / Lakhdar Belloumi (16)

16.03.1988

IVORY COAST - ZAIRE 1-1 (0-1)
Stade Mohamed V, Casablanca
Referee: Ali Benaceur (Tunisia), Attendance: 10.000
IVORY COAST: Pierre Alain Gouaméné, Boris Diecket (46 Basile Kouamé Aka), Patrice Lago, Diaby Sekana, Laurent Zahoui, Joseph Gadji-Celi, Serge-Alain Magui, François Zahoui, Didier Otokoré (62 Yéo Amani), Abdoulaye Traoré, Youssouf Fofana.
ZAIRE: Pangi Merikani, Mbai Kalau (39 Mbaki Mbala), Tshota Mutombo, John Buana, Danny Ngombo, Santos Muntubila, Mboté Ndinga, Mbaki Makengo, Jacques Kigambo (77 Vita Lutonadio), Eugène Kabongo, Gaston Mobati.
Goals: Abdoulaye Traoré (74) / Eugène Kabongo (37)

16.03.1988

MOROCCO - ALGERIA 1-0 (0-0)
Stade Mohamed V, Casablanca
Referee: Idrissa Sarr (Mauritania), Attendance: 40.000
MOROCCO: Ezaki Badou "Zaki", Tijani El Maatoui, Mustapha El Biaz, Hassan Mouhaid, Lahcen Ouadani "Hçina", Mustapha El Haddaoui, Mohammed Timoumi, Abdelmajid Lemriss, Aziz Bouderbala, Moulay El Gharef (81 Abderrahim Hamraoui), Abdelkrim Merry "Krimau".
ALGERIA: Nassereddine Drid, Chaâbane Merzekane, Abdelrrazak Belgherbi, Fodil Megharia, Mohammed Chaïb, Lakhdar Belloumi, Rachid Maatar, Mohammed Kaci-Said (32 Kamel Djahmoun), Abdelkader Ferhaoui, Djamel Menad, Ali Bouafia (75 Hakim Medane).
Goal: Mustapha El Haddadoui (52)

19.03.1988

ALGERIA - ZAIRE 1-0 (1-0)
Stade Mohamed V, Casablanca
Referee: Hugues-Joseph Mongbo (Benin), Attendance: 80.000
ALGERIA: Nassereddine Drid, Mokhtar Kechamli, Abdelrrazak Belgherbi, Fodil Megharia, Ali Ben Halima, Hocine Yahi, Abdelouahab Maiche, Lakhdar Belloumi, Abdelkader Ferhaoui, Hamidouche Bentayeb (70 Djamel Menad), Hakim Medane (83 Rachid Maatar).
ZAIRE: Pangi Merikani, Kalombo N'Kongolo (13 Malumba Mulamba), John Buana, Menayamé Tueba, Danny Ngombo, Tshota Mutombo, Santos Muntubila, Mboté Ndinga, Vita Lutonadio, Eugène Kabongo, Richard Mapuata (57 Ngole Kana).
Goal: Abdelkader Ferhaoui (36)

19.03.1988

MOROCCO - IVORY COAST 0-0
Stade Mohamed V, Casablanca
Referee: Hafid Tahir (Tanzania), Attendance: 80.000
MOROCCO: Ezaki Badou "Zaki", Tijani El Maatoui, Mustapha El Biaz, Hassan Mouhaid (87 Lahcen Ouadani "Hçina"), Abdelmajid Lemriss, Abdelrazzak Khairi, Mustapha El Haddaoui, Hassan Benhabicha, Aziz Bouderbala, Moulay El Gharef, Abdelkrim Merry "Krimau".
IVORY COAST: Pierre Alain Gouaméné, Basile Kouamé Aka, Lué Ruffin, Diaby Sekana, Laurent Zahoui (83 Arsène Hobou), Patrice Lago, Omar Ben Salah, Serge-Alain Magui, François Zahoui (64 Yéo Amani), Abdoulaye Traoré, Youssouf Fofana.

1.	MOROCCO	3	1	2	0	2	1	4
2.	ALGERIA	3	1	1	1	2	2	3
	Ivory Coast	3	0	3	0	2	2	3
4.	Zaire	3	0	2	1	2	3	2

Algeria finished level with Ivory Coast in the Group A placings and qualified for the semi-finals after lots were drawn.

GROUP B

14.03.1988

CAMEROON - EGYPT 1-0 (1-0)
Stade Prince Moulay Abdallah, Rabat
Referee: Idrissa Traoré (Mali), Attendance: 7000
CAMEROON: Jacques Songo'o, Victor N'Dip, Benjamin Massing, Emmanuel Kundé, Charles Ntamark, Eugène Ekéké (71 Bertin Ollé Ollé), André Kana-Biyik, Stephen Tataw, Cyrille Makanaky, François Omam-Biyik (28 Louis-Paul M'Fédé), Roger Milla. Trainer: Claude Le Roy (France)
EGYPT: Ahmed Shoubeir, Ibrahim Hassan, Mohamed Omar, Hamada Sedki, Rabei Yassin, Ismail Youssef Awanallah, Shawki Ghareeb (83 Mohammed Ramadan), Emad Soliman (65 Tarek Soliman), Osama Oraby, Hossam Hassan, Gamal Abdel Hamid. Trainer: Mike Smith (Wales).
Goal: Roger Milla (5)

14.03.1988

NIGERIA - KENYA 3-0 (3-0)
Stade Prince Moulay Abdallah, Rabat
Referee: Badra Sène (Senegal), Attendance: 4000
NIGERIA: Peter Rufai, Yisa Sofoluwe, Andrew Uwe, Sunday Eboigbe, Bright Omokaro, Ndubuisi Okosieme (82 Oluwole Odegbami), Samuel Okwaraji (67 Henry Nwosu), Ademola Adeshina, Augustine Eguavoen, Humphrey Edobor, Rashidi Yekini. Trainer: Manfred Höner (West Germany)
KENYA: Washington Muhanji, Tobias Ochola, Michael Wetche, Gabriel Olang, Hassan Juma, Ambrose Ayoyi, Douglas Mutua, David Ochieng, John Okello Zangi, Wilberforce Mulamba (61 Henry Motego), George Onyango (49 Peter Dawo). Trainer: Danilo Alves (Brazil)
Goals: Rashidi Yekini (6), Humphrey Edobor (13), Ndubuisi Okosieme (33)

17.03.1988

CAMEROON - NIGERIA 1-1 (1-1)
Stade Prince Moulay Abdallah, Rabat
Referee: Bester Kalombo (Malawi), Attendance: 12.000
CAMEROON: Joseph-Antoine Bell, Stephen Tataw, Benjamin Massing, Charles Ntamark, Emmanuel Kundé, Emile M'Bouh, Louis-Paul M'Fédé (77 Bertin Ollé Ollé), André Kana-Biyik, Cyrille Makanaky, Roger Milla, Eugène Ekéké (57 Bonaventure Djonkep),.
NIGERIA: Peter Rufai, Yisa Sofoluwe, Stephen Keshi, Sunday Eboigbe (34 Humphrey Edobor), Bright Omokaro, Andrew Uwe, Ademola Adeshina, Samuel Okwaraji, Augustine Eguavoen, Rashidi Yekini, Michael Obiku (73 Oluwole Odegbami).
Goals: Roger Milla (21) / Samuel Okwaraji (2)

17.03.1988

EGYPT - KENYA 3-0 (1-0)
Stade Prince Moulay Abdallah, Rabat
Referee: Simon Bantsimba (Congo), Attendance: 15.000
EGYPT: Ahmed Shoubeir, Ibrahim Hassan, Hesham Yakan, Mohamed Omar, Rabei Yassin, Ismail Youssef Awanallah, Shawki Ghareeb, Ayman Younis, Mohamed Ramadan, Hossam Hassan, Gamal Abdel Hamid (77 Tarek Yehia).
KENYA: David A. Ochieng, Tobias Ochola, Gabriel Olang, Austin Oduor, Charles Otieno (77 John Okello Zangi), Hassan Juma, John Odhiambo, Douglas Mutua (46 Sammy Onyango), Wilberforce Mulamba, Peter Dawo, Ambrose Ayoyi.
Goals: Gamal Abdelhamid (2, 65), Ayman Younis (58)

20.03.1988

CAMEROON - KENYA 0-0
Stade Prince Moulay Abdallah, Rabat
Referee: Badou Jasseh (Gambia), Attendance: 25.000
CAMEROON: Joseph-Antoine Bell, Stephen Tataw, Benjamin Massing, Charles Ntamark, Emmanuel Kundé, Cyrille Makanaky (84 Jean-Denis Mendengué), Emile M'Bouh, André Kana-Biyik, Louis-Paul M'Fédé, Bonaventure Djonkep (71 Bertin Ollé Ollé), Roger Milla.
KENYA: David Ochieng, Wycliffe Anyangu, Gabriel Olang, Austin Oduor, Hassan Juma, Ambrose Ayoyi (68 Henry Motego), Charles Otieno, John Odhiambo, George Nyangi (87 Johnston Taso), Wilberforce Mulamba, Peter Dawo.

20.03.1988

NIGERIA - EGYPT 0-0
Stade Prince Moulay Abdallah, Rabat
Referee: Aly Bangoura (Guinea), Attendance: 25.000
NIGERIA: Peter Rufai, Yisa Sofoluwe, Andrew Uwe, Sunday Eboigbe, Bright Omokaro, Samuel Okwaraji, Oluwole Odegbami (72 Ndubuisi Okosieme), Ademola Adeshina, Henry Nwosu, Rashidi Yekini, Folorunso Okenla (80 Humphrey Edobor).
EGYPT: Ahmed Shoubeir, Ibrahim Hassan, Hamada Sedki, Mohamed Omar, Rabei Yassin, Ismail Youssef Awanallah, Shawki Ghareeb, Ayman Younis, Tarek Yehia (68 Mohamed Ramadan), Hossam Hassan, Gamal Abdel Hamid.

1.	NIGERIA	3	1	2	0	4	1	4
2.	CAMEROON	3	1	2	0	2	1	4
3.	Egypt	3	1	1	1	3	1	3
4.	Kenya	3	0	1	2	0	6	1

Semi-finals

23.03.1988

NIGERIA - ALGERIA 1-1 (1-0,1-1), 9-8 on penalties
Stade Prince Moulay Abdallah, Rabat
Referee: Badra Sène (Senegal), Attendance: 35.000
ALGERIA: Nassereddine Drid, Chaâbane Merzekane (74 Abdelouahab Maiche), Fodil Megharia, Abdelrrazak Belgherbi, Rachid Maatar, Mohammed Chaïb, Abdelkader Ferhaoui (71 Ali Bouafia), Lakhdar Belloumi, Hocine Yahi, Djamel Menad, Hakim Medane.
NIGERIA: Peter Rufai, Yisa Sofoluwe, Andrew Uwe, Sunday Eboigbe (95 Michael Odu), Bright Omokaro, Augustine Eguavoen, Samuel Okwaraji, Ademola Adeshina, Henry Nwosu, Folorunso Okenla (84 Uchenna Okafor), Rashidi Yekini.
Goals: Abdelrrazak Belgherbi (39 own goal) / Rachid Maatar (86)
Adeshina sent off (84)

Algeria played with 10 men after substitute Abdelouahab Maiche was stretchered off in the 115th minute of the game. They were then eliminated when all players had taken their penalties. After Augustine Eguavoen scored for the second time, Lakhdar Belloumi missed the 22nd kick which was saved by Peter Rufai.

23.03.1988

MOROCCO - CAMEROON 0-1 (0-0)
Stade Mohamed V, Casablanca
Referee: Eganaden Cadressen (Mauritius), Attendance: 45.000
MOROCCO: Ezaki Badou "Zaki", Tijani El Maatoui, Mustapha El Biaz, Hassan Mouhaid (10 Lahcen Ouadani "Hçina"), Abdelmajid Lemriss, Mustapha El Haddaoui, Abdelmajid Dolmy, Abdelrazzak Khairi, Aziz Bouderbala, Moulay El Gharef, Abdelkrim Merry "Krimau".
CAMEROON: Joseph-Antoine Bell, Stephen Tataw, Richard Abena, Emmanuel Kundé, Charles Ntamark, Cyrille Makanaky, Bertin Ollé-Ollé, Emile M'Bouh, Louis-Paul M'Fédé, André Kana-Biyik, Roger Milla.
Goal: Cyrille Makanaky (78)

Third Place Match

26.03.1988

ALGERIA - MOROCCO 1-1 (0-0, 1-1), 4-3 on penalties
Stade Mohamed V, Casablanca
Referee: Hafid Tahir (Tanzania), Attendance: 40,000
MOROCCO: Khalid Azmi, Tijani El Maatoui, Mustapha El Biaz, Lahcen Ouadani "Hçina", Mourad Jabrane, Abdelmajid Dolmy (14 Abderrahim Hamraoui), Hassan Benhabicha, Abdelrazzak Khairi (104 Mohammed Timoumi), Moulay El Gharef, Hassan Nader, Mustapha Kiddi.
ALGERIA: Nassereddine Drid, Chaâbane Merzekane, Abdelrrazak Belgherbi, Fodil Megharia, Mohammed Chaïb, Rachid Maatar, Hocine Yahi, Lakhdar Belloumi, Abdelkader Ferhaoui, Hakim Medane (71 Kamel Djahmoun), Ali Bouafia (64 Hamidouche Bentayeb).
Goals: Lakhdar Belloumi (87) / Hassan Nader (67)

Final

27.03.1988

CAMEROON - NIGERIA 1-0 (0-0)
Stade Mohamed V, Casablanca
Referee: Idrissa Sarr (Mauritania), Attendance: 50.000
CAMEROON: Joseph-Antoine Bell, Stephen Tataw, Benjamin Massing, Emmanuel Kundé, Charles Ntamark, Emile Mbouh, Louis-Paul M'Fédé, André Kana-Biyik, Cyrille Makanaky, Roger Milla, Bertin Ollé-Ollé (33 Richard Abena). Trainer: Claude Le Roy (France).
NIGERIA: Peter Rufai, Yisa Sofoluwe, Stephen Keshi, Sunday Eboigbe, Bright Omokaro, Henry Nwosu, Ndubuisi Okosieme, Samuel Okwaraji, Augustine Eguavoen, Rashidi Yekini, Folorunso Okenla (76 Humphrey Edobor). Trainer: Manfred Höner (West Germany).
Goal: Emmanuel Kundé (55 penalty)

Seventeenth edition - 1990
Qualifying Tournament

For the 17th edition of the Africa Cup of Nations, 35 countries initially entered but seven then withdrew. Algeria hosted the finals tournament although there was a high level of political tension in the country which was on the verge of a civil war. Egypt, traditionally fierce rivals of Algeria, initially refused to play but eventually sent a team following pressure from the CAF. When the two teams came to meet in the group stage, the fact that Egypt had already been eliminated from the competition after losing their first two games did not stop unrest amongst the crowd and missiles were thrown before pitch invasions as Algeria won 1-0. Following this game, Algeria progressed to the final where they defeated Nigeria to win their only Continental title.

Preliminary Round

05.10.88 Angola - Equatorial Guinea 4-1
16.10.88 Equatorial Guinea - Angola 0-0

09.10.88 Gabon - Burkina Faso 3-0
23.10.88 Burkina Faso - Gabon 1-0

02.10.88 Liberia - Mali 0-1
16.10.88 Mali - Liberia 3-0

02.10.88 Mauritius - Seychelles 3-0
16.10.88 Seychelles - Mauritius 1-0

01.10.88 Tanzania - Swaziland 1-1
16.10.88 Swaziland - Tanzania 1-1, 3-1 on penalties

Ethiopia - Uganda w/o
Guinea - Gambia w/o
Libya - Mauritania w/o
Mozambique - Madagascar w/o

First Round

09.04.89 Angola - Ivory Coast 0-2
23.04.89 Ivory Coast - Angola 4-1

09.04.89 Ethiopia - Egypt 1-0
21.04.89 Egypt - Ethiopia 6-1

09.04.89 Gabon - Ghana 1-0
23.04.89 Ghana - Gabon 1-0, 3-5 on penalties

15.04.89 Guinea - Nigeria 1-1
22.04.89 Nigeria - Guinea 3-0

09.04.89 Mali - Morocco 0-0
23.04.89 Morocco - Mali 1-1

09.04.89 Mauritius - Zimbabwe 1-4
23.04.89 Zimbabwe - Mauritius 1-0

16.04.89 Mozambique - Zambia 0-1
30.04.89 Zambia - Mozambique 3-0

07.04.89 Sudan - Kenya 1-0
23.04.89 Kenya - Sudan 1-0, 6-5 on penalties

09.04.89 Swaziland - Malawi 0-2
23.04.89 Malawi - Swaziland 1-1

Senegal - Togo w/o
Tunisia - Libya w/o
Zaire - Sierra Leone w/o

Second Round

16.07.89 Egypt - Zaire 2-0
28.07.89 Zaire - Egypt 0-0

16.07.89 Nigeria - Zimbabwe 3-0
30.07.89 Zimbabwe - Nigeria 1-1

16.07.89 Malawi - Kenya 2-3
30.07.89 Kenya - Malawi 0-0

16.07.89 Mali - Ivory Coast 2-2
30.07.89 Ivory Coast - Mali 3-1

16.07.89 Senegal - Tunisia 3-0
30.07.89 Tunisia - Senegal 0-1

15.07.89 Zambia - Gabon 3-0
30.07.89 Gabon - Zambia 2-1

Final Tournament (Algeria)

GROUP A

02.03.1990

ALGERIA - NIGERIA 5-1 (1-0)
Stade du 5 Juillet, Alger
Referee: Shizuo Takada (Japan), Attendance: 65,000
ALGERIA: Anter Osmani, Abdelhakim Serrar, Fodil Megharia, Rachid Adghigh, Ali Benhalima, Tahar Cherif El-Ouazani, Djamel Amani, Moussa Saïb, Cherif Oudjani (79 Mohamed Rahim), Rabah Madjer, Djamel Menad. Trainer: Mohamed Kermali
NIGERIA: Alloysius Agu, Abdul Aminu, Uche Okechukwu, Ayodele Ogunlana (71 Baldwin Bazuaye), Andrew Uwe, Tajudeen Oyekanmi, Thompson Oliha (46 Emmanuel Okocha), Moses Kpakor, Ademola Adeshina, Rashidi Yekini, Daniel Amokachi. Trainer: Clemens Westerhoff (Netherlands).
Goals: Rabah Madjer (36, 58), Djamel Menad (69, 72), Djamel Amani (88) / Emmanuel Okocha (82)

03.03.1990

IVORY COAST - EGYPT 3-1 (0-0)
Olympique, Alger
Referee: Ali Hafidhi (Tanzania), Attendance: 65.000
IVORY COAST: Pierre Alain Gouaméné, Basile Kouamé Aka, Arsène Houbou, Rufin Biagné Lué, Omer Tiero, Joseph Gadji-Celi, Diaby Sékana, Serge Alain Maguy, Youssouf Fofana, Abdoulaye Traoré, Yao Amani. Trainer: Rade Ognanović (Yugoslavia)
EGYPT: Thabet El-Batal, Fawzy Gamal, Hamada Sedki, Hescham Ibrahim, Mohamed Saad, Taha El-Sayed, Abdel Azim El-Shoura, Mohamed Saad Shehata, Talaat Mansour, Adel Abdel Rahman, Tarek Yehia. Trainer: Hani Mustafa.
Goals: Abdoulaye Traoré (53, 60), Serge-Alain Magui (73) / Adel Abdel Rahman (75)

05.03.1990

ALGERIA - IVORY COAST 3-0 (1-0)
Stade du 5 Juillet, Alger
Referee: Idrissa Sarr (Mauritania), Attendance: 45,000
ALGERIA: Anter Osmani, Abdelhamid Serrar, Fodil Megharia, Rachid Adghigh (9 Kamel Adjas, 71 Tarek Lazizi), Ali Benhalima, Tahar Cherif El-Ouazani, Djamel Amani, Moussa Saïb, Cherif Oudjani, Rabah Madjer, Djamel Menad.
IVORY COAST: Pierre Alain Gouaméné, Basile Kouamé Aka, Omer Tiero, Diaby Sékana, Arsène Hobou, Rufin Biagné Lué, Joseph Gadji-Celi, Serge Alain Maguy, Oumar Ben Salah, Abdoulaye Traoré, Benoît Dali (64 Yao Lambert Amani).
Sent off: Abdoulaye Traoré (83)
Goals: Djamel Menad (23), Tahar Cherif El-Ouazani (81), Cherif Oudjani (82)

05.03.1990

NIGERIA - EGYPT 1-0 (1-0)
Olympique, Alger
Referee: Laurent Petcha (Cameroon), Attendance: 45,000

80

NIGERIA: Alloysius Agu, Abdul Aminu, Uche Okechukwu, Herbert Anijekwu, Isaac Semitoje, Ben Iroha, Thompson Oliha (86 Emmanuel Okocha), Moses Kpakor, Ayodele Ogunlana (61 Tajudeen Oyekanmi), Daniel Amokachi, Rashidi Yekini.
EGYPT: Thabet El-Batal, Fawzy Gamal, Hamada Sedki, Hescham Ibrahim, Mohamed Saad, Taha El-Sayed (51 Emad Salah), Abdel Azim El-Shoura, Mohamed Saad Shehata, Talaat Mansour, Adel Abdel Rahman, Tarek Yehia.
Goal: Rashidi Yekini (8)

08.03.1990

NIGERIA - IVORY COAST 1-0 (1-0)
Olympique, Alger
Referee: Abdelali Naciri (Morocco), Attendance: 80,000
NIGERIA: Alloysius Agu, Abdul Aminu, Uche Okechukwu, Herbert Anijekwu, Isaac Semitoje, Andrew Uwe, Emmanuel Okocha, Moses Kpakor (79 Ayodele Ogunlana), Thompson Oliha (46 Ademola Adeshima), Rashidi Yekini, Friday Elahor.
IVORY COAST: Pierre Alain Gouaméné, Basile Kouamé Aka, Omer Tiero, Diaby Sékana, Arsène Hobou, Georges Lignon (65 Lucien Kassy Kouadio), Joseph Gadji-Celi, Serge-Alain Maguy, Oumar Ben-Salah, Benoît Dali (35 Yao Amani), Youssouf Fofana.
Goal: Rashidi Yekini (3)

08.03.1990

ALGERIA - EGYPT 2-0 (2-0)
Stade du 5 Juillet, Alger
Referee: Eganaden Cadressen (Mauritius), Attendance: 80,000
ALGERIA: Kamel Kadri, Ait Abderahmane, Tarek Lazizi, Abdelhamid Serrar, Kamel Adjas, Tahar Cherif El-Ouazani, Mahiedine Meftah, Djamel Amani (60 Abderezzak Djahnit), Moussa Saïb, Mohamed Rahim, Djamel Menad (79 Nacer Bouiche).
EGYPT: Thabet El-Batal, Fawzy Gamal (46 Mosheer Hanafi), Hamada Sedki, Hescham Ibrahim, Mohamed Saad (63 Yasser Rayan), Abdel Azim El-Shoura, Mohamed Saad Shehata, Emad Salah, Talaat Mansour, Adel Abdel Rahman, Tarek Yehia.
Goals: Djamel Amani (39), Moussa Saïb (43)

1.	ALGERIA	3	3	0	0	10	1	6
2.	NIGERIA	3	2	0	1	3	5	4
3.	Ivory Coast	3	1	0	2	3	5	2
4.	Egypt	3	0	0	3	1	6	0

GROUP B

03.03.1990

ZAMBIA - CAMEROON 1-0 (0-0)
Stade 19 Mai 1956, Annaba
Referee: Hédi Jouini (Tunisia), Attendance: 8000
ZAMBIA: David Efford Chabala, Kapambwe Mulenga, Whiteson Changwe, Eston Mulenga, John Soko, Samuel Chomba, Wisdom Mumba Chansa, Lucky Msiska, Derby Makinka, Webster Chikabala, Timothy Mwitwa (87 Linos Makwaza). Trainer: Samuel Ndlovu
CAMEROON: Thomas N'kono, Stephen Tataw, Benjamin Massing, Emmanuel Kundé, Bertin Ebwelle, Thomas Libih, André Kana-Biyik, Cyrille Makanaky, Ernest Ebongue, François Omam-Biyick, Bonaventure Djonkep (80 Louis-Paul Mfédé). Trainer: Valeri Nepomniachi (USSR).
Goal: Webster Chikabala (58)

03.03.1990

SENEGAL - KENYA 0-0
Stade 19 Mai 1956, Annaba
Referee: Idrissa Traoré (Mali), Attendance: 8000
KENYA: Washington Muhanji, Wycliffe Anyangu, Paul Ochieng, Austin Oduor, Tobias Ochola, Paul Onyera, John Lukoye, Abbas Magongo, George Onyango, Peter Dawo, Henry Motego. Trainer: Mohammed Kheri.
SENEGAL: Cheikh Ahmed Seck, Papé Fall, Mamadou Teuw (72 Mamadou Diallo), Moustapha Lamine Diagné, Adolphe Mendy (69 Baytir Samb), Adama Cissé, Lamine Sagna, Mamadou Lamine Ndiaye, Abdoulaye Diallo, Moussa Ndaw, Souleymane Sane. Trainer: Claude Le Roy (France)

06.03.1990

ZAMBIA - KENYA 1-0 (1-0)
Stade 19 Mai 1956, Annaba
Referee: Mawukpona Hounnake-Kouassi (Togo), Attendance: 6000
ZAMBIA: David Efford Chabala, John Soko, Samuel Chomba, Eston Mulenga, Whiteson Changwe, Derby Makinka, Wisdom Mumba Chansa, Linos Makwaza, Lucky Msiska (80 Pearson Mwanza), Webster Chikabala, Geoffrey Mulenga (80 Kenneth Malitoli).
KENYA: Washington Muhanji, Wycliffe Anyangu, Paul Ochieng, Austin Oduor, Tobias Ochola, Abbas Magongo, Paul Onyera (52 John Odie), John Lukoye (52 Anthony Ndolo), George Onyango, Henry Motego, Peter Dawo,
Goal: Linos Makwaza (40)

06.03.1990

SENEGAL - CAMEROON 2-0 (1-0)
Stade 19 Mai 1956, Annaba
Referee: Jamal Al-Sharif (Syria).
SENEGAL: Cheikh Ahmed Seck, Mamadou Teuw, Moustapha Lamine Diagné, Mamadou Diallo, Papé Fall, Adama Cissé, Lamine Sagna, Mamadou Lamine Ndiaye, Moussa Ndaw (78 Baytir Samb), Jules-François Bocandé, Souleymane Sané (89 Mamadou Diarra).
CAMEROON: Thomas N'kono, Stephen Tataw, Benjamin Massing, Emmanuel Kundé, Bertin Ebwelle, Thomas Liibih (46 Ernest Ebongue), Jean-Claude Pagal, André Kana-Biyick, Cyrille Makanaky, Eugène Ekéké (76 Bonaventure Djonkep), François Omam-Biyick.
Goals: Mamadou Diallo (45), Moussa Ndaw (56)

09.03.1990

ZAMBIA - SENEGAL 0-0
Stade 19 Mai 1956, Annaba
Referee: Mohammed Hussam El-Din (Egypt), Attendance: 10.000
ZAMBIA: David Efford Chabala, John Soko, Samuel Chomba, Eston Mulenga, Kapambwe Mulenga, Derby Makinka, Phillimon Chisala, Wisdom Mumba Chansa, Linos Makwaza, Kenneth Malitoli (59 Lucky Msiska), Webster Chikabala.
SENEGAL: Cheikh Ahmed Seck, Lamine Diagné, Mamadou Teuw (31 Mamadou Diallo), Roger Mendy, Papé Fall, Adama Cissé, Lamine Sagna, Mamadou Lamine Ndiaye, Moustapha Abdoulaye Diallo, Jules-François Bocandé, Moussa Ndaw.

09.03.1990

CAMEROON - KENYA 2-0 (1-0)
Stade 19 Mai 1956, Annaba
Referee: Badou Jasseh (Gambia), Attendance: 6000
CAMEROON: William Andem, Stephen Tataw, Jules Onana, Emmanuel Kundé, Bertin Ebwelle,
Thomas Liibih, André Kana-Biyick, Cyrille Makanaky, Bonaventure Djonkep, François Omam-Biyick
(58 Louis-Paul Mfédé), Emmanuel Maboang.
KENYA: John Busolo, Mulupi Makuto, Micky Weche, Austin Oduor, Tobias Ochola, Paul Ochieng,
George Onyango (75 Paul Onyera), Henry Motego, Sammy Onyango (58 Khaduli), John Odie, Anthony
Ndolo.
Goals: Emmanuel Maboang (28, 69)

1.	ZAMBIA	3	2	1	0	2	0	5
2.	SENEGAL	3	1	2	0	2	0	4
3.	Cameroon	3	1	0	2	2	3	2
4.	Kenya	3	0	1	2	0	3	1

Semi-finals

12.03.1990

ZAMBIA - NIGERIA 0-2 (0-1)
Stade Omnisports, Annaba
Referee: Badara Sene (Senegal), Attendance: 30,000
NIGERIA: Alloysius Agu, Andrew Uwe, Uche Okechukwu, Herbert Anijekwu, Isaac Semitoje,
Ademola Adeshina (56 Wasiu Ipaye), Moses Kpakor, Emmanuel Okocha, Daniel Amokachi (56
Ayodele Ogunlana), Rashidi Yekini, Friday Elahor.
ZAMBIA: David Efford Chabala, John Soko, Samuel Chomba, Eston Mulenga, Whiteson Changwe,
Derby Makinka, Lucky Msiska (73 Kenneth Malitoli), Wisdom Mumba Chansa, Timothy Mwitwa (73
Pearson Mwanza), Linos Makwaza, Webster Chikabala.
Goals: Uche Okechukwu (18), Rashidi Yekini (77)

12.03.1990

ALGERIA - SENEGAL 2-1 (1-1)
Stade du 5 Juillet, Alger
Referee: Shizuo Takada (Japan), Attendance: 80,000
ALGERIA: Anter Osmani, Ali Benhalima, Fodil Megharia, Abdelhakim Serrar, Kamel Adjas (69
Mohamed Aït Abderrahmane), Tahar Cherif El-Ouazani, Djamel Amani, Moussa Saïb, Cherif Oudjani,
Rabah Madjer, Djamel Menad.
SENEGAL: Cheikh Ahmed Seck, Papé Fall, Mamadou Diallo, Roger Mendy, Moustapha Lamine
Diagné, Adolphe Mendy, Adama Cissé (79 Sylvester Coly), Lamine Sagna, Mamadou Lamine Ndiaye,
Abdoulaye Diallo, Jules-François Bocandé (69 Moussa Ndaw).
Goals: Djamel Menad (4), Djamel Amani (62) / Abdelhakim Serrar (20 own goal)

83

Third Place Match

15.03.1990

ZAMBIA - SENEGAL 1-0 (0-0)
Olympique, Alger
Referee: Hédi Jouini (Tunisia), Attendance: 8000
ZAMBIA: David Efford Chabala, Kapambwe Mulenga, Whiteson Changwe, Eston Mulenga, John Solo, Samuel Chomba, Derby Makinka, Linos Makwaza, Joël Bwalya (51 Pearson Mwanza), Webster Chikabala, Geoffrey Mulenga (40 Lucky Msiska).
SENEGAL: Abdou Mbaye, Papé Fall, Mamadou Diallo, Moustapha Lamine Diagné, Adolphe Mendy, Lamine Sagna, Baytir Samb (84 Mamadou Guèye), Mamadou Diarra, Abdoulaye Diallo, Sylvester Coly, Moussa Ndaw (84 Youssouf Mbengue).
Goal: Webster Chikabala (73)

Final

16.03.1990

ALGERIA - NIGERIA 1-0 (1-0)
Stade du 5 Juillet, Alger
Referee: Jean-Fidele Diramba (Gabon), Attendance: 80,000
ALGERIA: Antar Osmani, Ali Benhalima, Fodil Megharia, Abdelhakim Serrar, Mohamed Aït Abderrahmane, Tahar Cherif El-Ouazani (84 Mahieddine Meftah), Djamel Amani, Moussa Saïb, Djamel Menad, Cherif Oudjani (89 Mohamed Rahim), Rabah Madjer. Trainer: Mohamed Kermali
NIGERIA: Alloysius Agu, Ademola Adeshina, Herbert Anijekwu, Isaac Semitoje, Uche Okechukwu, Ayodele Ogunlana (69 Daniel Amokachi), Andrew Uwe (13 Abdul Aminu), Moses Kpakor, Thompson Oliha, Rashidi Yekini, Friday Elahor. Trainer: Clemens Westerhoff (Netherlands).
Goal: Cherif Oudjani (38)

Eighteenth edition - 1992
Qualifying Tournament

For the 18th edition of the African Cup of Nations, the format of both the qualifiers and the finals tournament was changed. For the first time (and for every subsequent edition since), a regional group system was introduced for the qualifying competition in place of knock-out stages used in previous editions. In total, 37 teams entered the qualifying competition, although three later withdrew.
The finals tournament for 1992 was held in Senegal, with twelve places available, divided into four groups of three teams playing a round-robin competition. The top two teams from each group then entered a quarter-final stage. The Ghanaian midfielder Abedi "Pelé" Ayew, who scored three goals, was voted best player of the tournament as he helped his team reach the final. Unfortunately, Abedi Pelé was suspended for the final and, without his talents, Ghana were unable to overcome the Ivory Coast who lifted the trophy following an 11-10 penalty shoot-out victory!

Preliminary Round

18.05.1990 Mauritania - Gambia 2-0
03.06.1990 Gambia - Mauritania 2-1

Group 1

18.08.1990 Guinea - Sierra Leone 1-2 (0-2)
Goals: Mohamed Sylla (70) / Deen (2), K. Mohamed (13)

19.08.1990 Cameroon - Mali 0-0
01.09.1990 Sierra Leone - Cameroon 1-1 (1-0)
Goals: Brimah (25) / Belle Belle (50)
02.09.1990 Mali - Guinea 1-1 (1-0)
Goals: Cheick Diallo (40) / Yansane (70)
14.04.1991 Guinea - Cameroon 0-0
14.04.1991 Mali - Sierra Leone 0-0
28.04.1991 Mali - Cameroon 0-2 (0-0)
Goals: Ewane (68), Oman-Biyik (86), match abandoned after 86 mins, result stood,
28.04.1991 Sierra Leone - Guinea 0-1 (0-1)
Goal: S. Touré (33)
14.07.1991 Cameroon - Sierra Leone 1-0 (0-0)
Goal: Ekeke (80)
14.07.1991 Guinea - Mali 2-1 (1-0)
Goals: Fodo Camara (17), Abubucar Tit Camara (70) / Kubilay (75)
28.07.1991 Cameroon - Guinea 1-0 (1-0)
Goal: Oman-Biyik (10)
28.07.1991 Sierra Leone - Mali 2-0

1.	CAMEROON	6	3	3	0	5	1	9
2.	Sierra Leone	6	2	2	2	5	4	6
3.	Guinea	6	2	2	2	5	5	6
4.	Mali	6	0	3	3	2	7	3

Group 2

17.08.1990 Egypt - Ethiopia 2-0 (0-0)
Goals: H. Ramzy (61), H.Hassan (85)
19.08.1990 Tunisia - Chad 2-1 (1-1)
Goals: Abid (27), Rouissi (82) / N'Doram (17)
02.09.1990 Chad - Egypt 0-0
18.11.1990 Ethiopia - Tunisia 0-2 (0-2)
Goals: Mahjoubi (39), Rouissi (41)
Ethiopia withdrawn after this match
14.04.1991 Tunisia - Egypt 2-2 (1-1)
Goals: Mahjoubi (44), Mahjoubi (87) / A. Ramzi (5), I. Hassan (47)
14.04.1991 Ethiopia – Chad awarded 0-2
28.04.1991 Ethiopia – Egypt awarded 0-2
28.04.1991 Chad - Tunisia 0-0
12.07.1991 Egypt - Chad 5-1 (1-1)
Goals: H. Hassan (35, 58), Ramzy (57, 60, 80) / Touré (18)
Tunisia – Ethiopia awarded 2-0
26.07.1991 Egypt - Tunisia 2-2 (1-0)
Goals: I. Youssef (44), Abdelghani (66) / Mahjoubi (46, 60)
Chad – Ethiopia awarded 2-0

1.	EGYPT	6	3	3	0	13	5	9
2.	Tunisia	6	3	3	0	10	5	9
3.	Chad	6	2	2	2	6	7	6
4.	Ethiopia	6	0	0	6	0	12	0

Group 3

NB: Liberia withdrew before playing a match
19.08.1990 Ivory Coast - Mauritania 2-0 (1-0)
Goals: Obou Arsène (34 penalties), Sié Donald (57)
19.08.1990 Morocco - Niger 2-0 (1-0)
Goals: Hababi (18), Laghrissi (89)
02.09.1990 Morocco - Mauritania 4-0 (3-0)
Goals: Hassan Nadir (8), Bouderbala (38), Rahib (44), Laghrissi (63)
30.09.1990 Niger - Ivory Coast 0-1
Goal: A. Traoré
14.10.1990 Niger - Mauritania 7-1 (1-1)
Goals: Amadou Dwaye (7, 62, 78, 79), Andre Zakari (46, 48), Doulla (86) / Papa Seck (10)
13.01.1991 Morocco - Ivory Coast 3-1 (1-0)
Goals: Laghrissi (9, 72), Lashaf (48), Amadou (77)
27.01.1991 Mauritania - Ivory Coast forfait
27.01.1991 Niger - Morocco 1-0 (1-0)
Goal: Douka (19)
12.04.1991 Mauritania - Morocco 0-2 (0-0)
Goals: Laghrissi (46), Bouderbala (66)
30.04.1991 Ivory Coast - Niger 1-0 (1-0)
Goal: A. Traoré (27 penalty)
26.07.1991 Mauritania - Niger 0-1
28.07.1991 Ivory Coast - Morocco 2-0 (1-0)
Goals: Lacina (24), A. Traoré (52)

1.	IVORY COAST	6	5	0	1	9	3	10
2.	MOROCCO	6	4	0	2	11	4	8
3.	Niger	6	3	0	3	9	5	6
4.	Mauritania	6	0	0	6	1	18	0

Group 4

19.08.1990 Burkina Faso - Benin 2-0 (1-0)
Goals: Ilboudo (20), Kadeba (70)
19.08.1990 Nigeria - Togo 3-0 (0-0)
Goals: Okechukwu (58), Amokachi (80), Lawal (87)
01.09.1990 Ghana - Nigeria 1-0 (1-0)
Goal: Mensah (32)
02.09.1990 Burkina Faso - Togo 2-0 (0-0)
Goals: Olboudo (48), Fofana (60)
30.09.1990 Benin - Nigeria 0-1
Goal: Ishaya Jatau
30.09.1990 Togo - Ghana 0-1 (0-0)
Goal: Mensah (46)
14.10.1990 Benin - Togo 1-1
14.10.1990 Ghana - Burkina Faso 2-0 (1-0)
Goals: Joe Addo (10), Prince Opoku (82)
13.01.1991 Burkina Faso - Nigeria 1-1 (1-0)
Goals: Aboubacar (24) / Epko (87)
13.01.1991 Ghana - Benin 4-0 (3-0)
Goals: Prince Opoku (8, 44), Armah (16), Naawu (60)
27.01.1991 Benin - Burkina Faso 1-2 (1-2)
Goals: Bossougbete (43) / Bakadou (9, 22)

27.01.1991 Togo - Nigeria 0-0
13.04.1991 Nigeria - Ghana 0-0
21.04.1991 Togo - Burkina Faso 1-0
27.04.1991 Nigeria - Benin 3-0 (3-0)
Goals: Siasia (5), Ekpo (17), Amokachi (28)
29.04.1991 Ghana - Togo 2-0 (1-0)
Goals: Lamptey (43), Baffoe (76)
13.07.1991 Burkina Faso - Ghana 2-1 (1-1)
Goals: Ilboudo (21), Gnimassou (87) / Teteh (17)
14.07.1991 Togo - Benin 2-0 (0-0)
Goals: Amegnizin (57), Flawoo (70 penalty)
27.07.1991 Nigeria - Burkina Faso 7-1 (2-1)
Goals: Yekini (13, 69, 71, 80), Siasia (14), Elahor (74), Sinidi (88) / Touré (20)
28.07.1991 Benin - Ghana 0-0

1.	GHANA	8	5	2	1	11	2	12
2.	NIGERIA	8	4	3	1	15	3	11
3.	Burkina Faso	8	4	1	3	10	13	9
4.	Togo	8	2	2	4	4	9	6
5.	Benin	8	0	2	6	2	15	2

Group 5

18.08.1990 Zambia - Swaziland 5-0 (2-0)
Goals: Chansa (39), Chikalala (40), Moselepeti (54), Masala (70), Changwe (84)
19.08.1990 Angola - Madagascar 0-1 (0-0)
Goal: Randranaivo (60)
01.09.1990 Swaziland - Angola 1-1 (0-1)
Goals: Terblanche (89) / Chilo (10)
01.09.1990 Madagascar - Zambia 0-0
14.04.1991 Angola - Zambia 1-2 (0-0)
Goals: Saavedra (62) / K. Bwalya (55), Mbasela (87)
14.04.1991 Swaziland - Madagascar 0-1 (0-1)
Goal: Raveloson (16)
28.04.1991 Swaziland - Zambia 2-1 (1-0)
Goals: Mambuza (44), Nkambule (50) / Makinka (60)
04.05.1991 Madagascar - Angola 0-0
14.07.1991 Zambia - Madagascar 2-1 (2-0)
Goals: Musonda (20), Bwalya (38) / Henry (49)
15.07.1991 Angola - Swaziland 1-1 (1-0)
Goals: Felito (40 penalty) / Dance Matse (48)
28.07.1991 Zambia - Angola 1-0 (0-0)
Goal: Musonda (89)

1.ZAMBIA	6	4	1	1	11	4	9
2.Madagascar	5	2	2	1	3	2	6
3.Swaziland	5	1	2	2	4	9	4
4.Angola	6	0	3	3	3	6	3

Group 6

Mauritius withdrew before playing a match
17.08.1990 Sudan - Mozambique 1-0 (1-0)
Goal: Atif Al-Quoz (85)

02.09.1990 Mozambique - Kenya 2-1 (0-0)
Goals: Nico (55), Nando (65) / Mutua (51)
14.04.1991 Sudan - Kenya 1-0 (1-0)
Goal: Mansour (8)
28.04.1991 Mozambique - Sudan 1-0 (1-0)
Goal: Zainadine (30)
14.07.1991 Kenya - Mozambique 1-0 (1-0)
Goal: Mwololo (32)
28.07.1991 Kenya - Sudan 2-1 (1-0)
Goals: Motego (13), Okoth (70) / Faraj (87)

1.	KENYA	4	2	0	2	4	4	4
2.	Mozambique	4	2	0	2	3	3	4
	Sudan	4	2	0	2	3	3	4

Group 7

NB: Seychelles withdrew before playing a match
18.08.1990 Malawi - Congo 0-1 (0-1)
Goal: Makita (5)
02.09.1990 Congo - Zimbabwe 2-0 (0-0)
Goals: Ndomba (55), Makita (86)
14.04.1991 Zimbabwe - Malawi 4-0
Goals: Mc Kop 2, Ndlovu, Chunga
28.04.1991 Congo - Malawi 2-1 (1-1)
Goals: Capy (35 penalty), Capy (85) / Gelard Phiri (41)
14.07.1991 Zimbabwe - Congo 2-2 (1-1)
Goals: McKop (9), Ndlovu (78) / Makita (40), Ndombe (89)
27.07.1991 Malawi - Zimbabwe 2-2 (1-1)
Goals: Rzwodzi (20 own goal), Chimodzi (86) / Nagoli (13), Ndlovu (89)

1.	CONGO	4	3	1	0	7	3	7
2.	Zimbabwe	4	1	2	1	8	6	4
3.	Malawi	4	0	1	3	3	9	1

Group 8

19.08.1990 Gabon - Uganda 1-0 (0-0)
Goal: Manon (65)
19.08.1990 Zaire - Tanzania 2-0 (1-0)
Goals: Eugene Kabongo (6, 75)
01.09.1990 Tanzania - Gabon 0-0
01.09.1990 Uganda - Zaire 2-1 (1-1)
Goals: Senoga (8), Musisi (62) / Kabongo (18)
14.04.1991 Uganda - Tanzania 3-2 (2-2)
Goals: Musisi (22), Musisi (26, 65), Haule (43, 45)
14.04.1991 Zaire - Gabon 2-1 (0-0)
Goals: Bwana (70), Mukanya (85) / Nzamba (74)
27.04.1991 Tanzania - Zaire 1-0 (0-0)
Goal: Haule (63)
27.04.1991 Uganda - Gabon 0-0
14.07.1991 Gabon - Tanzania 1-0 (1-0)
Goal: Anotho (37)
14.07.1991 Zaire - Uganda 1-0 (0-0)
Goal: Balenga (75 penalty)

28.07.1991 Gabon - Zaire 0-0
29.07.1991 Tanzania - Uganda 1-1 (1-1)

1.	ZAIRE	6	3	1	2	6	4	7
2.	Gabon	6	2	3	1	3	2	7
3.	Uganda	6	2	2	2	6	6	6
4.	Tanzania	6	1	2	3	4	7	4

Final Tournament (Senegal)

GROUP A

12.01.1992

NIGERIA - SENEGAL 2-1 (1-1)
Stade de l'Amitié, Dakar
Referee: Nizar Watti (Syria), Attendance: 60.000
NIGERIA: Alloysius Agu, Emeka Ezegou, Ajibade Babalade, Stephen Keshi, Reuben Agboola, Augustine Eguavoen, Mutiu Adepoju, Thompson Oliha (46 Friday Ekpo), Friday Elahor (83 Finidi George), Rashidi Yekini, Samson Siasia. Trainer: Clemens Westerhof (Netherlands)
SENEGAL: Cheikh Seck, Malick Fall, Roger Mendy, Mamadou Teuw, Adolphe Mendy, Victor Diagne, Oumar Gueye Sène, Lamine N'Diaye (46 Moussa N'Daw), Thiemo Youm, Jules Bocandé, Souleymane Sane. Trainer: Claude Le Roy (France)
Goals: Samson Siasia (13), Stephen Keshi (82) / Jules Bocandé (36)

14.01.1992

NIGERIA - KENYA 2-1 (2-0)
Stade de l'Amitié, Dakar
Referee: Abdelazim Kadry (Egypt), Attendance: 5000
NIGERIA: Alloysius Agu, Emeka Ezegou, Reuben Agboola, Mutiu Adepoju, Ajibade Babalade (78 Uche Okechukwu), Stephen Keshi, Friday Elahor (61 Finidi George), Augustine Eguavoen, Samson Siasia, Friday Ekpo, Rashidi Yekini
KENYA: John Busolo, Vitalis Owour, Tobias Ochulla, Micky Weche, Allan Odhiambo, George Sunguti, John Lukoye, Peter Mwololo, Anthony Lwanga (81 Henry Nyandoro), Simon Ndungu (82 Alfayo Odongo), Mike Okoth. Trainer: Gerry Saurer (Austria).
Goals: Rashidi Yekini (7, 15) / Micky Weche (89 penalty)

16.01.1992

SENEGAL - KENYA 3-0 (0-0)
Stade de l'Amitié, Dakar
Referee: Omar Yengo (Congo), Attendance: 50.000
SENEGAL: Cheikh Seck, Malick Fall, Mamadou Diallo, Roger Mendy, Adolphe Mendy, Adama Cissé, Oumar Gueye Sène (76 Lamine Sagna), Victor Diagne, Thiemo Youm, Jules Bocandé (85 Alboury Lah), Souleymane Sane.
KENYA: John Busolo, Tobias Ochulla, Micky Weche, Vitalis Owour, George Sunguti, Peter Mwololo, Anthony Lwanga (79 Elijah Koranga), John Lukoye (53 Simon Ndunga), Sammy Omolo, Mike Okoth, David Odhiambo.
Goals: Souleymane Sane (46), Jules Bocandé (68), Victor Diagne (89)

89

1.	NIGERIA	2	2	0	0	4	2	4
2.	SENEGAL	2	1	0	1	4	2	2
3.	Kenya	2	0	0	2	1	5	0

GROUP B

12.01.1992

CAMEROON - MOROCCO 1-0 (1-0)
Stade de l'Amitié, Dakar
Referee: Lim Kee Chong (Mauritius), Attendance: 60,000
CAMEROON: Joseph-Antoine Bell, Stephen Tataw, Bertin Ebwelle, Jules-Denis Onana, Emmanuel Kundé, Emile Mbouh, Jean-Claude Pagal, André Kana-Biyik (58 Eugene Ekeke), François Omam-Biyik, Louis-Paul Mfédé, Cyrille Makanaky,. Trainer: Philippe Redon (France)
MOROCCO: Badou Zaki (42 Khalid Azmi), Rachid Azzouzi, Noureddine Naybet, Mouhcine Bouhlal, Jilal Fadel (11 Moudaka Mouloud), Rachid Daoudi, Abdelmajid Bouyboud, Aziz Bouderbala, Khalid Raghib, Said Rokbi, Mohamed Chaouch. Trainer: Werner Olk (Germany)
Goal: André Kana-Biyik (23)

14.01.1992

MOROCCO - ZAIRE 1-1 (0-0)
Stade de l'Amitié, Dakar
Referee: Neji Jouini (Tunisia), Attendance: 5000
MOROCCO: Khalid Azmi, Rachid Azzouzi, Mouhcine Bouhlal, Noureddine Naybet, Rachid Daoudi, Abdelmajid Bouyboud, Moudaka Mouloud (82 Hicham Dmaei), Aziz Bouderbala, Fakhreddine Rajhy, Abdelslam Laghrissi (36 Said Rokbi), Mohamed Chaouch.
ZAIRE: Pangi Merikani, Mansoni Ngombo, Ngalula Buana, Epangala Lokose, Kabwe Kusongo, Kabeya Mukanya, Mbote Ndinga, Tyambo Mara Etshele (46 Tchang Ngombe), Kinkomba Kingambo, Mbala Henri Balenga, Ngole Kana. Trainer: Kalala Mukendi
Goals: Said Rokbi (89) / Ngole Kana (90)

16.01.1992

CAMEROON - ZAIRE 1-1 (1-1)
Stade de l'Amitié, Dakar
Referee: Rachid Medjiba (Algeria), Attendance: 10,000
CAMEROON: Joseph-Antoine Bell, Stephen Tataw, Benjamin Massing, Emmanuel Kundé, Bertin Ebwelle, Emile Mbouh, André Kana-Biyik, Jean-Claude Pagal, Louis-Paul Mfédé (69 Eugene Ekeke), François Omam-Biyik, Cyrille Makanaky (74 Ernest Ebongue).
ZAIRE: Pangi Merikani, Mansoni Ngombo, Ngalula Buana, Epangala Lokose (78 Ekanza Simba), Kabwe Kasongo, Kabeya Mukanya, Menayame Tueba, Mbote Ndinga (54 Ngondala Assombalanga), Kinkomba Kingambo, Mbala Henri Balenga, Shimbula Mayanga.
Goals: François Omam-Biyik (15) / Menayame Tueba (1)

1.	CAMEROON	2	1	1	0	2	1	3
2.	ZAIRE	2	0	2	0	2	2	2
3.	Morocco	2	0	1	1	1	2	1

GROUP C

13.01.1992

IVORY COAST - ALGERIA 3-0 (2-0)
Stade Aline Sitoe Diatta, Ziguinchor
Referee: Mohamed Hounnake-Kouassi (Togo), Attendance: 5000
IVORY COAST: Pierre Alain Gouaméné, Basile Kouamé Aka, Aboua Dominique Sam, Diaby
Sekana, Arsène Hobou, Oumar Ben Salah (43 Nagueu Lignon), Joseph Gadji-Celi, Didier Otokoré,
Abdoulaye Traoré (71 Serge-Alain Maguy), Joël Tiéhi, Youssouf Fofana. Trainer: Yeo Martial
ALGERIA: Antar Osmani, Mourad Rahmouni, Fodil Megharia, Omar Belatoui (65 Youssef Heraoui),
Ali Benhalima, Kamel Adjas, Tahar Cherif El-Ouazani, Moussa Saib, Rabah Madjer, Ali Bouafia,
Hakim Meddane (46 Liazad Sandjak). Trainer: Abdelhamid Kermali
Adjas sent off (27)
Goals: Abdoulaye Traoré (14), Youssouf Fofana (25), Joël Tiéhi (90)

15.01.1992

IVORY COAST - CONGO 0-0
Stade Aline Sitoe Diatta, Ziguinchor
Referee: Hafidhi Ali (Tanzania), Attendance: 5000
IVORY COAST: Pierre Alain Gouaméné, Basile Kouamé Aka, Abouo Dominique Sam, Diaby
Sekana, Arsène Hobou, Lué Rufin, Didier Otokoré, Serge-Alain Maguy, Joël Tiéhi (55 Moussa Traoré),
Abdoulaye Troaré, Youssouf Fofana.
CONGO: Brice Samba, Maurice Ntounou, Célestine Mouyabi, Icertain Tsoumou, Laurent Nsombi,
Simplice Nzamba Owomat, Florent Baloki, Jean-Claude Mbemba (58 Pierre Tchibota), Jean-Jacques
Ndomba (75 Jean-Michel Mbemba), François Makita, Ange N'Gapy. Trainer: Noel Minga

17.01.1992

ALGERIA - CONGO 1-1 (1-1)
Stade Aline Sitoe Diatta, Ziguinchor
Referee: Christopher Musaabi (Uganda), Attendance: 5000
ALGERIA: Kamel Kadir, Mourad Rahmouni, Fodil Megharia, Omar Belatoui, Ali Benhalima, Tahar
Cherif El-Ouazani, Moussa Saib, Rabah Madjer (69 Mohamed Rahim), Ali Bouafia (69 Abdelhafid
Tasfaout), Djamel Menad, Nasser Bouiche.
CONGO: Brice Samba, Appolinaire Bouketo, Icertain Tsoumou, Célestine Mouyabi, Laurent Nsombi,
Jean-Jacques Ndomba, Pierre Tchibota, Simplice Nzamba Owomat, Pierre Kallet Mbongo, Sylvain
Moukassa, François Makita (55 Aristide Amouzoud).
Goals: Nasser Bouiche (44) / Pierre Tchibota (6)

1.	IVORY COAST	2	1	1	0	3	0	3
2.	CONGO	2	0	2	0	1	1	2
3.	Algeria	2	0	1	1	1	4	1

GROUP D

13.01.1992

ZAMBIA - EGYPT 1-0 (0-0)
Stade Aline Sitoe Diatta, Ziguinchor
Referee: Badara Sene (Senegal), Attendance: 5000

91

ZAMBIA: David Chabala, John Soko, Whiteson Changwe, Samuel Chomba, Eston Mulenga, Ashios Melu (82 Robert Watiyakeni), Timothy Mwitwa, Derby Makinka, Webby Chikabala (60 Gibby Mbaseta), Kalusha Bwalya, Linos Makwaza. Trainer: Samuel Ndlovu
EGYPT: Ahmed Shoubier, Ibrahim Hassan, Hesham Yakan, Hani Ramzy, Ayman Ragab, Ahmed Ramzy, Magdi Abdel Ghani, Ismail Youssef, Ahmed El-Kass, Hossam Hassan, Gamal Abdel Hamid (80 Mohamed Abdelazim). Trainer: Mahmoud El-Gohary
Goal: Kalusha Bwalya (61)

15.01.1992

GHANA - ZAMBIA 1-0 (0-0)
Stade Aline Sitoe Diatta, Ziguinchor
Referee: Naciri Abdelali (Morocco), Attendance: 5000
GHANA: Edward Ansah, Nil Darko Ankrah, Stephen Frimpong Manso, Anthony Baffoe, Emmanuel Armah, Kwasi Appiah, Mohamed Gargo (55 Samuel Opoku-Nti), Nil Lamptey (89 Sarfo Gyamfi), Abedi Pelé, Anthony Yeboah, Ali Ibrahim. Trainer: Otto Pfister (Germany)
ZAMBIA: David Chabala, John Soko, Samuel Chomba, Eston Mulenga, Robert Watiyakeni, Whiteson Changwe, Derby Makinka, Linos Makwaza (82 Maybin Mugaiwa), Timothy Mwitwa (70 Pearson Mwanza), Gibby Mbaseta, Kalusha Bwalya.
Goal: Abedi Pelé (64)

17.01.1992
GHANA - EGYPT 1-0 (0-0)
Stade Aline Sitoe Diatta, Ziguinchor
Referee: Tachi Kiichiro (Japan), Attendance: 5000
GHANA: Edward Ansah, Nil Darko Ankrah, Stephen Frimpong Manso (61 Mohamed Gargo), Anthony Baffoe, Emmanuel Armah, Kwasi Appiah, Stanley Abroah, Nil Lamptey (70 Emmanuel Ampiah), Abedi Pelé, Anthony Yeboah, Ali Ibrahim.
EGYPT: Ahmed Shoubier, Ibrahim Hassan, Hesham Yakan, Hany Ramzy, Ayman Ragab, Ahmed Ramzy (58 Gamal Abdelhamid), Ismail Youssef, Magdy Abdelghani, Mohamed Abdelazim, Hossam Hassan (50 Fawzy), Ahmed El-Kass.
Sent off: Armah (64) / I. Hassan (64)
Goal: Anthony Yeboah (89)

1.	GHANA	2	2	0	0	2	0	4
2.	ZAMBIA	2	1	0	1	1	1	2
3.	Egypt	2	0	0	2	0	2	0

Quarter-finals

19.01.1992

NIGERIA - ZAIRE 1-0 (1-0)
Stade Aline Sitoe Diatta, Ziguinchor
Referee: Idrissa Sarr (Mauritania), Attendance: 10.000
NIGERIA: Alloysius Agu, Emeka Ezeugo, Nduka Ugbade, Stephen Keshi, Uche Okechukwu, Augustine Eguavoen, Mutiu Adepoju, Rashidi Yekini, Samson Siasia, Thompson Oliha, Friday Elahor (64 Finidi George).
ZAIRE: Pangi Merikani, Mbaki Makengo, Epangala Lokose, Mansoni Ngomba (84 Menayame Tueba), Ngalula Buana, Kabwe Kasongo, Ekanza Simba, Mbala Balenga (55 Ngondola Assombalanga), Ngole Kana, Kinkomba Kingambo, Mbote Ndinga.
Goal: Rashidi Yekini (17)

92

19.01.1992

CAMEROON - SENEGAL 1-0 (0-0)
Stade de l'Amitié, Dakar
Referee: Kiichiro Tachi (Japan), Attendance: 35.000
SENEGAL: Cheikh Seck, Malick Fall, Roger Mendy, Mamadou Teuw, Adolphe Mendy, Victor Diagne, Oumar Gueye Sène, Lamine Ndiaye, Thiemo Youm (81 Moussa Ndaw), Jules Bocandé, Souleymane Sane.
CAMEROON: Joseph-Antoine Bell, Hans Agbo, Emmanuel Kundé, Jules-Denis Onana, Bertin Ebwellé, Roger Feutmba, Guy Tapoko (59 Ernest Ebongué), Jean-Claude Pagal, Emile Mbouh, François Omam-Biyik, André Kana-Biyik (89 Victor Ndip),.
Goal: Ernest Ebongué (89)

20.01.1992

IVORY COAST - ZAMBIA 1-0 (0-0,0-0)
Stade Aline Sitoe Diatta, Ziguinchor
Referee: Pierre-Alain Mounguengui (Gabon), Sttendance: 3000
IVORY COAST: Pierre Alain Gouaméné, Basile Kouamé Aka, Diaby Sekana, Aboua Dominique Sam, Oumar Ben Salah (73 Donald Sié), Joseph Gadji-Celi (89 Nagueu Lignon), Serge-Alain Maguy, Arsène Hobou, Kouadio Lucien Kassy, Abdoulaye Traoré, Moussa Traoré
ZAMBIA: David Chabala, John Soko, Eston Mulenga, Whiteson Changwe, Ashios Melu, Samuel Chomba, Beston Chambeshi (66 Gibby Mbaseta), Derby Makinka, Timothy Mwitwa, Kalusha Bwalya, Webby Chikabala (86 Mwenya Matete)
Goal: Donald Sié (94)

20.01.1992

GHANA - CONGO 2-1 (1-0)
Stade de l'Amitié, Dakar
Referee: Ibrahim Faye (Gambia), Attendance: 15.000
GHANA: Edward Ansah, Anthony Baffoe, Kwesi Appiah, Samuel Opoku-Nti (88 Isaac Asare), Stanley Abroah, Emmanuel Ampiah, Stephen Frimpong Manso, Nil Lamptey, Abedi Pelé, Tony Yeboah, Ali Ibrahim (56 Sarfo Gyamfi).
CONGO: Brice Samba, Maurice Ntounou, Icertain Tsoumou, Célestine Mouyabi (86 Aristide Amouzoud), Simplice Nzamba Owomat (40 Yvon Okemba), Florent Baloki, Laurent Nsombi, Sylvain Mounkassa, Jean-Jacques Ndomba, Ange N'Gapy, Pierre Tchibota.
Goals: Tony Yeboah (29), Abedi Pelé (57) / Pierre Tchibota (52)

Semi-finals

23.01.1992

GHANA - NIGERIA 2-1 (1-1)
Stade de l'Amitié, Dakar
Referee: Neji Jouini (TUN), Attendance: 30.000,
GHANA: Edward Ansah, Anthony Baffoe, Kwasi Appiah (46 Nil Darko Ankrah), Stanley Abroah, Emmanuel Ampiah, Isaac Asare, Sarfo Gyamfi, Nil Lamptey, Abedi Pelé, Tony Yeboah, Ali Ibrahim (34 Prince Polley).
NIGERIA: Alloysius Agu, Reuben Agboola, Stephen Keshi, Ajibade Babalade, Emeka Ezeugo, Augustine Eguavoen, Thompson Oliha (82 Friday Elahor), Finidi George (67 Friday Ekpo), Mutiu Adepoju, Rashidi Yekini, Samson Siasia.
Babalade sent off (75)
Goals: Abedi Pelé (43), Prince Polley (54) / Mutiu Adepoju (11)

23.01.1992

CAMEROON - IVORY COAST 0-0 aet, 1-3 penalties
Stade de l'Amitié, Dakar
Referee: Lim Kee Chong (Mauritius), Attendance: 35.000
IVORY COAST: Pierre Alain Gouaméné, Basile Kouamé Aka, Nagueu Lignon, Abouo Dominique
Sam, Lassine Dao (66 Abdoulaye Troaré), Diaby Sekana, Serge-Alain Maguy, Oumar Ben Salah,
Didier Otokoré, Joël Tiéhi (85 Yago Eugene Beugre), Moussa Traoré.
CAMEROON: Joseph-Antoine Bell, Jules-Denis Onano, Bertin Ebwelle, Emmanuel Kundé, Hans
Agbo, Roger Feutmba, Guy Tapoko (59 Eugene Ekeke), André Kana-Biyik, Jean-Claude Pagal, Ernest
Ebongue (104 Cyrille Makanaky), François Omam-Biyik.
Penalties: 1-0 Diaby Sekana, Cyrille Makanaky, 2-0 Moussa Traoré, 2-1 Bertin Ebwelle, Yago Eugene
Beugre, François Omam-Biyik, 3-1 Abdoulaye Traoré, Joseph-Antoine Bell

Third Place Match

25.01.1992

NIGERIA - CAMEROON 2-1 (2-1)
Stade de l'Amitié, Dakar
Referee: Sinkoh Zeli (Ivory Coast), Attendance: 2000
NIGERIA: Alloysius Agu, Nduka Ubade, Augustine Eguavoen (34 Emeka Ezeugo), Abdul Aminu,
Reuben Agboola, Mutiu Adepoju, Friday Ekpo, Finidi George, John Okon (74 Oladotun Alatishe),
Victor Ikpeba, Rashidi Yekini.
CAMEROON: Jacques Songo'o, Stephen Tataw, Benjamin Massing, Victor Ndip, Jules-Denis Onana,
Bertin Ebwelle, Emile Mbouh, Jacob Ewane (46 Eugene Ekeke), Guy Tapoko, Cyrille Makanaky (75
Ernest Ebongue), Kessack Maboang.
Goals: Friday Ekpo (75), Rashidi Yekini (88) / Kessak Maboang (85)

Final

26.01.1992

IVORY COAST - GHANA 0-0 aet, 11-10 penalties
Stade de l'Amitié, Dakar
Referee: Badara Sene (Senegal), Attendance: 45,000
IVORY COAST: Pierre Alain Gouaméné, Basile Kouamé Aka, Abouo Dominique Sam, Diaby
Sekana, Arsène Hobou, Joseph Gadji-Celi, Serge-Alain Maguy, Donald Sié, Didier Otokoré (53 Moussa
Traoré), Joël Tiéhi, Abdoulaye Traoré (101 Kouadio Lucien Kassy).
GHANA: Edward Ansah, Emmanuel Ampiah, Stephen Frimpong Manso, Anthony Baffoe, Emmanuel
Armah, Sarfo Gyamfi (51 Richard Naawu), Stanley Abroah, Nil Lamptey, Isaac Asare, Tony Yeboah,
Samuel Opoku-Nti.
Penalties: 1-0 Basile Kouamé Aka, 1-1 Anthony Baffoe, 2-1 Arsène Hobou, 2-2 Nil Lamptey, 3-2
Diaby Sekana, 3-3 Richard Naawu, 4-3 Moussa Traoré, Isaac Asare (miss), Joël Tiéhi (miss), 4-4 Tony
Yeboah, 5-4 Joseph Gadji-Celi, 5-5 Stephen Frimpong Manso, 6-5 Kouadio Lucien Kassy, 6-6
Emmanuel Armah, 7-6 Abouo Dominique Sam, 7-7 Stanley Abroah, 8-7 Serge-Alain Maguy, 8-8
Emmanuel Ampiah, 9-8 Donald Sié, 9-9 Samuel Opoku-Nti, 10-9 Pierre Alain Gouaméné, 10-10
Edward Ansah, 11-10 Basile Kouamé Aka, 11-10 Anthony Baffoe (save).

Nineteenth edition - 1994
Qualifying Tournament

The 19th edition of the competition saw 37 teams enter the qualifiers once again although six teams then withdrew or were disqualified for a number of reasons. The twelve-team, four-group format was retained for the finals tournament once again although this time the hosts, Algeria, were embarrassed as they were eliminated at the group stage. Nigeria, who had qualified for the 1994 World Cup Finals for the first time just a few months earlier, won the title a second time after beating a spirited Zambia team 2-1 in the final. Particular credit was due to Zambia for reaching the final of the competition as a large part of their team had died in an aeroplane crash on 28th April 1993 while travelling to a World Cup qualifier.

Preliminary Round

14.06.1992 Lesotho - Botswana 0-0
28.06.1992 Botswana - Lesotho 0-4 (0-1)
Goals: Khali (20), Lekhotia (46), Mokhati (60), Mohale (85)

14.06.1992 Guinea Bissau - Cape Verde 3-1
28.06.1992 Cape Verde - Guinea Bissau 1-0
05.07.1992 Guinea Bissau - Cape Verde 1-0

Group 1

16.08.1992 Gabon - Cameroon 0-0
16.08.1992 Benin - Niger 1-2 (0-1)
Goals: Sossa (66), Jacques André Lembo (80) / Burkire (19)
30.08.1992 Cameroon - Benin 2-0 (1-0)
Goals: Jacob Ewane (27), Emmanuel Tiki (60)
30.08.1992 Niger - Gabon 1-3 (1-2)
Goals: Zakari (11) / Nzamba (4, 7, 83)
11.04.1993 Gabon - Benin 2-0 (2-0)
Goals: Tristan Mombo (20), Régis Manon (23)
11.04.1993 Niger - Cameroon 0-0
25.04.1993 Niger - Benin 4-1
25.04.1993 Cameroon - Gabon 0-0
11.07.1993 Benin - Cameroon 0-3 (0-2)
Goals: Alphonse Tchami (12), David Embé (21), Paul Loga (90)
11.07.1993 Gabon - Niger 3-0 (1-0)
Goals: Jean-Daniel Ndong-Nzé (15), Guy-Roger Nzamba (75), Brice Makaya (90)
25.07.1993 Benin - Gabon 1-2 (0-0)
Goals: Sacramento (52) / Guy-Roger Nzamba (54, 89)
25.07.1993 Cameroon - Niger 2-0

1.	GABON	6	4	2	0	10	2	10
2.	Cameroon	6	3	3	0	7	0	9
3.	Niger	6	2	1	3	7	10	5
4.	Benin	6	0	0	6	3	15	0

Group 2

15.08.1992 Uganda - Ethiopia 3-1 (2-0)
Goals: Mayanja (25, 30), Alolo (80) / Jemani (75)
16.08.1992 Sudan - Nigeria 0-0

95

29.08.1992 Nigeria - Uganda 2-0 (1-0)
Goals: Daniel Amokachi (16), Samson Siasia (87)
30.08.1992 Ethiopia - Sudan 3-0 (2-0)
Goals: Habtemariam Matewos (35), Kebede Mulugeta (43), Begashaw Milyon (83)
10.04.1993 Sudan - Uganda 1-1 (1-1)
Goals: Hamad Al-Nil (30) / Sambo (44)
11.04.1993 Ethiopia - Nigeria 1-0 (1-0)
Goal: Tasfaye Aurgecho (28)
24.04.1993 Nigeria - Sudan 4-0
Goals: Rashidi Yekini, Emmanuel Amunike, Thompson Oliha, Akinwunme Akinsehinde
25.04.1993 Ethiopia - Uganda 2-2
10.07.1993 Sudan - Ethiopia 1-0
17.07.1993 Uganda - Nigeria 0-0
24.07.1993 Uganda - Sudan 1-0
24.07.1993 Nigeria - Ethiopia 6-0 (3-0)
Goals: Barnabas Inenga (29) Rashidi Yekini (33, 44, 64), Nduka Ugbade (50), Peter Rufai (90 penalty)

1.	NIGERIA	6	3	2	1	12	1	8
2.	Uganda	6	2	3	1	7	6	7
3.	Ethiopia	6	2	1	3	7	12	5
4.	Sudan	6	1	2	3	2	9	4

Group 3

14.08.1992 Algeria - Guinea Bissau 3-1 (2-0)
Goals: Meziane (13), Mourad Rahmouni (20), Moussa Saib (49) / Sirou (60)
16.08.1992 Senegal - Togo 2-0 (2-0)
Goals: Mamadou Diallo (15, 36)
29.08.1992 Sierra Leone - Algeria 1-0 (0-0)
Goal: Mohamed Kallon (60)
30.08.1992 Senegal - Guinea Bissau 3-0 (1-0)
Goals: Mamadou Diallo (45, 50), Diop (67)
03.10.1992 Togo - Algeria 0-0
04.10.1992 Guinea Bissau - Sierra Leone 0-3
08.11.1992 Sierra Leone - Senegal 2-0
Goals: Kanu, Brima
08.11.1992 Togo - Guinea Bissau 0-0
09.01.1993 Sierra Leone - Togo 0-0
10.01.1993 Senegal - Algeria 1-2
24.01.1993 Togo - Senegal 1-1
24.01.1993 Guinea Bissau - Algeria 1-4
09.04.1993 Algeria - Sierra Leone 0-0
11.04.1993 Guinea Bissau - Senegal 0-3 (0-2)
Goals: Mamadou Diallo (9), Mamadou Diarra (30), Mame Birame Mangane (68)
23.04.1993 Algeria - Togo 4-0 (2-0)
Goals: Abdelhafid Tasfaout (34, 43), Mohammed Brahim (70), Nager Zekri (84)
24.04.1993 Sierra Leone - Guinea Bissau 2-0
11.07.1993 Senegal - Sierra Leone 1-1 (1-1)
Goals: Mame Birame Mangane (14) / Mohamed Mansareh (30)
25.07.1993 Algeria - Senegal 4-0 (2-0)
Goals: Abdelhafid Tasfaout (3, 62, 76), Nager Zekri (32)

96

1.	SIERRA LEONE	6	4	2	0	9	1	10
2.	Algeria	6	4	1	1	13	4	9
3.	SENEGAL	6	2	1	3	8	9	5
4.	Guinea Bissau	6	0	0	6	2	18	0

Algeria were disqualified from final tournament for fielding an ineligible player and their place was taken by Senegal. Togo withdrew, their record at withdrawal was:

Togo	6	0	4	2	1	7	4

Group 4

16.08.1992 Zaire - Mozambique 2-0 (1-0)
Goals: Ditunga Kabongo (20, 85)
16.08.1992 Lesotho - Kenya 2-2 (2-1)
Goals: Majoro (12), Khali (42) / Onyera (32), James Nandna (89)
29.08.1992 Kenya - Zaire 1-3 (0-1)
Goals: Patrick Nachok (55) / Mbole (32), Ndama Bapupa (49), Katshi Okitakatshi (57)
30.08.1992 Mozambique - Lesotho 3-0 (1-0)
11.04.1993 Mozambique - Kenya 0-0
11.04.1993 Lesotho - Zaire 1-1
24.04.1993 Kenya - Lesotho 3-0 (1-0)
Goals: Patrick Nachok (15, 54), Michael Okoth (71)
25.04.1993 Mozambique - Zaire 0-0
11.07.1993 Zaire - Kenya 0-1 (0-1)
Goal: Patrick Nanchok (30)
11.07.1993 Lesotho - Mozambique 1-1
24.07.1993 Kenya - Mozambique 4-1
25.07.1993 Zaire - Lesotho 7-0

1.	ZAIRE	6	3	2	1	13	3	8
2.	Kenya	6	3	2	1	11	6	8
3.	Mozambique	6	1	3	2	5	7	5
4.	Lesotho	6	0	3	3	4	17	3

Group 5

16.08.1992 Zambia - Mauritius 2-1 (0-1)
Goals: Nyirenda (55), Mankika (66) / Philogene (2)
16.08.1992 Zimbabwe - South Africa 4-1 (2-1)
Goals: Vitalis Takawaria (7), Rahman Gumbo (20), Peter Ndlovu (50 penalty, 62) / Sam Kambule (21)
30.08.1992 Mauritius - Zimbabwe 0-1 (0-1)
Goal: Rahman Gumbo (38)
30.08.1992 South Africa - Zambia 0-1 (0-1)
Goal: Timothy Mitwa (72)
10.04.1993 South Africa - Mauritius 0-0
11.04.1993 Zambia - Zimbabwe 0-0
24.04.1993 South Africa - Zimbabwe 1-1 (1-0)
Goals: Marks Maponyane (6) / Benjamin Nkonjera (80)
25.04.1993 Mauritius - Zambia 0-3
11.07.1993 Zimbabwe - Mauritius 2-0 (1-0)
Goals: Max Lunga (37), Agent Sawu (63)
11.07.1993 Zambia - South Africa 3-0 (1-0)
Goals: Aggrey Chiyangi (1), Kalusha Bwalya (66 penalty), Linos Makwaza (71)

25.07.1993 Zimbabwe - Zambia 1-1 (1-0)
Goals: Henry McKop (27) / Kalusha Bwalya (80)
25.07.1993 Mauritius - South Africa 1-3 (1-2)
Goals: Itthier (5) / Pitso Mosimane (31), Brendan Augustin (33), Phil Masinga (70)

1.	ZAMBIA	6	4	2	0	10	2	10
2.	Zimbabwe	6	3	3	0	9	3	9
3.	South Africa	6	1	2	3	5	10	4
4.	Mauritius	6	0	1	5	2	11	1

Group 6

16.08.1992 Burundi - Congo 1-0 (1-0)
Goal: Bernard Abdi (25)
16.08.1992 Chad - Guinea 0-3 (0-1)
Goals: Souleymane Oulare (10), Aboubacar Camara (50), Fode Camara (85)
30.08.1992 Guinea - Burundi 2-2 (2-2)
Goals: Camara (43), Oulare (44) / Nduwayo (7), Mbuyi (44)
30.08.1992 Congo - Chad 2-0 (0-0)
Goals: Pierre Tchibota-Zaou (49 penalty), Younga (70)
11.04.1993 Guinea - Congo 1-0 (0-0)
Goal: S. Kolobat (84)
25.04.1993 Congo - Burundi 0-0
11.07.1993 Burundi - Guinea 2-2 (1-0)
Goals: Kazadi Ngando (16, 86 penalty) / Titi Camara (58), Morlaye Soumah (70)
15.08.1993 Congo - Guinea 0-0

1.	Guinea	4	1	3	0	5	4	5
2.	Burundi	4	1	3	0	5	4	5
3.	Congo	4	0	2	2	0	2	2

Chad withdrew after two matches

Playoff
24.10.1993 Burundi - Guinea 0-0 aet, 4-5 on penalties

Group 7

15.08.1992 Burkina Faso - Liberia 1-1 (0-1)
Goals: Bambara (58) / Y. Traoré (30 own goal)
15.08.1992 Tanzania - Ghana 2-2 (1-1)
Goals: Machunga Bakari (35), Mwamba (53) / Paul Hasule (22 own goal), Koma Zblade (70)
30.08.1992 Ghana - Burkina Faso 3-0 (2-0)
Goals: Anthony Yeboah (2, 4), Mohamed Ahmed (84)
30.08.1992 Liberia - Tanzania 1-1 (0-0)
Goals: Sabwe (52) / Holder (86)
11.04.1993 Ghana - Liberia 1-0 (0-0)
Goal: Frimpong Manso (87)
25.07.1993 Liberia - Ghana 0-2
Goals: Abedi Ayew Pelé, Anthony Yeboah

1.	GHANA	2	2	0	0	3	0	4
2.	Liberia	2	0	0	2	0	3	0

Burkina Faso and Tanzania withdrew.

Group 8

15.08.1992 Malawi - Egypt 1-0 (0-0)
Goal: Mtawali (81)
29.08.1992 Malawi - Mali 1-1 (0-0)
04.10.1992 Mali - Morocco 2-1
08.11.1992 Morocco - Egypt 0-0
09.04.1993 Egypt - Mali 2-1 (1-0)
Goals: Hossam Hassan (25), Yasser Ezzat (47) / Makan Kite (47)
11.04.1993 Morocco - Malawi 0-1 (0-0)
Goal: Lawrence (89)
23.04.1993 Egypt - Malawi 2-0 (1-0)
Goals: Ibrahim Hassan (44), Yasser Rayan (54)
25.04.1993 Morocco - Mali 1-0 (1-0)
Goal: Youssef Fertout (76)
11.07.1993 Egypt - Morocco 1-1 (0-1)
Goals: Hamada (67) / Abdelslam Langhrissi (22)
11.07.1993 Mali - Malawi 2-1
25.07.1993 Malawi - Morocco 0-2 (0-1)
Goals: Simou (33 penalty), Robki (75)
25.07.1993 Mali - Egypt 2-1 (1-1)
Goals: Traoré (39), Modibo (85 penalty) / Ahmed El-Kass (40)

1.	MALI	6	3	1	2	8	7	7
2.	EGYPT	6	2	2	2	6	5	6
3.	Morocco	6	2	2	2	5	4	6
4.	Malawi	6	2	1	3	4	7	5

Libya and Mauritania withdrew without playing any matches

Final Tournament (Tunisia)

GROUP A

26.03.1994

MALI - TUNISIA 2-0 (2-0)
Stade Olympique El Menzah, Tunis
Referee: Lim Kee Chong (Mauritius), Attendance: 45.000
TUNISIA: Chokri El Ouaer, Tarek Thabet, Taoufik Hichri, Mourad Okbi, Imed Mizouri, Mohamed Mahjoubi, Mourad Gharbi (36 Skander Souayeh), Adel Sellimi, Raouf Bouzaène, Faouzi Rouissi, Ayadi Hamrouni (46 Ziad Tlemcani). Trainer: Youssef Zouaoui
MALI: Ousmane Farota, Moussa Keita, Souleymane Sangare, Abdoulaye Traoré, Modibo Sidibe, Amadou Pathe Biallo, Soumalia Traoré (81 Habib Sangare), Sekou Sangare, Yatouma Diop, Bassala Touré (81 Demba N'Diaye), Fernand Coulibaly. Trainer: Mamadou Keita
Goals: Fernand Coulibaly (25), Modibo Sidibe (35)

28.03.1994

ZAIRE - MALI 1-0 (0-0)
Stade Olympique El Menzah, Tunis
Referee: Mohamed Ali Bujsaim (United Arab Emirates), Attendance: 8000
ZAIRE: Mukuayanzo Bulayima, Mansoni Ngombo, Ntumba Danga, Epangala Lokose, Mbaki
Makengo, Kabeya Mukanya, Lemba Basuala, Mbote Ndinga, Kabwe Kasango, Lugomgola Mateso,
Menama Lukaku. Trainer: Kalala Mukendi
MALI: Ousmane Farota, Moussa Keita, Souleymane Sangare, Abdoulaye Traoré, Modibo Sidibe,
Amadou Biallo, Yatouma Diop, Sekou Sangare, Bassala Touré, Demba N'Diaye (60 Soumailia Traoré),
Fernand Coulibaly.
Goal: Lemba Basuala (48)

30.03.1994

TUNISIA - ZAIRE 1-1 (1-0)
Stade Olympique El Menzah, Tunis
Referee: Jamal Al-Sharif (Syria), Attendance: 45.000
TUNISIA: Chokri El-Ouaer, Tarek Thabet, Mourad Okbi, Imed Mizouri, Mohamed Ali Mahjoubi,
Adel Sellimi, Samir Sellimi, Skander Souayeh (76 Raouf Bouzaène), Faouzi Rouissi, Ayadi Hamrouni,
Ziad Tlemcani (6 Jamel Limam). Trainer: Faouzi Benzerti
ZAIRE: Mukuayanzo Bulayima, Mansoni Ngombo, Jose Nzau, Epangala Lokose, Kubu Lembi,
Kabeya Mukanya (78 Tamukini Lukima), Lemba Basuala, Mbote Ndinga, Kabwe Kasango, Elonga
Ekaklia (46 Ngoy Nsumbu), Menama Lukaku.
Goals: Faouzi Rouissi (43 penalty) / Ngoy Nsumbu (55)

1.	ZAIRE	2	1	1	0	2	1	3
2.	MALI	2	1	0	1	2	1	2
3.	Tunisia	2	0	1	1	1	3	1

GROUP B

26.03.1994

NIGERIA - GABON 3-0 (1-0)
Stade Olympique El Menzah, Tunis
Referee: Mohamed Bahar (Morocco), Attendance: 30.000
NIGERIA: Peter Rufai, Augustine Eguavoen, Ben Iroha, Stephen Keshi (75 Uchenna Okafor), Uche
Okechukwu, Thompson Oliha, Augustine 'Jay-Jay' Okocka (66 Mutiu Adepoju), Sunday Oliseh,
Samson Siasia, Daniel Amokachi, Rashidi Yekini. Trainer: Clemens Westerhoff (Netherlands)
GABON: Germain Mendome, Tristan Mombo, Etienne Kassa-Ngoma, Pierre Aubame, Jean-Daniel
Ndong-Nzé, Valery Ondo, Parfait Ndong, François Amegassé, Placide Nvangala (70 Brice Mackaya),
Guy-Roger Nzamba, Régis Manon. Trainer: Jean Thissen (Belgium)
Goals: Rashidi Yekini (18, 88), Mutiu Adepoju (72)

28.03.1994

EGYPT - GABON 4-0 (2-0)
Stade Olympique El Menzah, Tunis
Referee: Charles Massembe (Uganda), Attendance: 6000
EGYPT: Ahmed Shoubier, Hany Ramzy (68 Ashraf Kassem), Fawzi Gamal, Islam Fathi, Hamza El-
Gamal, Talaat Mansour, Ahmed El-Kass (46 Reda Abdelal), Yasser Rayan, Fakri Al-Saghir, Bashir
Abdel Samad, Ayman Mansour. Trainer: Taha Ismail

GABON: Germain Mendome, Tristan Mombo, Etienne Kassa-Ngoma, Pierre Aubame, Jean-Daniel Ndong-Nzé (68 Thierry Retoa), Valery Ondo, Parfait Ndong, François Amegassé (59 Jean Moutsinga), Jonas Ogandaga, Guy-Roger Nzamba, Brice Mackaya.
Goals: Ayman Mansour (1), Hamza El-Gamal (22), Bashir Abdel Samad (55, 69)

30.03.1994

NIGERIA - EGYPT 0-0
Stade Olympique El Menzah, Tunis
Referee: Lee Kim Chong (Mauritius), Attendance: 30.000
NIGERIA: Peter Rufai, Augustine Eguavoen, Ben Iroha, Uchenna Okafor, Uche Okechukwu, Thompson Oliha, Mutiu Adepoju (65 Augustine 'Jay-Jay' Okocha), Sunday Oliseh, Samson Siasia, Daniel Amokachi, Rashidi Yekini (70 Victor Ikpeba).
EGYPT: Ahmed Shoubier, Ashraf Kassem, Hamza El-Gamal, Islam Fathi, Fawzi Gamal, Talaat Mansour, Ahmed El-Kass (64 Reda Abdelal), Yasser Rayan, Fekri Al-Saghir, Bashir Abdel Samad, Ayman Mansour (83 Mohamed Ramadhan).

1.	EGYPT	2	1	1	0	4	0	3
2.	NIGERIA	2	1	1	0	3	0	3
3.	Gabon	2	0	0	2	0	7	0

GROUP C

27.03.1994

IVORY COAST - SIERRA LEONE 4-0 (2-0)
Stade Olympique, Sousse
Referee: Jamal Al-Sharif (Syria), Attendance: 10.000
IVORY COAST: Pierre Alain Gouaméné, Arsène Hobou, Vilasco Fallet, Dominique Sam Abou, Lassina Dao, Donald-Olivier Sié, Aliou Sidi Badra, Tchiressoa Guel, Serge-Alain Maguy, Michel Bassole (88 Abdoulaye Traoré), Joël Tiéhi (79 Eugene Yago). Trainer: Henryk Kasperczak (Poland)
SIERRA LEONE: Osaid Marah, Mohamed Kanu, Mohamed Mansaray, Abubakar Kamara, Abdulai Sessay, John Sama, Lamine Conteh (67 Kemokai Kallon), Ibrahim Koroma, Abdul Conteh, Leslie Allen (56 Musa Kanu), John Gbassay Sessay. Trainer: Raymond Zarpanelian (France)
Goals: Joël Tiéhi (19, 63, 70), Tchiressoa Guel (35)

29.03.1994

ZAMBIA - SIERRA LEONE 0-0
Stade Olympique, Sousse
Referee: Omer Yengo (Congo), Attendance: 6000
ZAMBIA: James Phiri, Harrison Chongo, Elijah Litana, John Lungu (60 Evans Sakala), Aggrey Chiyangi, Happy Sichikolo, Tenant Chilumba (78 Zeddy Saileti), Joël Bwalya, Johnson Bwalya, Kalusha Bwalya, Kenneth Malitoli. Trainer: Ian Portfield (Scotland)
SIERRA LEONE: Osaid Marah, Mohamed Kanu, Mohamed Mansaray, Abubakar Kamara, Lamine Bangoura (46 Basiru King), Kemokai Kallon, John Sama, Musa Kanu, Abu Kanu (58 Brima George), Amidu Karim, John Gbassay Sessay.

31.03.1994

ZAMBIA - IVORY COAST 1-0 (0-0)
Stade Olympique, Sousse
Referee: Petros Mathebela (South Africa), Attendance: 6000
ZAMBIA: James Phiri, Harrison Chongo, Elijah Litana, Kapambwe Mulenga, Aggrey Chiyangi,
Happy Sichikolo, Tenant Chilumba (78 Kenneth Malitoli), Evans Sakala, Johnson Bwalya (62 Gibby
Mbasela), Kalusha Bwalya, Zeddy Saileti.
IVORY COAST: Pierre Alain Gouaméné, Arsène Hobou, Vilasco Fallet, Dominique Sam Abou,
Lassina Dao, Donald-Olivier Sié, Aliou Sidi Badra (82 Abdoulaye Traoré), Tchiressoa Guel, Serge-
Alain Maguy, Eugene Yago (46 Basile Kouamé Aka), Joël Tiéhi.
Goal: Kenneth Malitoli (79)

1.	ZAMBIA	2	1	1	0	1	0	3
2.	IVORY COAST	2	1	0	1	4	1	2
3.	Sierra Leone	2	0	1	1	0	4	1

GROUP D

27.03.1994

GHANA - GUINEA 1-0 (0-0)
Stade Olympique, Sousse
Referee: Petros Mathebela (South Africa), Attendance: 10.000
GHANA: Edward Ansah, Frank Amankwah, Stephen Frimpong Manso, Emmanuel Ampeah, Agyeman
Duah, Samuel Johnson (18 Bernard Whyte), Nil Lamptey, Yaw Acheampong, Charles Akunnor, Abedi
'Pelé' Ayew, Kwame Ayew. Trainer: Emmanuel Aggrey-Finn
GUINEA: Saliou Diallo, Abdoul Karim Bangoura, Mohamed Ofei Sylla, Edgar Sylla, Morlaye
Soumah, Ousmane Camara (64 Sekou Soumah), Sekou Oumar Drame, Abdoul Sow, Demba Thiam,
Souleymane Ouiare, Aboubacar Camara. Trainer: Naby Camara
Goals: Charles Akunnor (87)

29.03.1994

SENEGAL - GUINEA 2-1 (0-1)
Stade Olympique, Sousse
Referee: H. Mousa (Egypt), Referee: 6000
SENEGAL: Cheikh Seck, Issa Tambedou, Adolphe Mendy, Moustapha Diagne, Lamine Cissé,
Momath Gueye, Mamadou Faye (52 Mamadou Diallo), Moussa Camara, Aly Male, Athanas Tendeng,
Soulemane Sane. Trainers: Jules Bocandé and Boubacar Sarr
GUINEA: Saliou Diallo, Abdoul Karim Bangoura, Mohamed Ofei Sylla, Edgar Sylla, Morlaye
Soumah, Ousmane Camara (64 Sekou Soumah), Sekou Oumar Drame, Abdoul Sow, Demba Thiam,
Souleymane Ouiare, Aboubacar Camara.
Goals: Momath Gueye (46 penalty), Athanas Tendeng (50) / Aboubacar Camara (44)

31.03.1994

GHANA - SENEGAL 1-0 (0-0)
Stade Olympique, Sousse
Referee: Mohamed Ali Bujsaim (United Arab Emirates), Attendance: 6000
GHANA: Edward Ansah, Frank Amankwah, Bernard Whyte, Stephen Frimpong Manso, Tony Baffoe,
Emmanuel Ampeah, Nil Lamptey (81 George Arthur), Charles Akunnor, Abedi 'Pelé' Ayew, Kwame
Ayew (66 Prince Opoku), Anthony Yeboah.

SENEGAL: Papa N'Diaye, Issa Tambedou, Adolphe Mendy, Mamadou Mariem Diallo, Lamine Sagna (46 Aly Male), Boubacar Gassama, Mamadou Diallo, Athanas Tendeng, Alassane Dione, Mamadou Diarra, Soulemane Sane (70 Mame Birame Mangane).
Goal: Prince Opoku (88)

1.	GHANA	2	2	0	0	2	0	4
2.	SENEGAL	2	1	0	1	2	2	2
3.	Guinea	2	0	0	2	1	3	0

Quarter-finals

02.04.1994

ZAIRE - NIGERIA 0-2 (0-0)
Stade Olympique El Menzah, Tunis
Referee: Lim Kee Chong (Mauritius), Attendance: 2000
ZAIRE: Bilolo Tambwe, Mansoni Ngombo, Jose Nzau, Ntumba Danga, Epangala Lokose, Tamukini Lukima, Kabwe Kasango, Mbote Ndinga, Lemba Basuala, Ekanza Nsimba (46 Ngoy Nsumbu), Menama Lukaku (71 Mpia Kasango).
NIGERIA: Peter Rufai, Augustine Eguavoen, Ben Iroha, Uchenna Okafor, Uche Okechukwu, Thompson Oliha, Finidi George, Sunday Oliseh (79 Nduka Ugbade), Efan Ekoku (61 Mutiu Adepoju), Daniel Amokachi, Rashidi Yekini.
Tambwe sent off (70)
Goals: Rashidi Yekini (51, 71 penalty)

02.04.1994

EGYPT - MALI 0-1 (0-0)
Stade Olympique El Menzah, Tunis
Referee: Charles Massembe (Uganda), Attendance: 3000
EGYPT: Ahmed Shoubier, Ashraf Kassem, Fawzi Gamal, Islam Fathi, Hamza El Gamal, Talaat Mansour, Ahmed El Kass, Yasser Rayan, Fekri El-Saghir, Bashir Abdel Samad (62 Mohamed Ramadhan), Ayman Mansour.
MALI: Ousmane Farota, Moussa Keita, Oumar Guindo, Sekou Sangare, Modibo Sidibe, Abdoulaye Traoré, Ibrahim Sory Toure (80 Brahima Traoré), Ousmane Soumano, Amadou Diallo, Soumailia Traoré (88 Habib Sangare), Fernand Coulibaly.
Goal: Soumailia Traoré (64)

03.04.1994

ZAMBIA - SENEGAL 1-0 (1-0)
Stade Olympique, Sousse
Referee: Jamal Al-Sharif (Syria), Attendance: 8000
ZAMBIA: James Phiri, Harrison Chongo, Elijah Litana, John Lungu, Aggrey Chiyangi, Happy Sichikolo (65 Mordon Malitoli), Evans Sakala, Johnson Bwalya (83 Tenant Chilumba), Kalusha Bwalya, Zeddy Saileti, Kenneth Malitoli.
SENEGAL: Cheikh Seck, Mustapha Diagne, Adolphe Mendy, Boubacar Gassama (53 Issa Tambedou), Lamine Cissé, Moussa Camara, Aly Male, Mamadou Faye, Athanas Tendeng (46 Mamadou Diallo), Amara Traoré, Soulemane Sane.
Goal: Evans Sakala (38)

03.04.1994

GHANA - IVORY COAST 1-2 (0-1)
Stade Olympique, Sousse
Referee: Mohamed Ali Bujsaim (United Arab Emirates), Attendance: 8000
GHANA: Edward Ansah, Frank Amankwah, Bernard Whyte, Stephen Frimpong Manso (46 Afo Dodoo), Tony Baffoe, Agyeman Duah, Yaw Acheampong, Charles Akunnor, Abedi Pelé, Prince Opoku, Anthony Yeboah.
IVORY COAST: Pierre Alain Gouaméné, Basile Kouamé Aka, Vilasco Fallet, Dominique Sam Abou, Lassina Dao, Donald-Olivier Sié, Tchiressoa Guel, Serge-Alain Maguy, Michel Bassole, Abdoulaye Traoré, Joël Tiéhi (63 Yao Lambert Amani).
Goals: Charles Akunnor (77) / Joël Tiéhi (30), Abdoulaye Traoré (81)

Semi-finals

06.04.1994

NIGERIA - IVORY COAST 2-2 (2-2, 2-2), 4-2 on penalties
Stade Olympique El Menzah, Tunis
Referee: Mohamed Ali Bujsaim (United Arad Emirates), Attendance: 2000
NIGERIA: Peter Rufai, Isaac Semitoje (74 Uchenna Okafor), Ben Iroha, Stephen Keshi (102 Nduka Ugbade), Uche Okechukwu, Sunday Oliseh, Finidi George, Augustine 'Jay-Jay' Okocha, Samson Siasia, Daniel Amokachi, Rashidi Yekini.
IVORY COAST: Pierre Alain Gouaméné, Basile Kouamé Aka, Vilasco Fallet, Dominique Sam Abouo, Lassina Dao, Donald-Olivier Sié, Tchiressoa Guel, Serge-Alain Maguy, Michel Bassole, Abdoulaye Traoré (44 Ahmed Ouattara), Joël Tiéhi (57 Yao Lambert Amani).
Goals: Ben Iroha (26), Rashidi Yekini (40) / Michel Bassole (19, 31)
Penalties: Finidi George, Samson Siasia (miss), Rashidi Yekini / Basile Kouamé Aka, Vilasco Fallet, Michel Bassole (miss), Yao Lambert Amani (miss).

06.04.1994

ZAMBIA - MALI 4-0 (2-0)
Stade Olympique El Menzah, Tunis
Referee: Charles Massembe (Uganda), Attendance: 2000
ZAMBIA: Martin Mwamba, Harrison Chongo, Elijah Litana, Mordon Malitoli, Aggrey Chiyangi, John Lungu (77 Tenant Chilumba), Joël Bwalya, Evans Sakala, Kalusha Bwalya, Zeddy Saileti (67 Linos Makwaza), Kenneth Malitoli.
MALI: Ousmane Farota, Moussa Keita, Souleymane Sangare, Abdoul Karim Sidibe (46 Sekou Sangare), Amadou Diallo, Abdoulaye Traoré, Sory Ibrahim Touré (49 Brahima Traoré), Bassala Touré, Ousmane Soumano, Soumailia Traoré, Fernand Coulibaly.
Goals: Elijah Litana (8), Zeddy Saileti (30), Kalusha Bwalya (47), Kenneth Malitoli (73)

Third Place Match

10.04.1994

IVORY COAST - MALI 3-1 (1-0)
Stade Olympique El Menzah, Tunis
Referee: Petros Mathebela (South Africa), Attendance: 15.000

IVORY COAST: Pierre Alain Gouaméné, Basile Kouamé Aka, Arsène Hobou, Dominique Sam Abouo, Celestin Amani, Donald-Olivier Sié, Tchiressoa Guel, Yao Lambert Amani, Adama Klofie Koné (87 Yacouba Camara), Eugene Yago (64 Michel Bassole), Ahmed Ouattara.
MALI: Ousmane Farota, Moussa Keita (78 Bassala Touré), Sekou Sangare, Modibo Sidibe, Oumar Guindo (15 Habib Sangare), Souleymane Sangare, Demba N'Diaye, Amadou Diallo, Yatouma Diop, Brahima Traoré, Ousmane Soumano.
Goals: Adama Klofie Koné (2), Ahmed Ouattara (67), Donald-Olivier Sié (70) / Amadou Diallo (46)

Final

10.04.1994

NIGERIA – ZAMBIA 2-1 (1-1)
Stade Olympique El Menzah, Tunis
Referee: Lim Kee Chong (Mauritius), Attendance: 25.000
NIGERIA: Peter Rufai, Augustine Eguavoen, Ben Iroha, Uche Okechukwu, Uchenna Okafor, Sunday Oliseh, Finidi George (41 Samson Siasia), Augustine 'Jay-Jay' Okocha (73 Nduka Ugbade), Daniel Amokachi, Emmanuel Amunike, Rashidi Yekini. Trainer: Clemens Westerhoff
ZAMBIA: James Phiri, Harrison Chongo, Elijah Litana, Mordon Malitoli, Aggrey Chiyangi, Kapambwe Mulenga (60 Linos Makwaza), Evans Sakala, Joël Bwalya (70 Johnson Bwalya), Kalusha Bwalya, Kenneth Malitoli, Zeddy Saileti. Trainer: Ian Portfield
Goals: Emmanuel Amunike (5, 47) / Elijah Litana (3)

Twentieth edition - 1996
Qualifying Tournament

The 20th edition of the Africa Cup of Nations saw the return of South Africa to the competition as hosts following decades of exclusion. The collapse of the country's apartheid regime in 1994 had led to their team becoming eligible to enter the competition once again but the team failed to progress through the qualifiers on that occasion. With Kenya originally scheduled to host the 1996 finals tournament, South Africa once again entered the qualifiers but, when Kenya subsequently withdrew from the competition citing a lack of resources, South Africa rode to the rescue by agreeing to be hosts and therefore qualified for the finals automatically.

Forty-three teams entered the qualifying competition but no fewer than 11 of them subsequently withdrew. The format of the finals tournament was changed in 1996 so that 16 places were available to be split between four groups of four. Each group was played as a round-robin and the top two teams from each group qualified for the quarter-finals stage. The format of the finals tournament for the Africa Cup of Nations remains the same as this to this day.

In the event, only fifteen nations were eventually involved in the finals tournament as Nigeria withdrew at the last minute, ostensibly on the grounds of insufficient safety guarantees but more probably due to a political dispute in 1995 between Nelson Mandela and Sani Abacha, the Nigerian premier. For refusing to play, Nigeria was consequently excluded from international competitions for four years although this ban was later reduced to two years. In an attempt to keep the full complement of 16 teams in the finals, Guinea were offered Nigeria's place as best losers from the qualifying competition but the country refused this invitation. The finals tournament proved to be a success in every way for South Africa as "Bafana Bafana" (the nickname of the South African team) won their first title after victory over Tunisia in the final. Notably, the South African captain Neil Tovey became the first white player to raise the trophy in their mixed-race team.

Group 1

04.09.1994 Zaire - Malawi 1-1 (0-0)
Goals: Liombi Essende (80) / John Maduka (85)
04.09.1994 Zimbabwe - Lesotho 5-0 (2-0)
Goals: Kennedy Nagoli (10), Francis Shonhayi (15), Adam Ndlovu (51), Vitalis Takawira (83, 89)
15.10.1994 Malawi - Zimbabwe 3-1 (0-1)
Goals: Hendrix Banda (62), John Maduka (83), Albert Mpinganjira (89) / Agent Sawu (35)
16.10.1994 Cameroon - Zaire 1-0 (1-0)
Goal: Georges Mouyémé (2)
13.11.1994 Lesotho - Cameroon 2-0 (0-0)
Goals: Lekoane Lekoane (48), Lefika Lekhotla (73)
13.11.1994 Zimbabwe - Zaire 2-1 (0-0)
Goals: Adam Ndlovu (52), Peter Ndlovu (89 penalty) / Liombe Essende (66)
08.01.1995 Cameroon - Malawi 0-0
08.01.1995 Zaire - Lesotho 3-0 (2-0)
Goals: Menama Lukaku (1 penalty), Kabye Mukanya (37), Kapela Mbiyavanga (82)
22.01.1995 Lesotho - Malawi 0-2 (0-0)
Goals: Lovemore Chanfunya (62), Hendrix Banda (64)
22.01.1995 Zimbabwe - Cameroon 4-1 (1-0)
Goals: Vitalis Takawira (12, 50, 88), Paul Gundani (47) / Hans Agbo (83)
09.04.1995 Malawi - Zaire 0-1 (0-1)
Goal: Liombi Essende (11)
09.04.1995 Lesotho - Zimbabwe 0-2 (0-2)
Goals: Agent Sawu (14), Isaac Riyano (16)
23.04.1995 Zaire - Cameroon 2-1 (0-0)
Goals: Philippe Mbote Ndinga (75), Andre Ngole Kona (82) / Georges Mouyème (68)
23.04.1995 Zimbabwe - Malawi 1-1 (1-1)
Goals: Peter Ndlovu (14 penalty) / Hendrix Banda (43)
04.06.1995 Cameroon - Lesotho 4-1 (1-0)
Goals: Nicolas Dikoumé (10, 73), Roland Njume Ntocko (49), Georges Mouyémé (87) / Lekoane Lekoane (80)
04.06.1995 Zaire - Zimbabwe 5-0 (3-0)
Goals: Nzelo Lembi (29, 35, 55), Zola Kiniambi (26), Lowata (77)
16.07.1995 Malawi - Cameroon 1-3 (0-0)
Goals: John Maduka (55) / Joseph Mbarga (5), Georges Mouyémé (42, 68)
30.07.1995 Cameroon – Zimbabwe 1-0 (0-0)
Goal: Augustine Simo (49)

1.	ZAIRE	6	3	1	2	10	5	7
2.	CAMEROON	6	3	1	2	7	7	7
3.	Malawi	6	1	3	2	6	7	5
4.	Zimbabwe	6	2	1	3	8	12	5

NB: Lesotho withdrew, their record at withdrawal:

Lesotho	6	1	0	5	3	16	2

Swaziland withdrew without playing any matches

Group 2

03.09.1994 Senegal - Mauritania 0-0
04.09.1994 Guinea Bissau - Tunisia 1-3 (1-2)
Goals: Pau (44 penalty) / Sami Trabelsi (5), Zoubeir.Beya (19), Hedi Ben Rekhissa (80)
04.09.1994 Liberia - Togo 1-0 (1-0)
Goals: George Weah (42)
14.10.1994 Mauritania - Guinea Bissau 1-1 (1-0)
Goals: Brahim Ould Malha (25) / Brahima Mane (87)
16.10.1994 Togo - Senegal 2-0 (0-0)
Goals: Koffi Fiawoo (50), Bachirou Salou (73)
11.11.1994 Nouakchott Mauritania - Liberia 1-1 (0-1)
Goals: Brahim Ould Malha (79) / Akoune Ndiaye (28 owngoal)
13.11.1994 Tunisia - Togo 1-1 (1-0)
Goals: Ayedi Hamrouni (24) / Lantam Sakihou Ouadja (56)
13.11.1994 Guinea Bissau - Senegal 1-4 (0-2)
Adelino Augusto Lopes Lino (68) / Mamadou Diallo (5), Souleymane Sane (38, 65), Seni Diatta (73)
07.01.1995 Senegal - Tunisia 0-0
08.01.1995 Togo - Mauritania 0-0
22.01.1995 Liberia - Senegal 1-1 (1-0)
Goals: Jonathan Sogbie (22 penalty) / Souleymane Sané (83)
29.01.1995 Tunisia - Mauritania 1-0 (0-0)
Goal: Mohamed Ali Mahjoubi (67)
10.02.1995 Tunisia - Liberia 0-0
07.04.1995 Mauritania - Senegal 0-1 (0-1)
Goal: Mamadou Diallo (14)
09.04.1995 Togo - Liberia 0-0
22.04.1995 Senegal - Togo 5-1 (2-1)
Goals: Mamadou Diallo (8 penalty, 60), Moussa Ndaw (19, 86), Amara Traoré (88) / Messam
Ametokodo (7)
23.04.1995 Liberia - Tunisia 1-0 (0-0)
Goal: Jonathan Sogbie (64)
04.06.1995 Liberia - Mauritania 2-0 (1-0)
Goals: James Debah (25, 67)
04.06.1995 Togo - Tunisia 0-1 (0-1)
Goal: Abdelkader Ben Hassan (9)
14.07.1995 Mauritania - Togo 2-1 (1-0)
Goals: Ahmed Sidibe (12), Magaye Wade (60) / Lantam Sakibou Ouadja (82)
15.07.1995 Tunisia - Senegal 4-0 (0-0)
Goals: Hedi Ben Rekhissa (47, 83), Zoubeir Beya (56), Abdelkader Ben Hassan (69)
30.07.1995 Mauritania - Tunisia 0-0
30.07.1995 Senegal - Liberia 3-0 (1-0)
Goals: Mamadou Diallo (40 penalty, 52), Amara Traoré (80)

1.	TUNISIA	8	3	4	1	7	2	10
2.	LIBERIA	8	3	4	1	6	5	10
3.	Senegal	8	3	3	2	10	8	9
4.	Mauritania	8	1	4	3	3	6	6
5.	Togo	8	1	3	4	5	10	5

NB: Guinea Bissau withdrew, their record at withdrawal:

	Guinea Bissau	3	0	1	2	3	8	1

Group 3

04.09.1994 Congo - Gambia 1-1 (0-1)
Goals: Sylvain Moukassa (64) / Peter Johnson (38)
04.09.1994 Ghana - Sierra Leone 4-1 (0-0)
Goals: Kasola Da Costa (55 penalty), Emmanuel Duah (63), Charles Akunnor (72), Felix Aboagye (88) / Lamine Conteh (87)
16.10.1994 Niger - Ghana 1-5 (1-1)
Goals: Hassana Hamidou (6 penalty) / Yaw Preko (2, 54, 87), Kwame Ayew (67), Daniel Addo (69)
16.10.1994 Sierra Leone - Congo 3-2 (2-1)
Goals: Alahji Jalloh (34), Lamine Conteh (43, 53) / Florent Baloki (33), Charles Nieux Imboula (86)
12.11.1994 Gambia - Ghana 1-2 (1-2)
Goals: Boubacar Manneh (20) / Charles Akunnor (34), Frank Amankwah (42)
13.11.1994 Niger - Sierra Leone 4-2 (2-1)
Goals: Brah Taher Djibo (5, 22), Ayikouto Ayiayiane (55), Garike Mounkaila Ide (65) / Mohammed Kanu (37), Lamine Conteh (60)
07.01.1995 Sierra Leone - Gambia 2-0 (0-0)
Goals: Francis Koroma (50), Musa Kanu (53)
08.01.1995 Congo - Niger 3-1 (1-1)
Goals: Charles Nieux Imboula (38, 50), Guillaume Ibara (74) / Moussa Yahaya (29)
22.01.1995 Ghana - Congo 3-1 (1-0)
Goals: Augustine Ahinful (39), Jean Tsoumou Mbele (69 own goal), Kwame Ayew (70) / Ruffin Oba (80)
22.01.1995 Niger - Gambia 1-1 (0-1)
Goals: Abdoulaye Hamidou (70) / Paring Jammeh (17)
08.04.1995 Sierra Leone - Ghana 1-0 (0-0)
Goal: Lamine Conteh (77 penalty)
09.04.1995 Gambia - Congo 1-1 (1-0)
Goals: Samuel Kargbo (44) / Charles Nieux Imboula (67)
22.04.1995 Congo - Sierra Leone 0-2 (0-0)
Goals: Mohammed Kallon (54), John Sama (90)
23.04.1995 Ghana - Niger 1-0 (1-0)
Goal: Anthony Yeboah (21)
03.06.1995 Sierra Leone - Niger 5-1 (1-1)
Goals: Mohamed Kallon (32), Musa Kallon (55, 69), Francis Koroma (75), John Sama (78) / Mounkaila Garike Ide (18)
30.07.1995 Congo - Ghana 0-2 (0-0)
Goals: Felix Aboagye (57, 89)

1.	GHANA	4	3	0	1	9	3	6
2.	SIERRA LEONE	4	3	0	1	7	6	6
3.	Congo	4	0	0	4	3	10	0

NB: Gambia and Niger withdrew, their records at withdrawal:

| Gambia | 5 | 0 | 3 | 2 | 4 | 7 | 3 |
| Niger | 5 | 1 | 0 | 4 | 8 | 16 | 2 |

Central African Republic withdrew without playing any matches

Group 4

03.09.1994 Tanzania - Uganda 4-0 (3-0)
Goals: Bure Salehe (5), Edibily Lunyamila (9, 88), John Nteze (13)
04.09.1994 Ethiopia - Algeria 0-0
04.09.1994 Sudan - Egypt 0-0
14.10.1994 Algeria - Sudan 1-1 (0-1)
Goals: Charif El-Ouazzani (64) / Sabri El-Hak (11)
14.10.1994 Egypt - Tanzania 5-1 (1-0)
Goals: Ahmed El-Kas (12, 52), Walid El-Salaheddine (64), Hossam Hassan (82 penalty), Islam Fathi (84) / Bure Salehe (55)
15.10.1994 Uganda - Ethiopia 4-1 (0-1)
Goals: Joseph Mutyaba (55), Fred Tamale (75), Ibrahim Buwembo (79), George Semogerere (84) / Eliyas Juhar (21)
11.11.1994 Egypt - Ethiopia 5-0 (3-0)
Goals: Hossam Hassan (24, 36), Ahmed Sary (30), Walid El-Salaheddine (56), Haytham Farouk (57)
12.11.1994 Tanzania - Sudan 2-0 (1-0)
Goals: Madaraka Selemany (26, 61)
12.11.1994 Uganda - Algeria 1-1 (0-1)
Goals: George Semwogerere (70 penalty) / Abdelhafid Tasfaout (43)
06.01.1995 Sudan - Uganda 3-1 (2-1)
Goals: Ahmed Said Nimery (9, 35), Ibrahim Amir Hussein (80) / Majid Musisi (22)
08.01.1995 Algeria - Egypt 1-0 (1-0)
Goal: Billal Dziri (16 penalty)
08.01.1995 Ethiopia - Tanzania 1-0 (1-0)
Goals: Eliyas Juhar (33)
21.01.1995 Tanzania - Algeria 2-1 (1-1)
Goals: Juma Bakari Kidishi (37), Madaraka Selemani (66) / Kamal Keci Said (13)
21.01.1995 Uganda - Egypt 0-0
22.01.1995 Ethiopia - Sudan 2-0 (1-0)
Goals: Kebede Yared (3), Ashenafe Sessaye (71)
07.04.1995 Algeria - Ethiopia 2-0 (2-0)
Goals: Abdelhafid Tasfaout (17, 32)
07.04.1995 Egypt - Sudan 3-1 (1-0)
Goals: Mahmoud Abou Al-Dahab (10), Mohamed El-Sawi (70), Ahmed El-Kass (88) / Edward Gido Fidda (71)
08.04.1995 Uganda - Tanzania 2-0 (2-0)
Goals: Phillip Obwiny (30), Joseph Mutyaba (38)
22.04.1995 Tanzania - Egypt 1-2 (0-1)
Goals: Madaraka Selemany (89) / Mahmoud Abou Al-Dahab (27, 68)
23.04.1995 Ethiopia - Uganda 0-0
24.04.1995 Sudan - Algeria 2-0 (1-0)
Goals: Musa El-Hilo Babiker (22 penalty), Amir Musa Khogali (74)
The match was later awarded 2-0 to Algeria (for poor organisation by Sudan), after a protest to CAF
02.06.1995 Algeria – Uganda 1-1 (1-0)
Goals: Abdelhafid Tasfaout (16) / Kigeto Mutyaba (76)
03.06.1995 Sudan - Tanzania 2-1 (1-1)
Goals: Abdullah Omer El-Tahir (13), Anas Abdel Magid (60) / John Ntzee (36)
04.06.1995 Ethiopia - Egypt 0-2 (0-2)
Goals: Mahmoud Abou Al-Dahab (7), Hady Khashaba (38)
14.07.1995 Egypt – Algeria 1-1 (0-1)
Goals: Ibrahim El-Masry (61) / Kamel Kaci Said (42)
15.07.1995 Tanzania - Ethiopia 2-0 (2-0)
Goals: Mohamed Hussein (8), Edibily Lunyamila (11)

15.07.1995 Uganda - Sudan 2-0 (0-0)
Goals: George Semwogerere (71), Augustine Barigye (74)
30.07.1995 Algeria - Tanzania 2-1 (1-1)
Goals: Aman Hussein Marsha (29 own goal), Rezki Amrouche (59) / Mohamed Hussein (21)
30.07.1995 Egypt - Uganda 6-0 (4-0)
Goals: Ahmed El-Kass (4, 65, 73), Ahmed Sary (8, 43), Mohamed Abu Greisha (36)
30.07.1995 Sudan - Ethiopia 3-0 (2-0)
Goals: Muntasir El-Zaki (15), Edward Gildo Fidda (36), Essam Osman (52)

1.	EGYPT	10	6	3	1	24	5	15
2.	ALGERIA	10	4	5	1	12	7	13
3.	Uganda	10	3	4	3	11	16	10
4.	Tanzania	10	4	0	6	14	15	8
5.	Sudan	10	3	2	5	10	14	8
6.	Ethiopia	10	2	2	6	4	18	6

Group 5

04.09.1994 Madagascar - South Africa 0-1 (0-1)
Goals: Phil Masinga (21)
15.10.1994 South Africa - Mauritius 1-0 (0-0)
Goal: Phil Masinga (51)
13.11.1994 Zambia - South Africa 1-1 (0-0)
Goals: Kenneth Malitoli (86 penalty) / Theophilus Khumalo (68)
13.11.1994 Gabon - Mauritius 3-0 (2-0)
Goals: François Amegasse (26 penalty), Aurelien Bekogo Zolo (28), Brice Mackaya (64)
20.11.1994 Gabon - Zambia 2-1 (0-0)
Goals: Valery Ondo (60 penalty), Guy-Roger Nzamba (73) / Wedson Nyirenda (89)
09.01.1995 Mauritius - Zambia 0-3 (0-1)
Goals: Kalusha Bwalya (32, 87), Johnson Bwalya (76)
08.04.1995 Zambia - Gabon 1-0 (0-0)
Goal: Kalusha Bwalya (83)
04.06.1995 Mauritius - Gabon 0-3 (0-1)
Goals: Brice Makaya (42), Valery Ondo (47, 88)
15.07.1995 Zambia - Mauritius 2-0 (0-0)
Goals: Denis Lota (57), Johnson Bwalya (72)

1.	GABON	4	3	0	1	8	2	6
2.	ZAMBIA	4	3	0	1	7	2	6
3.	Mauritius	4	0	0	4	0	11	0

South Africa withdrew after becoming hosts, their record at withdrawal:

	South Africa	2	1	1	0	2	1	3

Madagascar withdrew after its first match
Seychelles withdrew without playing any matches

Group 6

04.09.1994 Angola - Namibia 2-0 (2-0)
Goals: João Paulo Tubia (6), Quissango Merodac (40 penalty)
04.09.1994 Botswana - Guinea 0-1 (0-0)
Goal: Aboubacar Camara (89)

04.09.1994 Mali - Mozambique 2-1 (2-0)
Goals: Modiho Sidibe (20, 30) / Matola Nana (69)
15.10.1994 Namibia - Mali 2-1 (1-0)
Goals: Sylvester Goraseb (40), Ruben van Wyk (57) / Soumailia Traoré (89)
16.10.1994 Guinea - Angola 3-1 (2-0)
Goals: O. Suma (6, 59), Aboubacar Camara (9) / Martino Quessongo Castella (69)
16.10.1994 Mozambique - Botswana 3-1 (2-0)
Goals: Arnaldo Ouana (34, 39, 73) / Oliver Pikati (74)
30.10.1994 Mali - Guinea 2-0 (1-0)
Goals: Bassala Touré (45), Amadou Pathe Diallo (75)
13.11.1994 Mali - Angola 0-0
13.11.1994 Mozambique - Guinea 2-1 (0-1)
Goals: Tchaka Tchaka (64 penalty), Manuel José Luis Bucuane 'Tico-Tico' (89) / Mohammed Sylla
(20)
13.11.1994 Namibia - Botswana 1-1 (0-1)
Goals: Ruben van Wyk (89) / Buikago Modise (25)
07.01.1995 Botswana 1-3 Mali 1-3 (0-3)
Goals: Itumeleng Duiker (75) / B. Touré (5), Diawara (18, 26)
08.01.1995 Angola - Mozambique 1-0 (1-0)
Goal: João Paulo Ribeiro 'Tubia' (19)
08.01.1995 Guinea - Namibia 3-0 (0-0)
Goals: Abdoul Camara (62), Abdoul Salam Sow (69), Mohammed Sylla (88)
22.01.1995 Botswana - Angola 1-2 (1-0)
Goals: Mmoni Segopolo (44) / Pauoo António Alves 'Paulão' (55, 63)
22.01.1995 Mozambique - Namibia 4-2 (2-0)
Goals: Nuro Amiro Tualibudane (6, 30, 90), Eurico (68) / Ewald Hoeseb (72), Paul Boonstander (85)
08.04.1995 Namibia - Angola 2-2 (1-1)
Goals: Lucky Richter (11), Silvester Lolo Goraseb (61) / Paulo António Alves 'Paulão' (8), Joaquim
Alberto da Silva 'Quinzinho' (76)
09.04.1995 Guinea - Botswana 5-0 (2-0)
Goals: Fode Camara (6, 10), Mohamed Sylla (54), Tayfour Diane (60), Abdoul Salam Sow (88)
09.04.1995 Mozambique - Mali 1-0 (1-0)
Goal: Francisco Queriol 'Chiquinho' Conde (44)
23.04.1995 Angola - Guinea 3-0 (0-0)
Goals: Fabrice Alcebiades Maieco 'Akwá' (48, 75), Paulo Antônio Alves 'Paulão' (55)
23.04.1995 Botswana - Mozambique 0-3 (0-1)
Goals: Francisco Queriol 'Chiquinho' Conde (15, 53), Nuro Amiro Tualibudane (69)
23.04.1995 Mali - Namibia 2-0 (1-0)
Goals: Modibo Sidibe (16), Abdoula Karim Magassouba (66)
04.06.1995 Angola - Mali 1-0 (1-0)
Goal: Fabrice Alcebiades Maieco 'Akwá' (28 penalty)
04.06.1995 Botswana - Namibia 1-1 (1-1)
Goals: Tshenolo Mothelesi (5) / Frans Page Ananias (18)
04.06.1995 Guinea - Mozambique 0-0
15.07.1995 Namibia - Guinea 0-0
16.07.1995 Mali - Botswana 4-0 (1-0)
Goals: Djibril Diawara (12, 50), Seydou Lamine Traoré (46), Oumar Bagayogo (85)
16.07.1995 Mozambique - Angola 2-1 (1-0)
Goals: Sérgio Faife (15), Malo (46) / Paulo Antônio Alves 'Paulão' (75)
30.07.1995 Angola - Botswana 4-0 (2-0)
Goals: Osvaldo Roque Gonçalves Cruz 'Joni' (1, 9), Rosario (43), Paulo Antônio Alves 'Paulão' (50)
30.07.1995 Guinea - Mali 4-1 (2-1)
Goals: Aboubacar Camara (28, 45), Abdoul Salem Sow (65 penalty), Mohamed Camara (87) / Djibril
Diawara (13)

30.07.1995 Namibia - Mozambique 0-0

1.	ANGOLA	10	7	0	3	17	8	14
2.	MOZAMBIQUE	10	6	2	2	16	8	14
3.	Guinea	10	5	2	3	17	9	12
4.	Mali	10	5	1	4	15	10	11
5.	Namibia	10	1	5	4	8	16	7
6.	Botswana	10	0	2	8	5	27	2

Group 7

04.09.1994 Burkina Faso - Morocco 2-1 (0-1)
Goals: Aboubakari Ouédraogo (49), Abou Ouattara (68) / Tahar El-Khalej (32)
13.11.1994 Morocco - Ivory Coast 1-0 (1-0)
Goal: Nader Hassan (15)
22.01.1995 Ivory Coast - Burkina Faso 2-2 (2-0)
Goals: Joël Tiéhi (7, 43) / Sidi Napou (50), Seydou Traoré (80)
09.04.1995 Morocco - Burkina Faso 0-0
04.06.1995 Ivory Coast - Morocco 2-0 (1-0)
Goals: Joël Tiéhi (19), Sekou Bamba (65)
30.07.1995 Burkina Faso - Ivory Coast 1-1 (1-0)
Goals: Aboubakari Ouattara (22) / Joël Tiéhi (64)

1.	BURKINA FASO	4	1	3	0	5	4	5
2.	IVORY COAST	4	1	2	1	5	4	4
3.	Morocco	4	1	1	2	2	4	3

Benin, Cape Verde and Equatorial Guinea withdrew without playing any matches

Final Tournament (South Africa)

Nigeria withdrew before the final tournament citing insufficient safety guarantees as the reason. Guinea was asked by the CAF to replace them in Group 3 (as best losers in qualifying), but the country refused the invitation.

GROUP A

13.01.1996

SOUTH AFRICA - CAMEROON 3-0 (2-0)
First National Bank Stadium, Johannesburg
Referee: Said Belqola (Morocco), Attendance: 80.000
SOUTH AFRICA: André Arendse, Sizwe Motaung, Neil Tovey, Mark Fish, David Nyathi, Eric Tinkler, Linda Buthelezi (58 Helman Mkhalele), John Moshoeu, Theophilus Khumalo, Mark Williams (71 Shaun Bartlett), Phil Masinga (82 August Makalakalane). Trainer: Clive Barker
CAMEROON: William Andem, Sunday Jang, Hans Agbo, Tobie Mimboe, Rigobert Song, Pierre Wome (38 Roland Ntocko), François Oman-Biyik, Marie Jose Tchango (55 Augustine Simo), Marc-Vivien Foé, Georges Mouyeme, Alphonse Tchami (65 Joseph Mbarga). Trainer: Jules-Frederic Nyongha.
Goals: Phil Masinga (14), Mark Williams (37), John Moshoeu (55)

15.01.1996

EGYPT - ANGOLA 2-1 (2-0)
First National Bank Stadium, Johannesburg,
Referee: Sidi Bekaye Magassa (Mali), Attendance: 3000
EGYPT: Nader El-Sayed, Hany Ramzy, Samir Kamouna, Fawzi Gamal, Yasser Radwan, Hazem Emam, Ismail Youssef, Hady Khashaba, Abdel Sattar Sabry, Ahmed Aboul El-Kass (79 Medhat Abdel Hady), Aly Maher (59 Ibrahim El-Masry, 86 Moustapha Reyadh). Trainer: Ruud Krol (Netherlands)
ANGOLA: Orlando, Amadeu, Fua, Antonio Neto, Wilson, Walter (46 Abel Campos), Carlos Pedro, Joni, Paulão, Fabrice Alcebiades Maieco 'Akwá' (19 Quinzinho), Tubia. Trainer: Carlos Alhinho (Portugal).
Goals: Ahmed Aboul El Kass (30, 33) / Quinzinho (77)

18.01.1996

CAMEROON - EGYPT 2-1 (1-0)
First National Bank Stadium, Johannesburg,
Referee: Lim Kee Chong (Mauritius), Attendance: 4000
CAMEROON: Boukar Alioum, Tobie Mimboe, Hans Agbo, Rigobert Song, Sunday Jang, Roland Njume Ntocko, Marc-Vivien Foé (70 Marcel Mahouvre), Joseph Mbarga, Alphonse Tchami (85 Bernard Tchoutang), Augustine Simo, François Oman-Biyik.
EGYPT: Nader El-Sayed, Hany Ramzy, Samir Kamouna, Fawzi Gamal (84 Hamza El-Gamal), Yasser Radwan, Hazem Emam (89 Mohamed Kamouna), Ismail Youssef, Hady Khashaba, Abdel Sattar Sabry (57 Mohamed Salah Abougreisha), Ahmed Aboul El-Kass, Ali Maher.
Goals: François Oman-Biyik (36 penalty), Alphonse Tchami (59) / Ali Maher (48)

20.01.1996

SOUTH AFRICA - ANGOLA 1-0 (0-0)
First National Bank Stadium, Johannesburg
Referee: Fethi Boucetta (Tunisia), Attendance: 30.000
SOUTH AFRICA: Andre Arendse, Sizwe Motaung, David Nyathi, Mark Fish, Neil Tovey, Eric Tinkler, Linda Buthelezi (71 Helman Mkhalele), John Moshoeu, Theophilus Khumalo (76 Lucas Radebe), Phil Masinga, Mark Williams (88 Shaun Bartlett).
ANGOLA: Orlando, Helder Vicente, Antonio Neto, Carlos Pedro, Wilson, Fua (72 Luizinho), Castela, Joni, Paulão, Tubia, Abel Campos (58 Quinzinho).
Goal: Mark Williams (57)

24.01.1996

SOUTH AFRICA - EGYPT 0-1 (0-1)
First National Bank Stadium, Johannesburg,
Referee: Lucien Bouchardeau (Niger), Attendance: 40.000
SOUTH AFRICA: Andre Arendse, Sizwe Motaung, Neil Tovey, Mark Fish, David Nyathi, Eric Tinkler, Lucas Radebe (76 Zane Moosa), August Makalakalane (39 John Moshoeu), Helman Mkhalele, Mark Williams, Phil Masinga (71 Shaun Bartlett).
EGYPT: Nader El-Sayed, Hany Ramzy, Samir Kamouna, Medhat Abdel Hady, Yasser Radwan, Hazem Emam (85 Ahmed Khoushary), Ismail Youssef, Hady Khashaba, Abdel Sattar Sabry, Ahmed Aboul El-Kass (33 Fawzi Gamal), Ali Maher (74 Mohamed Kamouna).
Goal: Ahmed Aboul El-Kass (7)

24.01.1996

ANGOLA - CAMEROON 3-3 (1-1)
ABSA Stadium, Durban
Referee: Kouradji (Algeria), Attendance: 3000
ANGOLA: Orlando, Helder Vicente, Antonio Neto, Minhonha, Castella, Wilson (89 Antonio Diogo), Joni, Paulão, Fua, Quinzinho, Tubia (65 Abel Campos).
CAMEROON: Boukar Alioum, Hans Agbo, Tobie Mimboe, Roland Njume Ntocko, Sunday Jang, Rigobert Song, Marc-Vivien Foé (73 Marcel Mahouvre), Joseph Mbargo (62 Essa Mvondo), Augustine Simo, Alphonse Tchami (59 Georges Mouyeme), François Oman-Biyik.
Goals: Joni (41 penalty), Paulão (55), Quinzinho (80) / François Oman-Biyik (27), Georges Mouyeme (82), Helder Vicente (90 own goal)

1.	SOUTH AFRICA	3	2	0	1	4	1	6
2.	EGYPT	3	2	0	1	4	3	6
3.	Cameroon	3	1	1	1	5	7	4
4.	Angola	3	0	1	2	4	6	1

GROUP B

14.01.1996

ZAMBIA - ALGERIA 0-0
Free State Stadium, Bloemfontein
Referee: Ali Bujsaim (United Arab Emirates), Attendance: 6000
ZAMBIA: James Phiri, Harrison Chongo, Elijah Litana, Mordon Malitoli, Hillary Makasa, Johnson Bwalya, John Lungu (60 Kenneth Malitoli), Dennis Lota, Vincent Mutale (88 Zeddy Saileti), Joël Bwalya (60 Andrew Tembo), Kalusha Bwalya. Trainer: Roald Poulsen (Denmark)
ALGERIA: Mohamed Haniched, Faycal Hamdani, Mourad Slatni, Mahiddine Meftah, Kamal Kaci Said (58 Ali Messabih), Billal Dziri, Khaled Lounici (76 Ali Dahleb), Cherif El-Ouazani, Sidi Ahmed Zerrouki, Moussa Saib, Tarek Lazizi. Trainer: Ali Fergani.

15.01.1996

SIERRA LEONE - BURKINA FASO 2-1 (1-0)
Free State Stadium, Bloemfontein
Referee: Okoampa (Ghana), Attendance: 1500
SIERRA LEONE: Brima Kamara, Francis Koroma (62 Lamine Bangura), Kewulay Conteh, John Sama, Ibrahim Bah, Mohamed Kanu, Rashin Wurie (82 Amidu Karim), Bangura Gbassay, Musa Kallon (54 Mohamed Kallon), Lamine Conteh, John Gbassay Sessay. Trainer: Roger Palmgren (Sweden)
BURKINA FASO: Ibrahima Diarra, Pierre Kouada, Camille Palenfo, Hassane Kamagate, Ousseni Diop, Youssouf Traoré (66 Seydou Traoré), Aboubakri Ouattara (64 Sidi Napon), Salifou Traoré, Vincent Ye, Aboubakari Ouédraogo, Brahima Traoré (46 Ousmane Sanou). Trainer: Idrissa Traoré.
Goals: John Gbassay Sessay (11), Mohamed Kallon (89) / Aboubakari Ouédraogo (74)

18.01.1996

ALGERIA - SIERRA LEONE 2-0 (1-0)
Free State Stadium, Bloemfontein
Referee: McLeod (South Africa), Attendance: 1500
ALGERIA: Mohamed Haniched, Faycal Hamdani, Mourad Slatni, Tarek Lazizi, Sidi Ahmed Zerrouki, Cherif El-Ouazani, Billal Dziri, Moussa Saib, Khaled Lounici, Ali Dahleb (72 Mahiddine Meftah), Ali Messabih.

SIERRA LEONE: Brima Kamara, Bangura Gbassay, John Sama, Kewulay Conteh, Mohamed Kanu, Rashin Wurie, Ibrahim Bah, Amidu Karim, John Gbassay Sessay (79 Mohamed Sillah), Lamine Conteh, Mohamed Kallon (75 Musa Kallon).
Goals: Ali Messabih (44, 61)

20.01.1996

ZAMBIA - BURKINA FASO 5-1 (5-0)
Free State Stadium, Bloemfontein
Referee: Okada (Japan), Attendance: 2000
ZAMBIA: James Phiri, Harrison Chongo, Elijah Litana, Kenneth Malitoli, Hillary Makasa, Mordon Malitoli (78 Aggrey Chitangi), Johnson Bwalya, Dennis Lota (46 Zeddy Saileti), Vincent Mutale, Andrew Tembo (68 Joël Bwalya), Kalusha Bwalya.
BURKINA FASO: Ibrahima Diarra, Pierre Kouada, Salifou Traoré (63 Zakaria Zeba), Ousseni Diop, Camille Palenfo (19 Aboubakari Ouattara), Hassane Kamagate, Boureima Zongo, Sidi Napon, Vincent Ye, Seydou Traoré, Aboubakari Ouédraogo (50 Youssouf Traoré).
Hassane Kamagate sent off (31)
Goals: Kenneth Malitoli (18), Kalusha Bwalya (21, 32), Dennis Lota (44), Johnson Bwalya (45) / Youssouf Traoré (53)

24.01.1996

SIERRA LEONE - ZAMBIA 0-4 (0-2)
Free State Stadium, Bloemfontein
Referee: Lim Kee Chong (Mauritius), Attendance: 200
ZAMBIA: James Phiri, Harrison Chongo, Elijah Litana, Hillary Makasa, Mordon Malitoli, Kenneth Malitoli, Johnson Bwalya, Andrew Tembo, Vincent Mutale, Kalusha Bwalya, Dennis Lota (46 Mwape Miti).
SIERRA LEONE: Brima Kamara, John Sama, Lamine Bangura (58 Francis Koroma), Kewulay Conteh, Aboubacar Kamara, Ibrahim Bah, Mohamed Kanu, Rashin Wurie, John Gbassay Sessay, Abu Kanu (46 Musa Kallon), Lamine Conteh.
Goals: Kalusha Bwalya (2, 9, 84), Mordon Malitoli (87)

24.01.1996

BURKINA FASO - ALGERIA 1-2 (0-1)
Boet-Erasmus, Port Elizabeth
Referee: Charles Masembe (Uganda), Attendance: 1000
ALGERIA: Mohamed Haniched, Faycal Hamdani (46 Karim Bakhti), Mourad Slatni, Sidi Ahmed Zerrouki, Tarik Lazizi, Moussa Saib, Cherif El-Ouazani, Billal Dziri, Khaled Lounici, Abdelaziz Guechir, Ali Messabih (46 Mahiddine Meftah).
BURKINA FASO: Ibrahima Diarra, Ousseni Diop, Firmin Sanou, Zakaria Zeba, Mamadou Koné, Aboubakari Ouattara, Vincent Yé, Brahima Traoré, Seydou Traoré, Youssouf Traoré (76 Ousmane Sanou), Aboubakari Ouédraogo (43 Boureima Zongo). Trainer: Calixte Zagre
Goals: Khaled Lounici (3), Billal Dziri (75) / Boureima Zongo (83)

1.	ZAMBIA	3	2	1	0	9	1	7
2.	ALGERIA	3	2	1	0	4	1	7
3.	Sierra Leone	3	1	0	2	2	7	3
4.	Burkina Faso	3	0	0	3	3	9	0

GROUP C

16.01.1996

GABON - LIBERIA 1-2 (0-1)
ABSA Stadium, Durban
Referee: Gamal El Ghandour (Egypt), Attendance: 5000
GABON: Germain Mendome, Jonas Ogandaga (87 Jean-Daniel Ndong-Nze), Jean-Martin Moulongui, Guy Nzeng, Etienne Kassa-Ngoma, Pierre Aubame, François Amegasse, Brice Mackaya (77 Aurelien Bekogo), Valery Ondo (62 Constant Tamboucha), Francis Koumba, Guy-Roger Nzamba. Trainer: Alain da Costa
LIBERIA: Anthony Tokpah, Jenkins Cooper, Henry Beetoe, Kelvin Sebwe, Robert Clarke (74 Jonathan Sogbie), Joe Nagbe, George Weah, James Debbah, Mass Sarr (54 Chrstopher Wreh), Alexander Freeman, Fallah Johnson. Trainer: Wilfred Lardner.
Goals: Guy Nzeng (59) / Kelvin Sebwe (5 penalty), Mass Sarr (54)

19.01.1996

ZAIRE - GABON 0-2 (0-2)
ABSA Stadium, Durban
Referee: Yengo (Congo), Attendance: 4000
GABON: Germain Mendome, Jonas Ogandaga, Jean-Martin Moulongui, Guy Nzeng, Etienne Kassa-Ngoma, Pierre Aubame, François Amegasse, Brice Mackaya (80 Regis Manon), Francis Koumba, Guy-Roger Nzamba, Aurelien Bekogo (63 Constant Tamboucha).
ZAIRE: Pangi Merikani, Epangala Lukose, Ntumba Danga (68 Kabongo Mutamba), Nzelo Lembi, Kabeya Mukanya, Ngole Kona, Mbote Ndinga, Menana Lukaku, Felix Michel Ngonge (46 Liombi Essende), Roger Hitoto, Ndiaye Kalenga (37 Michel Dinzey). Trainer: Mushin Ertgal (Turkey).
Goals: Brice Mackaya (21 penalty), Aurelien Bekogo (34)

25.01.1996

LIBERIA - ZAIRE 0-2 (0-1)
First National Bank Stadium, Johannesburg,
Referee: Said Belqola (Morocco), Attendance: 1000
ZAIRE: Pangi Merikani, Epangala Lukose, Kabongo Mutamba, Nzelo Lembi, Zola Kiniambi, Kabeya Mukanya, Ntumba Danga (55 Ebanga Mamale), Kabwe Kasongo, Banga Kasongo, Menana Lukaku (68 Ngole Kona), Liombi Essende (77 Ndiaye Kalenga). Trainer: L. Basilwa
LIBERIA: Anthony Tokpah, Jenkins Cooper, Henry Beetoe (71 Fallah Johnson), Joe Nagbe, Alexander Freeman, Kelvin Sebwe, Robert Clarke (73 Arthur Fahr), Alexander Theo, George Weah, James Debbah, Jonathan Sogbie (59 Christopher Wreh).
Goals: Menana Lukaku (5 penalty), Liombi Essende (72)

1.	GABON	2	1	0	1	3	2	3
2.	ZAIRE	2	1	0	1	2	2	3
3.	Liberia	2	1	0	1	2	3	3

Nigeria withdrew, Guinea declined the invitation to participate.

GROUP D

14.01.1996

IVORY COAST - GHANA 0-2 (0-1)
Boet-Erasmus, Port Elizabeth
Referee: Okada (Japan) Attendance: 4000
GHANA: Simon Addo, Frank Amankwah, Issac Asare, Samuel Johnson, Afo Dodoo, Joseph Addo, Mallam Yahaya (90 Osei Kuffour), Abedi Pelé, Charles Akonnor (88 Ibrahim Tanko), Yaw Preko (46 Nil Lamptey), Anthony Yeboah. Trainer: Ismael Kurtz (Brazil)
IVORY COAST: Pierre Alain Gouaméné, Basile Kouamé Aka, Lassina Dao, Kpassagnon Gneto, Cyril Domoraud (82 Ibrahima Camara), Donald Olivier Sie, Ibrahima Koné, Moussa Traoré, Tchiressoa Guel (75 Serge Die), Joël Tiéhi, Aboulaye Traoré (46 Ibrahim Bakayoko). Trainer: Pierre Pleimelding (France)
Goals: Anthony Yeboah (20), Abedi Pelé (70)

16.01.1996

TUNISIA - MOZAMBIQUE 1-1 (1-1)
Boet-Erasmus, Port Elizabeth
Referee: Charles Masembe (Uganda), Attendance: 1000
TUNISIA: Chokri El Ouaer, Sami Trabelsi, Hedi Ben Rekhissa (74 Medhi Ben Slimane), Mounir Boukadida (87 Sabri Jaballah), Lassad Hanini, Ferid Chouhcane, Riadh Bouazizi, Khais Godhbane, Zoubier Beya, Adel Sellimi, Abdelkader Ben Hassen (58 Belhassen Aloui). Trainer: Henry Kasperczak (Poland)
MOZAMBIQUE: Rui Evora Alves, Sergio Faife, Luis, Zé Augusto, Pinto Barros, Antoninho (35 Ali Hassan), Nana, Jojo, Riquito, Chiquinho Conde, Manuel José Luis Bucuane 'Tico-Tico' (57 Arnaldo Ouana). Trainer: Rui Cacador (Portugal).
Goals: Hedi Ben Rekhissa (24) / Manuel José Luis Bucuane 'Tico-Tico' (4)

19.01.1996

GHANA - TUNISIA 2-1 (0-0)
Boet-Erasmus, Port Elizabeth
Referee: Mathabela (South Africa), Attendance: 250
GHANA: Simon Addo, Samuel Johnson, Afo Dodoo, Joseph Addo, Mallam Yahaya (67 Yaw Acheampong), Frank Amankwah, Charles Akonnor, Isaac Asare, Ibrahim Tanko (60 Felix Aboagye), Abedi Pelé, Anthony Yeboah.
TUNISIA: Chokri El Ouaer, Sami Trabelsi, Hedi Ben Rekhissa (57 Bechir Sahbani), Riadh Bouazizi, Ferid Chouhcane, Zoubier Beya, Khais Godhbane, Sofiane Fekhi (69 Imed Ben Younès), Lassad Hanini, Jameleddine Limam (35 Medhi Ben Slimane), Adel Sellimi.
Goals: Abedi Pelé (50), Charles Akonnor (77) / Imed Ben Younès (72)

21.01.1996

MOZAMBIQUE - IVORY COAST 0-1 (0-1)
Boet-Erasmus, Port Elizabeth
Referee: Gamal El Ghandour (Egypt), Attendance: 350
IVORY COAST: Pierre Alain Gouaméné, Basile Kouamé Aka, Lassaina Dao, Ibrahima Kamara, Kpassagnon Gneto, Ibrahima Koné, Michel Bassolé (88 Cyril Domoraud), Aliou Sidi Badra, Tchiressoa Guel, Joël Tiéhi (73 Moussa Traoré), Abdoulaye Traoré (54 Donald Olivier Sié).
MOZAMBIQUE: Rui Evora Alves, Sergio Faife, Zé Augusto, Luis, João Chissano, Antoninho, Jojo (55 Riquito), Nana (70 Ali Hassan), Pinto Barros (44 Manuel José Luis Bucuane 'Tico-Tico'), Chiquinho Conde, Arnaldo Ouana.
Goal: Joël Tiéhi (32)

25.01.1996

TUNISIA - IVORY COAST 3-1 (2-0)

Boet-Erasmus, Port Elizabeth
Referee: Sidi Bekaye (Mali).
TUNISIA: Chokri El Ouaer, Sami Trabelsi, Mounir Bouakadida, Hedi Ben Rekhissa, Ferid Chouhcane, Riadh Bouazizi, Zoubier Beya (81 Ahmed Trabelsi), Khais Godhbane, Adel Sellimi, Imed Ben Younès (61 Sofiane Fekhi), Abdelkader Ben Hassen (73 Medhi Ben Slimane).
IVORY COAST: Obou Macaire, Ibrahima Kamara, Lassina Dao, Kpassagnon Gneto, Basile Kouamé Aka, Ibrahima Koné (57 Donald Olivier Sié), Aliou Sidi Badra, Tchiressoa Guel, Abdoulaye Traoré (62 Ibrahim Bakayoko), Joël Tiéhi (71 Moussa Traoré), Michel Bassolé.
Goals: Imed Ben Younès (32, 38), Abdelkader Ben Hassen (48) / Moussa Traoré (87)

25.01.1996

MOZAMBIQUE - GHANA 0-2 (0-1)

Free State Stadium, Bloemfontein
Referee: Ali Bujsaim (United Arab Emirates), Attendance: 3500
GHANA: Simon Addo, Frank Amankwah, Isaac Asare (87 Stephen Baidoo), Afo Dodoo, Joseph Addo, Yaw Acheampong, Abedi Pelé (76 Ablade Kumah), Osei Kuffour, Felix Aboagye, Kwame Ayew (80 Daniel Addo), Anthony Yeboah.
MOZAMBIQUE: Rui Evora Alves, Sergio Faife, Zé Augusto, Antoninho (61 Buane Cachela), Jojo, Nana (74 Arnaldo Ouana), Chiquinho Conde, Luis, Manuel José Luis Bucuane 'Tico-Tico', João Chissano, Riquito (67 Luisinho).
Rui Evora Alves sent off (68)
Goals: Kwame Ayew (42), Felix Aboagye (68)

1.	GHANA	3	3	0	0	6	1	9
2.	TUNISIA	3	1	1	1	5	4	4
3.	Ivory Coast	3	1	0	2	2	5	3
4.	Mozambique	3	0	1	2	1	4	1

Quarter-finals

27.01.1996

SOUTH AFRICA - ALGERIA 2-1 (0-0)

First National Bank Stadium, Johannesburg,
Referee: Ali Bujsaim (United Arab Emirates), Attendance: 30.000
SOUTH AFRICA: Andre Arendse, Sizwe Motaung, Lucas Radebe, Mark Fish, Neil Tovey, Eric Tinkler, Linda Buthelezi, Theophilus Khumalo (79 Helman Mkhalele), John Moshoeu, Phil Masinga, Mark Williams (76 Shaun Bartlett).
ALGERIA: Mohamed Haniched, Karim Bakhti (60 Faycal Hamdani), Sidi Ahmed Zerrouki, Mourad Slatni, Tarek Lazizi, Mahiddine Meftah, Cherif El-Ouazani (81 Nacer Zekri), Moussa Saib, Billal Dziri, Khaled Lounici, Ali Messabih.
Goals: Mark Fish (72), John Moshoeu (85) / Tarek Lazizi (84)

27.01.1996

ZAMBIA - EGYPT 3-1 (0-1)

Free State Stadium, Bloemfontein
Referee: Charles Masembe (Uganda), Attendance: 10.000

EGYPT: Nader El Sayed, Hany Ramzy, Samir Kamouna, Medhat Abdel Hady, Yasser Radwan, Hazem Emam, Ismail Youssef, Hady Khashaba, Abdel Sattar Sabry, Ahmed Aboul El-Kass (76 Mohamed Abougreisha), Aly Maher (56 Fawzi Gamal).
ZAMBIA: James Phiri, Harrison Chongo, Elijah Litana, Mordon Malitoli, Hillary Makasa, Andrew Tembo, Vincent Mutale, Kenneth Malitoli (78 Bilton Musonda), Johnson Bwalya (28 John Lungu), Kalusha Bwalya, Dennis Lota.
Goals: Elijah Litana (58), Vincent Mutale (65), Dennis Lota (76) / Samir Kamouna (43)

28.01.1996

GHANA - ZAIRE 1-0 (1-0)
First National Bank Stadium, Johannesburg,
Referee: Sidi Bekaye (Mali), Attendance: 5000
GHANA: Simon Addo, Frank Amankwah, Afo Dodoo, Joseph Addo, Osei Kuffour, Samuel Johnson, Mallam Yahaya (51 Yaw Acheampong), Charles Akonnor, Felix Aboagye (88 Kwame Ayew), Anthony Yeboah, Abedi Pelé (81 Ibrahim Tanko).
ZAIRE: Pangi Merikani, Roger Hitoto, Kabongo Mutamba (58 Ngole Kona), Nzelo Lembi, Kabwe Kasongo, Kabeya Mukanya (46 Ngamala Monka), Ntumba Danga, Zola Kiniambi, Banga Kasongo, Ndiaye Kalenga (67 Emeka Mamale), Liombi Essende.
Nzeno Lembi sent off (20)
Goal: Anthony Yeboah (22)

28.01.1996

GABON - TUNISIA 1-1 (1-1, 1-1), 1-4 penalties
ABSA Stadium, Durban
Referee: Lee Kim Chong (Mauritius), Attendance: 5000
TUNISIA: Chokri El Ouaer, Sami Trabelsi (120 Sabri Jaballah), Ferid Chouhcane, Hedi Ben Rekhissa, Riadh Bouazizi, Khaled Badra, Khais Godhbane, Zoubier Beya, Medhi Ben Slimane, Adel Sellimi, Abdelkader Ben Hassen (46 Belhassen Aloui, 85 Sofiane Fekhi).
GABON: Germain Mendome, Jean-Martin Moulongui, François Amegasse, Guy Nzeng, Etienne Kassa-Ngoma, Francis Koumba, Jonas Ogandaga, Pierre Aubame (91 Constant Tamboucha), Brice Mackaya, Guy-Roger Nzamba, Albin Mbougha-Nze (108 Aurelien Bekogo).
Goals: Zoubier Beya (10) / Brice Mackaya (16)
Penalties: 1-0 Adel Sellimi, Brice Mackaya (miss), 2-0 Sofiane Fekhi, Etienne Kassa-Ngoma (miss), 3-0 Mehdi Ben Slimane, 3-1 Aurelien Bekogo, 4-1 Chokri El Ouaer.

Semi-finals

31.01.1996

TUNISIA - ZAMBIA 4-2 (0-2)
ABSA Stadium, Durban
Referee: Lucien Bouchardeau (Niger), Attendance: 6000
TUNISIA: Chokri El Ouaer, Mounir Boukadida, Sami Trabelsi, Ferid Chouhcane, Hedi Ben Rekhissa, Khaled Badra (75 Lassad Hanini), Khais Godhbane, Soufiane Fekhi, Zoubier Beya, Medhi Ben Slimane, Adel Sellimi.
ZAMBIA: James Phiri, Harrison Chongo (75 Johnson Bwalya), Elijah Litana, Hillary Makasa, Mordon Malitoli (48 Aggrey Chitangi), Kenneth Malitoli, John Lungu, Andrew Tembo, Vincent Mutale (53 Mwape Miti), Kalusha Bwalya, Dennis Lota.
Goals: Adel Sellimi (16, 85 penalty), Zoubier Beya (30), Khais Godhbane (47) / Dennis Lota (68), Hillary Makasa (89)

31.01.1996

SOUTH AFRICA – GHANA 3-0 (1-0)
First National Bank Stadium, Johannesburg,
Referee: Gamal El Ghandour (Egypt), Attendance: 70.000
SOUTH AFRICA: Andre Arendse, Sizwe Motaung, Lucas Radebe, Mark Fish, Neil Tovey, Linda
Buthelezi (76 John Moeti), Eric Tinkler, Theophilus Khumalo, John Moshoeu, Shaun Bartlett (84
Daniel Mudau), Mark Williams.
GHANA: Simon Addo, Frank Amankwah, Isaac Asare, Afo Dodoo, Joseph Addo, Samuel Johnson,
Yaw Acheampong (63 Ibrahim Tanko), Ablade Kumah, Charles Akonnor, Kwame Ayew (59 Nil
Lamptey), Anthony Yeboah.
Lamptey sent off (84)
Goals: John Moshoeu (22, 87), Shaun Bartlett (46)

Third Place Match

03.02.1996

ZAMBIA - GHANA 1-0 (0-0)
First National Bank Stadium, Johannesburg,
Referee: Omer Yengo (Congo), Attendance: 80.000
GHANA: Simon Addo, Frank Amankwah, Osei Kuffour, Joseph Addo, Stephen Baidoo, Mallam
Yahaya (46 Daniel Addo), Yaw Acheampong, Ablade Kumah, Charles Akonnor, Felix Aboagye,
Ibrahim Tanko (74 Isaac Asare). Trainer: Ismael Kurtz
ZAMBIA: James Phiri, Aggrey Chitangi, Elijah Litana, Jones Mwewa, Hillary Makasa (63 Allan
Kamwanga), John Lungu, Andrew Tembo (46 Vincent Mutale), Kalusha Bwalya, Johnson Bwalya,
Dennis Lota (70 Kenneth Malitoli), Mwape Miti. Trainer: Raoul Poulsen (Denmark).
Lungu sent off: (69)
Goal: Johnson Bwalya (52)

Final

03.02.1996

SOUTH AFRICA - TUNISIA 2-0 (2-0)
First National Bank Stadium, Johannesburg
Referee: Charles Masembe (Uganda), Attendance: 80.000
SOUTH AFRICA: Andre Arendse, Sizwe Motaung, Lucas Radebe, Mark Fish, Neil Tovey, Linda
Buthelezi (51 Helman Mkhalele), Eric Tinkler, John Moshoeu, Theophilus Khumalo, Shaun Bartlett,
Phil Masinga (64 Mark Williams). Trainer: Clive Barker
TUNISIA: Chokri El Ouaer, Mounir Boukadida, Hedi Ben Rekhissa, Ferid Chouhcane, Sabri Jaballah,
Zoubier Beya, Riadh Bouazizi (75 Abdelkader Ben Hassen), Sofiane Fekhi, Khais Godhbane (46
Lassad Hanini), Adel Sellimi, Medhi Ben Slimane. Trainer: Henry Kasperczak (Poland)
Goals: Mark Williams (73, 75)

Twenty-first edition - 1998
Qualifying Tournament

The 21st edition of the competition saw 36 countries enter the competition although three of them subsequently withdrew. This number was considerably lower than the previous edition due to a number of suspensions imposed by the CAF. The suspended countries were Nigeria (for their failure to participate in the final tournament in 1996) and Gambia, Guinea Bissau, Lesotho, Madagascar and Niger (for withdrawing during the qualifying stages of the 1996 tournament). Several other countries did not enter the competition, including Chad, Djibouti, Libya, Rwanda, Somalia and Swaziland. The finals in 1998 were held in in Burkina Faso and reigning champions, South Africa, reached the final once again. However, they were not able to retain the trophy as they were defeated by Egypt (with a 2-0 scoreline) who won the title for a fourth time. The most memorable game from the tournament came in the third place match between Burkina Faso and the Democratic Republic of Congo. With just four minutes of normal time remaining, the Congolese team led 4-1 but remarkably, Burkina Faso managed to score three goals in three just minutes to take the game to extra-time although the DR Congo finally clinched third place following a penalty shoot-out victory.

Preliminary Round

11.08.1996 Mauritius - Seychelles 1-0 (1-0)
Goal: Jean-Sébastien Bax (25)
24.08.1996 Seychelles - Mauritius 1-1 (0-1)
Goals: Paul Rose (50) / Antoine-Percy Mocude (20)

11.08.1996 Congo - Togo 0-0
25.08.1996 Togo - Congo 1-0 (0-0)
Goal: Bachirou Salou (57)

11.08.1996 Botswana - Namibia 0-0
25.08.1996 Namibia - Botswana 6-0
Goals: Sylvanus Ndjambari, Gervasius Uri Khob, Ruben van Wyk 2, Johannes Hindjou 2

Central African Republic - Burundi w/o

11.08.1996 Benin - Mauritania 4-1 (1-0)
Goals: Abdul Rahimi Coles (3), Leon Bessam (54, 72, 89) / Ahmed Ould Eleyo (67)
30.08.1996 Mauritania - Benin 0-0

11.08.1996 Uganda - Ethiopia 1-1 (0-0)
Goals: Ibrahim Buwembo (65) / Edward Kalungi (46 own goal)
25.08.1996 Ethiopia - Uganda 1-1 aet, 4-2 on penalties
Goals: / Ibrahim Kizito

Group 1

06.10.1996 Ghana - Angola 2-1 (2-1)
Goals: Felix Aboagye (7), Kim Grant (30) / Paulo Antônio Alves 'Paulão' (2)
06.10.1996 Sudan - Zimbabwe 0-3
Goals: Charles Yohane, Agent Sawu 2
26.01.1997 Zimbabwe - Ghana 0-0
23.02.1997 Zimbabwe - Angola 1-0 (1-0)
Goal: Wilfred Mugeyi (31 penalty)

22.06.1997 Angola - Ghana 1-0 (1-0)
Goal: Fabrice Alcebiades Maieco 'Akwá' (23)
13.07.1997 Ghana - Zimbabwe 2-1 (2-1)
Goals: Abedi 'Pelé' Ayew (22), Samuel Kuffour (39) / Shepherd Muradzikwa (24)
27.07.1997 Angola - Zimbabwe 2-1 (1-0)
Goals: Aurelio de Sousa Soares (9), Fabrice Alcebiades Maieco 'Akwá' (70) / Stewart Murisa (80)

1.	GHANA	4	2	1	1	4	3	7
2.	ANGOLA	4	2	0	2	4	4	6
3.	Zimbabwe	4	1	1	2	3	4	4

Sudan withdrew on January 16, 1997, due to political unrest in the east of the country.

Group 2

06.10.1996 Algeria - Ivory Coast 4-1 (2-0)
Goals: Ali Messabih (7, 69), Moussa Saib (41, 89) / Joël Tiéhi (71)
06.10.1996 Benin - Mali 1-2 (1-0)
Goals: Moussa Latoundji (38) / Bassala Touré (54), Brahima Traoré (78)
26.01.1997 Ivory Coast - Benin 1-0 (1-0)
Goal: Tchiressoa Guel (12)
26.01.1997 Mali - Algeria 1-0 (0-0)
Goals: Bassala Touré (63)
23.02.1997 Benin - Algeria 1-1 (1-0)
Goals: Moussa Latoundji (35) / Abdelhafid Tasfaout (51)
23.02.1997 Mali - Ivory Coast 1-2 (1-2)
Goals: Modibo Sidibe (14) / Ibrahima Bakayoko (13), Joël Tiéhi (22)
22.06.1997 Ivory Coast - Algeria 2-1 (1-1)
Goals: Joël Tiéhi (45), Michel Bassolé (87) / Kamel Kaci Said (17)
22.06.1997 Mali - Benin 3-1 (1-1)
Goals: Basala Touré (12), Soumaila Coulibaly (68), Sadio Traoré (85 penalty) / Michel Gbete Dossou (40)
13.07.1997 Algeria - Mali 1-0 (1-0)
Goal: Khaireddine Kherris (18)
13.07.1997 Benin - Ivory Coast 0-0
27.07.1997 Algeria - Benin 2-0 (2-0)
Goals: Abdelhafid Tasfaout (13), Cheikh Benzargha (27)
27.07.1997 Ivory Coast - Mali 4-2 (2-0)
Goals: Joël Tiéhi (22, 26), Tchiressoa Guel (51), Ibrahim Bakayoko (75) / Soumaila Coulibaly (47), Modibo Sidibe (69 penalty)

1.	IVORY COAST	6	4	1	1	10	8	13
2.	ALGERIA	6	3	1	2	9	5	10
3.	Mali	6	3	0	3	9	9	9
4.	Benin	6	0	2	4	3	9	2

Group 3

04.10.1996 Egypt - Morocco 1-1 (0-0)
Goals: Hossam Hassan (88) / Salaheddine Bassir (70)
06.10.1996 Ethiopia - Senegal 1-2 (1-2)
Goals: Eliyas Juhar (3) / Ibrahima Tete Diandy (17), Alassane Keita (36)
25.01.1997 Senegal - Egypt 0-0
22.02.1997 Senegal - Morocco 0-0

23.02.1997 Ethiopia - Egypt 1-1 (0-0)
Goals: Tesfaye Aseged (58) / Tarek Mustafa (71)
31.05.1997 Morocco - Ethiopia 4-0 (3-0)
Goals: Said Chiba (8), Ahmed Bahja (18), Noureddine Naybet (34), Abdelkrim El-Hadrioui (81)
21.06.1997 Morocco - Egypt 1-0 (0-0)
Goal: Salaheddine Bassir (71)
22.06.1997 Senegal - Ethiopia 3-0 (1-0)
Goals: Souleymane Sané (38, 53), Omar Traoré (68)
13.07.1997 Egypt - Senegal 2-0 (1-0)
Goals: Hazem Imam (12), Hady Khashaba (55 penalty)
13.07.1997 Ethiopia - Morocco 0-1 (0-1)
Goal: Salaheddine Bassir (21)
27.07.1997 Egypt - Ethiopia 8-1 (5-0)
Goals: Hady Khashaba (1 penalty), Hesham Hanefi (5), Hazem Imam (19, 36, 44), Hossam Hassan (55), Ahmed Hassan (62), Magdi El-Sayed (77) / Eliyas Juhar (60 penalty)
27.07.1997 Morocco - Senegal 3-0 (2-0)
Goals: Salaheddine Bassir (11, 67), Said Chiba (40)

1.	MOROCCO	6	4	2	0	10	1	14
2.	EGYPT	6	2	3	1	12	4	9
3.	Senegal	6	2	2	2	5	6	8
4.	Ethiopia	6	0	1	5	3	19	1

Group 4

06.10.1996 Tunisia - Sierra Leone 2-0 (1-0)
Goals: Sami Trabelsi (29), Skander Souayeh (69)
06.10.1996 Central African Republic - Guinea 2-3 (1-1)
Goals: Georges Matondo (30), Alain Azo (48 penalty) / Morlaye Soumah (27, 89), Mousa Keita (85)
26.01.1997 Guinea - Tunisia 1-0 (0-0)
Goal: Abdoul Sow (49)
23.02.1997 Guinea - Sierra Leone 1-0 (0-0)
Goal: Fode Camara (67)
13.07.1997 Tunisia - Guinea 1-0 (0-0)
Goal: Riadh Jelassi (90)
 Sierra Leone - Tunisia not played
 Sierra Leone - Guinea not played

1.	TUNISIA	3	2	0	1	3	1	6
2.	GUINEA	3	2	0	1	2	1	6
3.	Sierra Leone	2	0	0	2	0	3	0

Central African Republic were disqualified from the competition on 30th January, 1997, after the government had prevented the squad travelling for the away game in Sierra Leone on 25th January. Sierra Leone withdrew two matches before the end of the tournament.

Group 5

06.10.1996 Namibia – Kenya 1-0
Goal: Francis Raymond Oduor (own goal)
06.10.1996 Gabon - Cameroon 0-0
25.01.1997 Kenya - Gabon 1-0 (0-0)
Goal: Michael Muiruri (70)

26.01.1997 Cameroon - Namibia 4-0 (2-0)
Goals: Patrick Mboma (3, 85), Jean-Jacques Missé-Missé (35, 48)
22.02.1997 Kenya - Cameroon 0-0
22.02.1997 Namibia - Gabon 1-1 (0-1)
Goals: Ruben van Wyk (86) / Pierre Aubame Yang (19 penalty)
21.06.1997 Kenya - Namibia 0-1 (0-1)
Goal: Gervasius Uri Khob (35)
22.06.1997 Cameroon - Gabon 2-2 (2-1)
Goals: Bernard Tchoutang (12), Cyrille Mangan (33) / Pierre Aubame Yang (38 penalty), Aurelien Bekogo Zolo (87)
12.07.1997 Namibia - Cameroon 0-1 (0-0)
Goal: Joseph Tchango (69)
13.07.1997 Gabon - Kenya 1-0 (0-0)
Goal: Théodore Nzue Nguema (50)
27.07.1997 Cameroon - Kenya 1-1 (0-0)
Goals: Fabrice Moreau (89 penalty) / Francis Were (49)
27.07.1997 Gabon - Namibia 1-1 (1-0)
Goals: Pierre Aubame Yang (22 penalty) / Johannes Hindjou (60 penalty)

1.	CAMEROON	6	2	4	0	8	3	10
2.	NAMIBIA	6	2	2	2	4	7	8
3.	Gabon	6	1	4	1	5	5	7
4.	Kenya	6	1	2	3	2	4	5

Group 6

06.10.1996 Togo - Tanzania 2-1 (1-0)
Goals: Tadjou Salou (17), Yaovi Abalo (57) / Macho Yusuf Rwenda (72)
06.10.1996 Zaire - Liberia 0-0
26.01.1997 Tanzania - Zaire 1-2 (0-0)
Goals: Said Kizito (79) / Kibembe Mbayo (52), Siala Nzalambila (85)
26.01.1997 Liberia - Togo 1-2 (1-1)
Goals: Jonathan Sogbie (24) / Bachirou Salou (26), Komlan Assignon (67)
23.02.1997 Tanzania - Liberia 1-1 (0-1)
Goals: Saidi Duwa (75) / Jonathan Sogbie (27)
23.02.1997 Togo - Zaire 1-1 (0-1)
Goals: Kossi Noutsoudjé (90) / Ekanza Simba (26)
22.06.1997 Tanzania - Togo 1-0 (1-0)
Goal: Idelfonce Amlima (31)
22.06.1997 Liberia - DR Congo 2-1 (1-0)
Goals: Kelvin Sebwe (20), George Weah (66) / Nzangani Kidoda Buayi (81)
13.07.1997 Togo - Liberia 4-0 (0-0)
Goals: Tadjou Salou (52), Kossi Noutsoudjé (86), Komlan Assignon (89), Bachirou Salou (90)
13.07.1997 DR Congo - Tanzania 1-1 (0-1)
Goals: Nzangani Kidoda Buayi (90 penalty) / Macho Yusuf Rwenda (12)
27.07.1997 Liberia - Tanzania 1-0 (0-0)
Goal: Zizi Roberts (54)
27.07.1997 DR Congo – Togo 1-0 (1-0)
Goal: Nganzadi Kidoda Buayi (15)

1.	TOGO	6	3	1	2	9	5	10
2.	DR CONGO	6	2	3	1	6	5	9
3.	Liberia	6	2	2	2	5	8	8
4.	Tanzania	6	1	2	3	5	7	5

During the tournament, the country of Zaire were renamed DR Congo (Democratic Republic of Congo) following a change of regime. Their matches after the renaming are listed under the new name.

Group 7

06.10.1996 Mauritius – Malawi 1-2 (0-1)
Goals: Robert Rateau (75) / Bob Mpinganjira (29), Jonas France (90 own goal)
06.10.1996 Zambia – Mozambique 1-0 (1-0)
Goal: Mordon Malitoli (4)
25.01.1997 Malawi - Zambia 0-2 (0-1)
Goals: Elijah Litana (40), Andrew Tembo (83)
26.01.1997 Mozambique - Mauritius 3-0 (0-0)
Goals: Francisco Queriol Conde (55), Sérgio Faife Matsolo (62) / André Jossias Macamo (65)
22.02.1997 Malawi - Mozambique 2-0 (1-0)
Goals: John Maduka (6), Lawrent Kamanga (60)
23.02.1997 Mauritius - Zambia 0-0
21.06.1997 Malawi - Mauritius 3-2 (1-0)
Goals: John Maduka (19, 81), Hendrix Banda (76) / Joseph-Roël Philogene (87), Robert Rateau (89)
22.06.1997 Mozambique - Zambia 2-2 (1-1)
Goals: Manuel José Luis Bucuane 'Tico-Tico' (11), Francisco Queriol 'Chiquinho' Conde (62 penalty)
/ Frazer Kamwandi (25), Masautso Tembo (57)
12.07.1997 Zambia - Malawi 3-1 (1-0)
Goals: Hector Chilombo (30 penalty), Frazer Kamwandi (55), Freddie Mwila (75) / Hendrix Banda (89)
13.07.1997 Mauritius - Mozambique 1-3 (0-2)
Goals: Georges Hesman Appou (65), Francisco Queriol 'Chiquinho' Conde (6), Nuro Amiro
Tualibudine (33), Manuel José Luis Bucuane 'Tico-Tico' (89)
27.07.1997 Mozambique - Malawi 2-1 (0-0)
Goals: Pinto Barros (85), Manuel José Luís Bucuane 'Tico-Tico' (88) / Jones Nkhwazi (62)
27.07.1997 Zambia - Mauritius 1-0 (0-0)
Goal: Vincent Mutale (57)

1.	ZAMBIA	6	4	2	0	9	3	14
2.	MOZAMBIQUE	6	3	1	2	10	7	10
3.	Malawi	6	3	0	3	9	10	9
4.	Mauritius	6	0	1	5	4	12	1

Final Tournament (Burkina Faso)

GROUP A

07.02.1998

BURKINA FASO - CAMEROON 0-1 (0-1)
4 Août Stadium, Ouagadougou
Referee: Gamal El-Ghandour (Egypt), Attendance: 30.000
BURKINA FASO: Ibrahim Diarra, Seydou Traoré, Ibrahim Talle, Souleymane Doumbia (88 Oumar Barro), Ismael Koudou (69 Abdoulaye Traoré), Boureima Zongo, Ousmane Sanou, Alain Nana, Brahima Traoré, Romeo Kambou (68 Alassane Ouédraogo), Jean-Michel Gnonka Liadé. Trainer: Philippe Troussier (France)
CAMEROON: Jacques Songo'o, Tobie Mimboe, Raymond Kalla, Rigobert Song, Ernest Oben Etchi, Pierre Wome, Marc-Vivien Foé, Bernard Tchoutang (79 Joseph-Désiré Job), Romarin Billong, Alphonse Tchami, Salomon Olembé (58 Augustine Simo). Trainer: Jean-Manga-Onguené
Goal: Alphonse Tchami (20)

08.02.1998

ALGERIA - GUINEA 0-1 (0-0)
Municipal, Ouagadougou
Referee: Lim Kee Chong (Mauritius), Attendance: 3000
ALGERIA: Aomar Hamened, Tarek Ghoul (83 Cheikh Benzerga), Abdelatif Osmane, Mahieddine
Meftah, Mounir Zeghdoud, Billal Dziri, Moussa Saïb, Salem Harchache, Ali Dahlab (83 Sid Ahmed
Benamara), Kamel Kaci Saïd (66 Ishak Ali Moussa), Abdelhafid Tasfaout. Trainer: Abderrahmane
Mehdaoui
GUINEA: Saliou Diallo, Edgar Barbara Sylla, Abdoul Salam Sow, Mohamed Camara, Souleymane
Oularé (82 Taifour Diané), Sekou Oumar Dramé (86 Momo Wandel Soumah), Abdoul Karim
Bangoura, Morlaye Soumah, Keffing Dioubaté (82 Fode Camara), Ousmane N'Gom Camara,
Aboubacar 'Titi' Camara. Trainer: Vladimir Muntean (Ukraine).
Goal: Souleymane Oularé (61)

11.02.1998

CAMEROON - GUINEA 2-2 (2-0)
Municipal, Ouagadougou
Referee: Kim Young-Joo (South Korea), Attendance: 2000
CAMEROON: Jacques Songo'o, Ernest Oben Etchi, Pierre Womé, Rigobert Song, Timboe Mimboe,
Raymond Kalla (22 Geremi Fotso Njitap), Bernard Tchoutang (81 Joseph-Désiré Job), Alphonse
Tchami, Patrick Mboma (71 Samuel Ipoua), Augustine Simo, Marc-Vivien Foé.
GUINEA: Saliou Diallo (60 Kemoko Camara), Mohamed Ofei Sylla, Abdoul Salam Sow, Mohamed
Camara, Souleymane Oularé, Aboubacar 'Titi' Camara, Sekou Oumar Dramé, Ousmane N'Gom Camara
(46 Fodé Camara), Abdoul Karim Bangoura, Morlaye Soumah, Keffing Dioubaté.
Goals: Alphonse Tchami (9), Pierre Womé (44) / Souleymane Oularé (47, 76)

11.02.1998

BURKINA FASO - ALGERIA 2-1 (0-0)
4 Août Stadium, Ouagadougou
Referee: Pierre Alain Moungengui (Gabon), Attendance: 35.000
BURKINA FASO: Ibrahim Diarra, Seydou Traoré, Firmin Sanou (76 Ousmane Coulibaly), Ibrahima
Korbeogo (58 Ismael Koudou), Alain Nana, Abdoulaye Traoré, Romeo Kambou, Boureima Zongo,
Jean-Michel Gnonka Liadé, Ibrahim Talle, Oumar Barro (46 Kassoum Ouédraogo).
ALGERIA: Aomar Hamened, Cheikh Benzerga (75 Ali Dahlab), Abdelatif Osmane, Mahieddine
Meftah, Mounir Zeghdoud, Billal Dziri, Moussa Saïb, Sid Ahmed Benamara, Salem Harchache (82
Abdelaziz Benhamlat), Abdelhafid Tasfaout, Kamel Kaci Saïd.
Goals: Kassoum Ouédraogo (65), Seydou Traoré (77) / Moussa Saïb (80 penalty)

15.02.1998

BURKINA FASO - GUINEA 1-0 (0-0)
4 Août Stadium, Ouagadougou
Referee: Omer Yengo (Congo), Attendance: 40.000
BURKINA FASO: Ibrahim Diarra, Seydou Traoré, Firmin Sanou (73 Ousmane Sanou), Ismael
Koudou (67 Oumar Barro), Kassoum Ouédraogo, Alain Nana, Brahima Traoré, Romeo Kambou,
Boureima Zongo (51 Magan Diabaté), Jean-Michel Gnonka Liadé, Ibrahim Tallé.
GUINEA: Kemoko Camara, Mohamed Ofei Sylla, Abdoul Salam Sow (58 Ousmane N'Gom Camara),
Pablo Thiam, Mohamed Camara, Fodé Camara (76 Momo Wandel Soumah), Souleymane Oularé (65
Taifour Diané), Aboubacar 'Titi' Camara, Sekou Oumar Dramé, Abdoul Karim Bangoura, Morlaye
Soumah.
Sent off Thiam (38)
Goal: Romeo Kambou (85)

15.02.1998

CAMEROON - ALGERIA 2-1 (0-1)
Municipal, Ouagadougou
Referee: Tibebu Kine (Ethiopia), Attendance: 1000
CAMEROON: Vincent Ongandzi, Ernest Oben Etchi, Pierre Nlend Womé, Rigobert Song, Tobie Mimboe, Augustine Simo, Lucien Mettomo, Marc-Vivien Foé, Joseph-Désiré Job, Bernard Tchoutang (74 Geremi Fotso Njitap), Alphonse Tchami (78 Patrick Mboma).
ALGERIA: Aomar Hamened, Abdelaziz Benhamlat (70 Cheikh Benzerga), Kheireddine Kerris (88 Kamel Habri), Tarek Ghoul, Mahieddine Meftah, Mounir Zeghdoud, Billal Dziri, Abdelatif Osmane, Salem Harchache (70 Ali Dahlab), Ishak Ali Moussa, Abdelhafid Tasfaout.
Goals: Joseph-Désiré Job (47), Alphonse Tchami (65) / Billal Dziri (40)

1.	CAMEROON	3	2	1	0	5	3	7
2.	BURKINA FASO	3	2	0	1	3	2	6
3.	Guinea	3	1	1	1	3	3	4
4.	Algeria	3	0	0	3	2	5	0

GROUP B

09.02.1998

DR CONGO – TOGO 2-1 (0-0)
Municipal, Ouagadougou
Referee: Said Belqoba (Morocco), Attendance: 4000
DR CONGO: Nikombe Tokala, Mundaba Kisombe, Kabongo Mutamba, Banza Kasongo, Roger Hitoto (81 Dandou Selenge), Mbuilua Tondelua, Ekanza Simba, Litimba Botomoyiko (68 Kibembe Mbayo), Esele Bakasu, Epotele Bazamba, Ndama Bapupa. Trainer: Louis Watunda
TOGO: Nidombe Wake, Messan Ametokodo, Massamesso Tchangai, Abalo Yaovi, Ratei Takpara, Lantame Ouadja, Kossi Noutsoudje (64 Djima Oyawole), Bachirou Salou, Franck Dote (82 Abdelkader Coubadja Touré), Komlan Assignon, Cherif Mama-Touré (73 Koukouni Akpalo Gnavor). Trainer: Eberhard Vogel (Germany)
Goals: Mbuilua Tondelua (58 penalty, 72 penalty) / Massamesso Tchangai (89)

09.02.1998

GHANA – TUNISIA 2-0 (1-0)
4 Août Stadium, Ouagadougou
Referee: Ian McLeod (South Africa), Attendance: 12.000
GHANA: Simon Addo, Dan Edusei (89 Patrick Allotey), Samuel Osei Kuffour, Mohamed Gargo, Alex Nyarko, Emmanuel Tetteh (73 Eric Addo), Abedi Pelé, Charles Akonnor, Emmanuel Osei Kuffour, Samuel Johnson, Felix Aboagye. Trainer: Rinus Israel (Netherlands)
TUNISIA: Ali Boumnijel, Sami Trabelsi, Taoufik Hicheri, Ferid Chouchane, Tarek Thabet (71 Khais Godhbane), Zoubier Beya (67 Faouzi Rouissi), Riadh Bouazizi (67 Khaled Badra), Sirajeddine Chihi, Medhi Ben Slimane, Hassan Gabsi, Ziad Tlemcani. Trainer: Henry Kasperczak (Poland)
Goals: Alex Nyarko (12), Mohamed Gargo (89)

12.02.1998

TUNISIA - DR CONGO 2-1 (1-1)
Municipal, Ouagadougou
Referee: Tibebu Kine (Ethiopia), Attendance: 1000

127

TUNISIA: Ali Boumnijel, Khaled Badra, Sami Trabelsi, Ferid Chouchane, Faouzi Rouissi (46 Zied Tlemcani), Zoubier Beya (54 Kais Ghodhbane), Riadh Bouazizi (70 Maher Sediri), Sirajeddine Chihi, Tarek Thabet, Mehdi Ben Slimane, Hassan Gabsi.
DR CONGO: Nikombe Tokala, Okitankoyi Kimoto, Mundaba Kisombe (82 Epotele Bazamba), Kabongo Mutamba, Dandou Selenge, Banza Kasongo, Roger Hitoto (46 Emeka Mamale), Mbuilua Tondelua (69 Keve Bembuana), Ekanza Simba, Kibemba Mbayo, Ndama Bapupa.
Goals: Mehdi Ben Slimane (30), Zied Tlemcani (75) / Okitankoyi Kimoto (35)

12.02.1998

GHANA - TOGO 1-2 (0-1)
4 Août Stadium, Ouagadougou
Referee: Omer Yengo (Congo), Attendance: 3000
TOGO: Nidombe Wake, Yao Senayi (62 Messan Ametokodo), Massamesso Tchangai, Abalo Yaovi, Ratei Takpara, Lantame Ouadja, Kossi Noutsoudje, Bachirou Salou (77 Mohamed Coubabdja Touré), Franck Doté, Komlan Assignon, Cherif Mama-Touré.
GHANA: Simon Addo, Dan Edusei (53 Patrick Allotey), Samuel Osei Kuffour, Mohamed Gargo (26 Eric Addo), Alex Nyarko, Emmanuel Tetteh, Abedi Pelé, Charles Akonnor, Emmanuel Osei Kuffour (70 Peter Ofori-Quaye), Samuel Johnson, Felix Aboagye.
Goals: Franck Doté (26), Abdelkader Coubadja Touré (89) / Samuel Johnson (84 penalty)

16.02.1998

GHANA – DR CONGO 0-1 (0-0)
4 Août Stadium, Ouagadougou
Referee: Kim Young-Joo (South Korea), Attendance: 3000
GHANA: Simon Addo, Samuel Osei Kuffour, Eric Addo, Patrick Allotey, Alex Nyarko, Emmanuel Tetteh (66 Ablade Kumah), Abedi Pelé, Charles Akonnor, Emmanuel Osei Kuffour, Samuel Johnson, Felix Aboagye (46 Peter Ofori-Quaye).
DR CONGO: Nikombe Tokala, Okitankoyi Kimoto, Mundaba Kisombé, Kabongo Mutamba, Dandou Selenge, Banza Kasongo, Mbuilua Tondelua, Ekanza Simba, Epotele Bazamba, Ndama Bapupa (39 Esele Bakasu), Badibanga Ilunga (58 Emeka Mamale).
Goal: Mundaba Kisombé (77)

16.02.1998

TUNISIA - TOGO 3-1 (2-1)
Municipal, Ouagadougou
Referee: Pierre Alain Mougengui (Gabon), Attendance: 800
TOGO: Nidombe Wake, Messan Ametokodo (67 Djima Oyawolé), Massamesso Tchangai, Abalo Yaovi, Ratei Takpara, Abdoulaye Loukoumanou (46 Koukouni Akpalo), Bachirou Salou, Komlan Assignon (84 Rafael Patron Akakpo), Chérif Mama-Touré, Abdelkader Coubadja Touré, Franck Doté.
TUNISIA: Ali Boumnijel, Khaled Badra, Sami Trabelsi, Ferid Chouchane (34 Mohamed Mkacher), Khais Ghodhbane (76 Sofiane Fekih), Bechir Sahbani, Sirajeddine Chihi, Tarek Thabet (17 Taoufik Hicheri), Mehdi Ben Slimane, Zied Tlemcani, Hassan Gabsi.
Goals: Zied Tlemcani (9), Mehdi Ben Slimane (12), Hassan Gabsi (80) / Komlan Assignon (4 penalty)

1.	TUNISIA	3	2	0	1	5	4	6
2.	DR CONGO	3	2	0	1	4	3	6
3.	Ghana	3	1	0	2	3	3	3
4.	Togo	3	1	0	2	4	6	3

GROUP C

08.02.1998

SOUTH AFRICA - ANGOLA 0-0
Omnisport Stadium, Bobo-Dioulasso
Referee: Sidi Bekaye Magassa (Mali), Attendance: 20.000
SOUTH AFRICA: Brian Baloyi, Andrew Rabutla, David Nyathi, Willem Jackson, Mark Fish, Phil Masinga, John Moshoeu, Helman Mkhalele, Benedict McCarthy (9 Brendan Augustine), John Moeti, Lucas Radebe. Trainer: Jomo Sono
ANGOLA: Marito, Bodunha, Helder Vicente, Neto, Paulo Silva, Paulão (73 Luis Miguel), Sousa, Lito, Aurelio, Quinzinho (84 Zito), Miguel Pereira (56 Fabrice Alcebiades Maieco 'Akwá'). Trainer: Miguel Gomes (Portugal)
Sent off: Moeti (88) / Bodunha (88)

08.02.1998

IVORY COAST - NAMIBIA 4-3 (3-0)
Omnisport Stadium, Bobo-Dioulasso
Referee: Karim Dahou (Algeria), Trainer: 20.000
IVORY COAST: Pierre Alain Gouaméné, Ibrahima Diomande, Patrice Zéré, Lassina Diabaté, Cyrille Domoraud, Saliou Lassissi, Tchiressoa Guel, Sob Evariste Dibo (84 Bonaventure Kalou), Donald-Olivier Sie, Ibrahim Bakayoko, Joël Tiéhi (66 Sidi Badra Aliou). Trainer: Robert Nouzaret (France)
NAMIBIA: Fillemon Kanalelo, Bimbo Tjihero, Stanley Goagoseb, Robert Nauseb (46 Sandro de Gouveia), Phillip Gairiseb, Ricardo Mannetti, Mohamed Ouseb, Simon Uutoni, Johannes Hindjou (46 Silvester Goraseb), Gervatius Uri Khob, Eliphas Shivute. Trainer: Rusten Mogane
Goals: Joël Tiéhi (2, 39), Ibrahim Bakayoko (34), Lassina Diabaté (83) / Eliphas Shivute (46, 73), Ricardo Mannetti (70)

11.02.1998

SOUTH AFRICA - IVORY COAST 1-1 (0-1)
Omnisport Stadium, Bobo-Dioulasso
Referee: Charles Masembe (Uganda), Attendance: 10.000
IVORY COAST: Pierre Alain Gouaméné, Patrice Zéré, Didier Angan, Cyrille Domoraud, Saliou Lassissi, Lassina Diabaté, Tchiressoa Guel, Sob Evariste Dibo (46 Ibrahima Diomandé), Donald-Olivier Sié, Joël Tiéhi (76 Ahmed Ouattara), Ibrahim Bakayoko (76 Moussa Traoré).
SOUTH AFRICA: Brian Baloyi, Andrew Rabutla, David Nyathi, Willem Jackson, Mark Fish, Lucas Radebe, John Moshoeu, Helman Mkhalele, Brandan Silent (70 Benedict McCarthy), Brendan Augustine (57 Dumisa Ngobe), Pollen Ndlanya (70 Themba Mnguni).
Goals: Ahmed Ouattara (88) / Helman Mkhlalele (8 penalty)

12.02.1998

ANGOLA - NAMIBIA 3-3 (2-0)
Omnisport Stadium, Bobo-Dioulasso
Referee: Falla Ndoye (Senegal), Attendance: 2000
NAMIBIA: Fillemon Kanalelo, Bimbo Tjihero, Stanley Goagoseb, Robert Nauseb, Phillip Gairiseb, Ricardo Mannetti, Mohamed Ouseb, Simon Uutoni, Johannes Hindjou (46 Sandro de Gouveia), Gervatius Uri Khob (76 Berlin Auchumeb), Eliphas Shivute.
ANGOLA: Marito, Helder Vicente (77 Zito), Neto, Luis Miguel, Aurelio, Paulo Silva, Sousa, Lito, Paulão (46 Miguel Pereira), Fabrice Alcebiades Maieco 'Akwá' (10 Lazaro), Quinzinho.
Goals: Gervatius Uri Khob (20, 51), Robert Nauseb (33) / Lazaro (46), Paulo Silva (67 penalty), Miguel Pereira (86)

16.02.1998

SOUTH AFRICA - NAMIBIA 4-1 (4-0)
Omnisport Stadium, Bobo-Dioulasso
Referee: Karim Dahou (Algeria), Attendance: 9500
SOUTH AFRICA: Simon Gopane, Andrew Rabutla (65 Dumisa Ngobe), David Nyathi, Willem Jackson, Themba Mnguni, Lucas Radebe, John Moshoeu, Helman Mkhalele, Brendan Augustine (84 Quinton Fortune), Phil Masinga (37 Pollen Ndlanya), Benedict McCarthy.
NAMIBIA: Fillemon Kanalelo, Petrus Haraseb, Stanley Goagoseb, Phillip Gairiseb (46 Berlin Auchumeb), Robert Nauseb, Frans Ananias, Mohamed Ouseb, Simon Uutoni, Johannes Hindjou (30 Silvester Goraseb), Gervatius Uri Khob, Eliphas Shivute.
Goals: Benedict McCarthy (9, 11, 19, 21) / Simon Uutoni (68)

16.02.1998

IVORY COAST - ANGOLA 5-2 (3-1)
Stade Municipal, Ouagagoudou
Referee: Engage Camara (Guinea), Attendance: 4000
IVORY COAST: Pierre Alain Gouaméné, Ibrahima Diomande, Lassina Diabaté, Didier Angan, Tchiressoa Guel, Cyrille Domoraud, Koffi Blaise Kouassi (81 Ghislain Akassou), Ibrahim Bakayoko (85 Ahmed Ouattara), Donald-Olivier Sié (83 Sob Evariste Dibo), Saliou Lassissi, Joël Tiéhi.
ANGOLA: Marito, Raúl Barbosa (66 Paulão), Paulo Silva, Aurelio, Neto, Lito, Quinzinho, Zito, Luis Miguel, Lazaro (50 Miguel Pereira), Sousa (66 Assis).
Goals: Tchiressoa Guel (8, 23), Joël Tiéhi (43, 81 penalty), Ibrahim Bakayoko (56) / Paulão Silva (27), Quinzinho (52)

1.	IVORY COAST	3	2	1	0	10	6	7
2.	SOUTH AFRICA	3	1	2	0	5	2	5
3.	Angola	3	0	2	1	5	8	2
4.	Namibia	3	0	1	2	7	11	1

GROUP D

09.02.1998

ZAMBIA - MOROCCO 1-1 (1-0)
Stade Omnisport, Bobo-Dioulasso,
Referee: Abdul Rahman Al-Zeid (Saudi Arabia), Attendance: 10.000
MOROCCO: Abdelkader El-Brazi, Abdelilah Saber, Abdelkrim El-Hadrioui, Noureddine Naybet, Youssef Rossi, Mustapha Hadji, Said Chiba, Rachid Azzouzi, Ahmed Bahja (67 Abderrahim Ouakili), Salheddine Bassir (30 Abdeljalil Hadda), Youssef Chippo. Trainer: Henri Michel (France)
ZAMBIA: Davies Phiri, Harrison Chongo, Elijah Litana, Allan Kamwanga (67 Masauso Tembo), Peter Chitila, Mordon Malitoli (76 Rotson Kilambe), Kenneth Malitoli (46 Tenant Chilumba), Andrew Tembo, Moses Sichone, Kalusha Bwalya, Dennis Lota. Trainer: Burkhard Ziese (Germany).
Goals: Ahmed Bahja (37) / Tenant Chilumba (87)

10.02.1998

EGYPT - MOZAMBIQUE 2-0 (2-0)
Stade Omnisport, Bobo-Dioulasso,
Referee: Engage Camara (Guinea), Attendance: 20.000
EGYPT: Nader El Sayed, Yasser Radwan, Ibrahim Samir Kamouna, Mehdat Abdelhadi, Mohamed Youssef, Ahmed Hassan, Hany Ramzy, Abdelsatar Sabry (55 Tarek Mostafa), Yasser Rayan (71 Abdel Zaher El Saqqa), Hazem Imam (81 Walid Salah), Hossam Hassan. Trainer: Mahmoud El-Gohary
MOZAMBIQUE: Rui Evora, Adino, Tomas, Jojo, Pinto Barros, Paulito, Mario Artur (57 Dario), Jossias (82 Mavo), Avelino, Chiquinho Conde, Manuel José Luís Bucuane 'Tico-Tico' (63 Nuro).
Trainer: Arnaldo Salvado
Goals: Hossam Hassan (14, 43)

13.02.1998

ZAMBIA - EGYPT 0-4 (0-1)
Stade Omnisport, Bobo-Dioulasso,
Referee: Kim Milton Nielsen (Denmark), Attendance: 5000
EGYPT: Nader El-Sayed, Mohamed Omara, Ibrahim Samir Kamouna, Mehdat Abdelhadi (59 Sami El-Sheshini), Yasser Radwan, Mohamed Youssef (48 Abdel Zaher El-Saqqa), Hany Ramzy, Ahmed Hassan, Hazem Imam (80 Nabib Osama), Abdelsatar Sabry, Hossam Hassan.
ZAMBIA: Davies Phiri, Mordon Malitoli, Harrison Chongo, Allan Kamwanga, Moses Sichone, Elijah Litana, Peter Chitila (57 Kenneth Malitoli), Andrew Tembo, Rotson Kilambe (24 Tenant Chilumba), Dennis Lota (56 Masauso Tembo), Kalusha Bwalya.
Goals: Hossam Hassan (34, 57, 71), Yasser Radwan (80)

13.02.1998

MOROCCO - MOZAMBIQUE 3-0 (2-0)
Stade Omnisport, Bobo-Dioulasso,
Referee: Lucien Bouchardeau (Niger), Attendance: 3000
MOROCCO: Abdelkader El-Brazi, Abdelilah Saber (46 Lahcen Abrami), Abdelkrim El-Hadrioui, Noureddine Naybet, Youssef Rossi, Mustapha Hadji (64 Abderrahim Ouakili), Said Chiba, Youssef Chippo, Rachid Azzouzi, Ali El-Khattabi (82 Youssef Fertout), Ahmed Bahja.
MOZAMBIQUE: Luisinho, Adino, Tomás, Jojo, Pinto Barros (75 Jossias), Macamo, Paulito, Avelino, Mavo (46 Manuel José Luís Bucuane 'Tico-Tico'), Nuro, Chiquinho Condé (57 Dario).
Goals: Said Chiba (39), Ali El-Khattabi (40), Youssef Fertout (82)

17.02.1998

ZAMBIA - MOZAMBIQUE 3-1 (2-0)
Stade Omnisport, Bobo-Dioulasso,
Referee: Falla Ndoye (Senegal), Attendance: 3000
ZAMBIA: Collins Mbulo, Hillary Makasa (52 Numba Mumamba), Harrison Chongo, Elijah Litana, Allan Kamwanga, Tenant Chilumba (65 Masauso Tembo), John Lungu, Andrew Tembo, Rotson Kilambe (84 Kenneth Malitoli), Kalusha Bwalya, Dennis Lota. Trainer: George Mungwa
MOZAMBIQUE: Luisinho, Zé Augusto, Tomas, Jojo, Pinto Barros (60 Jossias), Macamo, Paulito (40 Nana), Avelino, Nuro, Manuel José Luís Bucuane 'Tico-Tico', Dario (67 Mavo).
Goals: Rotson Kilambe (16), Kalusha Bwalya (43), Masauso Tembo (73) / Avelino (57)

17.02.1998

MOROCCO - EGYPT 1-0 (0-0)
Municipal, Ouagadougou
Referee: Kim Milton Nielsen (Denmark), Attendance: 500
EGYPT: Nader El Sayed, Abdel Zaher El Saqqa, Mohamed Omara, Hany Ramzy, Sami El Sheshini, Mehdat Abdelhadi, Yasser Radwan, Abdelsatar Sabry (56 Yasser Rayan), Hazem Imam (82 Mohamed Youssef), Tarek Mostafa (59 Nabih Osama), Hossan Hassan.
MOROCCO: Abdelkader El Brazi, Noureddine Naybet, Lahcen Abrami, Abdelkrim El Hadrioui, Said Chiba, Abderrahim Ouakili (67 Youssef Fertout), Mustapha Khalif (80 Abdellatif Jrindou), Taher El Khalej, Youssef Chippo, Moustapha Hadji, Ali El Khattabi (73 Ahmed Bahja).
Sent off: Mehdat Abdelhadi (30)
Goal: Moustapha Hadji (90)

1.	MOROCCO	3	2	1	0	5	1	7
2.	EGYPT	3	2	0	1	6	1	6
3.	Zambia	3	1	1	1	4	6	4
4.	Mozambique	3	0	0	3	1	8	0

Quarter-finals

20.02.1998

CAMEROON – DR CONGO 0-1 (0-1)
Omnisport Stadium, Bobo-Dioulasso
Referee: Abdul Rahman Al-Zeid (Saudi Arabia), Attendance: 5000
DR CONGO: Nkweni Mayala, Okitankoyi Kimoto, Mundaba Kisombe, Mutamba Makenga, Esele Bakasu, Ekanza Simba, Epotele Bazamba (88 Kibemba Mbayo), Umba Kanokene (66 Banza Kasongo), Emeka Mamale, Dandou Selenge, Mbuilua Tondelua (71 Kabongo Mutamba).
CAMEROON: Vincent Ongandzi, Ernest Oben Etchi, Pierre Nlend Wome, Timboe Mimboe, Rigobert Song, Romarin Billong (84 Samuel Ipoua), Lucien Mettomo, Bernard Tchoutang, Augustine Simo (82 Salomon Olembé), Alphonse Tchami (54 Patrick Mboma), Joseph-Désiré Job.
Sent off: Bakasu (67), Kisombe (88)
Goal: Mbuilua Tondelua (30)

21.02.1998

BURKINA FASO - TUNISIA 1-1 (1-0, 1-1), 8-7 on penalties
4 Août Stadium, Ouagadougou
Referee: Lim Kee Chong (Mauritius), Attendance: 35.000
BURKINA FASO: Ibrahim Diarra, Firmin Sanou, Jean-Michel Gnonka Liadé, Ibrahim Tallé, Oumar Barro (54 Magan Diabaté), Alain Nana, Brahima Traoré, Romeo Kambou (64 Ousmane Sanou, 82 Ousmane Coulibaly), Boureima Zongo, Seydou Traoré, Kassoum Ouédraogo.
TUNISIA: Ali Boumnijel, Khaled Badra, Sami Trabelsi, Taoufik Hicheri, Riadh Bouazizi, Khais Ghodhbane, Bechir Sahbani (46 Zoubier Beya), Sirajeddine Chihi, Hassan Gabsi, Mehdi Ben Slimane (62 Riadh Jelassi), Zied Tlemcani (66 Faouzi Rouissi).
Goals: Hassan Gabsi (89) / Kassoum Ouédraogo (44 penalty)
Penalties: 1-0 Seydou Traoré, 1-1 Faouzi Rouissi, 2-1 Firmin Sanou, 2-2 Khaled Badra, 3-2 Alain Nana, 3-3 Riadh Bouazizi, Ibrahim Tallé (save), Sirajeddine Chihi (miss), 4-3 Kassoum Ouédraogo, 4-4 Riadh Jelassi, Boureima Zongo (save), Zoubier Beya (save), 5-4 Brahima Traoré, 5-5 Hassan Gabsi, 6-5 Magan Diabaté, 6-6 Khais Godhbane, 7-6 Jean-Michel Gnonka Liadé, 7-7 Taoufik Hicheri, 8-7 Ousmane Coulibaly, Sami Trabelsi (miss).

21.02.1998

IVORY COAST - EGYPT 0-0 aet, 4-5 on penalties
Municipal, Ouagadougou
Referee: Ian McLeod (South Africa), Attendance: 20.000
IVORY COAST: Pierre Alain Gouaméné, Ibrahima Diomandé, Patrice Zéré, Lassina Diabaté, Didier
Angan (46 Ghislain Akassou), Tchiressoa Guel, Cyrille Domoraud, Ibrahim Bakayoko, Donald-Olivier
Sié, Saliou Lassissi (87 Ibrahima Koné), Joël Tiéhi (73 Ahmed Ouattara).
EGYPT: Nader El-Sayed, Abdel Zaher El-Saqqa, Mohamed Omara (119 Tarek Mostafa), Hany
Ramzy, Ibrahim Samir Kamouna, Yasser Radwan, Ahmed Hassan, Sami El-Sheshini (65 Nabih
Osama), Abdelsatar Sabry (91 Yasser Rayan), Hazem Imam, Hossam Hassan.
Penalties: 1-0 Cyrille Domoraud, 1-1 Hany Ramzy, 2-1 Tchiressoa Guel, 2-2 Yasser Radwan, Ibrahima
Diomandé (save), 2-3 Samir Kamouna, 3-3 Ibrahim Bakayoko, 3-4 Tarek Mostafa, 4-4 Ahmed
Ouattara, 4-5 Hazem Imam.

22.02.1998

MOROCCO - SOUTH AFRICA 1-2 (1-1)
Municipal, Ouagadougou
Referee: Lucien Bouchardeau (Niger), Attendance: 2000
MOROCCO: Abdelkader El-Brazi, Abdelkrim El-Hadrioui, Youssef Rossi (56 Tahar El-Khalej),
Noureddine Naybet, Mustapha Hadji (68 Ahmed Bahja), Said Chiba, Lahcen Abrami, Rachid Azzouzi,
Youssef Chippo, Youssef Fertout, Ali El-Khattabi (80 Abderrahim Ouakili).
SOUTH AFRICA: Brian Baloyi, Andrew Rabutla, David Nyathi, Willem Jackson, Mark Fish, John
Moshoeu (82 Quinton Fortune), Helman Mkhlalele (32 Brandan Silent), Brendan Augustine, Benedict
McCarthy, John Moeti, Lucas Radebe.
Sent off: Andrew Rabutla (89)
Goals: Said Chiba (35) / Benedict McCarthy (21), David Nyathi (73)

Semi-finals

25.02.1998

DR CONGO - SOUTH AFRICA 1-2 (0-0, 1-1)
4 Août Stadium, Ouagadougou
Referee: Charles Masembe (Uganda), Attendance: 4000
DR CONGO: Nkweni Mayala, Okitankoyi Kimoto, Mutamba Makenga (58 Lokenge Mungongo),
Kabongo Mutamba, Roger Hitoto, Dandou Selenge, Ekanza Simba, Epotele Bazamba (91 Kibemba
Mbayo), Emeka Mamale, Mbuilua Tondelua (46 Keve Bembuana), Umba Kanokene.
SOUTH AFRICA: Brian Baloyi, David Nyathi (46 Quinton Fortune), Willem Jackson, Mark Fish,
John Moshoeu, Pollen Ndlanya, Benedict McCarthy, John Moeti, Lucas Radebe (120 Dumisa Ngobe),
Brandan Silent (77 Thabo Mooki), Themba Mnguni.
Goals: Keve Bembuana (48) / Benedict McCarthy (60, 112)

25.02.1998

BURKINA FASO - EGYPT 0-2 (0-1)
Omnisport, Bobo-Dioulasso
Referee: Kim Milton Nielsen (Denmark), Attendance: 40.000
BURKINA FASO: Ibrahim Diarra, Firmin Sanou, Souleymane Doumbia, Abdoulaye Traoré (64 Alassane Ouédraogo, 78 Romeo Kambou), Seydou Traoré, Ismael Koudou (46 Oumar Barro), Boureima Zongo, Ibrahim Tallé, Alain Nana, Magan Diabaté, Kassoum Ouédraogo.
EGYPT: Nader El-Sayed, Mohamed Omara, Hany Ramzy, Samir Kamouna, Mehdat Abdelhadi, Yasser Radwan, Hazem Imam, Ahmed Hassan, Tarek Mostafa, Nabih Osama (70 Yasser Rayan), Hossam Hassan.
Goals: Hossam Hassan (41, 65)

Third Place Match

27.02.1998

BURKINA FASO - DR CONGO 4-4 (1-0, 4-4), 1-4 on penalties
Municipal, Ouagadougou
Referee: Mahmoud El-Gandour (Egypt)
BURKINA FASO: Ibrahim Diarra, Firmin Sanou, Ibrahim Talle, Jean-Michel Gnonka Liadé, Magan Diabaté, Brahima Traoré, Romeo Kambou (57 Seydou Traoré), Oumar Barro, Sidi Napon (61 Ibrahima Korbeogo), Ousmane Sanou, Alassane Ouédraogo. Trainer: Phillip Troussier (France)
DR CONGO: Nkweni Mayala, Okitankoyi Kimoto (66 Lokenge Mungongo), Mundaba Kisombe, Kabongo Mutamba (46 Ndana Bapupa), Esele Bakasu, Dandou Selenge, Ekanza Simba, Emeka Mamale, Banza Kasongo, Mbuilua Tondelua, Keve Bembuana (46 Kibembe Mbayo). Trainer: Louis Watunda Iyolo
Goals: Alassane Ouédraogo (6), Oumar Barro (56), Sidi Napon (56), Ibrahim Talle (86) / Lokenge Mungongo (76, 89), Banza Kasongo (86), Mbuilua Tondelua (88)
Penalties: 0-1 Ekanza Simba, Seydou Traoré (save), 0-2 Emeka Mamale, 1-2 Firmin Sanou, 1-3 Mundaba Kisombe, Magan Diabate (save), 1-4 Dandou Selenge.

Final

28.02.1998

EGYPT - SOUTH AFRICA 2-0 (2-0)
4 Août Stadium, Ouagadougou
Referee: Said Belqola (Morocco), Attendance: 40.000
EGYPT: Nader El Sayed, Abdel Zaher El Saqqa, Mohamed Omara, Samir Kamouna, Mehdat Abdelhadi, Yasser Radwan, Hany Ramzy, Ahmed Hassan, Tarek Mostafa (78 Nabih Osama), Hazem Imam (55 Abdelsatar Sabry), Hossam Hassan. Trainer: Mahmoud El-Gohary
SOUTH AFRICA: Brian Baloyi, Andrew Rabutla, Willem Jackson, Mark Fish, Lucas Radebe, John Moeti, John Moshoeu, Helman Mkhlalele, Brendan Augustine (48 Quinton Fortune), Phil Masinga (81 Pollen Ndlanya), Benedict McCarthy. Trainer: Jomo Sono
Goals: Ahmed Hassan (5), Tarek Mostafa (13)

134

Twenty-second edition – 2000
Qualifying Tournament

Forty-seven teams entered the qualifying competition for the 22nd edition of the Africa Cup of Nations although four teams then withdrew. Zimbabwe were originally scheduled to be hosts in 2000 but were stripped of the competition by the CAF on 8th February 1999. On 15th March 1999, CAF selected Ghana and Nigeria as joint hosts and both teams therefore automatically qualifying for the finals as did holders of the trophy, Egypt. One of the hosts, Nigeria, progressed to the final where they were narrowly beaten by 'The Indomitable Lions' of Cameroon following extra-time and a penalty shoot-out.

Preliminary Round

31.07.1998 Libya - Algeria 1-3 (0-0)
Goals: Abdelhafid Tasfaout (65, 73), Fodil Dob (82)
14.08.1998 Algeria – Libya 3-0 (1-0)
Goals: Lakhdar Adjali (9), Kouider Boukessassa (57), Abdelhafid Tasfaout (65)

02.08.1998 Benin - Angola 2-1 (2-1)
Goals: Oumar Tchomogo (6, 32) / André Chicangada (36)
16.08.1998 Angola - Benin 2-0
Goal: Fabrice Alcebiades Maieco 'Akwá' 2

02.08.1998 Mali - Cape Verde 3-0
Goals: Mamadou Dissa Yaya, Harouna Diarra, Brahima Traoré
16.08.1998 Cape Verde - Mali 0-0

02.08.1998 Chad - Congo 1-1
Goals: Hisseine Abana / Denis Tsoumou
16.08.1998 Congo - Chad 0-0

02.08.1998 Equatorial Guinea - Gabon 0-2 (0-0)
Goals: Stéphane Bounguedza (60), Théodore Zué Nguéma (65)
16.08.1998 Gabon - Equatorial Guinea 3-0

31.07.1998 Djibouti - Kenya 0-3 (0-2)
Goals: Maurice Sunguti (4, 20), Eric Omondi (70)
15.08.1998 Kenya - Djibouti 9-1 (5-1)
Goals: Sammy Okoth (3, 6, 67), Maurice Sunguti (19, 26), Francis Odour (30, 85), Boniface Ambani (75, 83) / Dirieh Hamed (25)

02.08.1998 Niger - Liberia 2-1 (2-0)
Goals: Ide Moukaila (5 penalty), Yataga Soumaila (44) / Mass Sarr (87)
16.08.1998 Liberia - Niger 2-0 (2-0)
Goals: Christopher Wreh (30), Zizi Roberts (45)

02.08.1998 Swaziland - Madagascar 1-2 (1-1)
Goals: Mfanzile Dlamini (28) / Etienne Haja Rasoanaivo (22), Fabrice Mosa (61)
23.08.1998 Madagascar - Swaziland 1-1 (1-0)
Goals: Ruphin Menakely (15) / Siza Dlamini (49)

02.08.1998 Lesotho - Mauritius 1-1 (1-1)
Goals: Lehlohonolo Seema (30 penalty) / Jimmy Cundasamy (3)
23.08.1998 Mauritius - Lesotho 3-1 (1-0)
Goals: Jimmy Cundasamy (34), Christopher Perlé (65), Jean-Marc Ithier (90) / Motheo Mohapi (75)

02.08.1998 Botswana - Mozambique 0-0
15.08.1998 Mozambique - Botswana 2-1
Goals: Dario Monteiro 2 / Itumeleng Duiker

01.08.1998 Namibia - Malawi 2-1 (1-1)
Goals: Bobby Samaria (9), Robert Nauseb (60) / Cedric Nakumwa (22)
15.08.1998 Malawi - Namibia 0-1 (0-1)
Goal: Robert Nauseb (15)

02.08.1998 Burundi - Tanzania 1-0 (0-0)
Goal: Jean-Marie Mbuyi (55)
15.08.1998 Tanzania - Burundi 0-1 (0-0)
Goal: Shabani Daoudi (88)

02.08.1998 Sao Tome e Principe - Togo 0-4 (0-2)
Goals: Kossi Noutsoudje (9 penalty, 19), Jacques Goumani (54) / Libambani Yedibahoma (77)
18.08.1998 Togo - Sao Tome e Principe 2-0 (1-0)
Goals: Kossi Noutsoudje (4), Komi Adjamgba (71)

01.08.1998 Uganda - Rwanda 5-0 (3-0)
Goals: Majid Musisi (1, 43, 47), Phillip Obwinyi (42), Joseph Mutyaba (83)
16.08.1998 Rwanda - Uganda 0-0

Ethiopia withdrew, Eritrea qualified
Gambia withdrew, Senegal qualified
Mauritania withdrew, Sierra Leone qualified

Group 1

04.10.1998 Cameroon - Ghana 1-3 (1-2)
Goals: Salomon Olembé (35) / Charles Akonnor (12), Samuel Johnson (35), Alex Nyarko (89)
04.10.1998 Mozambique - Eritrea 3-1
Goals: / Amanneh Iyassan
23.01.1999 Eritrea - Cameroon 0-0
24.01.1999 Ghana - Mozambique 1-0 (0-0)
Goal: Charles Akonnor (54)
28.02.1999 Cameroon - Mozambique 1-0 (1-0)
Goal: Patrick Mboma (25)
28.02.1999 Ghana - Eritrea 5-0 (2-0)
Goals: Augustine Arhinful (5), Yaw Preko (27, 56, 84), Peter Ofori-Quaye (68)
11.04.1999 Mozambique - Cameroon 1-6 (0-4)
Goals: Manuel José Luis Bucuane 'Tico-Tico' (60) / Joseph-Désiré Job (26, 28), Patrick Mboma (33, 42), Pierre Njanka (74), Patrick Suffo (83)
06.06.1999 Cameroon - Eritrea 1-0 (1-0)
Goal: Rigobert Song (32)
19.06.1999 Eritrea – Mozambique 1-0 (0-0)
Goal: Yohane Fishaye (81)

1.	CAMEROON	4	3	1	0	8	1	10
2.	Eritrea	4	1	1	2	2	4	4
3.	Mozambique	4	1	0	3	4	9	3

Ghana qualified automatically after being selected as co-hosts on 15th March 1999.

Group 2

03.10.1998 Morocco - Sierra Leone 3-0 (2-0)
Goals: Youssef Chippo (22), Salaheddine Bassir (42), Abdeljalil Haddad (82)
04.10.1998 Togo - Guinea 2-0 (1-0)
Goals: Tadjou Salou (5), Lantame Ouadja (58)
24.01.1999 Guinea - Morocco 1-1 (1-0)
Goals: Souleymane Oularé (30) / Mustapha Hadji (46)
28.02.1999 Togo - Morocco 2-3 (1-2)
Goals: Kossi Noutsoudje (32), Jacques Goumai (63) / Abdeljelil Hadda (2, 72), Mustapha Hadji (39)
10.04.1999 Morocco - Togo 1-1 (1-0)
Goals: Youssef Chippo (40) / Djima Oyawole (67)
06.06.1999 Morocco - Guinea 1-0 (0-0)
Goal: Abdeljelil Hadda (60)
20.06.1999 Guinea - Togo 2-1 (0-0)
Goals: Fosé Camara (53, 64) / Abdelkader Coubadja Touré (6)

1.	MOROCCO	4	2	2	0	6	4	8
2.	TOGO	4	1	1	2	6	6	4
3.	Guinea	4	1	1	2	3	5	4

Sierra Leone were disqualified on 22nd March 1999.

Group 3

03.10.1998 Namibia - Congo 0-1 (0-0)
Goal: Brice Mokossi (72)
04.10.1998 Mali - Ivory Coast 0-1 (0-0)
Goal: Brahima Koné (87)
24.01.1999 Ivory Coast - Namibia 3-0
Goals: Modibo Diallo (1, 90), Ibrahim Diomandé (32)
24.01.1999 Congo – Mali 0-0
28.02.1999 Congo – Ivory Coast 1-0 (0-0)
Goal: Maurice Ntounou (10)
11.04.1999 Mali - Namibia 2-1
Goals: Mamadou Dissa / Mohamed Ouseb
11.04.1999 Ivory Coast - Congo 2-0 (2-0)
Goal: Ibrahima Bakayoko (20), Joël Tiéhi (25)
08.05.1999 Namibia - Mali 0-0
05.06.1999 Namibia - Ivory Coast 1-1 (0-0)
Goals: Quinton Jacobs (56) / Hamed Diallo (78)
06.06.1999 Mali - Congo 3-1
Goals: / Roland Buitys (20)
20.06.1999 Ivory Coast - Mali 0-0
20.06.1999 Congo – Namibia 3-0 (1-0)
Goals: Richard Bokatola (24), Roland Buitys (53), Rolf Guié-Mien (87)

1.	IVORY COAST	6	3	2	1	7	2	11
2.	CONGO	6	3	1	2	6	5	10
3.	Mali	6	2	3	1	5	3	9
4.	Namibia	6	0	2	4	2	10	2

Group 4

03.10.1998 South Africa - Angola 1-0 (0-0)
Goal: Shaun Bartlett (86)
04.10.1998 Gabon - Mauritius 2-0 (2-0)
Goals: Dieudonné Londo (17), Jonas Ogandaga (42)
23.01.1999 Mauritius - South Africa 1-1 (0-1)
Goals: Désiré Periatambée (55) / Phil Masinga (44)
24.01.1999 Angola - Gabon 3-1 (1-1)
Goals: Fabrice Alcebiades Maieco 'Akwá' (7, 51, 87) / Jean-Martin Mouloungui (34)
27.02.1999 South Africa - Gabon 4-1 (1-1)
Goals: John Moeti (44), Phil Masinga (50), Shaun Bartlett (57), Benedict McCarthy (80) / Théodore
Nzué Nguéma (27)
28.02.1999 Angola - Mauritius 0-2 (0-1)
Goals: Christopher Perlé (29), Jean-Sébastien Bax (84)
10.04.1999 Gabon - South Africa 1-0 (0-0)
Goal: Dieudoné Londo (90 penalty)
10.04.1999 Mauritius - Angola 1-1 (1-1)
Goals: Christopher Perle (31) / Mateus Agostinho (16)
05.06.1999 South Africa - Mauritius 2-0 (0-0)
Goals: Thabo Mngomeni (56), Benedict McCarthy (77)
06.06.1999 Gabon - Angola 3-1 (2-0)
Goals: Théodore Nzué Nguéma (17, 36), François Amégasse (80) / Valente (81)
20.06.1999 Angola - South Africa 2-2 (0-0)
Goals: Zico (67), Jabaru (69) / Hekman Mkhalele (48), Daniel Mudau (54)
20.06.1999 Mauritius - Gabon 2-2 (1-1)
Goals: Tony François (45), Christopher Perlé (73) / Yves Nzanboutamba (37), Théodore Nzué Nguéma
(69)

1.	SOUTH AFRICA	6	3	2	1	10	5	11
2.	GABON	6	3	1	2	10	10	10
3.	Mauritius	6	1	3	2	6	8	6
4.	Angola	6	1	2	3	7	10	5

Group 5

04.10.1998 Burkina Faso - Nigeria 0-0
13.12.1998 Burundi - Senegal 1-0 (1-0)
Goal: Sutche Wembo (18)
23.01.1999 Nigeria - Burundi 2-0 (1-0)
Goal: George Lawal (38), Finidi George (70)
23.01.1999 Senegal - Burkina Faso 1-1 (1-0)
Goals: Salif Keita (31) / Alain Nana (54)
28.02.1999 Senegal - Nigeria 1-1 (0-0)
Goals: Salif Keita (69) / Jonathan Akpoborie (75)
28.02.1999 Burundi – Burkina Faso 1-2 (1-1)
Goals: Debo Kitenge (24 penalty) / Mamadou Zongo (40), Romeo Kambou (56)
11.04.1999 Burkina Faso - Burundi 3-1 (3-1)
Goals: Boureima Zongo (4, 19), Mamadou Zongo (10 penalty) / Juma Mossi (29)
06.06.1999 Burkina Faso - Senegal 2-2 (1-1)
Goals: Kassoum Ouédraogo (22), Mamadou Koné (81) / Henri Camara (20), Pape Malick Diop (59)
19.06.1999 Senegal - Burundi 1-0 (1-0)
Goal: Salif Keita (10)

1.	BURKINA FASO	4	2	2	0	8	5	8
2.	Senegal	4	1	2	1	4	4	5
3.	Burundi	4	1	0	3	3	6	3

Nigeria qualified automatically after being selected as co-hosts on 15th March 1999.

Group 6

03.10.1998 Kenya - Madagascar 1-1 (1-0)
Goals: Musa Otieno (11 penalty) / Ruphin Menakely (64)
04.10.1998 Zambia - Congo 1-1 (0-1)
Goals: Kilambe Rotson (46) / Simba Ekanzi (44)
24.01.1999 Madagascar - Zambia 1-2 (0-0)
Goals: Etienne Rado Rasonaivo (65) / Harry Milanzi (85), Rotson Kilembe (87)
24.01.1999 DR Congo - Kenya 2-1 (1-0)
Goals: Kampami Wa Kanyengele (15, 73) / Michael Otoch (66)
28.02.1999 Kenya - Zambia 0-1 (0-1)
Goal: Dennis Lota (9)
28.02.1999 Madagascar - DR Congo 3-1 (1-0)
Goals: Ruphin Menakely (42), Etienne Fidi Rasonaivo (64), Etienne Rado Rasoanaivo (74) / Essele Bakasu (81)
10.04.1999 Zambia - Kenya 1-0 (1-0)
Goal: Rotson Kilambe (4)
11.04.1999 DR Congo - Madagascar 2-0 (1-0)
Goals: Kimoto Okidankoyi (7), Lokose Epangala (46)
05.06.1999 Zambia - Madagascar 3-0 (2-0)
Goals: Cosmos Banda (2, 23), Dennis Lota (77)
06.06.1999 Kenya – DR Congo 0-1 (0-1)
Goal: Ezekiel Akwana (26 own goal)
20.06.1999 DR Congo - Zambia 0-1 (0-0)
Goal: Andrew Sinkala (47 penalty)
20.06.1999 Madagascar - Kenya 1-1 (1-1)
Goals: / Mark Serengo (25)

1.	ZAMBIA	6	5	1	0	9	2	16
2.	DR CONGO	6	3	1	2	7	6	10
3.	Madagascar	6	1	2	3	6	10	5
4.	Kenya	6	0	2	4	3	7	2

Group 7

02.10.1998 Uganda - Algeria 2-1 (0-0)
Goals: Hassan Mubiru (75, 90) / Billal Dziri (71)
04.10.1998 Tunisia - Liberia 2-1 (1-1)
Goals: Adel Sellimi (41 penalty, 89) /, Kelvin Sebwe (32)
22.01.1999 Algeria - Tunisia 0-1 (0-1)
Goal: Faouzi Rouissi (44)
24.01.1999 Liberia - Uganda 2-0 (2-0)
Goals: Zizi Roberts (20), George Jebrow (38)
28.02.1999 Tunisia - Uganda 6-0 (2-0)
Goals: Maher Kanzari (16), Radhi Jaïdi (33), Mounir Boukadida (57), Adel Sellimi (61 penalty), Faouzi Roussi (83), Hassan Gabsi (85)
28.02.1999 Liberia - Algeria 1-1
Goals: Zizi Roberts / Rafik Saifi (69)

139

09.04.1999 Algeria - Liberia 4-1 (2-0)
Goals: Hamid Merrakchi (40, 44), Rafik Saïfi (60), Yarmah Kpoto (87 own goal) / Victor Konwlo (61)
10.04.1999 Uganda - Tunisia 0-2 (0-2)
Goals: Hassan Gabsi (18), Faouzi Rouissi (40)
05.06.1999 Uganda - Liberia 1-0 (0-0)
Goal: Phillip Ssozi (84)
06.06.1999 Tunisia - Algeria 2-0 (0-0)
Goals: Imed Mhadhebi (55), Tarek Thabet (90)
20.06.1999 Algeria - Uganda 2-0 (1-0)
Goals: Hamid Merakchi (45, 56)
20.06.1999 Liberia - Tunisia 2-0 (0-0)
Goals: Oliver Makor (50 penalty), George Weah (85)

1.	TUNISIA	6	5	0	1	13	3	15
2.	ALGERIA	6	2	1	3	8	7	7
3.	Liberia	6	2	1	3	7	8	7
4.	Uganda	6	2	0	4	3	13	6

Play-off Group

The runners-up of groups 1 and 5 joined Zimbabwe in a play-off for a place in the final tournament.

04.07.1999 Eritrea - Zimbabwe 0-1 (0-1)
Goal: Adam Ndlovu (25)
18.07.1999 Senegal - Eritrea 6-2 (4-0)
Goals: Papé Daouda Sene (2), Salif Keita (21, 52), Omar Traoré (30, 40), Moussa Ndiaye (60) / Fassil
Abraha (58), Tshesalan (68)
30.07.1999 Zimbabwe - Senegal 2-1 (1-0)
Goals: Peter Ndlovu (8), Agent Sawu (55) / Omar Traoré (77)
08.08.1999 Senegal - Zimbabwe 2-0 (1-0)
Goals: Moussa Ndiaye (15), Ousmane Diop (86)
15.08.1999 Zimbabwe - Eritrea 4-0 (0-0)
Goals: Adam Ndlovu (61), Agent Sawu (69, 75, 90)
21.08.1999 Eritrea - Senegal 0-2 (0-0)
Goals: Henri Camara (55), Mama Touré (90)

1.	SENEGAL	4	3	0	1	11	4	9
2.	Zimbabwe	4	3	0	1	7	3	9
3.	Eritrea	4	0	0	4	2	13	0

Final Tournament (Ghana and Nigeria)

GROUP 1

22.01.2000

GHANA - CAMEROON 1-1 (0-1)
Accra Sports Stadium, Accra
Referee: Mohammed Ali Bujsaim (United Arab Emirates), Attendance: 45000
GHANA: Richard Kingson, Samuel Osei Kuffour, Stephen Baidoo, Mohammed Gargo (55 Mark Edusei), Alex Nyarko, Augustine Ahinful (31 Peter Ofori-Quate), Charles Akonnor, Christian Gyan, Samuel Johnson, Kwame Ayew, Otto Addo (67 Stephen Appiah). Trainer: Giuseppe Dossena (Italy)
CAMEROON: Boukar Alioum, Lauren Etame-Mayer, Rigobert Song, Raymond Kalla, Pierre Wome, Pierre Njanka, Geremi Fotso Njitap, Marc-Vivien Foé, Salomon Olembé (81 Lucien Mettomo), Joseph-Désiré Job (64 Pius N'Diefi), Patrick Mboma (80 Samuel Eto'o). Trainer: Lechantre (France)
Goals: Kwame Ayew (56) / Marc-Vivien Foé (19)

24.01.2000

IVORY COAST - TOGO 1-1 (1-0)
Accra Sports Stadium, Accra
Referee: Tessema Hailemalak (Ethiopia), Attendance: 13.000
IVORY COAST: Pierre Alain Gouaméné, Patrice Zere, Lassina Diabaté, Serge Die, Ibrahima Koné, Didier Angan, Bonaventure Kalou (84 Charles Dago), Cyrille Domoraud, Ibrahima Bakayoko (76 Hamed Modibo Diallo), Tchiressoa Guel, Donald-Olivier Sie (73 Aliou Siby Badra). Trainer: Martin Gbonke Tia
TOGO: Kossi Agassa, Messan Amétokodo (46 Franck Atsou), Massamesso Tchangai, Yaovi Abalo, Yao Senaya, Yao Aziawonou (36 Komlan Assignon), Tadjou Salou, Lantame Ouadja, Chérif Maman-Touré, Abdelkader Coubadja Touré, Koffi Fiawoo (46 Djima Oyawolé). Trainer: Gottlieb Goller (Germany)
Goals: Tchiresso Guel (38 penalty) / Lantame Ouadja (62)

27.01.2000

GHANA - TOGO 2-0 (2-0)
Accra Sports Stadium, Accra
Referee: Abderahim El Arjoune (Morocco), Attendance: 30.000
GHANA: Richard Kingson, Eben Dugbarthey, Samuel Osei Kuffour, Samuel Johnson, Mark Edusei, Otto Addo (85 Daniel Addo), Alex Nyarko, Christian Gyan (81 Stephen Baidoo), Charles Akonnor, Kwame Ayew, Yaw Preko (67 Emmanuel Osei Kuffour).
TOGO: Kossi Agassa, Massamesso Tchangai, Tadjou Salou, Yaovi Abalo, Yao Senaya, Komlan Assignon, Franck Atsou (84 Franck Doté), Lantame Ouadja, Chérif Mamam-Touré (71 Rafael Patron Akakpo), Abdelkader Coubadja Touré, Koffi Fiawoo (48 Djima Oyawolé). Trainer: Kodjovi Mawuena
Sent off: Dugbarthey (66)
Goals: Kwame Ayew (28), Otto Addo (37)

28.01.2000

CAMEROON - IVORY COAST 3-0 (2-0)

Accra Sports Stadium, Accra
Referee: Mourad Daami (Tunisia), Attendance: 5000
CAMEROON: Boukar Alioum, Pierre Njanka, Raymond Kalla, Rigobert Song, Pierre Wome, Geremi Fotso Njitap (65 Joseph Ndo), Lauren Etame-Mayer, Marc-Vivien Foé, Salomon Olembé (59 Innocent Hamga), Samuel Eto'o (46 Pius N'Diefi), Patrick Mboma.
IVORY COAST: Pierre Alain Gouaméné, Olivier Tebily, Cyrille Domoraud, Dominique Sam Aboun, Lassina Dao (46 Ibrahima Koné), Lassina Diabaté (73 Serge Die), Aliou Siby Badra, Tchiressoa Guel, Donald-Olivier Sie, Charles Dago (62 Bonaventure Kalou), Ibrahima Bakayoko.
Goals: Raymond Kalla (29), Samuel Eto'o (44), Patrick Mboma (89)

31.01.2000

GHANA - IVORY COAST 0-2 (0-1)

Accra Sports Stadium, Accra
Referee: Gamal El-Ghandour (Egypt), Attendance: 40.000
GHANA: Richard Kingson, Samuel Osei Kuffour, Samuel Johnson, Stephen Baidoo, Emmanuel Osei Kuffour (61 Mohammed Gargo), Mark Edusei, Otto Addo (78 Yaw Preko), Alex Nyarko, Charles Akonnor, Kwame Ayew, Augustine Ahinful (60 Peter Ofori-Quaye).
IVORY COAST: Pierre Alain Gouaméné, Olivier Tebily, Ghislain Akassou, Dominique Sam Abouo, Ibrahima Koné (90 Blaise Kouassi Koffi), Serge Die, Aliou Siby Badra, Tchiressoa Guel, Bonaventure Kalou, Hamed Modibo Diallo (72 Ibrahima Bakayoko), Zéphirin Zoko (67 Donald-Olivier Sie).
Goals: Bonaventure Kalou (44), Donald-Olivier Sie (84)

31.01.2000

CAMEROON - TOGO 0-1 (0-1)

Kumasi Sports Stadium, Kumasi
Referee: Olaniyan Olufunmi (Nigeria), Attendance: 2000
CAMEROON: Boukar Alioum, Rigobert Song, Lucien Mettomo, Pierre Njanka, Innocent Hamga (62 Salomon Olembé), Geremi Fotso Njitap, Lauren Etame-Mayer, Marc-Vivien Foé, Patrick Mboma, Marcel Mahouvre, Joseph-Désiré Job (46 Bernard Tchoutang).
TOGO: Kossi Agassa, Yao Senaya, Massamesso Tchangai, Yaovi Abalo, Yao Aziawonou, Komlan Assignon, Tadjou Salou, Lantame Ouadja, Djima Oyawolé, Chérif Maman-Touré (80 Rafael Patron Akakpo), Abdelkader Coubadja Touré.
Goal: Massamesso Tchangai (19)

1.	CAMEROON	3	1	1	1	4	2	4
2.	GHANA	3	1	1	1	3	3	4
3.	Ivory Coast	3	1	1	1	3	4	4
4.	Togo	3	1	1	1	2	3	4

GROUP 2

23.01.2000

SOUTH AFRICA - GABON 3-1 (1-1)

Kumasi Sports Stadium, Kumasi
Referee: Gamal El-Ghandour (Egypt), Attendance: 35.000
GABON: Jacques Deckousshoud, Guy-Roger Nzeng, Dieudonne Mouyouma, François Amégasse, Eric Endo, Jonas Ogandaga, Chiva Star Nzighou, Bruno Mbanangoye Zita, Dieudonné Londo (61 René Nsi-Akué), Théodore Nzué-Nguéma, Daniel Cousin. Trainer: Antonio Dumas (Brazil)

142

SOUTH AFRICA: Andre Arendse, Lucas Radebe, Mark Fish, Pierre Issa, Quinton Fortune (74 Steve Lekoelea), John Moshoeu, Helman Mkhalele, Dumisa Ngobe, Erick Tinkler, Shaun Bartlett, Siyabonga Nomvete (79 Pollen Ndlanya). Trainer: Trott Moloto
Goals: Dumisa Ngobe (42), Shaun Barlett (54, 77) / Chiva Star Nzigou (20)

24.01.2000

ALGERIA – DR CONGO 0-0
Kumasi Sports Stadium, Kumasi
Referee: Monteiro Duarte (Ivory Coast), Attendance: 7000
ALGERIA: Abdesslam Benabdellah, Maamar Mamouni (79 Yacine Slatni), Rezki Amrouche, Mahieddine Meftah, Abdelaziz Benhamlat, Rafik Saïfi (70 Abdelhafid Tasfaout), Nasreddine Kraouche, Billal Dziri, Moussa Saïb, Farid Ghazi, Faouzi Moussouni (63 Brahim Mezouar). Trainer: Nasser Sandjak (France)
DR CONGO: Mkueni Mayala, Kabwe Kasongo, Kitutele Yuvuladio, Esele Bakasu, Ndjeka Mukando, Emeka Mamale (88 Apataki Kifu), Missilou Mangituka, Michel Dinzey, Makaya Nsilulu (63 Ndompetelo Mbabu), Jean-Banza Kasongo, Felix Michel Ngonge. Trainer: Basilua Lusadusu

27.01.2000

SOUTH AFRICA - DR CONGO 1-0 (1-0)
Kumasi Sports Stadium, Kumasi
Referee: Olaniyan Olufumi (Niger), Attendance: 3500
DR CONGO: Mkueni Mayala, Kabwe Kasongo, Kitutele Yuvuladio, Esele Bakasu, Ndjenka Mukando, Mubama Kibwey (53 Ngidi Yemwewi), Missilou Mangituka (67 Dikilu Bageta), Michel Dinzey, Makaya Nsilulu (63 Ndompetelo Nbabu), Jean-Banza Kasongo, Felix Michel Ngonge.
SOUTH AFRICA: Andre Arendse, Lucas Radebe, Mark Fish, Pierre Issa, Quinton Fortune, John Moshoeu (10 Alex Bapela), Helman Mkhalele, Dumisa Ngobe, Eric Tinkler, Shaun Bartlett (86 Pollen Ndlanya), Siyabonga Nomvete.
Goal: Shaun Bartlett (44)

29.01.2000

GABON - ALGERIA 1-3 (0-2)
Kumasi Sports Stadium, Kumasi
Referee: Isaack Omar Abdulkadir (Tanzania), Attendance: 5000
GABON: Germain Mendome, Jean-Martin Mouloungui (46 Bruno Mbanangoye Zita), Guy-Roger Nzeng, Theirry-Dieudonné Mouyouma, François Amégasse, Eric Endo, Jonas Ogandaga, Chiva Nzighou (32 René Nsi-Akué), Chantry Muie Nguéma, Daniel Cousin (68 Henri Antchouet), Théodore Nzué-Nguéma.
ALGERIA: Abdesslam Benabdellah, Maamar Mamouni, Abdelaziz Benhamlat, Rezki Amrouche, Mahieddine Meftah, Nasreddine Kraouche (65 Moulay Haddou), Billal Dziri, Farid Ghazi (77 Rafik Saïfi), Moussa Saïb, Abdelhafid Tasfaout, Faouzi Moussouni (66 Brahim Mezouar).
Sent off: Endo (26)
Goals: Bruno Mbanangoye Zita (89) / Farid Ghazi (12), Abdelhafid Tasfaout (41), Billel Dziri (90)

02.02.2000

SOUTH AFRICA - ALGERIA 1-1 (1-0)
Kumasi Sports Stadium, Kumasi
Referee: Tessema Hailemalik (Ethiopia), Attendance: 2000
ALGERIA: Abdesslam Benabdellah, Maamar Mamouni, Rezki Amrouche, Mahieddine Meftah, Abdelaziz Benhamlat, Abdelhafid Tasfaout, Nasreddine Kraouche, Billal Dziri, Moussa Saïb, Farid Ghazi, Faouzi Moussouni (57 Moulay Haddou).

SOUTH AFRICA: Hans Vonk, Lucas Radebe, Mark Fish, Pierre Issa, Eric Tinkler (60 Papi Khomane), Dumisa Ngobe, Helman Mkhalele, Thabo Mngomeni (46 Alex Bapela), Quinton Fortune (46 Steve Lekoelea), Shaun Bartlett, Glen Salmon.
Goals: Shaun Bartlett (2) / Faouzi Moussouni (52)

02.02.2000

GABON - DR CONGO 0-0
Accra Sports Stadium, Accra
Referee: El Arjoune (Morocco), Attendance: 2000
GABON: Germain Mendome, Thierry-Dieudonné Mouyouma, Chantry Muie Nguéma, René Nsi-Akué, Cédric Moubamba, Tristan Mombo, Jonas Ogandaga (67 Armanel Ossey), Chiva Nzighou, Bruno Mbanangoye Zita, Dieudonné Londo (77 Daniel Cousin), Théodore Nzué-Nguéma.
DR CONGO: Mkueni Mayala, Kabwe Kasongo, Kitutele Yuvuladio (82 Dikilu Bageta), Esele Bakasu, Michel Dinzey, Ndjeka Mukando, Missilou Mangituka, Epotele Bazamba, Apataki Kifu, Ngidi Yemwewi (72 Makaya Nsilulu), Jean-Banza Kasongo (59 Mputu Mbungu).
Sent off: Kabwe Kasongo (64)

1.	SOUTH AFRICA	3	2	1	0	5	2	7
2.	ALGERIA	3	1	2	0	4	2	5
3.	DR Congo	3	0	2	1	0	1	2
4.	Gabon	3	0	1	2	2	6	1

GROUP 3

23.01.2000

EGYPT - ZAMBIA 2-0 (1-0)
Stade Sani Abacha, Kano
Referee: Bonaventure Coffi Codja (Benin), Attendance: 18.000
EGYPT: Nader El-Sayed, Ibrahim Hassan, Mohamed Omara, Hady Khashaba, Abdezaher El-Saqqa, Yasser Radwan (79 Ahmed Hassan), Tarek El-Said, Ibrahim Said, Ayman Abdelaziz, Hossam Hassan, Ahmed Salah Hosni (87 Abdelhalim Ali). Trainer: Gerard Gili (France)
ZAMBIA: Davies Phiri, Laughter Chilembi, Elijah Litana, Moses Sichone, Elijah Tana, Mannaseh Mwanza, Dennis Lota, Kalusha Bwalya, Andrew Tembo, Andrew Sinkala, Mwape Miti. Trainer: Ben Bamfuchile
Goals: Yasser Radwan (36), Hossam Hassan (49)

25.01.2000

BURKINA FASO - SENEGAL 1-3 (0-2)
Stade Sani Abacha, Kano
Referee: Abdel Hakin Shelmani (Libya), Attendance: 12.000
BURKINA FASO: Abdoulaye Soulama Traoré, Brahima Cissé, Issa Sanogo, Brahima Korbeogo, Ismael Koudou (78 Moumouni Dagano), Mamadou Zongo, Ousmane Sanou, Jean-Michel Gnonka Liadé (52 Ousmane Traoré), Rahim Ouédraogo (60 Oumar Barro), Mahamadou Kéré, Seydou Traoré. Trainer: René Taelman (Belgium)
SENEGAL: Oumar Diallo, Omar Daf, Pape Malick Diop, Henri Camara, Mbaye Badji, Assane Ndiaye, Khalilou Fadiga (62 Salif Keita), Ousmane Diop (71 Pape Niokhor Fall), Cheikh Sidy Ba, Pape Sarr (74 Moussa Ndiaye), Fary Faye. Trainer: Peter Schnittger (Germany)
Goals: Ousmane Sanou (65) / Henri Camara (3), Papa Sarr (44), Salif Keita (85)

144

28.01.2000

EGYPT - SENEGAL 1-0 (1-0)
Stade Sani Abacha, Kano
Referee: Petros Mathabela (South Africa), Attendance: 30.000
EGYPT: Nader El-Sayed, Ibrahim Hassan, Mohamed Omara, Abdel Zaher El-Saqqa, Yasser Radwan, Hossam Hassan, Tarek Al-Said (71 Hany Ramzi), Ibrahim Said, Ahmed Salah Hosni (26 Mohamed Farouk, 85 Hazem Emam), Hady Khashaba, Ayman Abdelaziz.
SENEGAL: Oumar Diallo, Omar Daf, Pape Malick Diop, Henri Camara, Assane Ndiaye, Khalilou Fadiga, Ousmane Diop (78 Moussa Ndiaye), Pape Niokhor Fall, Cheikh Sidy Ba, Pape Sarr (72 Oumar Traoré), Fary Faye (63 Salif Keita).
Goal: Hossam Hassan (39)

29.01.2000

ZAMBIA - BURKINA FASO 1-1 (1-0)
Stade Sani Abacha, Kano
Referee: Abdel Hakin Shelmani (Libya), Attendance: 5000
ZAMBIA: Davies Phiri, Laughter Chilembi, Elijah Litana, Moses Sichone, Elijah Tana, Mannaseh Mwanza, Dennis Lota (71 Mumamba Numba), Kalusha Bwalya, Andrew Tembo, Andrew Sinkala, Bernard Makufi (88 Perry Mutapa).
BURKINA FASO: Abdoulaye Traoré Soulama, Issa Sanogo, Madou Dossama, Brahima Korbeogo, Ismael Koudou, Mamadou Zongo, Ousmane Sanou (73 Oumar Barro), Jean-Michel Gnonka Liadé (28 Brahima Traoré), Ousmane Traoré, Amadou Tidiane Fall, Mahamadou Kéré (46 Alassane Ouédraogo).
Sent off: Litana (75)
Goal: Dennis Lota (16) / Alassane Ouédraogo (90)

01.02.2000

EGYPT - BURKINA FASO 4-2 (1-2)
Stade Sani Abacha, Kano
Referee: Pierre Alain Mounguegui (Gabon), Attendance: 17.000
EGYPT: Nader El-Sayed, Mohamed Omara, Hany Ramzy, Hossam Hassan, Abdel Sattar Sabry (46 Sayed Abdel Hafiz), Hossam Abdel Monem, Hazem Emam, Ibrahim Said, Ahmed Hassan (80 Tarek El-Said), Ahmed Salah Hosni (60 Abdel Halim Ali), Hady Khashaba.
BURKINA FASO: Abdoulaye Traoré Soulama, Issa Sanogo, Madou Dossama, Brahima Korbeogo, Ismael Koudou (74 Seydou Traoré), Mamadou Koné (59 Amadou Tidiane Fall), Mamadou Zongo, Ousmane Sanou (72 Alassane Ouédraogo), Brahima Traoré, Ousmane Traoré, Mahamadou Kéré.
Goals: Ahmed Salah Hosni (29), Hossam Hassan (73 penalty), Hany Ramzi (84), Abdel Halim Ali (88) / Ismael Koudou (9), Ousmane Sanou (23)

01.02.2000

SENEGAL – ZAMBIA 2-2 (0-0)
National Stadium, Lagos
Referee: Alex Quartey (Ghana), Attendance: 2000
SENEGAL: Oumar Diallo, Omar Traoré, Pape Malick Diop, Henri Camara, Assane Ndiaye, Khalilou Fadiga (70 Mame Ibra Touré), Salif Keita (57 Abdoulaye Mbaye), Ousmane Diop, Pape Niokhor Fall, Cheikh Sidy Ba, Pape Sarr (46 Mbaye Badji).
ZAMBIA: Emmanuel Misichilli, Laughter Chilembi, Moses Sichone, Elijah Tana, Mannaseh Mwanza, Dennis Lota (69 Mwape Miti), Kalusha Bwalya, Andrew Tembo (70 Rotson Kilambe), Andrew Sinkala, Jones Mwewa, Bernard Makufi (63 Mumamba Numba).
Coaches: Senegal: Peter Schnittger (Germany)
Goals: Henri Camara (47), Abdoulaye Mbaye (80) / Laughter Chilembi (52), Kalusha Bwalya (87 penalty)

1.	EGYPT	3	3	0	0	7	2	9
2.	SENEGAL	3	1	1	1	5	4	4
3.	Zambia	3	0	2	1	3	5	2
4.	Burkina Faso	3	0	1	2	4	8	1

GROUP 4

23.01.2000

NIGERIA - TUNISIA 4-2 (1-0)
National Stadium, Lagos
Referee: Alain Sars (France), Attendance: 80.000
NIGERIA: Ike Shorunmu, Gbenga Okunowo, Celestine Babayaro, Nwankwo Kanu, Furo Iyenemi, Taribo West, Finidi George (50 Benedict Akwuegbu), Austin Okocha, Garba Lawal (65 Tijani Babangida), Sunday Oliseh, Victor Ikpeba (87 Emmanuel Amunike). Trainer: Jo Bonfrere (Netherlands)
TUNISIA: Chokri El Ouaer, Khaled Badra (60 Bechir Mogaadi), Sami Trabelsi, Mounir Boukadida (46 Walid Azaiez), Zoubier Beya, Khais Ghodbane, Adel Sellimi, Sirajeddine Chihi, Radhi Jaidi, Tarek Thabet, Ziad Jaziri (46 Imed Mehdhebi). Trainer: Francesco Scoglio (Italy)
Goals: Austin Okocha (27, 62), Victor Ikpeba (68, 74) / Adel Sellimi (49), Zoubeir Beya (90)

25.01.2000

MOROCCO - CONGO 1-0 (0-0)
National Stadium, Lagos
Referee: Alex Quartey (Ghana), Attendance: 8000
MOROCCO: Khalid Fouhami, Abdelilah Saber, Rachid Neqrouz, Noureddine Naybet, Tahar El Khalej (76 Rachid Benmahmoud), Youssef Mariana, Mustapha Hadji, Said Chiba, Abdeljilil Hadda (83 Salaheddine Bassir), Ahmed Bahja (76 Adil Ramzi), Youssef Chippo. Trainer: Henri Michel (France)
CONGO: Brice Samba, Luc-Arsene Diamesso, Camille Oponga, Toussaint Service, Jules Tchimbakala, Jean-Sylvestre Nkeoua, Bedel Moyimbouabeka, Rock Embingou (77 Richard Bokatola-Lossombo), Rolf-Christel Guie-Mien, Oscar Ewolo, Macchambes Younga-Mouhani (84 Modeste Eta). Trainer: David Memy
Goal: Salaheddine Bassir (85)

28.01.2000

NIGERIA - CONGO 0-0
National Stadium, Lagos
Referee: Felix Tangawarima (Zimbabwe), Attendance: 60.000
NIGERIA: Ike Shorunmu, Gbenga Okunowo, Celstine Babayaro, Nwankwo Kanu, Furo Iyenemi, Taribo West, Finidi George, Austin Okocha, Garba Lawal (56 Tijani Babangida), Sunday Oliseh, Victor Ikpeba (61 Benedict Akwuegbu).
CONGO: Brice Samba, Luc-Arsene Diamesso, Camille Oponga, Toussaint Service, Jules Tchimbakala, Jean-Sylvestre Nkeoua, Bedel Moyimbouabeka, Richard Bokatola-Lossombo (82 Eock Embingou), Rolf-Christel Guie-Mien (35 Francis Mackaya), Oscar Ewolo, Macchambes Younga-Mouhani.

29.01.2000

TUNISIA - MOROCCO 0-0
National Stadium, Lagos
Referee: Ndoye Falla (Senegal), Attendance: 5000
MOROCCO: Khalid Fouhami, Abdelilah Saber, Abdelkrim El Hadrioui, Noureddine Naybet, Tahar El Khalej, Mustapha Hadji (88 Hassan Kachloul), Said Chiba, Adil Ramzi (67 Salaheddine Bassir), Youssef Chippo (11 Rachid Benmahmoud), Abdeljilil Hadda, Jamal Sellimi.
TUNISIA: Chokri El Ouaer, Khaled Badra, Sami Trabelsi, Zoubeir Beya, Adel Sellimi, Sirajeddine Chihi, Radhi Jaidi, Tarek Thabet (72 Maher Kanzari), Hassan Gabsi, Ziad Jaziri (80 Ali Zitouni), Walid Azaier (81 Mounir Boukadida).

03.02.2000

NIGERIA - MOROCCO 2-0 (1-0)
National Stadium, Lagos
Referee: Mohamed Ali Bujsaim (United Arab Emirates), Attendance: 40.000
NIGERIA: Ike Shorunmu, Celstine Babayaro, Nwankwo Kanu, Furo Iyenemi (46 Gbenga Okunowo), Taribo West, Finidi George, Mutiu Adepoju (77 Garba Lawal), Austin Okocha, Tijani Babangida, Benedict Akwuegbu (46 Julius Aghahowa), Godwin Okpara.
MOROCCO: Khalid Fouhami, Abdelilah Saber, Rachid Neqrouz, Moustapha Hadji, Said Chiba, Ahmed Bahja (70 Adil Ramzi), Salaheddine Bassir (46 Mohamed El Badraoui), Lahcen Abrami, Youssef Mariana, Jamal Sellimi, Tahar El Khalej (77 Rachid Benmahmoud).
Goals: Finidi George (29), Julius Aghahowa (82)

03.02.2000

TUNISIA – CONGO 1-0 (1-0)
Stade Sani Abacha, Kano
Referee: Bonaventure Coffi Codja (Benin), Attendance: 12.000
CONGO: Brice Samba, Luc-Arsene Diamesso, Jean-Sylvestre Nkeoua, Camille Oponga, Bedel Moyimboubeka (76 Murice Ntounou), Richard Bokatola-Lossombo (73 Modeste Eta), Oscar Ewolo, Maurice Ntounou, Toussaint Service, Georges Ngoma Nanitelamio, Jules Tchimbakala.
TUNISIA: Chokri El Ouaer, Khaled Badra, Sami Trabelsi, Ali Zitouni, Adel Sellimi (64 Ziad Jaziri), Raouf Bouazaine (77 Imed Mehdhebi), Sirajeddine Chihi, Radhi Jaidi, Tarek Thabet, Maher Kanzari (81 Zoubier Beya), Hassan Gabsi.
Goal: Rahdi Jaidi (17)

1.	NIGERIA	3	2	1	0	6	2	7
2.	TUNISIA	3	1	1	1	3	4	4
3.	Morocco	3	1	1	1	1	2	4
4.	Congo	3	0	1	2	0	2	1

Quarter-finals

06.02.2000

CAMEROON - ALGERIA 2-1 (2-0)
Accra Sports Stadium, Accra
Referee: Ndoye Falla (Senegal), Attendance: 15,000
CAMEROON: Boukar Alioum, Rigobert Song, Raymond Kalla, Pierre Njanka, Marc-Vivien Foé, Geremi Fotso Njitap, Lauren Etame-Mayer, Salomon Olembé, Bernard Tchoutang (72 Joseph Ndo), Patrick Mboma (61 Pius N'Diefi), Samuel Eto'o (46 Joseph-Désiré Job).
ALGERIA: Abdesslam Benabdellah, Maamar Mamouni, Rezki Amrouche, Mahieddine Meftah, Abdelaziz Benhamlat (46 Moulay Haddou), Abdelhafid Tasfaout, Nasreddine Kraouche, Billal Dziri, Moussa Saïb, Farid Ghazi (66 Brahim Mezouar), Faouzi Moussouni (51 Rafik Saïfi).
Goals: Samuel Eto'o (8), Marc-Vivien Foé (24) / Abdelhafid Tasfaout (79)

06.02.2000

SOUTH AFRICA - GHANA 1-0 (1-0)
Kumasi Sports Stadium, Kumasi
Referee: Mourad Daami (Tunisia), Attendance: 40,000
GHANA: Richard Kingson, Eben Dugbarthey, Emmanuel Osei Kuffour (75 Ohene Kennedy), Samuel Osei Kuffour, Samuel Johnson, Christian Gyan, Otto Addo (46 Peter Ofori-Quaye), Mark Edusei, Charles Akonnor (53 Stephen Appiah), Yaw Preko, Kwame Ayew.
SOUTH AFRICA: Andre Arendse, Lucas Radebe, Mark Fish, Pierre Issa, Erick Tinkler, Dumisa Ngobe, John Moshoeu, Helman Mkhalele, Quinton Fortune, Shaun Bartlett, Siyabonga Nomvete (85 Pollen Ndlanya).
Sent off: Tinkler (48)
Goal: Siyabonga Nomvete (42)

07.02.2000

EGYPT - TUNISIA 0-1 (0-1)
Stade Sani Abacha, Kano
Referee: Alain Sars (France), Attendance: 12.000
EGYPT: Nader El-Sayed, Ibrahim Hassan (46 Abdelsatar Sabry), Hany Ramzi, Abdel Zaher El-Saqqa (79 Abdelhalim Ali), Mohamed Omara, Hady Khashaba, Yasser Radwan, Tarek El-Said (62 Ahmed Hassan), Ibrahim Said, Hossam Hassan, Ahmed Salah Hosni.
TUNISIA: Chokri El Ouaer, Khaled Badra, Sami Trabelsi (78 Mounir Boukadida), Radhi Jaidi, Tarek Thabet, Zoubier Beya (66 Riadh Bouazizi), Sirajeddine Chihi, Raouf Bouazaine, Maher Kanzari, Ziad Jaziri, Ali Zitouni (46 Hassan Gabsi).
Goal: Khaled Badra (22 penalty)

07.02.2000

NIGERIA - SENEGAL 2-1 (0-1, 1-1)
National Stadium, Lagos
Referee: Felix Tangawarima (Zimbabwe), Attendance: 60.000
NIGERIA: Ike Shorunmu, Gbenga Okunowo (80 Sunday Oliseh), Godwin Okpara, Taribo West, Celestine Babayaro, Tijani Babangida (68 Julius Aghahowa), Mutiu Adepoju, Austin Okocha, Finidi George, Nwankwo Kanu, Benedict Akwuegbu (61 Emmanuel Amunike).
SENEGAL: Oumar Diallo, Omar Daf (70 Mbaye Badji), Omar Traoré (67 Pape Daouda Sene), Cheikh Sidy Ba, Assane Ndiaye, Pape Malick Diop, Ousmane Diop, Moussa Ndiaye, Pape Niokhor Fall, Henri Camara, Khalilou Fadiga (99 Abdoulaye Mbaye).
Austin Okocha sent off (111)
Goals: Julius Aghahowa (84, 92) / Kalidou Fadiga (6)

Semi-finals

10.02.2000

CAMEROON - TUNISIA 3-0 (0-0)
Accra Sports Stadium, Accra
Referee: Mohamed Ali Bujsaim (United Arab Emirates), Attendance: 6000
CAMEROON: Boukar Alioum, Rigobert Song, Raymond Kalla, Pierre Njanka, Marc-Vivien Foé, Geremi Fotso Njitap, Lauren Etame-Mayer, Salomon Olembé, Bernard Tchoutang (46 Pierre Wome), Patrick Mboma, Samuel Eto'o.
TUNISIA: Chokri El Ouaer, Khaled Badra, Sami Trabelsi, Radhi Jaidi, Tarek Thabet, Sirajeddine Chihi, Raouf Bouazaine, Maher Kanzari (64 Ali Zitouni), Hassan Gabsi, Ziad Jaziri (60 Riadh Bouazizi), Adel Sellimi (73 Imed Mehdhebi).
Goals: Patrick Mboma (49, 88), Samuel Eto'o (83)

10.02.2000

NIGERIA - SOUTH AFRICA 2-0 (2-0)
National Stadium, Lagos
Referee: Gamal El-Ghandour (Egypt), Attendance: 60.000
NIGERIA: Ike Shorunmu, Celstine Babayaro, Furo Iyenemi (89 Gbenga Okunowo), Taribo West, Godwin Okpara, Finidi George, Sunday Oliseh, Mutiu Adepoju, Tijana Babangida (74 Victor Ikpeba), Nwankwo Kanu, Raphael Chukwu (68 Julius Aghahowa).
SOUTH AFRICA: Andre Arendse, Lucas Radebe, Mark Fish, Pierre Issa, Dumisa Ngobe, Thabo Mngomeni (46 Alex Bapela), John Moshoeu, Quinton Fortune (76 Steve Lekoelea), Helman Mkhalele, Shaun Bartlett, Siyabonga Nomvete (79 Pollen Ndlanya).
Goals: Tijani Babangida (1, 34)

Third Place Match

12.02.2000

SOUTH AFRICA - TUNISIA 2-2 (1-1, 2-2), 4-3 on penalties
Accra Sports Stadium, Accra
Referee: Bonaventure Coffi Codja (Benin), Attendance: 1000
SOUTH AFRICA: Andre Arendse, Papi Khomane, Lucas Radebe (40 Frank Schoeman), Pierre Issa, Eric Tinkler, Alex Bapela, Isaac Shai, Dumisa Ngobe (21 John Moshoeu), Helman Mkhalele, Shaun Bartlett, Pollen Ndlamya (52 Siyabonga Nomvete). Trainer: Trott Moloto
TUNISIA: Chokri El Ouaer, Khaled Badra, Mounir Boukadida, Radhi Jaidi, Tarek Thabet, Sirajeddine Chihi, Hassan Gabsi, Maher Kanzari (73 Zoubier Beya), Walid Azaiez (60 Imed Mehdhebi), Ali Zitouni, Adel Sellimi (70 Ziad Jaziri). Trainer: Francesco Scoglio (Italy)
Goals: Shaun Bartlett (11), Siyabonga Novmete (62) / Ali Zitouni (28, 90)
Penalties: Sirajeddine Chihi, Siyabonga Nomvete, Ziad Jaziri, 1-0 Helman Mkhalele, 1-1 Hassan Gabsi, 2-1 Eric Tinkler, 2-2 Mounir Boukadida, Shaun Bartlett, 2-3 Khaled Badra, 3-3 John Moshoeu, Ali Zitouni, 4-3 Alex Bapela

Final

13.02.2000

NIGERIA – CAMEROON 2-2 (1-2, 2-2), 3-4 on penalties
National Stadium, Lagos
Referee: Mourad Daami (Tunisia), Attendance: 60,000
NIGERIA: Ike Shorunmu, Godwin Okpara, Furo Iyenemi, Taribo West, Celstine Babayaro, Sunday Oliseh, Mutiu Adepoju (98 Victor Ikpeba), Austin Okocha, Finidi George (70 Tijana Babangida), Nwankwo Kanu, Raphael Chukwu (46 Julius Aghahowa). Trainer: Jo Bonfrere (Netherlands)
CAMEROON: Boukar Alioum, Rigobert Song, Raymond Kalla (94 Lucien Mettomo), Pierre Njanka, Marc-Vivien Foé, Pierre Wome, Geremi Fotso Njitap, Lauren Etame-Mayer, Salomon Olembé, Patrick Mboma, Samuel Eto'o (72 Joseph-Désiré Job). Trainer: Pierre Lechantre (France)
Goals: Raphael Chukwu (44), Austin Okocha (47) / Samuel Eto'o (26), Patrick Mboma (31)
Penalties: 1-0 Austin Okocha, 1-1 Patrick Mboma, 2-1 Godwin Okpara, 2-2 Pierre Wome, Nwankwo Kanu, 2-3 Geremi Fotso Njitap, Victor Ikpeba, Marc-Vivien Foé, 3-3 Sunday Oliseh, 3-4 Rigobert Song.

Twenty-third edition - 2002
Qualifying Tournament

Fifty-one countries entered the 23rd edition of the competition and just 2 of them subsequently withdrew. Mali hosted the finals tournament and reached the semi-final stage where they lost to reigning champions, Cameroon. Senegal, who had recently qualified for the FIFA World Cup Finals, also reached the final but Cameroon retained the trophy, once again winning the final by penalty shoot-out following a goalless draw.

Preliminary Round

Guinea Bissau - Morocco w/o

01.07.2000 Gambia - Guinea 2-2 (2-1)
Goals: Abdoulie Corr (31 penalty, 44 penalty) / Diane Talfour (39), Souleymane Yula (87)
16.07.2000 Guinea - Gambia 2-0 (1-0)
Goals: Titi Camara (8), Souleymane Youla (90)

02.07.2000 Equatorial Guinea - Angola 0-1 (0-0)
Goal: Isaac (72)
16.07.2000 Angola - Equatorial Guinea 4-1 (2-1)
Goals: Paulão (14), Fabrice Alcebiades Maieco 'Akwá' (18), Mendonça (83), Isaac (88) / Mba Casiano (33)

03.07.2000 Cape Verde - Liberia 1-0
Goal: Antonio Duarte
16.07.2000 Liberia - Cape Verde 3-0 (1-0)
Goals: George Weah (3, 77), Alex Brown (71)

30.06.2000 Mauritania - Burkina Faso 0-0
16.07.2000 Burkina Faso - Mauritania 3-0 (1-0)
Goals: Omar Barro (23, 71), Manga Diabate (76)

20.08.2000 Sierra Leone - Togo 2-0 (1-0)
Goals: Ibrahim Bah (33), Abu Kanu (51)
03.09.2000 Togo - Sierra Leone 2-0 (1-0,2-0), 4-2 penalties
Goals: Kader Kougbadja-Toure (26), Tadjou Salou (60 penalty)

02.07.2000 Benin - Namibia 2-0 (0-0)
Goals: Leon Bessan (46), Moussa Latoundji (50)
15.07.2000 Namibia - Benin 8-2 (7-2)
Goals: Robert Nauseb (4), Silvester Goraseb (8, 20, 36), Razundura Tjikuzu (25, 43), Quinton Jacobs (31 penalty), Colin Benjamin (77) / Eric Assouma (6, 12)

02.07.2000 Niger - Ivory Coast 0-1 (0-0)
Goal: Harouna Dindane (55)
16.07.2000 Ivory Coast - Niger 6-0 (2-0)
Goals: Bamba Siaka (9), Serge Alain Yoffou (42, 65, 68), Venance Zeze (77), Zephirin Zoko (84)

01.07.2000 São Tome e Principe - Gabon 1-1 (1-1)
Goals: Touga (5) / Constant Tamboucha (12)
15.07.2000 Gabon - São Tome e Principe 4-1 (2-0)
Goals: Etienne Bito'o (17, 21, 70), Valery Ondo (50) / Amilcar Ramos (88)

02.07.2000 Central African Republic - DR Congo 1-1 (1-1)
Goals: Nazaire Malo (25) / Jean-Jacques Yemweni (12)
16.07.2000 DR Congo - Central African Republic 2-0 (1-0)
Goals: Jean-Jacques Yemweni (6), Janson Mayele (82)

02.07.2000 Sudan - Eritrea 5-1 (2-1)
Goals: Khalid Bakheit (4), James Joseph (11), Mohamed Musa (54), Hisham Seeni (56), Amir Mustafa (86) / Basili Abraham (6)
15.07.2000 Eritrea - Sudan 2-1 (2-0)
Goals: Fassil Abreha (33), Yonekachew Shimangus (45) / Samson Rtshard (66)

02.07.2000 Rwanda - Congo 2-1
16.07.2000 Congo - Rwanda 5-1 (3-0)
Goals: Lebali Eder (6), Goma Amoros (8 penalty), Pedel Moyimouadeka (26), Ngoma de Nanitelamio (61), Tsoumou Benis (61) / Mayele (80)

30.06.2000 Djibouti - Burundi 1-3 (0-2)
Goals: C.Kongolo (47 own goal) / N'Dayiragije (30), K.Kongolo (40), Mossi (74)
15.07.2000 Burundi - Djibouti 1-0 (1-0)
Goal: Damas Amuyali (34)

01.07.2000 Botswana - Madagascar 1-0 (1-0)
Goal: Diphethogo Selolwane (25)
15.07.2000 Madagascar - Botswana 2-0 (1-0)
Goals: Harry Randriannaivo (3), C. Ralaitafika (48)

30.06.2000 Chad - Libya 3-1
Goals: Loko Lokossinbaye 2 / A. Al-Hammali
14.07.2000 Libya - Chad 3-1 aet, 8-7 on penalties
Goals: T. Al-Taeb, N. Al-Terhouni, A. Al-Masli, Loko Lokossinbaye

02.07.2000 Ethiopia - Zambia 1-0 (1-0)
Goal: Sentayhu Getachew (34)
15.07.2000 Zambia - Ethiopia 2-0 (1-0)
Goals: Bernard Makufi (2), Gift Kampamba (67)

01.07.2000 Seychelles - Zimbabwe 0-1 (0-1)
Goal: Mwaruwari (35)
16.07.2000 Zimbabwe - Seychelles 5-0
Goals: Luke Petros 2, Blessing Makunike, Peter Ndlovu, Nqobizitha Ncube

01.07.2000 Tanzania - Mauritius 0-1 (0-0)
Goal: Naboh (57)
16.07.2000 Mauritius - Tanzania 3-2 (0-2)
Goals: Sebastian Bax (77), Tony François (79), Christopher Perle (88) / Cassim Tembele (24), Ntese Lungu (28)

01.07.2000 Uganda - Malawi 3-1 (2-0)
Goals: Hassan Mubiru (3), Hakim Magumba (14), Andrew Mukasa (52 penalty) / Dan Chitsulo (89)
15.07.2000 Malawi - Uganda 1-2 (0-1)
Goals: Ernest Mtawali (51) / Hassan Mubiru (30), Majid Musisi (81)

02.07.2000 Lesotho - Mozambique 1-0 (0-0)
Goal: Teele Ntsonyana (85)
16.07.2000 Mozambique - Lesotho 1-0 (0-0,1-0), 2-3 on penalties
Goal: Dario (82)

151

02.07.2000 Swaziland - Kenya 3-2 (1-1)
Goals: Dumisa Dlamini (43, 75 penalty), M. Dlamini (56) / Bernard Onyango (38), Mike Okoth (86)
15.07.2000 Kenya - Swaziland 3-0 (1-0)
Goals: Bernard Onyango (19), Mike Okoth (78), Sammy Simiyu (83)

Group 1

02.09.2000 Nigeria - Namibia 4-0 (1-0)
Goals: Victor Ikpeba (39, 73, 88), Pascal Ojigwe (55)
02.09.2000 Zambia - Madagascar 1-2 (1-1)
Goals: Dennis Lota (34) / Jean Natal (42), Hary Randrianaivo (75)
07.10.2000 Madagascar - Nigeria 0-0
08.10.2000 Namibia - Zambia 1-2 (1-0)
Goals: Augustinus Mukwoya (9) / Chanda Mwape (80), Philemon Chipata (81)
13.01.2001 Nigeria - Zambia 1-0 (1-0)
Goal: Victor Agali (33)
13.01.2001 Namibia - Madagascar 2-2 (0-2)
Goals: Johannes Hindjou (77), George Hummel (89) / Hary Randrainaivo (33), Jean-Louis Ratsimialona (44)
24.03.2001 Zambia - Nigeria 1-1 (1-1)
Goals: Isaac Okoronowo (42 own goal) / Benedict Akwuegbu (30)
24.03.2001 Madagascar - Namibia 1-2 (1-2)
Goals: Ruphin Menakely (30) / Michael Pienaar (5), Floris Dieergardt (10)
02.06.2001 Zambia - Namibia 0-0
02.06.2001 Nigeria - Madagascar 1-0 (1-0)
Goal: Benedict Akwuegbu (4)
16.06.2001 Namibia - Nigeria 0-2 (0-0)
Goals: Yakubu Aiyegbeni 89, Ishola Shaibu 90]
16.06.2001 Madagascar - Zambia 0-1 (0-1)
Goal: Mishek Lungu (13)

1.	NIGERIA	6	4	2	0	9	1	14
2.	ZAMBIA	6	2	2	2	5	5	8
3.	Madagascar	6	1	2	3	5	7	5
4.	Namibia	6	1	2	3	5	11	5

Group 2

03.09.2000 Liberia - Mauritius 4-0 (1-0)
Goals: Roberts Zizi (25), James Debbah (47, 79), Kelvin Lebwe
03.09.2000 Congo.- South Africa 1-2 (0-1)
Goals: Rolf-Christel Guie-Mien (70 penalty) / Thabo Mngomeni (21), Bradley August (59)
08.10.2000 Mauritius - Congo 1-2 (0-2)
Goals: Jean Marc Ithier (47) / Rolf-Christel Guie-Mien (27, 29)
16.12.2000 South Africa - Liberia 2-1 (0-0)
Goals: Shaun Bartlett (49), Phil Masinga (73) / Prince Daye (80)
13.01.2001 Mauritius - South Africa 1-1 (0-1)
Goals: Pascal François (60 penalty) / Delron Buckley (43)
14.01.2001 Liberia - Congo 5-1 (2-0)
Goals: James Debbah (23, 60), Oliver Makor (30), Zizi Roberts (51), Prince Daye (62) / Dongo Christ (21)
24.03.2001 South Africa - Mauritius 3-0 (3-0)
Goals: Benedict McCarthy (4), Alfred Phiri (14), Sibusiso Zuma (20)
25.03.2001 Congo - Liberia 0-1 (0-0)
Goal: Prince Daye (62)

03.06.2001 Congo - Mauritius 0-0
03.06.2001 Liberia - South Africa 1-1 (0-1)
Goals: Oliver Makor (48 penalty) / Andrew Rabutla (39)
16.06.2001 Mauritius - Liberia 0-2 (0-1)
Goals: Isaac Tondo (1, 61)
17.06.2001 South Africa - Congo 0-0

1.	LIBERIA	6	4	1	1	14	4	13
2.	SOUTH AFRICA	6	3	3	0	9	4	12
3.	Congo	6	1	2	3	4	9	5
4.	Mauritius	6	0	2	4	2	12	2

Group 3

02.09.2000 Gabon - Morocco 2-0 (1-0)
Goals: Guy-Roger Nzeng (38), Etienne Bito'o (56)
03.09.2000 Kenya - Tunisia 0-0
07.10.2000 Tunisia - Gabon 4-2 (2-2)
Goals: Ziad Jaziri (3), Radhi Jaidi (42), Hassen Gabsi (58), Tarek Thabet (75) / Cédric Moubamba (14), Etienne Bito'o (25)
08.10.2000 Morocco - Kenya 1-0 (1-0)
Goal: Youssef Chippo (43)
13.01.2001 Tunisia - Morocco 0-1 (0-0)
Goal: Abdeljelil Hadda Camacho (49)
13.01.2001 Kenya - Gabon 2-1 (1-1)
Goals: Bonaventure Maruti (16), Robert Mambo (72) / Etienne Bito'o (12)
24.03.2001 Morocco - Tunisia 2-0 (1-0)
Goals: Youssef Chippo (20), Abdeljelil Hadda (60)
24.03.2001 Gabon - Kenya 1-1 (0-0)
Goals: Valery Ondo (67 penalty) / Sammy Wanyanyi (85)
02.06.2001 Kenya - Morocco 1-1 (1-1)
Goals: Michael Okoth (5) / Salleh Eddine Bassir (43)
02.06.2001 Gabon - Tunisia 1-1 (0-0)
Goals: Daniel Cousin (57) / Riadh Jelassi (67)
16.06.2001 Morocco - Gabon 0-1 (0-1)
Goal: Due Nguema (43)
17.06.2001 Tunisia - Kenya 4-1 (3-0)
Goals: Ali Zitouni (33, 62), Ziad Jaziri (42, 44) / Mulama Simon (61)

1.	MOROCCO	6	3	1	2	5	4	10
2.	TUNISIA	6	2	2	2	9	7	8
3.	Gabon	6	2	2	2	8	8	8
4.	Kenya	6	1	3	2	5	8	6

Group 4

03.09.2000 Burundi - Angola 0-0
03.09.2000 Algeria - Burkina Faso 1-1 (0-0)
Goals: Abdelhafid Tasfaout (62) / Mamadou Zongo (52)
07.10.2000 Burkina Faso - Burundi 1-0 (0-0)
Goal: Ousmane Sanou (52)
08.10.2000 Angola - Algeria 2-2 (0-2)
Goals: Souza (52), Mendonça (66) / Abdelhafid Tasfaout (10, 26)
12.01.2001 Algeria - Burundi 2-1 (2-0)
Goals: Mehdi Meniri (6), Abdelhafid Tasfaout (45) / Masbi Jamamassi (60)

13.01.2001 Burkina Faso - Angola 1-0 (1-0)
Goal: Mamadou Zongo (38)
25.03.2001 Burundi - Algeria 0-1 (0-1)
Goal: Issaad Bourahli (17)
25.03.2001 Angola - Burkina Faso 2-0 (1-0)
Goals: Quinzinho (44), Fabrice Alcebiades Maieco 'Akwá' (75)
01.06.2001 Algeria - Angola 3-2 (2-1)
Goals: Rafik Saifi (6, 41 penalty), Mohamed Kherkhache (80) / Djiberato (29), Paulo Mendonça (60)
03.06.2001 Burundi - Burkina Faso 0-0
17.06.2001 Burkina Faso - Algeria 1-0 (1-0)
Goal: Seydou Traoré (38)
17.06.2001 Angola - Burundi 2-1 (1-0)
Goals: Paulão (25), FLÁVIO da Silva Amado (52) / Selemane (50)

1.	ALGERIA	6	3	2	1	9	7	11
2.	BURKINA FASO	6	3	2	1	4	3	11
3.	Angola	6	2	2	2	8	7	8
4.	Burundi	6	0	2	4	2	6	2

Group 5

02.09.2000 Uganda - Guinea 3-1 (2-1)
Goals: Hassan Mubiru (14, 31), Andrew Mukasa (77) / Pascal Feindouno 44]
24.09.2000 Senegal - Togo 0-0
08.10.2000 Togo - Uganda 3-0 (1-0)
Goals: Tadjou Salou (29 penalty), Kossi Noutsoudjin (49), Kader Cougbadja-Toure (73)
08.10.2000 Guinea - Senegal 1-0 (0-0)
Goal: Balde (59)
13.01.2001 Uganda - Senegal 1-1 (0-1)
Goals: Mathias Kawesa (69) / Thiaw Pape (6)
14.01.2001 Guinea - Togo 0-0
24.03.2001 Senegal - Uganda 3-0 (2-0)
Goals: El Hadj Diouf (18, 85), Henri Camara (40)
25.03.2001 Togo - Guinea n/p
02.06.2001 Uganda - Togo 0-3 (0-1)
Goals: Abdelkader Coubadja (34, 70), Dogbe Kouadji (48)
03.06.2001 Senegal - Guinea n/p
17.06.2001 Guinea - Uganda n/p
17.06.2001 Togo - Senegal 1-0 (1-0)
Goal: Kossi Nousoudjin (32)

1.	TOGO	4	3	1	0	7	0	10
2.	SENEGAL	4	1	2	1	4	2	5
3.	Uganda	4	0	1	3	1	10	1

Guinea were excluded from the competition after 3 matches when their record stood at:

	Guinea	3	1	1	1	2	3	4

Guinea were excluded from the competition on 19th March, 2001, after the Guinean sports minister failed to meet a third FIFA deadline to re-install the Guinean FA functionaries.

Group 6

03.09.2000 Zimbabwe - DR Congo 3-2 (2-1)
Goals: Luke Petros (6, 73), Peter Ndlovu (22) / Mayele Nono (29 penalty), Kambamu Wakanyenkele (67)
03.09.2000 Lesotho - Ghana 3-3 (0-1)
Goals: Seth Lephoto (47), Majara Masupha (49), Molefe Makhele (61) / Matthew Amoah (27), Nawa Duah (80, 88)
08.10.2000 Ghana - Zimbabwe 4-1 (2-0)
Goals: Stephen Appiah (28), Emmanuel Duah (42), Matthew Amoah (48), Charles Akunnor (78 penalty) / Benjamin Mwarawan (47)
10.10.2000 DR Congo – Lesotho 1-1 (0-0)
Goals: Moro Nvula (57) / Mpakanyane (65)
14.01.2001 Zimbabwe - Lesotho 1-2 (1-1)
Goals: Benjamin Mwaruwaru (21) / Masupha Majara (40), Leholohnolo Seema (87 penalty)
14.01.2001 DR Congo – Ghana 2-1 (2-0)
Goals: Michel Dinsey (10), Mputu Bandu (13) / Kwame Ayew (77)
24.03.2001 Lesotho - Zimbabwe 0-1 (0-0)
Goal: Peter Ndlovu (88)
25.03.2001 Ghana - DR Congo 3-0 (1-0)
Goals: Charles Allotey (17, 84), Stephen Appiah (49)
03.06.2001 Lesotho - DR Congo 0-0
03.06.2001 Zimbabwe - Ghana 1-2 (1-1)
Goals: Wilfred Mugeyi (15) / Princeton Owusu-Ansah (39), Isaac Boakye (89)
17.06.2001 DR Congo – Zimbabwe 2-1 (0-0)
Goals: Mulangu Bafwafwa (54), Kanku Mulekelayi (56) / Benjamin Mwaruwari
17.06.2001 Ghana - Lesotho 3-1 (3-0)
Goals: Stephen Appiah (25), Baffour Gyan (31), Matthew Amoah (37) / Ntronyona Teela (63)

1.	GHANA	6	4	1	1	16	8	13
2.	DR CONGO	6	2	2	2	7	9	8
3.	Lesotho	6	1	3	2	7	9	6
4.	Zimbabwe	6	2	0	4	8	12	6

Group 7

02.09.2000 Egypt - Ivory Coast 1-0 (1-0)
Goal: Sayed Abdel Hafiz (15)
10.09.2000 Libya - Sudan 1-0 (1-0)
Goals: Ezzedine Al-Masrati (44)
08.10.2000 Sudan - Egypt 0-1 (0-1)
Goal: Hossam Hassan (22)
19.11.2000 Ivory Coast - Libya 2-1 (1-1)
Goals: Bakayoko Ibrahim (17), Zephirin Zoko (87) / Ahmed Masli (8)
14.01.2001 Egypt - Libya 4-0 (1-0)
Goals: Ibrahim Hassan (27), Ahmed Hassan (47, 62), Abdelsattar Sabry (66 penalty)
20.01.2001 Ivory Coast - Sudan 2-0 (1-0)
Goals: Abdul Kader Keita (38), Zephirin Zoko (80)
23.03.2001 Libya - Egypt 2-0 (0-0)
Goals: Ahmed Abu Kubba (53), Ahmed Elmosly (65)
25.03.2001 Sudan - Ivory Coast 0-0
03.06.2001 Egypt – Sudan 3-2 (1-0)
Goals: Ahmed Hossam (20, 51), Ahmed Salah Hosni (58) / James Joseph (69), Farouk Gabra (89 penalty)

155

03.06.2001 Libya - Ivory Coast 0-3 (0-2)
Goals: Kader Keita (21), Ibrahima Bakayoko (31), Djah Ettien (67)
17.06.2001 Ivory Coast - Egypt 2-2 (0-0)
Goals: Ibrahim Bakayoko (70 penalty), Nader El Sayed (83 own goal) / Ahmed Salah (56), Ibrahim
Said (84)
17.06.2001 Sudan - Libya 1-0 (1-0)
Goal: Edward Gildo (45)

1.	EGYPT	6	4	1	1	11	6	13
2.	IVORY COAST	6	3	2	1	9	4	11
3.	Libya	6	2	0	4	4	10	6
4.	Sudan	6	1	1	4	3	7	4

Final Tournament (Mali)

GROUP A

19.01.2002

MALI - LIBERIA 1-1 (0-1)
Stade 26 Mars, Bamako
Referee: Abdel Hakim Shelmani (Libya), Attendance: 60.000
MALI: Mamadou Sidibe, Adama Coulibaly, Fousseini Diawara, Boubacar Diarra, Abdoulaye Camara
(21 Adama Diakite), Seydou Keita, Bassala Touré, Soumaila Coulibaly (60 Mamadou Dissa),
Mamadou Diarra, Djibril Sidibe (71 David Coulibaly), Mamadou Bagayoko. Trainer: Henryk
Kasperczak (Poland)
LIBERIA: Louis Crayton, Zizi Roberts, George Gebro, Jimmy Dixon, Thomas Kojo, Kelvin Sebwe,
Oliver Makor, George Weah, Prince Daye, Frank Seator (79 John Menyongar), James Debbah. Trainer:
George Weah
Goals: Seydou Keita (87) / George Weah (45)

21.01.2002

ALGERIA - NIGERIA 0-1 (0-1)
Stade 26 Mars, Bamako
Referee: Felix Tangawarima (Zimbabwe), Attendance: 15.000
ALGERIA: Lounes Gaouaoui, Moulay Haddou, Brahim Zafour, Mahieddine Meftah, Mohamed
Bradja, Yazid Mansouri, Nasreddine Kraouche, Billal Dziri (79 Omar Belbey), Farid Ghazi, Abdelhafid
Tasfaout (64 Nassim Akrour), Rafik Saïfi (85 Kamel Kherkhache). Trainer: Rabah Madjer
NIGERIA: Ike Shorunmu, Taribo West, Isaac Okoronkwo, Ifeanyi Udeze, Joseph Yobo, Sunday
Oliseh, Austin Okocha (79 Garba Lawal), Finidi George, Julius Aghahowa, Yakubu Ayegbeni (79
Tijani Babangida), Victor Agali (46 Nwankwo Kanu). Trainer: Amodu Shuaibu
Goal: Julius Aghahowa (43)

24.01.2002

MALI - NIGERIA 0-0
Stade 26 Mars, Bamako
Referee: Alex Quartey (Ghana), Attendance: 50.000
MALI: Mamadou Sidibé, Adama Coulibaly, Fousseini Diawara, Boubacar Diarra, Daouda Diakite, Seydou Keita, Bassala Touré (86 David Coulibaly), Soumaila Coulibaly (74 Mamadou Dissa), Mamadou Diarra, Djibril Sidibé, Mamadou Bagayoko.
NIGERIA: Ike Shorunmu, Joseph Yobo, Taribo West, Isaac Okoronkwo, Celestine Babayaro, Sunday Oliseh, Finidi George, Austin Okocha (78 Garba Lawal), Nwankwo Kanu, Julius Aghahowa, Victor Agali (65 Tijani Babangida).

25.01.2002

LIBERIA - ALGERIA 2-2 (1-1)
Stade 26 Mars, Bamako
Referee: Divine Raphaël Evehe (Cameroon), Attendance: 3000
LIBERIA: Louis Crayton, Jimmy Dixon, Zizi Roberts (71 Dionysius Sebwe), George Gebro, Thomas Kojo (47 Fallah Johnson), Kelvin Sebwe, Oliver Makor, Edward Dixon (70 John Menyongar), George Weah, James Debbah, Prince Daye.
ALGERIA: Lounes Gaouaoui, Yacine Slatni (54 Slimane Raho), Moulay Haddou, Mounir Zeghdoud, Mahieddine Meftah, Mohamed Bradja, Yazid Mansouri, Nasreddine Kraouche, Billal Dziri (65 Abdelhafid Tasfaout), Farid Ghazi (25 Nassim Akrour), Rafik Saïfi.
Goals: Prince Daye (7), Kelvin Sebwe (72) / Nassim Akrour (45), Nasseredine Kraouche (90)

28.01.2002

MALI - ALGERIA 2-0 (2-0)
Stade 26 Mars, Bamako
Referee: Lim Kee Chong (Mauritius), Attendance: 55.000
MALI: Mamadou Sidibé, Daouda Diakite (46 Vincent Doukantie), Fousseini Diawara, Boubacar Diarra, Adama Diakité, Djibril Sidibé, Seydou Keita, Bassala Touré, Soumaila Coulibaly, Mamadou Diarra, Mamadou Bagayoko.
ALGERIA: Lounes Gaouaoui, Mahieddine Meftah, Mohamed Bradja, Brahim Zafour, Moulay Haddou, Omar Belbey, Yazid Mansouri, Lounes Bendahmane (41 Billal Dziri), Abdelhafid Tasfaout (44 Nassim Bounekdja), Kamel Kherkhache (41 Slimane Raho), Nassim Akrour.
Goals: Mamadou Bagayoko (18), Bassala Touré (24)

28.01.2002

LIBERIA - NIGERIA 0-1 (0-0)
Barema Bocoum Stadium, Mopti
Referee: Falla Ndoye (Senegal), Attendance: 9000
LIBERIA: Louis Crayton, Jimmy Dixon, Dionysius Sebwe, George Gebro (81 Fallah Johnson), Thomas Kojo, Kelvin Sebwe, Oliver Makor, Josephus Yenay, George Weah, Frank Seator (71 Mass Sarr), Prince Daye.
NIGERIA: Ike Shorunmu, Joseph Yobo, Taribo West, Isaac Okoronkwo, Sunday Oliseh, Ifeanyi Udeze, Austin Okocha, Finidi George (66 Tijani Babangida), Garba Lawal, Julius Aghahowa (90 Yakubu Ayegbeni), Nwankwo Kanu.
Goal: Julius Aghahowa (63)

1.	NIGERIA	3	2	1	0	2	0	7
2.	MALI	3	1	2	0	3	1	5
3.	Liberia	3	0	2	1	3	4	2
4.	Algeria	3	0	1	2	2	5	1

GROUP B

20.01.2002

SOUTH AFRICA - BURKINA FASO 0-0
Stade Amary Ndaou, Segou
Referee: Falla Ndoye (Senegal), Attendance: 12.000
SOUTH AFRICA: Hans Vonk, Mbulelo Mabizela, Bradley Carnell, Pierre Issa, Aaron Mokoena, Eric Tinkler, Quinton Fortune (59 Thabo Mngomeni), Sibusiso Zuma, Delron Buckley, Benni McCarthy (69 Siyabonga Nomvete), Shaun Bartlett (19 Bradley August). Trainer: Carlos Queiroz (Portugal)
BURKINA FASO: Mohamed Kabore, Brahima Cissé, Mamadou Tall, Soumalia Tassembedo, Boureima Ouattara, Madou Dossama, Saifou Panandetiguiri, Amadou Touré (51 Romeo Kambou), Narcissé Yameogo (53 Wilfred Sanou), Oumar Barro (67 Alassane Ouédraogo), Moumouni Dagano. Trainer: Jacques-Michel Yameogo

21.01.2002

MOROCCO - GHANA 0-0
Stade Amary Ndaou, Segou
Referee: Domenico Messina (Italy), Attendance: 4000
GHANA: Sammy Adjei, Samuel Osei Kuffour, John Mensah, Amankwah Mireku, Princeton Owusu-Ansah (52 George Blay), Kofi Amponsah, Michael Essien, Emmanuel Duah, Abdul Razak Ibrahim, Isaac Boakye (55 Matthew Amoah), Baffour Gyan (72 Alex Tachie-Mensah). Trainer: Fred Osman Duodu
MOROCCO: Driss Benzekri, Akram Roumani, Abdelilah Fahmi, Noureddine Naybet, Gharib Amzine, Youssef Chippo, Adil Ramzi, Youssef Safri, Abdel Hadda (89 Faouzi El-Brazi), Hitchem Zerouali (79 Rabi Lafoui), Salaheddine Bassir (59 Rachid Rokki). Trainer: Humberto Coelho (Portugal)

24.01.2002

SOUTH AFRICA - GHANA 0-0
Stade Amary Ndaou, Segou
Referee: Mourad Daami (Tunisia), Attendance: 5000
GHANA: Sammy Adjei, John Mensah, George Blay, Princeton Owusu-Ansah (72 Amankwah Mireku), Kofi Amponsah (81 John Pantsil), Abdul Razak Ibrahim, Michael Essien, Emmanuel Duah (77 Matthew Amoah), Baffour Gyan, Derek Boateng, Ishmael Addo.
SOUTH AFRICA: Hans Vonk, Mbulelo Mabizela, Bradley Carnell, Pierre Issa, Aaron Mokoena, Eric Tinkler, Quinton Fortune (59 Thabo Mngomeni), Siyabonga Nomvete (59 Bradley August), Delron Buckey, Sibusiso Zuma, Benni McCarthy.

26.01.2002

BURKINA FASO - MOROCCO 1-2 (0-1)
Stade Amary Ndaou, Segou
Referee: Lim Kee Chong (Mauritius), Attendance: 6000
BURKINA FASO: Mohamed Kabore, Lamine Traoré, Brahima Cisse (67 Boueima Ouattara), Mamadou Tall, Madou Dossama, Soumaila Tassembedo, Saifou Panandetiguiri, Ali Ouédraogo (54 Narcisse Yameogo), Wilfred Sanou (72 Alassane Ouédraogo), Oumar Barro, Moumouni Dagano.
MOROCCO: Driss Benzekri, Akram Roumani, Abdelilah Fahmi, Noureddine Naybet, Gharib Amzine (32 Faouzi El-Brazi), Noureddine Boukhari (74 Rabi Lafoui), Youssef Safri (66 Rachid Benhammoud), Youssef Chippo, Adil Ramzi, Hichem Zerouali, Saleheddine Bassir.
Goals: Moumouni Dagano (58), Hichem Zerouali (22, 85)

30.01.2002

SOUTH AFRICA - MOROCCO 3-1 (1-0)
Stade Amary Ndaou, Segou
Referee: Gamal El Ghandour (Egypt), Attendance: 2000
SOUTH AFRICA: Hans Vonk, Mbulelo Mabizela, Bradley Carnell, Pierre Issa, Aaron Mokoena, Eric Tinkler, Thabo Mngomeni, Bennett Mnguni (70 Dillon Sheppard), Sibusiso Zuma, Delron Buckley (32 Siyabonga Nomvete), Benedict McCarthy (82 Ntutukho MacBeth Sibaya).
MOROCCO: Driss Benzekri, Akram Roumani, Abdelilah Fahmi, Noureddine Naybet, Faouzi El-Brazi, Youssef Safri, Youssef Chippo (56 Rachid Benmahmoud), Adil Ramzi, Hisham Zerouali, Nourdin Bouhkari (53 Abdeljelil Hadda), Salaheddine Bassir (85 Rachid Rokki).
Goals: Sibusiso Zuma (42), Thabo Mngomeni (48), Siyabonga Nomvete (51) / Rachid Benmahmoud (77 penalty)

30.01.2002

BURKINA FASO - GHANA 1-2 (0-0)
Stade Barema Bogoum, Mopti
Referee: Chukwudi Chukwujekwu (Nigeria), Attendance: 15.000
BURKINA FASO: Mohamed Kabore, Mamadou Tall, Brahima Cissé, Soumaila Tassembedo (64 Firmin Sanou), Ousmane Traoré, Madou Dossana, Narcisse Yameogo (48 Wilfried Sanou), Mady Saidou Panandetiguiri, Amadou Touré, Oumar Barro (39 Alassane Ouédraogo), Moumouni Beli Dagano.
GHANA: Sammy Adjei, Yaw Amankwah Mireku, Kofi Amponsah, John Mensah, George Blay (46 John Pantsill), Princeton Owusu-Ansah, Abdul Razak Ibrahim, Emmanuel Duah (46 Prince Koranteng Amoako), Emmanuel Osei-Kuffour, Dereck Boateng, Ishmael Addo (60 Isaac Boakye).
Goals: Amadou Touré (81) / Isaac Boakye (90, 90+2)

1.	SOUTH AFRICA	3	1	2	0	3	1	5
2.	GHANA	3	1	2	0	2	1	5
3.	Morocco	3	1	1	1	3	4	4
4.	Burkina Faso	3	0	1	2	2	4	1

GROUP C

20.01.2002

CAMEROON – DR CONGO 1-0 (1-0)
Stade Babemba Traoré, Sikasso
Referee: Bonaventure Coffi Codja (Benin), Attendance: 15,000
CAMEROON: Boukar Alioum, Geremi Fotso Njitap, Rigobert Song, Raymond Kalla, Tchato, Marc-Vivien Foé, Lauren Etame-Mayer, Salomon Olembé (60 Jean Dika Dika), Pierre Wome, Patrick Mboma, Samuel Eto'o (90 Patrick Suffo). Trainer: Winfried Schäfer (Germany)
DR CONGO: Paulin Tokala, Muyaya Kayembé, Mundaba Kisombé, Yvos Yuvuladio, Esele Bakasu, Jason Mayele (62 Kapela Mbiyavanga), Marcel Mbayo, Patrick Kifu (69 Alexis Tekumu), Belix Bukasa, Shabani Nonda (85 Boeka-Lisasi), Lomano Treso Lua Lua. Trainer: Louis Watunda
Goal: Patrick Mboma (40)

21.01.2002

TOGO - IVORY COAST 0-0
Stade Babemba Traoré, Sikasso
Referee: Chukwudi Chukwujekwu (Nigeria), Attendance: 15,000
IVORY COAST: Losseni Konaté, Ibrahima Koné, Kolo Touré, Blaise Kouassi, Mamadou Coulibaly,
Lassina Diabaté, Tchiressoua Guel, Siby Badra Aliou (46 Didier Zokora), Kader Keita, Ibrahima
Bakayoko (65 Kandia Traoré), Aruna Dindane (69 Bonaventure Kalou). Trainer: Lama Bamba
TOGO: Kossi Agassa, Eric Akoto, Yaovi Abalo, Koffi Olympio, Zanzan Atte-Oudeyi, Lantame
Ouadja, Michel Dogbe (70 Thomas Dossévi), Adekanmi Olufade, Komlan Assignon (82 Abdul Gafar
Maman), Yao Senaya, Abdelkader Coubadja Touré (57 Djima Oyawolé). Trainer: Tchanile Bana

25.01.2002

CAMEROON - IVORY COAST 1-0 (0-0)
Stade Babemba Traoré, Sikasso
Referee: Gamal El Ghandour (Egypt), Attendance: 15,000
CAMEROON: Boukar Alioum, Geremi Fotso Njitap, Raymond Kalla, Rigobert Song, Bill Tchato,
Marc-Vivien Foé, Lauren Etame-Mayer, Salomon Olembé (66 Daniel Ngom Kome), Pierre Wome,
Samuel Eto'o, Patrick Mboma.
IVORY COAST: Losseni Konate, Ibrahima Koné, Habib Toure Kolo, Didier Zokora, Blaise Kouassi,
Lassina Diabate (87 Zéphrin Zoko), Siby Badra Aliou, Mamadou Coulibaly, Tchiressoua Guel (87
Bonaventure Kalou), Ibrahima Bakayoko (76 Kandia Traoré), Kader Keita.
Goal: Patrick Mboma (85)

26.01.2002

DR CONGO - TOGO 0-0
Stade Babemba Traoré, Sikasso
Referee: Tessema Hailemelak (Ethiopia)
DR CONGO: Paulin Tokala, Dikilu Bageta, Essele Bakasu, Mundaba Kisombé, Felix Muamba, Papy
Kimoto, Marcel Mbayo (58 Kifu Apataki), Jason Mayele, Lomana Tresor Lua Lua, Jean-Paul Boeka
Lisasi (65 Pathy Nsele Esengo), Kapela Mbiyavanga (53 Alexis Tekumu).
TOGO: Kossi Agassa, Eric Akoto, Yaovi Abalo, Koffi Olympio, Atte Oudeyi, Lantame Ouadja,
Komlan Assignon, Koffi Noutsoudje, Yao Senaya, Djima Oyawolé (50 Abdelkader Coubadja Tourét),
Michel Dogbe (63 Thomas Dossevi, 85 Adekbani Olufadé),.

29.01.2002

CAMEROON - TOGO 3-0 (0-0)
Stade Babemba Traoré, Sikasso
Referee: Petros Mathabela (South Africa), Attendance: 6000
CAMEROON: Boukar Alioum, Rigobert Song, Raymond Kalla, Bill Tchato, Geremi Fotso Njitap,
Marc-Vivien Foé, Daniel Ngom Kome, Eric Djemba-Djemba (46 Joseph Ndo), Lucien Mettomo (63
Salomon Olembé), Patrick Mboma (82 Pius Ndiefi), Samuel Eto'o.
TOGO: Kossi Agassa, Eric Akoto, Yaovi Abalo, Koffi Olympio, Atte Oudéyi Zanzan (62 Djima
Oyawolé), Abdul Gafar Maman, Emmanuel Adebayor (72 Adekanmi Olufadé), Yao Senaya,
Moustapha Salifou, Michel Dogbe, Abdelkader Coubadja Touré (77 Thomas Dossevi).
Goals: Lucien Mettomo (52), Samuel Eto'o (79), Salomon Olembé (89)

29.01.2002

DR CONGO - IVORY COAST 3-1 (1-0)
Stade Abdoulaye Makoro Sissoko, Kayes
Referee: Felix Tangawarima (Zimbabwe), Attendance: 10,000
DR CONGO: Paulin Tokala, Mundaba Kisombe, Dikilu Bageta, Félix Muamba, Kituftei Yuvuladio, Okitankoyi Kimoto, Jason Mayele (62 Singa Manzagala), Kanku Mulekelayi (81 Kifu Apataki), Pathy Essengo (60 Alexis Tekumu), Lomana Lua Lua, Shabani Nonda.
IVORY COAST: Losseni Konate, Kolo Touré, Mamadou Coulibaly, Blaise Kouassi, Brahima Koné, Lassina Diabate (37 Ibrahima Bakayoko), Ghislain Akassou (25 Seydou Badjan Kante), Siby Badra Aliou, Gilles Yapi Yapo, Kader Keita, Bonaventure Kalou (72 Kandia Traoré).
Goals: Yves Yuvuladio (28), Shabani Nonda (66), Papy Kimoto (80 penalty) / Kandia Traoré (86)

1.	CAMEROON	3	3	0	0	5	0	9
2.	DR CONGO	3	1	1	1	3	2	4
3.	Togo	3	0	2	1	0	3	2
4.	Ivory Coast	3	0	1	2	1	4	1

GROUP D

20.01.2002

EGYPT - SENEGAL 0-1 (0-0)
Stade Modibo Keita, Bamako
Referee: Mohamed Guezzaz (Morocco), Attendance: 25.000
EGYPT: Essam El-Hadary, Yasser Radwan, Abdel Zaher El-Saqqa, Hani Said, Mohamed Emara, Mohamed Barakat (75 Amr Fahim), Hani Ramzy, Ahmed Hassan, Tarek El-Said (80 Tarek El-Sayed), Khaled Bebo (75 Hazem Emam), Ahmed Hossam. Trainer: Mahmoud El-Gohary
SENEGAL: Tony Sylva, Omar Daf, Pape Sarr (84 Pape Bouba Diop), Ferdinand Coly, Aliou Cissé, Henri Camara, Khalilou Fadiga, El Hadji Diouf (86 Habib Bèye), Lamine Diatta, Moussa N'Diaye (68 Pape Thiaw), Salif Diao. Trainer: Bruno Metsu (France)
Goal: Lamine Diatta (82)

21.01.2002

ZAMBIA - TUNISIA 0-0
Stade Modibo Keita, Bamako
Referee: Koman Coulibaly (Mali), Attendance: 5000
TUNISIA: Chokri El-Ouaer, Radhi Jaidi, Khaled Badra, Hamdi Marzouki, Raouf Bouzaiene, Mehdi Nafti (46 Hassen Gabsi), Zoubier Beya, Riadh Bouazizi, Hatem Trabelsi (76 Khais Godhbane), Imed Mhadhebi (64 Bessam Daasi), Jamel Zabi. Trainer: Henri Michel (France)
ZAMBIA: Davies Phiri, Laughter Chilembe, Moses Sichone, Elijah Tana, Mark Sinyangwe (68 Hillary Makasa), Charles Lota, Gift Kampamba (88 Jones Mwewa), Andrew Sinkala, Numba Mumamba (68 Nsofwa Chaswe), Misheck Lungu, Dennis Lota. Trainer: Roald Poulsen (Denmark)

25.01.2002

EGYPT - TUNISIA 1-0 (1-0)
Stade Modibo Keita, Bamako
Referee: Arturo Duaden Ibáñez (Spain), Attendance: 3000
EGYPT: Essam El-Hadary, Yasser Radwan, Abdel Zaher El-Saqqa, Hani Said, Mohamed Emara, Mohamed Barakat, Hani Ramzy, Ahmed Hassan, Hazem Emam (71 Tarek El-Sayed), Ahmed Hossam (36 Khaled Bebo), Ahmed Salah Hosni (82 Amr Fahim).
TUNISIA: Chokri El-Ouaer, Khaled Badra, Hatem Trabelsi (68 Hassen Gabsi), Hamdi Marzouki, Radhi Jaidi, Raouf Bouzaiene (46 Emir Mkademi), Raidh Bouazizi, Zoubier Beya, Khais Godhbane, Jamel Zabi, Mourad Melki (56 Imed Mhadhebi).
Goal: Hazem Emam (23)

26.01.2002

SENEGAL - ZAMBIA 1-0 (0-0)
Stade Modibo Keita, Bamako
Referee: Abdulhakim Shelmani (Libya), Attendance: 20,000
SENEGAL: Tony Sylva, Pape Sarr, Aliou Cissé, Ferdinand Coly, Lamine Diatta, Alassane Ndour, Salif Diao, Henri Camara (83 Souleymane Camara), Khalilou Fadiga (46 Makhtar N'diaye), El Hadj Diouf, Pape Thiaw (46 Sylvain N'diaye).
ZAMBIA: Davies Phiri, Hillary Makasa, Moses Sichone, Elijah Tana, Mark Sinyangwe, Numba Mumamba (83 Laughter Chilembe), Ian Bakala (74 Nsofwa Chaswe), Gift Kampamba, Charles Lota, Andrew Sinkala, Harry Milanzi (88 Cosmas Banda).
Goal: Souleymane Camara (90)

31.01.2002

EGYPT - ZAMBIA 2-1((1-0)
Stade Modibo Keita, Bamako
Referee: Bonaventure Coffi Codja (Benin), Attendance: 8000
EGYPT: Essam El-Hadary, Yasser Radwan, Abdel Zaher El-Saqqa, Amr Fahim, Mohamed Emara, Mohamed Barakat (81 Wael Goma'a), Hani Ramzy (49 Tarek El-Said), Ahmed Hassan, Hazem Emam, Hossam Hassan (76 Ahmed Salah Hosni), Ahmed Hossam.
ZAMBIA: Davies Phiri, Laughter Chilembe, Hillary Makasa, Moses Sichone, Elijah Tana, Ian Bakala, Charles Lota (65 Gift Kampamba), Numba Mumamba (85 Nsofwa Chaswe), Andrew Sinkala, Cosmos Banda (65 Harry Milanzi), Dennis Lota.
Goals: Ahmed Hossam (35), Hazem Emam (53) / Gift Kampamba (89)

31.01.2002

SENEGAL - TUNISIA 0-0
Stade Abdoulaye Makoro Sissoko, Kayes
Referee: Domenico Messina (Italy), Attendance: 8000
SENEGAL: Omar Diallo, Omar Daf, Pape Malick Diop, Pape Bouba Diop, Aliou Cissé (46 Souleymane Camara), Sylvain N'Diaye, Amadou Faye, Habib Bèye, Makhtar N'Diaye, Moussa N'Diaye (80 Salif Diao), Amara Traoré (65 El Hadj Diouf),.
TUNISIA: Chokri El-Ouaer, Hatem Trabelsi, Mounir Boukadida, Radhi Jaidi, Emir Mkademi (46 Raouf Bouzaiene), Riadh Bouazizi, Mehdi Nafti (81 Mourad Melki), Zoubeir Beya, Imed Mhadhebi, Slimane Benachour, Jamel Zabi (55 Bassam Daasi).

1.	SENEGAL	3	2	1	0	2	0	7
2.	EGYPT	3	2	0	1	3	2	6
3.	Tunisia	3	0	2	1	0	1	2
4.	Zambia	3	0	1	2	1	3	1

Quarter-finals

03.02.2002

SOUTH AFRICA - MALI 0-2 (0-0)
Stade Abdoulaye Makoro Sissoko, Kayes
Referee: Arturo Ibáñez (Spain), Attendance: 15.000
MALI: Mahamadou Sidibé, Adama Diakité, Adama Coulibaly, Boubacar Diarra, Fousseini Diawara, Bassala Touré, Mamadou Diarra, Djibril Sidibe, Seydou Keita, Mamadou Bagayoko, Soumaila Coulibaly (81 Dramane Coulibaly).
SOUTH AFRICA: Hans Vonk, Mbulelo Mabizela (85 Bradley August), Pierre Issa, Aaron Mokoena, Bradley Carnell, Sibusiso Zuma, Eric Tinkler, Thabo Mngomeni, Quinton Fortune (72 Delron Buckley), Benedict McCarthy, Siyabonga Nomvete (65 Shaun Bartlett).
Goals: Bassala Touré (60), Dramane Coulibaly (90)

03.02.2002

NIGERIA - GHANA 1-0 (0-0)
Stade 26 Mars, Bamako
Referee: Mohamed Guezzaz (Morocco), Attendance: 25,000
NIGERIA: Ike Shoronmu (35 Murphy Akanji), Joseph Yobo, Taribo West, Isaac Okoronkwo, Ifeanyi Udeze, Sunday Oliseh, Augustine Okocha (90 Wilson Oruma), Finidi George (90 Yakubu Ayebeni), Garba Lawal, Julius Aghahowa, Nwankwo Kanu.
GHANA: Sammy Adjei, Yaw Amankwah Mireku, Kofi Amponsah, John Mensah, Princeton Owusu-Mensah, John Pantsil, Prince Amoako (87 Matthew Amoah), Abdul Razak Ibrahim, Emmanuel Osei-Kuffour, Isaac Boakye, Dereck Boateng (87 Emmanuel Duah).
Goal: Garba Lawal (80)

04.02.2002

CAMEROON - EGYPT 1-0 (0-0)
Stade Babemba Traoré, Sikasso
Referee: Mourad Daami (Tunisia), Attendance: 15,000
CAMEROON: Boukar Alioum, Bill Tchato, Raymond Kalla, Rigobert Song, Geremi Fotso Njitap, Pierre Wome, Marc-Vivien Foé, Lauren Etame-Mayer, Salomon Olembé (72 Daniel Ngom Kome), Samuel Eto'o (90 Patrick Suffo), Patrick Mboma.
EGYPT: Essam El-Hadary, Yasser Radwan, Abdel Zaher El-Saqqa, Amr Fahim (52 Wael Gomaa), Mohamed Emara, Mohamed Barakat, Hani Ramzy, Ahmed Hassan (79 Khaled Bebo), Hazem Emam, Ahmed Hossam, Ahmed Salah Hosni (65 Hossam Hassan).
Goal: Patrick Mboma (62)

04.02.2002

SENEGAL – DR CONGO 2-0 (1-0)
Stade Modibo Keita, Bamako
Referee: Domenico Messina (Italy), Attendance: 15,000
SENEGAL: Tony Sylva, Omar Daf, Aliou Cissé, Lamine Diatta, Ferdinand Coly, Pape Sarr, Salif Diao, Sylvain N'Diaye (75 Pape Bouba Diop), Henri Camara (80 Souleymane Camara), Khalilou Fadiga, El Hadj Diouf.
DR CONGO: Paulin Tokala, Kituftei Yuvuladio, Bageta Dikilu, Félix Muamba, Essele Bakasu, Kimoto Obitankoyi, Kimemba Mbayo (81 Kifu Apataki), Kanku Mulekelayi (25 Singa Manzangala), Pathy Esengo, Lomana Lua Lua, Boeka Lisasi (46 Alexis Tekumu).
Sent off: Alexis Tekumu (90)
Goals: Salif Diao (30), El Hadj Diouf (86)

Semi-finals

07.02.2002

SENEGAL - NIGERIA 2-1 (0-0, 1-1)
Stade Modibo Keita, Bamako
Referee: Bonaventure Coffi Codja (Benin), Attendance: 20,000
SENEGAL: Tony Sylva, Ferdinand Coly, Omar Daf, Aliou Cissé, Lamine Diatta, Pape Sarr, Salif Diao
(113 Amdy Faye), Pape Bouba Diop, Khalilou Fadiga, Henri Camara (90 Souleymane Camara), El
Hadj Diouf
NIGERIA: Ike Shoronmu, Joseph Yobo, Isaac Okoronkwo, Taribo West, Ifeanyi Udeze, Finidi George
(67 Tijani Bangida), Garba Lawal (104 Karibe Ojigwe), Augustine Okocha (72 Wilson Oruma), Sunday
Oliseh, Julius Aghahowa, Nwankwo Kanu.
Sent off: Aghahowa (112), Udeze (120) / Sarr (34)
Goals: Pape Bouba Diop (54), Salif Diao (97) / Julius Aghahowa (88)

07.02.2002

MALI - CAMEROON 0-3 (0-2)
Stade du 26 Mars, Bamako
Referee: Lim Kee Chong (Mauritius), Attendance: 50,000
CAMEROON: Boukar Alioum, Bill Tchato, Pierre Wome, Rigobert Song, Raymond Kalla, Geremi
Fotso Njitap, Lauren Etame-Mayer, Marc-Vivien Foé, Salomon Olembé (89 Daniel Ngom Kome),
Samuel Eto'o (90 Eric Djemba-Djemba), Pius N'Diefi (81 Patrick Suffo).
MALI: Mahamadou Sidibé, Daouda Diakité (46 Vincent Doukantie), Adama Coulibaly, Fousseini
Diawara, Boubacar Diarra (46 Samba Diawara), Djibril Sidibe (73 Mamadou Dissa), Seydou Keita,
Bassala Touré, Soumaila Coulibaly, Mamadou Diarra, Mamadou Bagayoko.
Goals: Salomon Olembé (39, 45), Marc-Vivien Foé (84)

Third Place Match

09.02.2002

MALI - NIGERIA 0-1 (0-1)
Stade Barema Bogoum, Mpoti
Referee: Abdelhakim Shelmani (Libya), Attendance: 15,000
MALI: Mahamadou Sidibé (33 Karamoko Keita), Samba Diawara, Adama Coulibaly, Fousseini
Diawara, Adama Diakité, Djibril Sidibe, Seydou Keita, Bassala Touré, Mamadou Diarra, Soumaila
Coulibaly (46 Mamadou Dissa), Mamadou Bagayoko (79 Cheikh Oumar Dabo). Trainer: Henryk
Kasperczak (Poland)
NIGERIA: Murphy Akanji, Joseph Yobo, Karibe Ojigwe, Eric Ejiofor, Justice Christopher, Sunday
Oliseh, Wilson Oruma (89 Finidi George), Garba Lawal, Tijani Babangida (74 Nwankwo Kanu),
Yakubu Ayegbeni, Victor Ikpeba,. Trainer: Shuaibu Amodu
Goal: Yakubu Aiyegbeni (31)

Final

10.02.2002

CAMEROON - SENEGAL 0-0 aet, 3-2 penalties
Stade du 26 Mars, Bamako
Referee: Gamal El Ghandour (Egypt), Attendance: 60,000
CAMEROON: Boukar Alioum, Bill Tchato, Pierre Wome, Rigobert Song, Raymond Kalla, Geremi
Fotso Njitap, Lauren Etame-Mayer, Marc-Vivien Foé, Salomon Olembé, Samuel Eto'o, Pius Ndiefi
(104 Patrick Suffo). Trainer: Winfried Schäfer (Germany)
SENEGAL: Tony Sylva, Omar Daf, Aliou Cissé, Lamine Diatta, Ferdinand Coly, Salif Diao, Henri
Camara (106 Souleymane Camara), El Hadj Diouf, Khalilou Fadiga, Pape Bouba Diop (91 Amdy
Faye), Makhtar Ndiaye (46 Moussa Ndiaye). Trainer: Bruno Metsu (France)
Penalties: Pierre Wome, 0-1 Ferdinand Coly, 1-1 Patrick Suffo, 1-2 Khalilou Fadiga, 2-2 Lauren
Etame-Mayer, Amdy Faye, 3-2 Geremi Fotso Njitap, El Hadj Diouf, Rigobert Song, Aliou Cissé.

Twenty-fourth edition - Cup 2004
Qualifying Tournament

Once again, 51 teams entered the 24th edition of the Africa Cup of Nations although three then
withdrew. The qualifiers were played in 13 groups with the winners of each progressing to the finals
together with the best second-placed team from groups 2 to 9. Tunisia hosted the tournament and lifted
the trophy for the first time after beating their Maghreb neighbours, Morocco, by a 2-1 scoreline in the
final.

Group 1

08.09.2002 Angola - Nigeria 0-0
12.10.2002 Malawi - Angola 1-0 (0-0)
Goal: Russell Mwafulirwa (85)
29.03.2003 Malawi - Nigeria 0-1 (0-1)
Goal: John Utaka (10)
07.06.2003 Nigeria - Malawi 4-1 (4-1)
Goals: Yakubu Aiyegbeni (10, 16), Nwankwo Kanu (22, 35) / Esau Kanyenda (8)
21.06.2003 Nigeria - Angola 2-2 (0-1)
Goals: Uche Kalu (57), Peter Odemwigie (62 penalty) / Figueiredo (9), Fabrice Alcebiades Maieco
'Akwá' (55)
06.07.2003 Angola - Malawi 5-1 (3-0)
Goals: Maupo Msowoya (2), Fabrice Alcebiades Maieco 'Akwá' (3), Flávio Amado (33), Stopirra (76),
Chinho (89) / Peter Mgangira (78)

1.	NIGERIA	4	2	2	0	7	3	8
2.	Angola	4	1	2	1	7	4	5
3.	Malawi	4	1	0	3	3	10	3

NB: Djibouti withdrew

Group 2

07.09.2002 Niger - Ethiopia 3-1 (0-1)
Goals: Ibrahim Tankari (55, 61), Garba Abdoulaye (80) / Achenafi Guirma (16)
08.09.2002 Guinea - Liberia 3-0 (1-0)
Goals: Titi Camara (1), Fode Mansare (54), Ibrahima Sory (69)
12.10.2002 Liberia - Niger 1-0 (0-0)
Goal: Prince Daye (80)
13.10.2002 Ethiopia - Guinea 1-0 (0-0)
Goal: Abege Yared (63)
30.03.2003 Ethiopia - Liberia 1-0 (0-0)
Goal: Antenehe Feleke (80)
30.03.2003 Guinea - Niger 2-0 (1-0)
Goals: Fode Mansare (40 penalty), Abdoulaye Sylla (90)
07.06.2003 Niger - Guinea 1-0 (0-0)
Goal: Yahaya Tankari (69)
08.06.2003 Liberia - Ethiopia 1-0 (0-0)
Goal: Steve Mennoh (57)
21.06.2003 Liberia - Guinea 1-2 (1-1)
Goals: Daye Prince (20) / Souleymane Youla (11, 50)
22.06.2003 Ethiopia - Niger 2-0 (1-0)
Goals: Abdulahi Azad (15 own goal), Ermias Kidanu (51)
05.07.2003 Niger - Liberia 1-0 (0-0)
Goal: Soumaila Alhassan (90 penalty)
06.07.2003 Guinea - Ethiopia 3-0 (1-0)
Goals: Souleymane Youla (32, 72), Pascal Feindouno (55)

1.	GUINEA	6	4	0	2	10	3	12
2.	Niger	6	3	0	3	5	6	9
3.	Ethiopia	6	3	0	3	5	7	9
4.	Liberia	6	2	0	4	3	7	6

Group 3

08.09.2002 Benin - Tanzania 4-0 (2-0)
Goals: Anicet Adjamounsi (9, 38), Oumar Tchomogo (75 penalty), Moussa Latoundji (85)
08.09.2002 Sudan - Zambia 0-1 (0-0)
Goal: Chaswe Nsfowa (89)
12.10.2002 Tanzania - Sudan 1-2 (1-1)
Goals: Abdallah Rajab (17) / Jasten Lado (27), Khalid Mussa (55)
12.10.2002 Zambia - Benin 1-1 (0-1)
Goals: Rotson Kilambe (75) / Wassion Oladikpikpo (45)
29.03.2003 Tanzania - Zambia 0-1 (0-1)
Goal: Meshack Lungu (25)
29.03.2003 Sudan - Benin 3-0 (1-0)
Goals: Tambal (35, 70), Kabir (68)
07.06.2003 Zambia - Tanzania 2-0 (1-0)
Goals: Harry Milanzi (44, 81)
08.06.2003 Benin - Sudan 3-0 (0-0)
Goals: Omar Tchmogo (55 penalty, 72), Moure Ogoudiyi (90)
21.06.2003 Zambia - Sudan 1-1 (0-1)
Goals: Songwe Chalwe (72) / Abedi Dalag (23)
22.06.2003 Tanzania - Benin 0-1 (0-0)
Goal: Moussoro Kabirou (66)

166

06.07.2003 Benin - Zambia 3-0 (2-0)
Goals: Omar Tchomogo (9, 26), Moussa Latoundji (75)
06.07.2003 Sudan - Tanzania [Tanzania withdrew]

1.	BENIN	6	4	1	1	12	4	13
2.	Zambia	6	3	2	1	6	5	11
3.	Sudan	5	2	1	2	6	6	7
4.	Tanzania	5	0	0	5	1	10	0

Group 4

08.09.2002 Congo.- Burkina Faso 0-0
09.09.2002 Central African Republic - Mozambique 1-1 (0-0)
Goals: Marcelin Tamboula (72), Gonçalves Fumo (60)
13.10.2002 Burkina Faso - Central African Republic 2-1 (0-1)
Goals: Amadou Touré (60), Dieudonné Minougou (75) / Berede Dehandé Ouefio (38)
13.10.2002 Mozambique - Congo 0-3 (0-0)
Goals: Madza Tsoumou (49), Rolf-Christel Guié-Mien (70), Walter Bakouma (73)
30.03.2003 Mozambique - Burkina Faso 1-0 (0-0)
Goal: Dário (89)
04.05.2003 Congo - Central African Republic 2-1 (1-0)
Goals: Roch Embingou (6), Oscar Owolo (52) / Igor Makita (84)
07.06.2003 Burkina Faso - Mozambique 4-0 (3-0)
Goals: Moumouni Dagano (6, 8), Amadou Touré (34), Dieudonné Minoungou (88)
08.06.2003 Central African Republic - Congo 0-0
21.06.2003 Burkina Faso - Congo 3-0 (0-0)
Goals: Amadou Touré (54 penalty), Rahim Ouédraogo (61), Dieudonné Minoungou (75)
22.06.2003 Mozambique - Central African Republic 1-0 (0-0)
Goal: Jossias (73 penalty)
06.07.2003 Central African Republic - Burkina Faso 0-3 (0-1)
Goals: Moumouni Dagano (30, 71), Dieudonne Minoungou (90)
06.07.2003 Congo - Mozambique 0-0

1.	BURKINA FASO	6	4	1	1	12	2	13
2.	Congo	6	2	3	1	5	4	9
3.	Mozambique	6	2	2	2	3	8	8
4.	Central African Republic	6	0	2	4	3	9	2

Group 5

06.09.2002 Mauritania - Cape Verde 0-1 (0-1)
Goals: Clavio Zelilo (45), Antonio Duarte (60)
07.09.2002 Kenya - Togo 3-0 (0-0)
Goals: John Baraza (62), Musa Otieno (68), Denis Oliech (90)
12.10.2002 Cape Verde - Kenya 0-1 (0-0)
Goal: John Baraza (58)
12.10.2002 Togo - Mauritania 1-0 (1-0)
Goal: Emmanuel Adabyo Sheyi (23)
29.03.2003 Kenya - Mauritania 4-0 (2-0)
Goals: Robert Mambo (15, 70), Paul Oyuga (43), Dennis Oliech (46)
29.03.2003 Cape Verde - Togo 2-1 (0-1)
Goals: Duca (68), Calo (80) / Azia Wondu (37)

167

06.06.2003 Mauritania - Kenya 0-0
08.06.2003 Togo - Cape Verde 5-2 (3-2)
Goals: Alexandro Sania (2), Sherif Touré (23, 32), Paulo De Souza (72), Emmanuel Adebayor (78) /
Claudio Aguiar (6), Carlos Morais (26)
21.06.2003 Cape Verde - Mauritania 3-0 (0-0)
Goals: Claudio 'Lito' Agguar (65), Carlos Morais (76 penalty, 82)
match was stopped for 20 minutes before penalty kick and abandoned at 3-0 in 85' when Mauritania
were reduced to six players following 5 red cards, result will presumably stand
22.06.2003 Togo - Kenya 2-0 (1-0)
Goals: Alexandro Paria (23, 57 penalty)
05.07.2003 Mauritania - Togo 0-0
05.07.2003 Kenya - Cape Verde 1-0 (0-0)
Goal: Dennis Oliech (84)

1.	KENYA	6	4	1	1	9	2	13
2.	Togo	6	3	1	2	9	7	10
3.	Cape Verde	6	3	0	3	9	8	9
4.	Mauritania	6	0	2	4	0	10	2

Group 6

08.09.2002 Seychelles - Eritrea 1-0 (0-0)
Goal: Roddy Victor (50)
08.09.2002 Zimbabwe - Mali 1-0 (1-0)
Goal: Lazarus Muhoni (30)
12.10.2002 Eritrea - Zimbabwe 0-1 (0-1)
Goal: Peter Ndlovu (10)
13.10.2002 Mali - Seychelles 3-0 (1-0)
Goals: Seydou Keita (30), Mamady Sidibe (75), Dramane Coulibaly (85)
30.03.2003 Eritrea - Mali 0-2 (0-0)
Goals: Ibrahim Thiam (54), Dramane Coulibaly (89)
30.03.2003 Zimbabwe - Seychelles 3-1 (1-0)
Goals: Peter Ndlovu (19 penalty, 90 penalty), Adam Ndlovu (86) / Brian Methe (87)
07.06.2003 Seychelles - Zimbabwe 2-1 (0-0)
Goals: Alpha Balde (75 penalty), Philip Zialor (81) / Adam Ndlovu (86)
07.06.2003 Mali - Eritrea 1-0 (1-0)
Goal: Coulibaly Soumaila (20)
21.06.2003 Eritrea - Seychelles 1-0 (0-0)
Goal: Yonas Fessehaye (62)
22.06.2003 Mali - Zimbabwe 0-0
05.07.2003 Seychelles - Mali 0-2 (0-0)
Goals: Sammy Traoré (60), Bassala Touré (85)
05.07.2003 Zimbabwe - Eritrea 2-0 (2-0)
Goals: Peter Ndlovu (11, 17 penalty)

1.	MALI	6	4	1	1	8	1	13
2.	ZIMBABWE	6	4	1	1	8	3	13
3.	Seychelles	6	2	0	4	4	10	6
4.	Eritrea	6	1	0	5	1	7	3

Group 7

07.09.2002 Gabon - Morocco 0-1 (0-1)
Goal: Youssef Chippo (16)
08.09.2002 Equatorial Guinea - Sierra Leone 1-3 (0-1)
Goals: Ricardo Mavidi (82) / Mamadou Bah (38), Sesay (46), Menssary (68)
12.10.2002 Sierra Leone - Gabon 2-0 (1-0)
Goals: Paul Kpaka (45), Mamadou Alpha Jor Bah (52)
13.10.2002 Morocco - Equatorial Guinea 5-0 (4-0)
Goals: Adil Ramzi (8), Mustapha Bidodane (24), Youssef Safri (27), Rachid Roki (45), Noureddine Kacemi (70)
29.03.2003 Sierra Leone - Morocco 0-0
29.03.2003 Gabon - Equatorial Guinea 4-0 (2-0)
Goals: Eric Mouloungui (8), Yannick Lary (40, 49), Etienne Bito'o (65 penalty)
08.06.2003 Morocco - Sierra Leone 1-0 (1-0)
Goal: Youssef Chippo (25)
08.06.2003 Equatorial Guinea - Gabon 2-1 (1-1)
Goals: Jesus Mba (22), Andres Mangongo (50) / Dissikadie Alain (43)
20.06.2003 Morocco - Gabon 2-0 (1-0)
Goals: Mohamed El Yaacoubi (22), Zaid Jaziri (75)
22.06.2003 Sierra Leone - Equatorial Guinea 2-0 (0-0)
Goals: Mohammed Kallon (71), Amed Kabbah (90)
06.07.2003 Equatorial Guinea - Morocco 0-1 (0-0)
Goal: Houcine Kharja (60)
06.07.2003 Gabon - Sierra Leone 2-0 (1-0)
Gals: Bruno Zita Mbanangoye (33), Nde Mintsa

1.	MOROCCO	6	5	1	0	10	0	16
2.	Sierra Leone	6	3	1	2	7	4	10
3.	Gabon	6	2	0	4	7	7	6
4.	Equatorial Guinea	6	1	0	5	3	16	3

Group 8

08.09.2002 Lesotho - Senegal 0-1 (0-1)
Goal: Henri Camara (35)
13.10.2002 Gambia - Lesotho 6-0 (3-0)
Goals: Aziz Corr Nyang (7, 40), Tapha Sarr (45), Jatto Ceesay (55, 88), Sefo Soli (80)
30.03.2003 Gambia - Senegal 0-0
07.06.2003 Senegal - Gambia 3-1 (2-0)
Goals: Lamine Diatta (8), Henry Camara (36), El Hadji Diouf (73) / Ebou Sillah (63)
14.06.2003 Senegal - Lesotho 3-0 (1-0)
Goals: Hadji Diouf (26 penalty), Henry Camara (66, 70)
06.07.2003 Lesotho - Gambia 1-0 (0-0)
Goal: Molefe Makhele (87)

1.	SENEGAL	4	3	1	0	7	1	10
2.	Gambia	4	1	1	2	7	4	4
3.	Lesotho	4	1	0	3	1	10	3

São Tome and Principe withdrew.

Group 9

07.09.2002 Botswana - Swaziland 0-0
08.09.2002 Libya - DR Congo 3-2 (3-1)
Goals: Ani Al-Mallian (16), Gehad Muntaser (36), Essam Belal (41 penalty) / Shabani Nonda (22), Kikeba (52)
13.10.2002 DR Congo - Botswana 2-0 (2-0)
Goals: Lomano Trésor Lua Lua (6), Merlin Mpaina (21)
13.10.2002 Swaziland - Libya 2-1 (0-1)
Goals: Jerry Gamedze (81), Wonder Nhleko (83) / Mohamed Marhbelo Salah (20 penalty)
30.03.2003 Libya - Botswana 0-0
30.03.2003 Swaziland - DR Congo 1-1 (1-0)
Goals: Mfanzile Dlamini (10) / Kampamba Musasa (65)
07.06.2003 Botswana - Libya 0-1 (0-0)
Goal: Ahmed Masli (89)
08.06.2003 DR Congo - Swaziland 2-0 (1-0)
Goals: Marlin Piana (18), Kambamba Musasa (71)
22.06.2003 DR Congo - Libya 2-1 (1-0)
Goals: Alain Masudi (29), Merlin Mpiana (83) / Ilid Hamed (49)
22.06.2003 Swaziland - Botswana 3-2 (3-1)
Goals: Siza Dlamini (7, 25), Sibusiso Dlamini (18) / Michael Mogaladi (41), Pius Kolagano (56)
05.07.2003 Libya - Swaziland 6-2
Goals: Tarek Taib 2, Khaleb al-Mirghan, Nader Tarhouni, Ahmed Saad, Ali al-Milyan / Bongali Dlamini 2
05.07.2003 Botswana - DR Congo 0-0

1.	DR CONGO	6	3	2	1	9	5	11
2.	Libya	6	3	1	2	12	8	10
3.	Swaziland	6	2	2	2	8	12	8
4.	Botswana	6	0	3	3	2	6	3

Group 10

07.09.2002 Madagascar - Egypt 1-0 (0-0)
Goal: Menahely Ruphin (73)
12.10.2002 Mauritius - Madagascar 0-1 (0-1)
Goal: Ruphin Menaleky (26)
29.03.2003 Mauritius - Egypt 0-1 (0-1)
Goal: Ahmed Hossan (43)
08.06.2003 Egypt - Mauritius 7-0 (3-0)
Goals: Ahmed Hossam (7 penalty, 22), Tarek El Sayed (18), Gamal Hamza (53), Hazem Emam (61), Ahmed Hassan (72, 89)
20.06.2003 Egypt - Madagascar 6-0 (4-0)
Gals: Bechir Al Tabei (1), Ahmed Bilal (9, 24, 56, 83), Ahmed Hossam (41)
06.07.2003 Madagascar - Mauritius 0-2 (0-2)
Goals: Christopher Perle (16), Kersley Appou (31 penalty)

1.	EGYPT	4	3	0	1	14	1	9
2.	Madagascar	4	2	0	2	2	8	6
3.	Mauritius	4	1	0	3	2	9	3

Guinea Bissau withdrew.

Group 11

08.09.2002 Ivory Coast - South Africa 0-0
13.10.2002 South Africa - Burundi 2-0 (2-0)
Goals: Patrick Mayo (13), Delron Buckley (39)
30.03.2003 Burundi - Ivory Coast 0-1 (0-1)
Goal: Dagui Bakari (11)
08.06.2003 Ivory Coast - Burundi 6-1 (3-0)
Goals: Didier Drogba (7, 27, 32), Dagui Bakari (56, 78), Aruna Dindane (70) / Sadi Shabani (88)
22.06.2003 South Africa - Ivory Coast 2-1 (1-1)
Goals: Shaun Bartlett (21), Siyabonga Nomvete (65) / Bonaventure Kalou (41)
06.07.2003 Burundi - South Africa 0-2 (0-2)
Goals: Teboho Mokoena (1), Stanton Fredericks (30)

1.	SOUTH AFRICA	4	3	1	0	6	1	10
2.	Ivory Coast	4	2	1	1	8	3	7
3.	Burundi	4	0	0	4	1	11	0

Group 12

07.09.2002 Namibia - Algeria 0-1 (0-1)
Goal: Collen Benjamin (36 own goal)
11.10.2002 Algeria - Chad 4-1 (1-0)
Goals: Nassim Akrour (26, 72 penalty), Djamel Belmadi (54, 69) / Naama Naay (70)
30.03.2003 Chad - Namibia 2-0 (0-0)
Goals: Mahamad Hisseine (57, 90)
07.06.2003 Namibia - Chad 2-1 (1-1)
Goals: Floris Diergaardt (24), George Hummel (76 penalty) / Mahamat Hussein (35)
20.06.2003 Algeria - Namibia 1-0 (1-0)
Goal: Nasreddine Kraouche (5)
06.07.2003 Chad - Algeria 0-0

1.	ALGERIA	4	3	1	0	6	1	10
2.	Chad	4	1	1	2	4	6	4
3.	Namibia	4	1	0	3	2	5	3

Group 13

07.09.2002 Uganda - Ghana 1-0 (0-0)
Goal: Philip Obwiny (52)
13.10.2002 Ghana - Rwanda 4-2 (2-2)
Goals: Elias Ntaganda (24 own goal), Mohammed Hamza (42), Charles Taylor (58), Derek Boateng (70 penalty) / Hassan Milly (16), Hamao Ndijumama (43 penalty)
29.03.2003 Rwanda - Uganda 0-0
07.06.2003 Uganda - Rwanda 0-1 (0-1)
Goal: Jimmy Gatete (40)
22.06.2003 Ghana - Uganda 1-1 (0-1)
Goals: Charles Amoah (84) / Assani Bajoba (16)
06.07.2003 Rwanda - Ghana 1-0 (0-0)
Goal: Jimmy Gatete (49)

1.	RWANDA	4	2	1	1	4	4	7
2.	Uganda	4	1	2	1	2	2	5
3.	Ghana	4	1	1	2	5	5	4

Final Tournament (Tunisia)

GROUP A

24.01.2004

TUNISIA - RWANDA 2-1 (1-1)
Stade du 7 Novembre, Radès
Referee: Divine Evehe (Cameroon), Attendance: 60,000
TUNISIA: Ali Boumnijel, Karim Hagui, Anis Ayari, Radhi Jaidi, Khaled Badra, Jawhar Mnari (86 Hatem Trabelsi), Mehdi Nafti, Adel Chedli (66 Riadh Bouazizi), Slim Benachour, Francileudo dos Santos, Ziad Jaziri (81 Mohamed Jedidi). Trainer: Roger Lemerre (France)
RWANDA: Ramadhané Nkunzingoma, Hamad Ndikumana, Canesius Bizimana, Leandre Bizagwira, Elias Ntaganda, Abdul Sibomana, Raphael Elias, Eric Nshimiyimana, Said Abed Makasi (69 Jean Lomani), Désiré Mbonabucya (69 Jimmy Gatete), Olivier Karekezi. Trainer: Ratomir Dujković (Serbia/Montenegro).
Sent off: Benachour (60) / Sibomana (56)
Goals: Ziad Jaziri (27), Francileudo dos Santos (56) / João Rafael Elias (32)

25.01.2004

DR CONGO - GUINEA 1-2 (1-0)
Stade Olympique d'El Menzah, Tunis
Referee: Sharaf Aboubacar (Ivory Coast), Attendance: 3000
GUINEA: Kemoko Camara, Dian Bobo Baldé, Schumann Bah, Ibrahim Sory Conté, Morlaye Soumah, Pascal Feindouno, Abdoul Salam Sow, Souleymane Youla, Ousmane N'Gom Camara, Aboubacar 'Titi' Camara (69 Sambegou Bangoura), Fodé Mansaré. Trainer: Michel Dussuyer (France)
DR CONGO: Paulin Tokala, Camille Muzinga, Cyrille Mubiala, Jean-Paul Kamudimba, Michel Dinzey (85 Kangana Ndiwa), Trésor Lutala, Herita Ilunga, Alain Masudi, Merlin M'Piana (73 Dieudonné Kalulika), Lomana Trésor Lua Lua, Marcel Mbayo (76 Kabamba Musasa). Trainer: Mick Wadsworth (England).
Goals: Alain Masudi (30) / Aboubacar 'Titi' Camara (68), Pascal Feindouno (81)

28.01.2004

TUNISIA - DR CONGO 3-0 (0-0)
Stade du 7 Novembre, Radès
Referee: Jerome Damon (South Africa), Attendance: 20.000
TUNISIA: Ali Boumnijel, Khaled Badra, Karim Hagui, Karim Saidi, Anis Ayari, Mehdi Nafti (46 Hatem Trabelsi), Jawhar Mnari, Khais Ghodhbane, Najeh Braham, Mohamed Jedidi (17 Francileudo dos Santos) , Imed Mhedhebi (77 Riadh Bouazizi).
DR CONGO: Papy Lukata Shumu, Herita Ilunga, Camille Muzinga, Cyrille Mubiala, Jean-Paul Kamudimba, Michel Dinzey (45 Franck Matingou), Trésor Luntala, Alain Masudi (69 Olivier Nzuzi), Marcel Mbayo (59 Bomboko N'Goy), Dieudonné Kalulika, Lomana Trésor Lua Lua.
Sent off: Lomana Trésor Lua Lua (38)
Goals: Francileudo dos Santos (54, 87), Najeh Braham (65)

28.01.2004
RWANDA - GUINEA 1-1 (0-0)
Stade 15 Octobre, Bizerte
Referee: Modou Sowe (Gambia), Attendance: 4000
RWANDA: Ramadhané Nkunzingoma, Hamad Ndikumana, Leandre Bizagwira, Elias Ntaganda, Jean-Remi Bitana, Michel Kamanzi, Eric Nshimiyimana, Raphael Elias, Olivier Karekezi (64 Désiré Mbonabucya), Jimmy Gatete (46 Said Abed Makasi), Jean Lomani (74 Karim Kamanzi).
GUINEA: Kemoko Camara, Dian Bobo Baldé, Schumann Bah, Ibrahim Sory Conté, Morlaye Soumah, Pascal Feindounou, Abdoul Salam Sow (78 Abdel Kader Camara), Ousmane N'Gom Camara, Souleymane Youla (86 Sambegou Bangoura), Aboubacar 'Titi' Camara, Fodé Mansaré.
Goals: Karim Kamanzi (90) / Aboubacar 'Titi' Camara (48)

01.02.2004
TUNISIA - GUINEA 1-1 (0-0)
Stade du 7 Novembre, Radès
Referee: Hailemalak Tessama (Ethiopia), Attendance: 18.000
TUNISIA: Khaled Azaiez, Hatem Trabelsi (46 Anis Ayari), Karim Saidi, Radhi Jaidi, Alaeddine Yahia, Adel Chédli, Riadh Bouazizi, Slim Benachour, Imed Mhedhebi (67 Jawhar Mnari), Francileudo dos Santos, Ziad Jaziri (90 Karim Hagui).
GUINEA: Kemoko Camara, Dian Bobo Baldé, Schumann Bah, Ibrahim Sory Conté, Kanfory Sylla, Pascal Feindouno (80 Souleymane Youla), Abdoulkarim Sylla (63 Fodé Mansaré), Abdoul Salam Sow, Ousmane N'Gom Camara, Aboubacar 'Titi' Camara (89 Sekou Oumar Dramé), Sambegou Bangoura.
Goals: Slim Benachour (58) / Aboubacar 'Titi' Camara (84)

01.02.2004
RWANDA – DR CONGO 1-0 (0-0)
Stade 15 Octobre, Bizerte
Referee: Falla N'Doye (Senegal), Attendance: 700
RWANDA: Ramadhani Nkunzingoma, Canesius Bizimana, Hamad Ndikumana, Elias Ntaganda, Frederic Risanganwa (55 Jean-Paul Habyarimana), Michel Kamanzi, Olivier Karekezi (30 Jimmy Mulisa), Karim Kamanzi (65 Henri Munyaneza), Abdul Sibomana, Said Abed Makazi, Désiré Mbonabucya.
DR CONGO: Muteba Kidiaba, Musasa Mwamba, Camille Muzinga, Cyrille Mubiala (61 Jean-Paul Kamudimba), Mundaba Kisombé, Herita Ilunga, Franck Matingou, Olivier Nzuzi (80 Alain Masudi), Mbuta Mbala (65 Marcel Mbayo), Musasa Kabamba, Merlin M'Piana.
Goal: Said Abed Makasi (74)

1.	TUNISIA	3	2	1	0	6	2	7
2.	GUINEA	3	1	2	0	4	3	5
3.	Rwanda	3	1	1	1	3	3	4
4.	DR Congo	3	0	0	3	1	6	0

GROUP B

26.01.2004
SENEGAL - BURKINA FASO 0-0
Stade Olympique d'El Menzah, Tunis
Referee: Mohamed Guezzaz (Morocco), Attendance: 2000
SENEGAL: Tony Sylva, Omar Daf, Pape Malick Diop, Souleymane Diawara, Ferdinand Coly (58 Habib Bèye), Aliou Cissé, Henri Camara, Salif Diao, El Hadji Diouf, Ousmane N'Doye (80 Papa Bouba Diop), Mamadou Niang (69 Diomansy Kamara). Trainer: Guy Stephan (France)
BURKINA FASO: Abdoulaye Soulama, Moussa Ouattara, Lamine Traoré, Amadou Coulibaly, Rahim Ouédraogo, Mahamadou Kéré, Saidou Madi Panandetiguiri, Bébé Kambou, Amadou Touré, Moumouni Dagano, Abdoulaye Cissé (65 Tanguy Barro). Trainer: Jean-Paul Rabier (France).

26.01.2004

KENYA - MALI 1-3 (0-1)
Stade 15 Octobre, Bizerte
Referee: Tessema Hailemelak (Ethiopia), Attendance: 6000
MALI: Mahamadou Sidibé, Souleymane Diamoutène (67 Djibril Sidibé), Fousseiny Diawara, Adama Coulibaly, Brahim Thiam, Sammy Traoré, Mahamadou Diarra, Soumaila Coulibaly, Seydou Keita (88 Bassala Touré), Mohamed Lamine Sissoko, Frédéric Kanouté. Trainer: Henri Stambouli (France)
KENYA: Franciso Onyiso, George Waweru (88 Philip Opiyo), Issa Kassim, Musa Otieno, Tom Juma, Titus Mulama, Adam Shaban, John Muiruri (73 Emmanuel Ake), Robert Mambo, Michael Okoth, Dennis Oliech. Trainer: Jacob Mulee.
Goals: Titus Mulama (58) / Mohamed Laminé Sissoko (28), Frédéric Kanouté (63, 82)

30.01.2004

BURKINA FASO - MALI 1-3 (0-2)
Stade Olympique d'El Menzah, Tunis
Referee: Abdul Hakim Shelmani (Libya), Attendance: 1500
MALI: Mahamadou Sidibé, Djibril Sidibé, Fousseiny Diawara, Adama Coulibaly, Brahim Thiam, Sammy Traoré, Mahamadou Diarra, Soumaila Coulibaly (90 Abdoulaye Demba), Bassala Touré (82 Souleymane Diamoutène), Mohamed Lamine Sissoko (60 Daouda Coulibaly), Frédéric Kanouté.
BURKINA FASO: Abdoulaye Soulama, Moussa Ouattara, Lamine Traoré, Amadou Coulibaly, Rahim Ouédraogo (82 Abdoulaye Cissé), Mahamadou Kéré, Saidou Madi Panandetiguiri, Bébé Kambou, Amadou Touré (46 Dieudonné Minoungou), Moumouni Dagano, Tanguy Barro (69 Patrick Zoundi).
Goals: Dieudonné Minoungou (50) / Frédéric Kanouté (34), Mahamadou Diarra (38), Soumaila Coulibaly (78)

30.01.2004

SENEGAL - KENYA 3-0 (3-0)
Stade 15 Octobre, Bizerte
Referee: Abdel Fatah Essam (Egypt), Attendance: 13,500
SENEGAL: Tony Sylva, Lamine Diatta, Pape Malick Diop, Ibrahim Fayé, Omar Daf (85 Habib Bèye), Salif Diao, Aliou Cissé, Papa Bouba Diop, Henri Camara, Mamadou Niang (69 Fréderic Mendy), El Hadji Diouf (69 Diomansy Kamara).
KENYA: Francis Onyiso, Issa Kassim, Musa Otieno, Moses Gikenyi, Tom Juma, Titus Mulama, Emmanuel Ake (60 James Omondi), Philip Opiyo, Robert Mambo (79 John Muiruri), Michael Okoth (89 Maurice Sunguti), Dennis Oliech.
Goals: Mamadou Niang (4, 30), Papa Bouba Diop (19)

02.02.2004

SENEGAL - MALI 1-1 (1-1)
Stade Olympique d'El Menzah, Tunis
Referee: Divine Evehe (Cameroon), Attendance: 7.550
SENEGAL: Tony Sylva, Habib Bèye, Lamine Diatta, Ibrahim Fayé, Salif Diao, Sylvain N'Diaye (79 Ousmane N'Doye), Pape Malick Diop, Papa Bouba Diop, El Hadji Diouf, Henri Camara, Mamadou Niang (65 Lamine Sakho).
MALI: Mahamadou Sidibé, Sammy Traoré, Fousseiny Diawara, Souleymane Diamoutène, Adama Coulibaly, Daouda Coulibaly (61 Djibril Sidibé), Seydou Keita, Mahamadou Diarra, Mohamed Lamine Sissoko (75 Bassala Touré), Abdoulaye Demba (82 Soumaila Coulibaly), Dramane Traoré.
Goals: Habib Beye (45) / Dramane Traoré (33)

174

02.02.2004

BURKINA FASO - KENYA 0-3 (0-0)
Stade 15 Octobre, Bizerte
Referee: Modou Sowe (Gambia), Attendance: 4550
KENYA: Duncan Ochieng, Musa Otieno, Adam Shabaan, Moses Gikenyi (38 Andrew Oyombe), Tom Juma, Titus Mulama, Emmanuel Ake (81 Maurice Sunguti), Philip Opiyo, Robert Mambo, Michael Okoth (57 John Barasa), Dennis Oliech.
BURKINA FASO: Mohamed Kaboré, Moussa Ouattara, Adama Coulibaly, Ousmane Traoré (66 Patrick Zoundi), Rahim Ouédraogo, Amadou Tidiané Tall (46 Tanguy Barro), Amara Ouattara, Dieudonné Minoungou, Mahamadou Kéré, Moumouni Dagano, Hamidou Balboné (36 Abdoulaye Cissé).
Sent off: Ouédraogo (76)
Goals: Emmanuel Ake (50), Dennis Oliech (63), John Baraza (84)

1.	MALI	3	2	1	0	7	3	7
2.	SENEGAL	3	1	2	0	4	1	5
3.	Kenya	3	1	0	2	4	6	3
4.	Burkina Faso	3	0	1	2	1	6	1

GROUP C

25.01.2004

ZIMBABWE - EGYPT 1-2 (0-0)
Stade Taieb Mhiri, Sfax
Referee: Lassina Paré (Burkina Faso), Attendance: 22.000
EGYPT: Nader El-Sayed, Ahmed Hassan, Besheer El-Tabei, Hani Said, Abdel Zaher El-Saqua, Tarek El-Sayed, Hazem Emam (62 Mohamed Barakat), Tamer Abdel Hamid, Tarek El-Said (71 Ahmed Fathi), Ahmed Belal (84 Hady Khashaba), Ahmed Hossam. Trainer: Mohsen Saleh
ZIMBABWE: Energy Murambadoro, Dumisani Mpofu, Dazzy Kapenya, Kaitano Tembo, George Mbwando, Esrom Nyandoro, Lazarus Muhoni (67 Joël Luphahala), Charles Yohane, Tinashe Nengomasha, Agent Sawu (55 Wilfred Mugeyi), Peter Ndlovu. Trainer: Sunday Marimo
Goals: Peter Ndlovu (47) / Tamer Abdel Hamid (58), Mohamed Barakat (62)

25.01.2004

CAMEROON - ALGERIA 1-1 (1-0)
Stade Olympique, Sousse
Referee: Bonaventure Coffi Codja (Benin), Attendance: 20.000
ALGERIA: Lounes Gaouaoui, Samir Beloufa (46 Brahim Zafour), Salim Aribi, Karim Ziani, Antar Yahia, Yazid Mansouri, Nasreddine Kraouche (85 Foadi Hadjadj), Djamel Belmadi (78 Hocine Achiou), Maamar Mamouni, Abdelmalek Chérrad, Mansour Boutabout. Trainer: Rabah Saâdane
CAMEROON: Idriss Kameni, Jean-Joël Doumbé, Lucien Mettomo, Rigobert Song, Bill Tchato (64 Timothée Atouba), Geremi Fotso Njitap, Modeste Mbami, Eric Djemba-Djemba, Mohamadou Idrissou (86 Daniel N'Gom), Samuel Eto'o, Patrick Mboma. Trainer: Winfried Schäfer (Germany).
Goals: Patrick Mboma (44) / Brahim Zafour (51)

175

29.01.2004

CAMEROON - ZIMBABWE 5-3 (3-1)
Stade Taieb Mhiri, Sfax
Referee: Sharaf Aboubacar (Ivory Coast), Attendance: 15,000
CAMEROON: Idriss Kameni, Bill Tchato, Rigobert Song, Timothée Atouba, Jean-Joël Doumbé, Geremi Fotso Njitap (86 Daniel N'Gom), Eric Djemba-Djemba, Jean Makoun (76 Valery Mezague), Modeste Mbami, Samuel Eto'o, Patrick Mboma (71 Mohamadou Idrissou).
ZIMBABWE: Energy Murambadoro, Dumisani Mpofu, Dazzy Kapenya, George Mbwando (71 Adam Ndlovu), Dixon Choto, Esrom Nyandoro, Charles Yohane, Wilfred Mugeyi, Tinashe Nengomasha, Joël Luphahla, Peter Ndlovu.
Goals: Patrick Mboma (31, 44, 65), Modeste Mbami (39, 66) / Peter Ndlovu (8, 47 penalty), Esrom Nyandoro (89)

29.01.2004

ALGERIA - EGYPT 2-1 (1-1)
Stade Olympique, Sousse
Referee: Alain Hamer (Luxembourg), Attendance: 15,000
ALGERIA: Lounes Gaouaoui, Salim Aribi, Brahim Zafour, Antar Yahia, Karim Ziani (82 Fodil Hadjadj), Yazid Mansouri, Nasreddine Kraouche, Djamel Belmadi (56 Hocine Achiou), Maamar Mamouni, Abdelmalek Cherrad, Mansour Boutabout (63 Moulay Haddou).
EGYPT: Nader El-Sayed, Ahmed Fathi, Besheer El-Tabei, Hani Said, Abdel Zaher El-Saqua (78 Hady Khashaba), Tarek El-Sayed, Ahmed Hassan (72 Mohamed Barakat), Tamer Abdel Hamid, Tarek El-Said (84 Hazem Emam), Ahmed Belal, Ahmed Hossam.
Sent off: Mamouni (59)
Goals: Mamar Mamouni (13), Hocine Achiou (86) / Ahmed Belal (26)

03.02.2004

CAMEROON - EGYPT 0-0
Stade Mustapha Ben Jannet, Monastir
Referee: Mohamed Ali Bujsaim (United Arab Emirates), Attendance: 20,000
CAMEROON: Idriss Kameni, Jean-Joël Perrier Doumbe, Rigobert Song, Lucien Mettomo, Timothée Atouba, Geremi Fotso Njitap, Modeste Mbami, Eric Djemba-Djemba, Jean Makoun (53 Salomon Olembé), Samuel Eto'o (81 Pius Ndiefi), Patrick Mboma (64 Mohamadou Idrissou).
EGYPT: Abdel Wahed El-Sayed, Ahmed Fathi, Besheer El-Tabei, Wael El-Quabbani, Abdel Zaher El-Saqua, Tarek El-Sayed, Ahmed Hassan, Hossam Ghali, Tamer Abdel Hamid (46 Ahmed Belal), Tarek El-Sayed, Ahmed Hossam.

03.02.2004

ALGERIA - ZIMBABWE 1-2 (0-0)
Stade Olympique, Sousse
Referee: Eddy Maillet (Seychelles), Attendance: 10.000
ZIMBABWE: Tapuwa Kapini, Dixon Choto, Dumisani Mpofu, Bekhitemba Ndlovu, Kaitano Tembo, Ronald Sibanda (83 Esrom Nyandoro), Harlington Shereni (87 Charles Yohane), Tinashe Nengomasha, Joël Luphahla, Adam Ndlovu (85 Wilfred Mugeyi), Peter Ndlovu.
ALGERIA: Lounes Gaouaoui, Salim Aribi, Brahim Zafour, Moulay Haddou (75 Djamel Belmadi), Samir Zaoui (24 Antar Yahia), Karim Ziani, Nasreddine Kraouche, Fodil Hadjadj, Hocine Achiou, Nassim Akrour, Fares Fellahi (66 Abdelmalek Cherrad).
Goals: Hocine Achiou (72) / Joël Luphahla (65, 71)

1.	CAMEROON	3	1	2	0	6	4	5
2.	ALGERIA	3	1	1	1	4	4	4
3.	Egypt	3	1	1	1	3	3	4
4.	Zimbabwe	3	1	0	2	6	8	3

GROUP D

27.01.2004

NIGERIA - MOROCCO 0-1 (0-0)
Stade Mustapha Ben Jannet, Monastir
Referee: Falla Ndoye (Senegal), Attendance: 15,000
MOROCCO: Khalid Fouhami, Abdeslam Ouaddou, Talal El-Karkouri, Noureddine Naybet, Oualid Regragui, Abdelkrim Kaissi, Jaouad Zairi (58 Youssef Hadji), Hocine Kharja, Youssef Safri, Youssef Mokhtari (71 Mohamed El-Yaccoubi), Marouane Chamkh. Trainer: Badou Zaki
NIGERIA: Vincent Enyeama, Joseph Yobo, Isaac Okoronkwo, George Abbey, Celestine Babayaro, Nwankwo Kanu (72 Pius Ikedia), Augustine 'Jay-Jay' Okocha, Seyi Olofinjana, John Utaka, Yakubu Aiyegbeni, Julius Aghahowa (79 Victor Agali). Trainer: Christian Chukwu.
Goal: Youssef Hadji (77)

27.01.2004

SOUTH AFRICA - BENIN 2-0 (0-0)
Stade Taieb Mhiri, Sfax
Referee: Koman Coulibaly (Mali), Attendance: 12,000
SOUTH AFRICA: Emile Baron, Thabang Molefe (81 Neil Winstanley), Jacob Lekgetho, Aaron Mokoena, Mbulelo Mabizela, Benson Mhlongo, John Moshoeu, Delron Buckley, Sibusiso Zuma, Siyabonga Nomvete, Patrick Mayo. Trainer: April Phumo
BENIN: Rachid Chitou, Damien Chrysostome, Tony Toklomety, Anicet Adjamonsi, Seidath Tchomogo, Moussa Latoundji, Jonas Okétola, Romauld Bocco, Jocelyn Ahoueya, Muri Ogunbiyi (63 Wassiou Oladikpikpo), Alain Gaspoz (79 Kabirou Moussoro). Trainer: Cecil Jones Attuquayefio (Ghana).
Goals: Siyabonga Nomvete (58, 76)

31.01.2004

NIGERIA - SOUTH AFRICA 4-0 (1-0)
Stade Mustapha Ben Jannet, Monastir
Referee: Mohamed Ali Bujsaim (United Arab Emirates), Attendance: 15,000
NIGERIA: Vincent Enyeama, George Abbey, Joseph Yobo, Isaac Okoronkwo, Garba Lawal, Ifeanyi Ekwueme, Augustine 'Jay-Jay' Okocha, Seyi Olofinjana, John Utaka, Nwankwo Kanu (67 Osaze Odemwingie), Julius Aghahowa (83 Pius Ikedia).
SOUTH AFRICA: Emile Baron, Thabang Molefe, Jacob Lekgetho, Aaron Mokoena, Mbulelo Mabizela, Benson Mhlongo (46 Bernard Mnguni), John Moshoeu (86 Jabu Pule), Delron Buckley, Sibusiso Zuma (74 Stanton Fredericks), Siyabonga Nomvete, Patrick Mayo.
Goals: Joseph Yobo (4), Augustine 'Jay-Jay' Okocha (64 penalty), Osaze Odemwingie (80, 82)

31.01.2004

MOROCCO - BENIN 4-0 (1-0)
Stade Taieb Mhiri, Sfax
Referee: Eddy Maillet (Seychelles), Attendance: 20,000
MOROCCO: Khalid Fouhami, Abdeslam Ouaddou, Talal El-Karkouri, Noureddine Naybet, Oualid Regragui, Abdelkrim Kaissi (62 Youssef Mokhtari), Hocine Kharja, Mohamed El-Yaccoubi (77 Hassan Alla), Youssef Safri, Marouane Chamakh, Jaouad Zairi (46 Youssef Hadji).
BENIN: Rachid Chitou, Anicet Adjamossi, Tony Toklimety, Sylvain Rémy (57 Muri Ogunbiyi), Damien Chrysostome, Seidath Tchomogo Jocelyn Ahoueya, Romuald Bocco (90 Samuel Suka), Alain Gaspoz (72 Laurent Djaffo), Moussa Latoundji, Oumar Tchomogo.
Goals: Marouane Chamakh (15), Youssef Mokhtari (73), Abdeslam Ouaddou (75), Talal El Karkouri (80)

04.02.2004

MOROCCO - SOUTH AFRICA 1-1 (1-1)
Stade Olympique, Sousse
Referee: Hichem Guirat (Tunisia), Attendance: 6000
MOROCCO: Khalid Fouhami, Abdeslam Ouaddou, Talal El-Karkouri, Noureddine Naybet, Oualid Regragui, Youssef Mokhtari (82 Mohamed El-Yaccoubi), Youssef Hadji (90 Mourad Hdiouad), Abdelkrim Kaissi, Houcine Kharja, Youssef Safri, Jaouad Zairi.
SOUTH AFRICA: André Arendse, Thabang Molefe, Jacob Lekgetho, Aaron Mokoena, Mbulelo Mabizela, Neil Winstanley, Tehoho Mokoena (82 Jabu Pule), Delron Buckley (61 Nkosinathi Nhleko), Sibusiso Zuma, Siyabonga Nomvete, Patrick Mayo.
Goals: Youssef Safri (37 penalty) / Patrick Mayo (29)

04.02.2004

NIGERIA - BENIN 2-1 (1-0)
Stade Taieb Mhiri, Sfax
Referee: Abdel Fatah Essam (Egypt), Attendance: 15,000
NIGERIA: Vincent Enyeama, George Abbey, Joseph Yobo, Isaac Okoronkwo, Seyi George Olofinjana (88 Ikpe Ekong), John Utaka (85 Pius Ikedia), Augustine 'Jay-Jay' Okocha, Garba Lawal, Ifeanyi Udeze, Nwankwo Kanu, Julius Aghahowa (66 Peter Osaze Odemwingie).
BENIN: Maxime Agueh, Samuel Suka, Seidah Tchomogo (70 Sylvain Rémy), Tony Toklomety, Damien Chrysostome, Wassiou Oladipupo (74 Moustapha Agnide), Jonas Okétola, Jocelyn Ahoueya, Anicet Adjamossi, Oumar Tchomogo, Moussa Latoundji.
Goals: Garba Lawal (35), John Utaka (76) / Moussa Latoundji (90)

1.	MOROCCO	3	2	1	0	6	1	7
2.	NIGERIA	3	2	0	1	6	2	6
3.	South Africa	3	1	1	1	3	5	4
4.	Benin	3	0	0	3	1	8	0

Quarter-finals

07.02.2004

TUNISIA - SENEGAL 1-0 (0-0)
Stade du 7 Novembre, Radès,
Referee: Mohamed Ali Bujsaim (United Arab Emirates), Atendance: 57,000
TUNISIA: Ali Boumnijel, Anis Ayari, Radhi Jaidi, Karim Hagui, Khaled Badra, Slim Benachour, Riadh Bouazizi, Jawhar Mnari (88 Adel Chédli), Mehdi Nafti, Francileudo dos Santos (90 Imed Mhedhebi), Ziad Jaziri (78 Najeh Braham).
SENEGAL: Tony Sylva, Habib Bèye, Lamine Diatta, Pape Malick Diop, Ibrahim Fayé, Papa Bouba Diop, Salif Diao (73 Mamadou Niang), Henri Camara, Aliou Cissé, El Hadj Diouf, Lamine Sakho (85 Diomansy Kamara).
Goal: Jawhar Mnari (65)

07.02.2004
MALI - GUINEA 2-1 (1-1)
Stade Olympique d'El Menzah, Tunis
Referee: Essam Abdel Fatah (Egypt), Attendance: 1,450
MALI: Mahamadou Sidibé, Sammy Traoré, Adama Coulibaly, Fousseiny Diawara, Souleymane Diamoutène (90 Mamary Traoré), Mahamadou Diarra, Bassala Touré (79 Seydou Keita), Soumaila Coulibaly, Djibril Sidibé, Frédéric Kanouté, Dramane Traoré (61 Mohamed Lamine Sissoko).
GUINEA: Kemoko Camara, Dian Bobo Baldé, Schumann Bah, Morlaye Soumah (74 Ibrahim Sory Conté), Ousmane Ngom Camara, Kanfory Sylla, Pascal Feindouno, Abdoul Salam Sow (90 Sambegou Bangoura), Fodé Mansare, Aboubacar 'Titi' Camara, Souleymane Youla.
Goals: Frédéric Kanouté (45+2), Mahamadou Diarra (90+1) / Pascal Feindouno (15)

08.02.2004

CAMEROON - NIGERIA 1-2 (1-1)
Stade Moustapha Ben Jannet, Monastir
Referee: Mohamed Guezzaz (Morocco), Attendance: 14.750
NIGERIA: Vincent Enyeama, Joseph Yobo, Isaac Okoronkwo, George Abbey, Ifeanyi Udeze, Nwankwo Kanu (90 Joseph Enakahire), Augustine 'Jay-Jay' Okocha, Garba Lawal, Seyi Olofinjana, John Utaka, Peter Odemwingie (89 Pius Ikedia).
CAMEROON: Idriss Kameni, Jean-Joël Perrier Doumbe, Bill Tchato (62 Mohamadou Idrissou), Rigobert Song, Lucien Mettomo, Timothée Atouba, Modeste Mbami, Geremi Fotso Njitap, Eric Djemba-Djemba, Samuel Eto'o, Patrick Mboma (78 Pius N'Diefi).
Goals: Samuel Eto'o (42) / Augustine 'Jay Jay' Okocha (45+3), John Utaka (73)

08.02.2004

MOROCCO - ALGERIA 3-1 (0-0, 1-1)
Stade Taieb Mhiri, Sfax
Referee: Abdulhakim Shelmani (Libya), Attendance: 22.000
MOROCCO: Khalid Fouhami, Oualid Regragui, Abdeslam Ouaddou, Talal El-Karkouri (86 Youssef Hadji), Noureddine Naybet, Abdelkrim Kaissi (69 Mohamed El-Yaacoubi), Houcine Kharja (90 Jamal Alioui), Youssef Safri, Marouane Chamakh, Youssef Mokhtari, Jaouad Zairi.
ALGERIA: Lounes Gaouaoui, Samir Beloufa, Salim Aribi, Antar Yahia, Yazid Mansouri, Nasreddine Kraouche, Djamel Belmadi (72 Karim Ziani), Hocine Achiou, Maamar Mamouni (98 Brahim Zafour), Mansour Boutabout (78 Nassim Akrour), Abdelmalek Cherrad.
Goals: Marouane Chammakh (90+4), Youssef Hadji (113), Jawad Zairi (120+1) / Abdelmalek Cherrad (84)

Semi-finals

11.02.2004

TUNISIA - NIGERIA 1-1 (0-0, 1-1), 5-3 penalties
Stade du 7 Novembre, Radès
Referee: Bonaventure Coffi Codja (Benin), Attendance: 56,000
TUNISIA: Ali Boumnijel, Karim Hagui, Radhi Jaidi, Khaled Badra, José Clayton (91 Hatem Trabelsi), Adel Chédli (105 Imed Mhedhebi), Riadh Bouazizi, Mehdi Nafti, Jawhar Mnari (73 Slim Benachour), Ziad Jaziri, Francileudo dos Santos.
NIGERIA: Vincent Enyeama, George Abbey, Joseph Yobo, Isaac Okoronkwo, Ifeanyi Udeze, Seyi Olofinjana, John Utaka, Augustine 'Jay-Jay' Okocha, Garba Lawal (68 Ifeanyi Ekwueme), Nwankwo Kanu (86 Pius Ikedia), Peter Odemwingie.
Goals: Khaled Badra (82 penalty) / Augustine 'Jay Jay' Okocha (67 penalty)
Penalties: 1-0 Khaled Badra, 1-1 John Utaka, 2-1 Francileudo dos Santos, Peter Odemwingie (save), 3-1 Imed Mhedhebi, 3-2 Joseph Yobo, 4-2 Slim Ben Achour, 4-3 Ifeanyi Udeze, 5-3 Karim Hagui.

11.02.2004

MOROCCO - MALI 4-0 (1-0)
Stade Olympique, Sousse
Referee: Sharaf Aboubacar (Ivory Coast), Attendance: 15,000
MOROCCO: Khalid Fouhami, Akram Roumani, Noureddine Naybet, Abdeslam Ouaddou, Oualid Regragui (68 Mourad Hdioued), Abdelkrim Kaissi, Mohamed El-Yaccoubi (59 Tareq Chihab), Youssef Safri, Youssef Mokhtari, Youssef Hadji (86 Nabil Baha), Marouane Chamakh.
MALI: Mahamadou Sidibé, Fousseiny Diawara (70 Mamary Traoré), Adama Couliably, Ibrahim Thiam, Sammy Traoré, Daouda Coulibaly (46 Bassala Touré), Mahamadou Diarra, Djibril Sidibé (60 Seydou Keita), Soumaila Coulibaly, Frédéric Kanouté, Dramane Traoré.
Goals: Youssef Mokhtari (13, 57), Youssef Hadji (80), Nabil Baha (90+1)

Third Place Match

13.02.2004

NIGERIA - MALI 2-1 (1-0)
Stade Moustapha Ben Jannet, Monastir
Referee: Modou Sowe (Gambia), Attendance: 2500
NIGERIA: Vincent Enyeama, George Abbey (46 Romanus Orjinta), Joseph Yobo, Joseph Enakahire, Ifeanyi Udeze, Augustine 'Jay-Jay' Okocha, Ikpe Ekong, Ifeanyi Ekwueme (90 Garba Lawal), Pius Ikedia (78 Nwankwo Kanu), John Utaka, Peter Odemwingie. Trainer: Christian Chukwu
MALI: Mahamadou Sidibé, Souleymane Diamoutène (90 Ibrahima Koné), Sammy Traoré, Adama Coulibaly, Fousseiny Diawara, Mahamadou Diarra, Djibril Sidibé, Dramane Traoré, Mohamed Lamine Sissoko (90 Daouda Coulibaly), Frédéric Kanouté (65 Mamady Sidibé), Sedonoude Abouta. Trainer: Henri Stambouli (France).
Goals: Augustine 'Jay Jay' Okocha (17), Osaze Odemwingie (47) / Janvier Abouta (70)

Final

14.02.2004
TUNISIA - MOROCCO 2-1 (1-1)
Stade du 7 Novembre, Radès
Referee: Falla Ndoye (Senegal), Attendance: 60,000
TUNISIA: Ali Boumnijel, Hatem Trabelsi, Karim Hagui, Radhi Jaidi, José Clayton, Riadh Bouazizi, Mehdi Nafti (46 Jawhar Mnari), Adel Chédli, Slim Benachour (57 Khais Ghodhbane), Ziad Jaziri (70 Imed Mhedhebi), Francileudo dos Santos. Trainer: Roger Lemerre (France)
MOROCCO: Khalid Fouhami, Abdeslam Ouaddou, Noureddine Naybet, Talal El-Karkouri, Oualid Regragui, Abdelkrim Kaissi, Youssef Safri (63 Mohamed El-Yaccoubi), Youssef Hadji (87 Nabil Baha), Marouane Chamakh, Akram Roumani (73 Jaouad Zairi), Youssef Mokhtari. Trainer: Badou Zaki.
Goals: Francileudo dos Santos (4), Ziad Jaziri (51) / Youssef Mokhtari (38)

Twenty-fifth edition - 2006
Qualifying Tournament

Fifty-one teams entered the qualification competition for the 25th edition of the Africa Cup of Nations. Notably, these qualifiers also doubled as the qualifying tournament for the finals of the FIFA World Cup 2006, so holders Tunisia and hosts Egypt were also required to participate. Despite failure to qualify for the FIFA World Cup Finals, Egypt soon found solace as they won the Africa Cup of Nations for the fifth time, defeating the Ivory Coast 4-2 on penalties in the final after a goalless draw.

Qualifying Round

10.10.2003 Guinea Bissau - Mali 1-2 (0-1)
Goals: Dionisio Fernandes (50 penalty) / Dramane Traoré (8), Soumala Coulibaly (72)
14.11.2003 Mali - Guinea-Bissau 2-0 (1-0)
Goals: Soumaila Coulibaly (15), Djibril Sidibe (82 penalty)

11.10.2003 Equatorial Guinea - Togo 1-0 (1-0)
Goal: José Luis Barila (25 penalty)
16.11.2003 Togo - Equatorial Guinea 2-0 (1-0)
Goals: Emmanuel Adebayor (45+2), Moustapha Salifou (57)

11.10.2003 Seychelles - Zambia 0-4 (0-2)
Goals: Gift Kampamba (8), Dudley Fichite (44), Harry Milanzi (52), Mumamba Numba (57)
15.11.2003 Zambia - Seychelles 1-1 (1-1)
Goals: Harry Milanzi (5) / Robert Suezetta (30)

11.10.2003 São Tomé e Principe – Libya 0-1 (0-0)
Goal: Ciraje (87)
16.11.2003 Libya - São Tomé e Príncipe 8-0 (4-0)
Goals: Ahmed al-Masli (15, 20, 25), Tarek al-Taeb (45, 60), Marei al-Ramly (54), Ahmed Saad (75), Mohammed al-Kakly (85)

11.10.2003 Niger - Algeria 0-1 (0-0)
Goal: Boutabou Mansour (65)
14.11.2003 Algeria 6-0 Niger 6-0 (3-0)
Goals: Abdelmalek Cherrad (16, 22), Mansour Boutabout (43, 71), Mamer Mamouni (47), Nassim Akrour (81)

11.10.2003 Tanzania - Kenya 0-0
15.11.2003 Kenya - Tanzania 3-0 (3-0)
Goals: Denis Oliech (10, 32), Michael Okoth (30)

Burkina Faso - Central African Republic (withdrew)

11.10.2003 Madagascar - Benin 1-1 (1-0)
Goals: Robert Edmond (30) / Jean Jaurs Corea (73)
16.11.2003 Benin - Madagascar 3-2 (1-2)
Goals: Omar Tchomogo (33 penalty, 62, 90+2 penalty) / Jean-Jacques Radonamahafalison (16), Alain Patrick Andriantaina (23)

11.10.2003 Botswana - Lesotho 4-1 (2-0)
Goals: Tshepiso Molwantwa (6), Nelson Gabolwelwe (44), Diphetogo Selolwane (48, 62) / Moses Ramafole (75)
16.11.2003 Lesotho - Botswana 0-0

11.10.2003 Uganda - Mauritius 3-0 (0-0)
Goals: Asani Bajope (52), Hassan Mubiru (67), David Obua (89)
16.11.2003 Mauritius - Uganda 3-1 (1-0, 3-0)
Goals: Ricardo Naboth (36), Cyril Mourgine (61), Jerry Louis (89) / David Obua (112)

12.10.2003 Zimbabwe - Mauritania 3-0 (1-0)
Goals: Adam Ndlovu (24), Kaitano Tembo (77), Peter Ndlovu (83)
14.11.2003 Mauritania - Zimbabwe 2-1 (2-0)
Goals: Yohan Langlet (3), Bilal Sidibe (10) / George Mbwando (81)

12.10.2003 Chad - Angola 3-1 (0-0)
Goals: Francis Oumar (65, 75, 89) / Bruno Mauro (63)
16.11.2003 Angola - Chad 2-0 (1-0)
Goals: Fabrice Alcebiades Maieco 'Akwá' (32), Bruno Mauro (61)

12.10.2003 Ethiopia - Malawi 1-3 (0-1)
Goals: Getu Teshome (81) / Esau Kawyenda (39), Esau Kawyenda (55), Peter Mgangira (89)
15.11.2003 Malawi - Ethiopia 0-0

12.10.2003 Guinea - Mozambique 1-0 (0-0)
Goal: Sambegou Bangoura (47)
16.11.2003 Mozambique - Guinea 3-4 (0-3)
Goals: Dario (71, 77, 87) / Souleymane Youla (17), Sambegou Bangoura (25, 35, 60)

12.10.2003 Congo- Brazzaville - Sierra Leone 1-0 (0-0)
Goal: Gerard Lebaly (89 penalty)
16.11.2003 Sierra Leone - Congo-Brazzaville 1-1
Goals: Ibrahima Koroma (penalty) / Rolf-Christel Guié-Mien

12.10.2003 Sudan - Eritrea 3-0 (0-0)
Goals: Haitham Tumbul (71), Haitham Al-Rasheed (75), Mujahid Ahmed (88)
16.11.2003 Eritrea - Sudan 0-0

12.10.2003 Swaziland - Cape Verde 1-1 (0-0)
Goals: Siza Dlamini (65) / Calo (53)
16.11.2003 Cape Verde - Swaziland 3-0 (1-0)
Goals: Cafu (31, 65), Calo (89 penalty)

12.10.2003 Rwanda - Namibia 3-0 (1-0)
Goals: Jean-Pierre Manamana (42), Olivier Kalekezi (50), Jean Lomami (58)
15.11.2003 Namibia - Rwanda 1-1 (1-1)
Goals: Paulus Shipanga (41) / Jean Lomani (39)

12.10.2003 Gambia - Liberia 2-0 (0-0)
Goals: Abou Njie (62), Edrissa Sonko (70)
16.11.2003 Liberia - Gambia 3-0 (1-0)
Goals: Zizi Roberts (10), Isaac Tondo (75, 85)

12.10.2003 Burundi - Gabon 0-0
15.11.2003 Gabon - Burundi 4-1 (3-0)
Goals: Sylvain Nzingou Chidan Star (2), Valery Twite (17 own goal), Stephane Nguema (37, 80) /
Gabriel Nzeyimana Longo (90)

16.11.2003 Somalia - Ghana 0-5 (0-1)
Goals: Nana Arhin Duah (25, 56), Isaac Boakye (69, 89), Asamoah Gyan (82)
19.11.2003 Ghana - Somalia 2-0 (1-0)
Goals: Stephen Appiah (27), Lawrence Adjei (89)

Group Stage

Group 1

05.06.2004 Zambia - Togo 1-0 (1-0)
Goal: Jacob Mulenga (10)
05.06.2004 Senegal - Congo 2-0 (0-0)
Goals: Lamine Diatta (59), Moussa Ndiaye (77)
06.06.2004 Liberia - Mali 1-0 (1-0)
Goal: Alvin Kieh (88)
19.06.2004 Mali - Zambia 1-1 (0-1)
Goals: Frédéric Kanouté (80) / Harry Milanzi (16)
20.06.2004 Congo 3-0 Liberia 3-0 (0-0)
Goals: Michel Clauga Bouanga (52 penalty), Armel Mamouna-Ossila (57), Makita-Passy (65)
20.06.2004 Togo - Senegal 3-1 (1-0)
Goals: Emmanuel Sheyi Adebayor (29), Junior Senaya (78, 89) / Pape Bouba Diop (83)
03.07.2004 Senegal - Zambia 1-0 (1-0)
Goal: Babacar Gueye (21)
04.07.2004 Congo - Mali 1-0 (1-0)
Goal: Armel Mamouna-Ossila (30)
04.07.2004 Liberia - Togo 0-0
04.09.2004 Zambia – Liberia 1-0 (0-0)
Goal: Kalusha Bwalya (89)
05.09.2004 Mali - Senegal 2-2 (1-1)
Goals: Mamadou Diallo (4), Frédéric Kanouté (52) / Henri Camara (44), Pape Cire Dia (89)
05.09.2004 Togo - Congo 2-0 (1-0)
Goals: Fabry Makita-Passy (39 own goal), Emmanuel Sheyi Adebayor (70)
10.10.2004 Congo - Zambia 2-3 (0-2)
Goals: Claude Bouanga (77), Armel Mamouna-Ossila (83) / Collins Mbesuma (2, 36, 67)
10.10.2004 Liberia - Senegal 0-3 (0-1)
Goals: Pape Bouba Diop (41), Henri Camara (50, 73)
10.10.2004 Togo - Mali 1-0 (1-0)
Goal: Emmanuel Sheyi Adebayor (23)
26.03.2005 Senegal - Liberia 6-1 (2-0)
Goals: Khalilou Fadiga (17), El Hadji Diouf (42 penalty, 84), Abdoulaye Diagne Faye (52), Henri
Camara (69), Moussa Ndiaye (73) / Isaac Tondo (88)
26.03.2005 Zambia - Congo 2-0 (2-0)
Goals: Elijah Tana (2), Collins Mbesuma (44)

183

27.03.2005 Mali - Togo 1-2 (1-0) [abandoned at 1-2 in 90' due to crowd trouble, resul stood
Goals: Soumaila Coulibaly (16) / Moustapha Salifou (83), Souleymane Maman (90)
05.06.2005 Congo - Senegal 0-0
05.06.2005 Mali - Liberia 4-1 (2-0)
Goals: Dramane Coulibaly (5 penalty, 34), Souleymane Diamoutene (48 penalty), Mahamadou Diarra
(75) / Shelton Barlee (58)
05.06.2005 Togo - Zambia 4-1 (2-1)
Goals: Emmanuel Shéyi Adébayor (15 penalty, 88 penalty), Chérif Maman Touré (44), Abdelkader
Coubadja Touré (60) / Gift Kampamba (17)
18.06.2005 Senegal - Togo 2-2 (2-1)
Goals: Mamadou Niang (14), Henri Camara (30) / Adekambi Olufade (11), Emmanuel Sheyi Adebayor
(73)
18.06.2005 Zambia - Mali 2-1 (1-0)
Goals: Linos Chalwe (27), Collins Mbesuma (85) / Soumaila Coulibaby (72)
19.06.2005 Liberia - Congo 0-2 (0-1)
Goals: Rudy Bhebey (3, 73)
03.09.2005 Mali - Congo 2-0 (0-0)
Goals: Abdoulaye Demba (48), Mohamed Lamine Cissoko (51)
03.09.2005 Zambia - Senegal 0-1 (0-0)
Goal: El Hadji Diouf (54)
04.09.2005 Togo - Liberia 3-0 (0-0)
Goals: Emmanuel Adebayor (57, 85), Cherif Mamam Touré (75)
01.10.2005 Liberia - Zambia 0-5 (0-0)
Goals: Ignatius Luipa (50, 81), Nchimunya Mweetwa (52, 62), Mumamba Numba (60)
08.10.2005 Senegal - Mali 3-0 (2-0)
Goals: Henri Camara (18, 65), El Hadji Diouf (23)
08.10.2005 Congo - Togo 2-3 (1-1)
Goals: Bertrand Bouity (26), Armel Mamouna-Ossila (56) / Emmanuel Adebayor (40), Abdelkader
Coubadja Touré (60, 70)

1.	TOGO	10	7	2	1	20	8	23
2.	SENEGAL	10	6	3	1	21	8	21
3.	ZAMBIA	10	6	1	3	16	10	19
4.	Congo	10	3	1	6	10	14	10
5.	Mali	10	2	2	6	11	14	8
6.	Liberia	10	1	1	8	3	27	4

Group 2

05.06.2004 South Africa - Cape Verde 2-1 (1-0)
Goals: Mbulelo Mabizela (42, 70) / Janicio Martins (78)
05.06.2004 Burkina Faso - Ghana 1-0 (0-0)
Goal: Mamadou Zongo (80)
06.06.2004 Uganda - DR Congo 1-0 (0-0)
Goal: Ibrahim Sekajja (76)
19.06.2004 Cape Verde - Uganda 1-0 (1-0)
Goal: Cafu (41)
20.06.2004 Ghana - South Africa 3-0 (1-0)
Goals: Sulley Muntari (14), Stephen Appiah (55, 78)
20.06.2004 DR Congo - Burkina Faso 3-2 (1-1)
Goals: Marcel Mbayo (13), Mbuta Mbala Biscotte (76), Dikilu Bageta (90 penalty) / Amadou Touré
(27), Moumoni Dagano (89)
03.07.2004 Cape Verde - DR Congo 1-1 (1-1)
Goals: Jimmy Modeste (26) / Kaluyitukadioko (2)

184

03.07.2004 South Africa - Burkina Faso 2-0 (2-0)
Goals: Steven Pienaar (13), Shaun Bartlett (41)
03.07.2004 Uganda - Ghana 1-1 (1-0)
Goals: David Obua (45) / Asamoah Gyan (86)
04.09.2004 Burkina Faso - Uganda 2-0 (1-0)
Goals: Moumouni Dagano (34), Abdoul Aziz Nikiema (79)
05.09.2004 DR Congo - South Africa 1-0 (0-0)
Goal: Kabamba Musasa (87)
05.09.2004 Ghana - Cape Verde 2-0 (1-0)
Goals: Michael Essien (23 penalty), Nelson Viega (62 own goal)
09.10.2004 Cape Verde - Burkina Faso 1-0 (1-0)
Goal: Cafu (3)
10.10.2004 Ghana - DR Congo 0-0
10.10.2004 Uganda - South Africa 0-1 (0-0)
Goal: Benni McCarthy (63 penalty)
26.03.2005 Burkina Faso - Cape Verde 1-2 (0-0)
Goals: Moumouni Dagano (70) / Carlos Morais (48, 88)
26.03.2005 South Africa - Uganda 2-1 (1-0)
Goals: Quinton Fortuna (19 penalty), Steven Pienaar (71) / David Obua (62 penalty)
27.03.2005 DR Congo - Ghana 1-1 (0-1)
Goals: Shabani Nonda (51) / Asamoah Gyan (31)
04.06.2005 Cape Verde - South Africa 1-2 (0-2)
Goals: Arlindo Cafu (78) / Benedict McCarthy (11), Delron Buckley (13)
05.06.2005 DR Congo - Uganda 4-0 (1-0)
Goals: Shabani Nonda (4, 85 penalty), Ngasanya Ilunga (62), Zola Matumona (87)
05.06.2005 Ghana - Burkina Faso 2-1 (0-1)
Goals: Stephen Appiah (66 penalty), Matthew Amoah (81) / Moumouni Dagano (25)
18.06.2005 Burkina Faso - DR Congo 2-0 (1-0)
Goals: Saidou Panandetiguiri (4), Beli Moumouni Dagano (68)
18.06.2005 South Africa - Ghana 0-2 (0-0)
Goals: Matthew Amoah (59), Michael Essien (90)
18.06.2005 Uganda - Cape Verde 1-0 (1-0)
Goal: Geofrey Sserunkuma (36)
03.09.2005 Burkina Faso - South Africa 3-1 (2-0)
Goals: Abdoulaye Cissé (31, 48 penalty), Kebé Yahia (39) / Sibusiso Zuma (75)
04.09.2005 DR Congo - Cape Verde 2-1 (1-1)
Goals: Kitambala Mubiala (21), Trésor Mabi Mputu (48) / Carlos Morais (22)
04.09.2005 Ghana - Uganda 2-0 (2-0)
Goals: Michael Essien (11), Matthew Amoah (15)
08.10.2005 Cape Verde - Ghana 0-4 (0-2)
Goals: Frimpong Asamoah (5), Sulley Muntari (35), Asamoah Gyan (75), Godwin Attram (87)
08.10.2005 South Africa - DR Congo 2-2 (1-2)
Goals: Sibusiso Zuma (5, 52) / Mabi Mputu (11), Shabani Nonda (44)
08.10.2005 Uganda - Burkina Faso 2-2 (1-1)
Goals: Simon Masaba (30 penalty), Geoffrey Serunkuma (71) / Yahia Kebe (15), Florent Rouamba (75)

1.	GHANA	10	6	3	1	17	4	21
2.	DR CONGO	10	4	4	2	14	10	16
3.	SOUTH AFRICA	10	5	1	4	12	14	16
4.	Burkina Faso	10	4	1	5	14	13	13
5.	Cape Verde	10	3	1	6	8	15	10
6.	Uganda	10	2	2	6	6	15	8

185

Group 3

06.06.2004 Cameroon - Benin 2-1 (2-1)
Goals: Samuel Eto'o Fils (43), Rigobert Song (45+2) / Seidah Konabe (11)
06.06.2004 Ivory Coast - Libya 2-0 (1-0)
Goals: Aruna Dindane (36), Didier Drogba (62 penalty)
06.06.2004 Sudan - Egypt 0-3 (0-1)
Goals: Abdelhalim Ali (6), Mohamed Aboutraika (52), Mohamed Abdelwahab (86)
18.06.2004 Libya - Cameroon 0-0
20.06.2004 Benin - Sudan 1-1 (1-1)
Goals: Muri Ogunbiyi (33) / Ahmed El Fatih (44)
20.06.2004 Egypt - Ivory Coast 1-2 (0-1)
Goals: Mohamed Aboutraika (55) / Aruna Dindane 22, Didier Drogba (75)
03.07.2004 Sudan - Libya 0-1 (0-0)
Goal: Nader Kara (90+2)
04.07.2004 Benin - Egypt 3-3 (1-0)
Goals: Oumar Tchomogo (23 penalty), Jocelyn Ahoueya (48), Laurent D'Jaffo (68) / Hassan Mustafa (66, 79), Hossam Ghali (75)
04.07.2004 Cameroon - Ivory Coast 2-0 (0-0)
Goals: Samuel Eto'o (80), Guy Feutchine (82)
03.09.2004 Libya - Benin 4-1 (1-1)
Goals: Younus Al Shibani (9), Nader Kara (47), Ahmed Osman (49), Marei Suliman (69) / Bachirou Osseni (14)
05.09.2004 Ivory Coast - Sudan 5-0 (3-0)
Goals: Didier Drogba (11 penalty), Aruna Dindane (15, 64), Giles Yapi Yapo (25) / Bakary Koné (55)
05.09.2004 Egypt - Cameroon 3-2 (1-0)
Goals: Mohamed Shawki (44), Ahmed Hassan (74 penalty), Tarek El-Sayed (89) / Bill Tchato (90), Samuel Eto'o (90+1)
08.10.2004 Libya - Egypt 2-1 (1-0)
Goals: Nader Kara (31), Ahmed Osman (84) / Amr Zaki (51)
09.10.2004 Sudan - Cameroon 1-1 (1-0)
Goals: Hamouda Bachir (18) / Joseph-Désiré Job (90)
10.10.2004 Benin - Ivory Coast 0-1 (0-0)
Goal: Aruna Dindane (48)
27.03.2005 Cameroon - Sudan 2-1 (1-1)
Goals: Geremi (35), Achille Webo (90+2) / Haytham Tambal (42)
27.03.2005 Ivory Coast - Benin 3-0 (2-0)
Goals: Bonaventure Kalou (12), Didier Drogba (18 penalty, 59)
27.03.2005 Egypt - Libya 4-1 (0-0)
Goals: Ahmed Hossam 'Mido' (55), Emad Abdel Nabi 'Moteab' (57, 80), Ahmed Hassan (77) / Osman El Fergani (52)
03.06.2005 Libya - Ivory Coast 0-0
04.06.2005 Benin - Cameroon 1-4 (0-1)
Goals: Coffi Agbessi (82) / Rigobert Song (19), Achile Webo (52), Geremi Fotso Njitap (66), Samuel Eto'o (67 penalty)
05.06.2005 Egypt - Sudan 6-1 (3-0)
Goals: Abdelhalim Ali (8, 31), Amr Zaki (28, 51), Tarek El Sayed (64), Ahmed Eid (72) / Haitham Tambal (81)
19.06.2005 Cameroon - Libya 1-0 (1-0)
Goal: Achille Webo (27)
19.06.2005 Ivory Coast - Egypt 2-0 (1-0)
Goals: Didier Drogba (42, 49)
17.08.2005 Sudan - Benin 1-0 (1-0)
Goal: Haytham Tambal (20)

02.09.2005 Libya - Sudan 0-0
04.09.2005 Ivory Coast - Cameroon 2-3 (1-2)
Goals: Didier Drobga (38, 47) / Achille Webo (30, 45+2, 85)
04.09.2005 Egypt - Benin 4-1 (2-0)
Goals: Amr Zaki (12, 16, 84), Ahmed Hossam (65) / Stephane Sessegnon (59)
08.10.2005 Sudan - Ivory Coast 1-3 (0-1)
Goals: Haytham Tambal (89) / Kanga Akale (22), Aruna Dindane (51, 73)
08.10.2005 Cameroon - Egypt 1-1 (1-0)
Goals: Rodolphe Douala (20) / Mohamed Shawki (79)
09.10.2005 Benin - Libya 1-0 (0-0)
Goal: Rachad Chitou (60)

1.	IVORY COAST	10	7	1	2	20	7	22
2.	CAMEROON	10	6	3	1	18	10	21
3.	EGYPT	10	5	2	3	26	15	17
4.	LIBYA	10	3	3	4	8	10	12
5.	Sudan	10	1	3	6	6	22	6
6.	Benin	10	1	2	7	9	23	5

Group 4

05.06.2004 Gabon - Zimbabwe 1-1 (0-0)
Goals: Thierry Issiemou (52), Shingayi Kaondera (84)
05.06.2004 Nigeria - Rwanda 2-0 (0-0)
Goals: Obafemi Martins (56, 87)
05.06.2004 Algeria - Angola 0-0
19.06.2004 Rwanda - Gabon 3-1 (2-1)
Goals: Said Abed (3, 63), Jimmy Mulisa (26) / Theo Ngwema (19)
20.06.2004 Angola - Nigeria 1-0 (0-0)
Goal: Fabrice Alcebiades Maieco 'Akwá' (85)
20.06.2004 Zimbabwe - Algeria 1-1 (0-1)
Goals: Madjid Bougherra (59 own goal) / Abdelmalek Cherrad (5)
03.07.2004 Gabon - Angola 2-2
Goals: Thierry Issiemou, Theodore Nze Nguema / Fabrice Alcebiades Maieco 'Akwá', Marco Paulo
03.07.2004 Nigeria - Algeria 1-0 (0-0)
Goal: Joseph Yobo (80)
03.07.2004 Rwanda - Zimbabwe 0-2 (0-1)
Goals: Peter Ndlovu (40), Tinashe Nengomasha (79)
05.09.2004 Algeria - Gabon 0-3 (0-0)
Goals: Catalina Aubame (56), Georges Akiremy (74), Etienne Bito'o (88)
05.09.2004 Angola - Rwanda 1-0 (0-0)
Goal: Freddy (51)
05.09.2004 Zimbabwe - Nigeria 0-3 (0-2)
Goals: Julius Aghahowa (4), Joseph Enakhahire (27), Yakubu Aiyegbeni (50 penalty)
09.10.2004 Gabon - Nigeria 1-1 (1-0)
Goals: Thierry Issiemou (35) / Yakubu Ayegbeni (70)
09.10.2004 Rwanda - Algeria 1-1 (1-1)
Goals: Said-Abed Makasi (8) / Assad Bourahili (13)
10.10.2004 Angola - Zimbabwe 1-0 (0-0)
Goal: Amado Flávio (52)
26.03.2005 Nigeria - Gabon 2-0 (0-0)
Goals: Julius Aghahowa (84), Nwankwo Kanu (86)
27.03.2005 Algeria - Rwanda 1-0 (0-0)
Goal: Mansour Boutabout (48)

27.03.2005 Zimbabwe - Angola 2-0 (0-0)
Goals: Shingirai Kawondera (60), Benjamin Mwaruwaru (71)
05.06.2005 Rwanda - Nigeria 1-1 (0-0)
Goals: Jimmy Gatete (53) / Obafemi Martins (79)
05.06.2005 Zimbabwe - Gabon 1-0 (0-0)
Goal: Peter Ndlovu (66 penalty)
05.06.2005 Angola - Algeria 2-1 (0-0)
Goals: Flávio Amado (48), Fabrice Alcebiades Maieco 'Akwá' (57) / Mansour Boutabout (66)
18.06.2005 Gabon - Rwanda 3-0 (1-0)
Goals: Alain Djissikadie (11), Dieudonne Londo (56), Theodore Zue (60)
18.06.2005 Nigeria - Angola 1-1 (1-0)
Goals: Austin 'Jay-Jay' Okocha (5) / Paulo Figuereido (60)
19.06.2005 Algeria - Zimbabwe 2-2 (1-1)
Goals: Antar Yahia (17), Sofiane Daoud (48) / Shingayi Kawondera (33), Peter Ndlovu (87)
04.09.2005 Algeria - Nigeria 2-5 (0-2)
Goals: Hanza Yacef (48), Mansour Boutabout (58) / Obafemi Martins (20 penalty), 89, 90), John Utaka
(39), Christian Obodo (81)
04.09.2005 Angola - Gabon 3-0 (2-0)
Goals: Rene Nsi Akoue (22 own goal), Mantorras (42), Zé Kalanga (89)
04.09.2005 Zimbabwe - Rwanda 3-1 (2-1)
Goals: Shingarai Kawondera (3), Benjani Mwaruwari (44), Ashley Rambanapasi (75) / Zyenika
Makonese (32 own goal)
08.10.2005 Gabon - Algeria 0-0
08.10.2005 Nigeria - Zimbabwe 5-1 (1-0)
Goals: Obafemi Martins (35, 75 penalty), Yusuf Ayila (62), Nwankwo Kanu (80 penalty), Peter
Odemwingie (89) / Benjamin Mwaruwari (70)
08.10.2005 Rwanda - Angola 0-1 (0-0)
Goal: Fabrice Alcebiades Maieco 'Akwá' (79)

1.	ANGOLA	10	6	3	1	12	6	21
2.	NIGERIA	10	6	3	1	21	7	21
3.	ZIMBABWE	10	4	3	3	13	14	15
4.	Gabon	10	2	4	4	11	13	10
5.	Algeria	10	1	5	4	8	15	8
6.	Rwanda	10	1	2	7	6	16	5

Group 5

05.06.2004 Malawi - Morocco 1-1 (1-1)
Goals: Heston Munthali (45) / Youssef Safri (26)
05.06.2004 Tunisia - Botswana 4-1 (2-0)
Goals: Jose Clayton (9), Karim Hagui (35, 78), Ali Zitouni (74) / Debhelogo Selolwane (65)
19.06.2004 Botswana - Malawi 2-0 (2-0)
Goals: Diphetogo Selolwane (5), Nelson Gabolwelwe (24)
20.06.2004 Guinea - Tunisia 2-1 (1-0)
Goals: Kaba Diawara (10, 46), Najeh Braham (55)
03.07.2004 Botswana - Morocco 0-1 (0-1)
Goal: Youssef Mokthari (27)
03.07.2004 Malawi - Guinea 1-1 (0-0)
Goals: Albert Mpinganjira (72) / Kaba Diawara (80)
04.09.2004 Kenya - Malawi 3-2 (3-1)
Goals: John Baraza (22, 31), Dennis Oliech (26), Malupo Mkhandawire (43) / Heston Munthali (89
penalty)
04.09.2004 Morocco - Tunisia 1-1 (0-1)

Goals: Talal El Karkouri (89) / Francileudo dos Santos (13)
05.09.2004 Guinea - Botswana 4-0 (1-0)
Goals: Pascal Feindouno (44 penalty), Souleymane Youla (54), Kaba Diawara (60), Fode Mansare (80)
09.10.2004 Botswana - Kenya 2-1 (0-1)
Goals: Tshepiso Molwantwana (50), Diphetego Selolwane (55) / Dennis Oliech (6)
09.10.2004 Malawi - Tunisia 2-2 (2-0)
Goals: Russell Mwafulirwa (20), Emmanuel Chipatalala (37) / Riadh Bouazizi (82), Jawhar Mnari (90)
10.10.2004 Guinea - Morocco 1-1 (0-1)
Goals: Foge Mansare (52) / Marouane Chamakh (5)
17.11.2004 Kenya - Guinea 2-1 (1-1)
Goals: Dennis Oliech (9), Edwin Mkenya (70) / Pascal Feindouno (18 penalty)
09.02.2005 Morocco - Kenya 5-1 (2-0)
Goals: Jawad Zairi (12, 39, 90), Mounir Diane (46), Youssef Hadji (81) / Musa Otieno (90)
26.03.2005 Kenya - Botswana 1-0 (1-0)
Goal: Dennis Oliech (45)
26.03.2005 Morocco - Guinea 1-0 (0-0)
Goal: Youssef Hadji (65)
26.03.2005 Tunisia - Malawi 7-0 (2-0)
Goals: Haykel Guemamdia (2), Francileudo dos Santos (13, 52, 76, 77), José Clayton (60 penalty), Kais Ghodhbane (79)
04.06.2005 Botswana - Tunisia 1-3 (1-2)
Goals: Mogogi Gabonamong (13) / Mehdi Nafti (28), Francileudo dos Santos (44), Wissem El Abdi (78)
04.06.2005 Morocco - Malawi 4-1 (2-1)
Goals: Youssef Safri (16 penalty), Youssef Hadji (21, 76), Hocine Kharja (72) / Essau Kanyenda (11)
05.06.2005 Guinea - Kenya 1-0 (0-0)
Goal: Sambegou Bangoura (67)
11.06.2005 Tunisia - Guinea 2-0 (1-0)
Goals: Jose Clayton (36 penalty), Adel Chedli (79)
18.06.2005 Kenya - Morocco 0-0
18.06.2005 Malawi - Botswana 1-3 (0-2)
Goals: Russel Mwafulirwa (48) / Tshepiso Molwantwa (10), Diphetogo Selolwane (40), Tshepo Motlhabankwe (87)
17.08.2005 Tunisia - Kenya 1-0 (1-0)
Goal: Haykel Guemamdia (2)
03.09.2005 Kenya - Tunisia 0-2 (0-1)
Goals: Haykel Guemamdia (2), Issam Jomaa (85)
03.09.2005 Morocco - Botswana 1-0 (0-0)
Goal: Talal El Karkouri (55)
04.09.2005 Guinea - Malawi 3-1 (2-1)
Goals: Pascal Feindouno (12), Kaba Diawara (35), Sambegou Bangoura (67) / Noel Mkandawire (36)
08.10.2005 Botswana - Guinea 1-2 (1-0)
Goals: Tshepiso Molwantwa (35) / Ousmane Bangoura (73, 76)
08.10.2005 Malawi - Kenya 3-0 (1-0)
Goals: Jimmy Zakazaka (6), Noel Mkandawire (49, 61)
08.10.2005 Tunisia - Morocco 2-2 (1-2)
Goals: José Clayton (18), Adel Chadli (69) / Marouane Chamarh (3), Talal El Karkouri (42)

1.TUNISIA	10	6	3	1	25	9	21
2.MOROCCO	10	5	5	0	17	7	20
3.GUINEA	10	5	2	3	15	10	17
4.Kenya	10	3	1	6	8	17	10
5.Botswana	10	3	0	7	10	18	9
6.Malawi	10	1	3	6	12	26	6

The top three teams of each group qualified for final tournament together with the team finishing 4th in Group 3 which contained hosts Egypt.

Final Tournament (Egypt)

GROUP A

20.01.2006

EGYPT - LIBYA 3-0 (2-0)
Cairo International Stadium
Referee: Lassina Pare (Burkina Faso), Attendance: 65,000
EGYPT: Essam El-Hadary, Mohamed Barakat, Wael Gomaa, Ibrahim Said, Abdel Zaher El-Saqqa, Mohamed Abdel Wahab (88 Tarek El-Sayed), Ahmed Hassan, Mohamed Shawki, Mohamed Aboutraika (79 Hassan Moustafa), Ahmed Hossam 'Mido', Amr Zaki (81 Emad Abdel Nabi 'Moteab').
LIBYA: Luis de Agustini, Omar Dawood, Younes Alshibani, Osama Hamadi, Mahmoud Maklouf, Jehad Muntaser (75 Muftah Ghzalla), Abdulnaser Slil, Nader Atrhoni, Ahmed Saed (63 Tarek El-Taib), Marei Ramli, Salem Rewani.
Sent off: Agustini (74)
Goals: Ahmed Hossam 'Mido' (17), Mohamed Aboutraika (22), Ahmed Hassan (76)

21.01.2006

MOROCCO - IVORY COAST 0-1 (0-1)
Cairo International Stadium
Referee: Jerome Damon (South Africa), Attendance: 8,000
MOROCCO: Tarik El-Jarmouni, Badr El-Kaddouri, Noureddine Naybet, Talal El-Karkouri, Youssef Chippo, Oualid Regragui, Youssef Hadji, Houssine Kharja (83 Ali Boussaboun), Mohamed Yaacoubi (85 Hicham Aboucherouane), Youssef Safri, Marouane Chamakh.
IVORY COAST: Jean-Jacques Tizie, Kolo Toure, Arthur Boka, Emmanuel Eboue, Blaise Kouassi, Emerse Fae, Yaya Toure, Kanga Akale, Didier Zokora, Bonaventure Kalou (75 Bakary Koné), Didier Drogba (65 Arouna Koné).
Goal: Didier Drogba (37 penalty)

24.01.2006

LIBYA - IVORY COAST 1-2 (1-1)
Cairo International Stadium
Referee: Shamsul Maidin (Singapore), Attendance: 42,000
LIBYA: Muftah Ghzalla, Younes Alshibani, Osama Hamadi, Waled Osman, Naje Shushan, Jehad Muntaser (72 Salem Rewani), Tarek El-Taib (78 Ahmed Saed), Abdesalam Khamis, Marei Ramli (83 Khaled Hussen), Nader Atrhoni, Nader Karra.
IVORY COAST: Jean-Jacques Tizie, Abdoulaye Meite, Kolo Toure, Arthur Boka, Marc Zoro, Yaya Toure (88 Emerse Fae), Kanga Akale, Didier Zokora, Gilles Yapi Yapo (69 Bonaventure Kalou), Didier Drogba, Arouna Koné (82 Bakary Koné).
Goals: Abdesalam Khamis (41) / Didier Drogba (10), Yaya Toure (74)

24.01.2006

EGYPT - MOROCCO 0-0
At Cairo International Stadium
Referee: Bonaventure Coffi Codja (Benin), Attendance: 75,000
EGYPT: Essam El-Hadary, Ahmed Fathi (49 Hassan Moustafa), Ibrahim Said, Abdel Zaher El-Saqqa, Wael Gomaa, Mohammed Abdel Wahab, Mohamed Barakat, Mohamed Shawki, Ahmed Hassan (66 Mohamed Aboutraika), Amr Zaki, Ahmed Hossam 'Mido' (79 Emad Abdel Nabi 'Moteab').
MOROCCO: Tarik El-Jarmouni, Noureddine Naybet, Talal El-Karkouri, Oualid Regragui (76 Youssef Chippo), Youssef Hadji (71 Ali Boussaboun), Badr El-Kaddouri, Houssine Kharja, Amine Erbati, Mohamed Yaacoubi, Youssef Safri, Marouane Chamakh (84 Hicham Aboucherouane).

28.01.2006

EGYPT - IVORY COAST 3-1 (1-1)
Cairo International Stadium
Referee: Eddy Maillet (Seychelles), Attendance: 74,000
EGYPT: Essam El-Hadary, Mohamed Barakat, Ibrahim Said, Abdel Zaher El-Saqqa, Wael Gomaa, Mohammed Abdel Wahab (62 Tarek El-Sayed), Mohamed Shawki, Ahmed Hassan, Mohamed Aboutraika (75 Hassan Moustafa), Ahmed Hossam 'Mido' (24 Hossam Hassan), Emad Abdel Nabi 'Moteab'.
IVORY COAST: Jean-Jacques Tizie (59 Boubacar Barry), Cyril Domoraud, Emmanuel Eboue, Blaise Kouassi, Guy Demel (67 Bakary Koné), Siaka Tiene, Emerse Fae, Yaya Toure (85 Kanga Akale), Bonaventure Kalou, Romaric N'Dri, Arouna Koné.
Goals: Emad Abdel Nabi 'Moteab' (8, 69), Mohamed Aboutraika (61) / Arouna Koné (43)

28.01.2006

LIBYA - MOROCCO 0-0
Military Academy Stadium, Cairo
Referee: Mourad Daami (Tunisia), Attendance: 5,000
LIBYA: Luis de Agustini, Omar Dawood, Osama Hamadi, Walid Osman, Naje Shushan, Tarek El-Taib, Abdesalam Khamis, Marei Ramli, Nader Atrhoni, Ahmed Saed, Nader Karra.
MOROCCO: Tarek El-Jarmouni, Noureddine Naybet, Talal El-Karkouri, Oualid Regragui, Youssef Hadji, Badr El-Kaddouri, Houssine Kharja, Mohamed Yaacoubi (73 Mohamed Madihi), Youssef Safri (86 Amine Erbati), Marouane Chamakh, Hicham Aboucherouane (58 Ali Boussaboun).

1.	EGYPT	3	2	1	0	6	1	7
2.	IVORY COAST	3	2	0	1	4	4	6
3.	Morocco	3	0	2	1	0	1	2
4.	Libya	3	0	1	2	1	5	1

GROUP B

21.01.2006

CAMEROON - ANGOLA 3-1 (2-1)
At Military Stadium, Cairo
Referee: Mohamed Guezzaz (Morocco), Attendance: 8,000
CAMEROON: Hamidou Souleymanou, Rigobert Song, Raymond Kalla, Timothee Atouba, Geremi Fotso Njitap, Alioum Saidou, Jean Makoun, Daniel Ngom Kome (83 Salomon Olembé), Samuel Eto'o (89 Achille Emana), Achille Webo (75 Pierre Boya), Roudolphe Douala.

ANGOLA: Joao Ricardo, Jamba, Jacinto, Lebo-Lebo, Marco Abreu (72 Delgado), Andre, Figueiredo, Mendonça, Edson (65 José Nsimba Baptista 'Zé Kalanga'), FLÁVIO da Silva Amado (60 Pedro Manuel Torres Mantorras), Fabrice Alcebiades Maieco 'Akwá'.
Goals: Samuel Eto'o (21, 39, 78) / FLÁVIO da Silva Amado (31 penalty)

21.01.2006

TOGO - DR CONGO 0-2 (0-1)
At Military Stadium, Cairo
Referee: Mourad Daami (Tunisia), Attendance: 6,000
TOGO: Kossi Agassa, Jean-Paul Yaovi Abalo, Junior Yao Senaya, Emmanuel Mathias, Zanzan Atte-Oudeyi, Eric Akoto, Yao Aziawonou, Alaixys Romao (55 Moustapha Salifou), Cherif Toure Mamam (85 Mikael Dogbe), Kader Cougbadja, Adekanmi Olufade (59 Emmanuel Adebayor).
DR CONGO: Pascal Kalemba, Herita Ilunga, Christian Kinkela, Gladys Bokese, Felicien Kabundi, Marcel Mbayo, Tshinyama Tshiolola, Zola Matumona (84 Ngasanya Ilongo), Biscotte Mbala (86 Tshatsho Kabamba), Tresor Mputu (62 Franck Matingou), Lomana Lua Lua.
Goals: Tresor Mputu (42), Lomana Lua Lua (61)

25.01.2006

ANGOLA - DR CONGO 0-0
At Military Stadium, Cairo
Referee: Badra Diatta (Senegal), Attendance: 2,000
ANGOLA: Joao Ricardo, Jamba, Carlos Manuel Gonçalves Alonso 'Kali', Delgado, Andre, Loco, Figueiredo (75 Miloy), Mendonça (46 Jonhson), Edson, FLÁVIO da Silva Amado (46 Maurito), Fabrice Alcebiades Maieco 'Akwá'.
DR CONGO: Pascal Kalemba, Herita Ilunga, Christian Kinkela, Gladys Bokese, Felicien Kabundi, Marcel Mbayo (90 Mutamba Milambo), Tshinyama Tshiolola, Zola Matumona (68 Franck Matingou), Biscotte Mbala (82 Ngandu Kasongo), Tresor Mputu, Lomana Lua Lua. Sent off: Mputu (19)

25.01.2006

CAMEROON - TOGO 2-0 (0-0)
At Military Stadium, Cairo
Referee: Modou Sowe (Gambia), Attendance: 3,000
CAMEROON: Hamidou Souleymanou, Rigobert Song, Raymond Kalla (55 Andre Bikey), Timothee Atouba, Geremi Fotso Njitap, Alioum Saidou, Jean Makoun, Daniel Ngom Kome, Samuel Eto'o, Achille Webo (69 Albert Meyong Ze), Roudolphe Douala (75 Salomon Olembé).
TOGO: Kossi Agassa, Jean-Paul Yaovi Abalo, Junior Yao Senaya (80 Alaixys Romao), Emmanuel Mathias, Ludovic Assemoassa, Yao Aziawonou (84 Adekanmi Olufade), Massamasso Tchangai, Cherif Toure Mamam (71 Kader Cougbadja), Gouyazou Kassim, Moustapha Salifou, Emmanuel Adebayor.
Goals: Samuel Eto'o (68), Albert Meyong Ze (86)

29.01.2006

ANGOLA - TOGO 3-2 (2-1)
Cairo International Stadium
Referee: Abderrahim El-Arjoun (Morocco), Attendance: 4,000
ANGOLA: Joao Ricardo, Jamba, Carlos Manuel Gonçalves Alonso 'Kali', Loco (72 Love), Delgado, Andre, Maurito, Figueiredo, Edson (55 José Nsimba Baptista 'Zé Kalanga'), FLÁVIO da Silva Amado, Fabrice Alcebiades Maieco 'Akwá' (61 Pedro Manuel Torres Mantorras).
TOGO: Ourou-Nimini Tchagnirou, Jean-Paul Yaovi Abalo, Junior Yao Senaya (85 Adekanmi Olufade), Ludovic Assemoassa, Gafarou Mamam, Massamasso Tchangai, Alaixys Romao (60 Yao Aziawonou), Cherif Toure Mamam, Gouyazou Kassim, Moustapha Salifou (78 Cougbadja Sherif), Kader Cougbadja. Sent off: Kassim (29)
Goals: FLÁVIO da Silva Amado (9, 39), Maurito (86) / Kader Cougbadja (24), Cherif Toure (67)

29.01.2006

CAMEROON - DR CONGO 2-0 (2-0)
At Military Stadium, Cairo
Referee: Koman Coulibaly (Mali), Attendance: 5,000
CAMEROON: Idris Carlos Kameni, Rigobert Song, Benoit Angbwa, Andre Bikey, Timothee Ateba, Salomon Olembé (89 Guy Feutchine), Geremi Fotso Njitap, Alioum Saidou, Samuel Eto'o, Albert Meyong Ze (46 Achille Webo), Pierre Boya (64 Achille Emana).
DR CONGO: Pascal Kalemba, Herita Ilunga, Christian Kinkela, Gladys Bokese, Felicien Kabundi, Marcel Mbayo (46 Tshatsho Kabamba), Tshinyama Tshiolola, Zola Matumona, Biscotte Mbala (79 Cyrille Mubiala), Mbele Lelo (46 Mutamba Milambo), Lomana Lua Lua.
Sent off: Bokese (70)
Goals: Geremi Fotso Njitap (31), Samuel Eto'o (33)

1.	CAMEROON	3	3	0	0	7	1	9
2.	DR CONGO	3	1	1	1	2	2	4
3.	Angola	3	1	1	1	4	5	4
4.	Togo	3	0	0	3	2	7	0

GROUP C

22.01.2006

TUNISIA - ZAMBIA 4-1 (1-1)
Harras al-Hedoud Stadium, Alexandria
Referee: Eddy Maillet (Seychelles), Attendance: 16,000.
TUNISIA: Ali Boumnijel, Hatem Trabelsi, Radhi Jaidi, Karim Hagui, Jose Clayton (69 Anis Ayari), Adel Chedli, Kaies Ghodhbane, Riadh Bouazizi, Sofiane Melliti (79 Hamed Namouchi), Francileudo dos Santos, Ziad Jaziri (72 Jouhar Mnari).
ZAMBIA: George Kolola, Clive Hachilensa, Joseph Musonda, Kennedy Nketani, Elijah Tana, Mumamba Numba (65 Felix Katongo), Chris Katongo, Isaac Chansa (65 Andrew Sinkala), James Chamanga, Collins Mbesuma, Lameck Njovu (88 Rainford Kalaba).
Goals: Francileudo dos Santos (35, 82, 90), Riadh Bouazizi (51) / James Chamanga (9)

22.01.2006

SOUTH AFRICA - GUINEA 0-2 (0-0)
Harras al-Hedoud Stadium, Alexandria
Referee: Mohamed Benouza (Algeria), Attendance: 10,000
SOUTH AFRICA: Calvin Marlin, Pierre Issa, Mbulelo Mabizela, Ricardo Katza, Jimmy Tau, Daniel Tshabalala, Benedict Vilakazi, Benni McCarthy, Siyabonga Nomvete (57 Siphiwe Tshabalala), Lebohang Mokoena (66 Siyabonga Nkosi), Sibusiso Zuma.
GUINEA: Naby Diarso, Bobo Balde, Ibrahima Camara, Kanfory Sylla, Oumar Kalabane, Daouda Jabi, Pascal Feindouno, Pablo Thiam, Kaba Diawara (69 Sambegou Bangoura), Fode Mansare (83 Ousmane Bangoura), Ismael Bangoura (73 Ibrahima Bangoura).
Goals: Sambegou Bangoura (76), Ousmane Bangoura (87)

26.01.2006

ZAMBIA - GUINEA 1-2 (1-0)
Harras al-Hedoud Stadium, Alexandria
Referee Emmanuel Imiere (Nigeria), Attendance: 24,000
ZAMBIA: George Kolola, Joseph Musonda, Kennedy Nketani, Billy Mwanza, Elijah Tana, Andrew Sinkala, Chris Katongo, James Chamanga, Felix Katongo (77 Isaac Chansa), Collins Mbesuma, Lameck Njovu.
GUINEA: Naby Diarso, Bobo Balde, Ibrahima Camara, Oumar Kalabane, Daouda Jabi, Mohamed Sylla, Pascal Feindouno, Pablo Thiam (90 Kanfory Sylla), Fode Mansare, Ibrahima Bangoura (55 Ibrahima Yattara), Sambegou Bangoura (75 Kaba Diawara).
Goals: Elijah Tana (34) / Pascal Feindouno (74 penalty, 90)

26.01.2006

TUNISIA - SOUTH AFRICA 2-0 (1-0)
Harras al-Hedoud Stadium, Alexandria
Referee: Divine Evehe (Cameroon), Attendance: 10,000
TUNISIA: Ali Boumnijel, Hatem Trabelsi, Radhi Jaidi, Anis Ayari, Karim Hagui, Adel Chedli, Jouhar Mnari, Slim Benachour (78 Issam Jemaa), Hamed Namouchi, Francileudo dos Santos (82 Haikel Guemamdia), Chaouki Ben Saada.
SOUTH AFRICA: Calvin Marlin, Pierre Issa, Mbulelo Mabizela, Ricardo Katza (65 Siboniso Gaxa), Vuyo Mere, Elrio Van Heerden (81 Katlego Mphela), Daniel Tshabalala, Benedict Vilakazi, Benni McCarthy, Siyabonga Nomvete, Sibusiso Zuma (73 Siyabonga Nkosi).
Goals: Francileudo dos Santos (32), Slim Benachour (57)

30.01.2006

TUNISIA - GUINEA 0-3 (0-1)
Harras al-Hedoud Stadium, Alexandria
Referee: Shamsul Maidin (Singapore). Attendance: 18,000
TUNISIA: Hamdi Kasraoui, Jose Clayton, Radhi Jaidi (59 Karim Hagui), Amir Haj Massaoud, Issam Merdassi, Kaies Ghodhbane, Jouhar Mnari, Sofiane Melliti, Hamed Namouchi (79 Adel Chedli), Haikel Guemamdia, Amine Ltifi (55 Issam Jemaa).
GUINEA: Naby Diarso, Kanfory Sylla, Oumar Kalabane (57 Ibrahima Camara), Mamadou Alimou Diallo, Mamadi Kaba, Morlaye Cisse, Ousmane Bangoura (79 Sekouba Camara), Ibrahima Souare, Kaba Diawara, Ismael Bangoura, Ibrahima Yattara (56 Pascal Feindouno).
Sent off: Merdassi (83)
Goals: Ousmane Bangoura (16), Pascal Feindouno (69), Kaba Diawara (90)

30.01.2006

ZAMBIA - SOUTH AFRICA 1-0 (0-0)
Al-Ittihad Stadium, Alexandria
Referee: Essam Abdel Fatah (Egypt), Attendance: 4,000
ZAMBIA: Kennedy Mweene, Clive Hachilensa, Joseph Musonda, Kennedy Nketani, Elijah Tana, Andrew Sinkala, Chris Katongo, James Chamanga, Felix Katongo (64 Dube Phiri), Collins Mbesuma (77 Linos Chalwe), Lameck Njovu (69 Ian Bakala).
SOUTH AFRICA: Calvin Marlin, Pierre Issa, Mbulelo Mabizela, Tshepo Masilela, Jimmy Tau, Daniel Tshabalala (63 Elrio Van Heerden), Siphiwe Tshabalala, Mlungisi Gumbi, Siyabonga Nkosi (80 Lebohang Mokoena), Siyabonga Nomvete (68 Joseph Makhanya), Katlego Mphela.
Goal: Chris Katongo (75)

1.	GUINEA	3	3	0	0	7	1	9
2.	TUNISIA	3	2	0	1	6	4	6
3.	Zambia	3	1	0	2	3	6	3
4.	South Africa	3	0	0	3	0	5	0

GROUP D

23.01.2006

NIGERIA - GHANA 1-0 (0-0)
Al-Masry Stadium, Port Said
Referee: Essam Abdel Fatah (Egypt), Attendance: 20,000
NIGERIA: Vincent Enyeama, Yussuf Ayila, Chidi Odiah, Taye Taiwo, Joseph Yobo, Joseph Enakarhire, Wilson Oruma, Christian Obodo (89 Obinna Nwaneri), Julius Aghahowa (80 Nwankwo Kanu), Obafemi Martins, Peter Odemwingie (83 Obinna Nsofor).
GHANA: Sammy Adjei, Samuel Kuffour, John Mensah, John Paintsil, Emmanuel Pappoe (89 Joetex Frimpong), Issah Ahmed, Haminu Dramani, Stephen Appiah, Abubakari Yakubu (75 Hans Sarpei), Laryea Kingston, Matthew Amoah.
Goal: Taye Taiwo (86)

23.01.2006

ZIMBABWE - SENEGAL 0-2 (0-0)
Al-Masry Stadium, Port Said
Referee: Khalid Abdel Rahman (Sudan), Attendance: 15,000
ZIMBABWE: Gift Muzadzi, George Mbwando, Zvenyika Makonese, James Matola, Esrom Nyandoro, Cephas Chimedza, Edelbert Dinha (61 Tinashe Nengomasha), Edzai Kasinauyo (85 Brian Badza), Benjani Mwaruwari, Shingi Kawondera, Peter Ndlovu (67 Joël Luphahla).
SENEGAL: Tony Sylva, Habib Beye, Ferdinand Coly, Lamine Diatta, Souleymane Diawara, Abdoulaye Diagne-Faye, Amdy Faye (85 Pape Bouba Diop), El Hadji Diouf (79 Issa Ba), Henri Camara, Rahmane Barry, Diomansy Kamara (63 Mamadou Niang).
Goals: Henri Camara (60), Issa Ba (80)

27.01.2006

GHANA - SENEGAL 1-0 (1-0)
Al-Masry Stadium, Port Said
Referee: Abderrahim El-Arjoun (Morocco), Attendance: 20,000
GHANA: Sammy Adjei, John Mensah, John Paintsil, Emmanuel Pappoe, Issah Ahmed, Haminu Dramani, Stephen Appiah (90 Daniel Edusei), Abubakari Yakubu, Laryea Kingston, Matthew Amoah (87 Prince Tagoe), Joetex Frimpong (83 Hamza Mohammed).
SENEGAL: Tony Sylva, Habib Beye, Ferdinand Coly, Lamine Diatta, Souleymane Diawara, Abdoulaye Diagne-Faye (46 Pape Bouba Diop), Amdy Faye, Issa Ba (67 Diomansy Kamara), Rahmane Barry, El Hadji Diouf (66 Mamadou Niang), Henri Camara.
Sent off: Kingston (62) / Beye (62)
Goal: Matthew Amoah (13)

27.01.2006

NIGERIA - ZIMBABWE 2-0 (0-0)
Al-Masry Stadium, Port Said
Referee Koman Coulibaly (Mali), Attendance: 10,000
NIGERIA: Vincent Enyeama, Yussuf Ayila, Chidi Odiah, Taye Taiwo, Joseph Yobo, Joseph Enakarhire, Wilson Oruma (54 John Obi Mikel), Christian Obodo (86 Garba Lawal), Julius Aghahowa (54 Nwankwo Kanu), John Utaka, Obafemi Martins.
ZIMBABWE: Gift Muzadzi, Zvenyika Makonese, James Matola, Tinashe Nengomasha, Esrom Nyandoro, Charles Yohane, Joël Luphahla (87 Gilbert Mushangazhike), Cephas Chimedza, Edelbert Dinha (70 Bekithemba Ndlovu), Benjani Mwaruwari, Shingi Kawondera (79 Peter Ndlovu).
Goals: Christian Obodo (57), John Obi Mikel (61)

31.01.2006

NIGERIA - SENEGAL 2-1 (0-0)
Al-Masry Stadium, Port Said
Referee: Jerome Damon (South Africa), Attendance: 5,000
NIGERIA: Vincent Enyeama, Yussuf Ayila, Chidi Odiah, Taye Taiwo, Joseph Yobo, Joseph Enakarhire, Christian Obodo (57 Garba Lawal), John Obi Mikel, Stephen Makinwa (52 Nwankwo Kanu), John Utaka (77 Obinna Nsofor), Obafemi Martins,.
SENEGAL: Tony Sylva, Ferdinand Coly (68 Pape Malickou Diakhate), Omar Daf, Lamine Diatta, Souleymane Diawara, Amdy Faye, Pape Bouba Diop, El Hadji Diouf, Henri Camara, Rahmane Barry (44 Souleymane Camara), Diomansy Kamara (79 Abdoulaye Diagne-Faye).
Goals: Obafemi Martins (79, 88) / Souleymane Camara (59)

31.01.2006

GHANA - ZIMBABWE 1-2 (0-0)
Ismailia Stadium, Ismailia
Referee: Rene Louzaya (Congo), Attendance: 14,000
GHANA: Sammy Adjei, John Mensah, John Paintsil, Emmanuel Pappoe, Daniel Edusei, Stephen Appiah, Abubakari Yakubu (56 Hamza Mohammed), Issah Ahmed, Haminu Dramani (65 Godwin Attram), Prince Tagoe (46 Baba Armando), Joetex Frimpong.
ZIMBABWE: Tapuwa Kapini, Zvenyika Makonese, James Matola, Tinashe Nengomasha, Esrom Nyandoro, Joël Luphahla, Cephas Chimedza, Edelbert Dinha, Benjani Mwaruwari, Gilbert Mushangazhike (86 Shingi Kawondera) , Peter Ndlovu (51 Edzai Kasinauyo).
Goals: Baba Armando (90+4) / Cephas Chimedza (60), Benjani Mwaruwari (68)

1.	NIGERIA	3	3	0	0	5	1	9
2.	SENEGAL	3	1	0	2	3	3	3
3.	Ghana	3	1	0	2	2	3	3
4.	Zimbabwe	3	1	0	2	2	5	3

Quarter-finals

03.02.2006

EGYPT - DR CONGO 4-1 (2-1)
Cairo International Stadium
Referee: Modou Sowe (Gambia), Attendance: 74,000
EGYPT: Essam El-Hadary, Mohamed Barakat, Ibrahim Said, Abdel Zaher El-Saqqa, Wael Gomaa, Tarek El-Sayed (79 Mohamed Abdel Wahab), Mohamed Shawki, Ahmed Hassan, Amr Zaki (72 Abdelhalim Ali), Hossam Hassan (66 Hassan Moustafa), Emad Abdel Nabi 'Moteab'.
DR CONGO: Pascal Kalemba, Herita Ilunga, Christian Kinkela, Cyrille Mubiala (46 Nono Lubanzadio), Dituabanza Nsumbu, Tshinyama Tshiolola, Zola Matumona, Marcel Mbayo, Ngandu Kasongo (53 Tshatsho Kabamba), Biscotte Mbala, Lomana Lua Lua.
Goals: Ahmed Hassan (33 penalty, 89), Hossam Hassan (41), Emad Abdel Nabi 'Moteab' (58) / Abdel Zaher El-Saqqa (45+2 own goal)

03.02.2006

GUINEA - SENEGAL 2-3 (1-0)
Harras al-Hedoud Stadium, Alexandria
Referee: Bonaventure Coffi Codja (Benin), Attendance: 17,000
GUINEA: Naby Diarso, Bobo Balde, Ibrahima Camara, Oumar Kalabane, Kanfory Sylla, Daouda Jabi, Ousmane Bangoura (81 Ismael Bangoura), Pascal Feindouno, Pablo Thiam (53 Ibrahima Souare), Kaba Diawara (68 Sambegou Bangoura), Fode Mansare.
SENEGAL: Tony Sylva, Ferdinand Coly (39 Pape Malickou Diakhate), Omar Daf, Lamine Diatta, Souleymane Diawara, Amdy Faye, Pape Bouba Diop, Henri Camara, Souleymane Camara (59 Mamadou Niang), Diomansy Kamara, Frederic Mendy (88 Issa Ba).
Goals: Kaba Diawara (24), Pascal Feindouno (90+5) / Pape Bouba Diop (60), Mamadou Niang (82), Henri Camara (90+3)

04.02.2006

CAMEROON - IVORY COAST 1-1 (0-0, 0-0), 11-12 on penalties
Military Academy Stadium, Cairo
Referee: Mohamed Guezzaz (Morocco), Attendance: 4,000
CAMEROON: Souleymanou Hamidou, Rigobert Song, Thimothee Atouba, Andre Bikey, Salomon Olembé (80 Roudolphe Douala), Geremi Fotso Njitap, Alioum Saidou, Jean Makoun, Daniel Ngom Kome, Samuel Eto'o, Achille Webo (34 Albert Meyong Ze).
IVORY COAST: Jean-Jacques Tizie, Kolo Toure, Arthur Boka, Emmanuel Eboue (111 Marc Zoro), Blaise Kouassi, Emerse Fae, Yaya Toure (88 Bakary Koné), Kanga Akale (98 Romaric N'Dri), Didier Zokora, Didier Drogba, Arouna Koné.
Penalties: 1-0 Eto'o, 1-1 Drogba, 2-1 Geremi, 2-2 Toure, 3-2 Atouba, 3-3 Bakaty Koné, 4-3 Ngom Kome, 4-4 Fae, 5-4 Meyong Ze, 5-5 Arouna Koné, 6-5 Makoun, 6-6 Kouassi, 7-6 Song, 7-7 N'Dri, 8-7 Saidou, 8-8 Boka, 9-8 Douala, 9-9 Zokora, 10-9 Bikey, 10-10 Zoro, 11-10 Souleymanou, 11-11 Tizie, Eto'o, 11-12 Drogba
Goals: Albert Meyong Ze (94) / Bakary Koné (92)

04.02.2006

NIGERIA - TUNISIA 1-1 (1-0, 1-1), 6-5 on penalties
Al-Masry Stadium, Port Said
Referee: Eddy Maillet (Seychelles), Attendance: 15,000
NIGERIA: Vincent Enyeama, Yussuf Ayila, Chidi Odiah (96 Obinna Nwanneri), Taye Taiwo, Joseph Yobo, Joseph Enakarhire, John Obi Mikel, Stephen Makinwa (91 Garba Lawal), John Utaka (58 Nwankwo Kanu), Obafemi Martins, Obinna Nsofor.
TUNISIA: Ali Boumnijel, Jose Clayton, Hatem Trabelsi (46 Amir Hadj Massaoud), Radhi Jaidi, Karim Hagui, Adel Chedli, Riadh Bouazizi, Sofiane Melliti (67 Slim Benachour), Hamed Namouchi, Francileudo dos Santos (80 Haikel Guemamdia), Ziad Jaziri.
Goals: Obinna Nsofor (6) / Karim Hagui (49)
Penalties: Yobo, 0-1 Namouchi, 1-1 Taiwo, 1-2 Guemamdia, Ayila, Chedli, 2-2 Nsofor, Benachour, 3-2 Martins, 3-3 Clayton, 4-3 Mikel, 4-4 Boumnijel, 5-4 Enyeama, 5-5 Massaoud, 6-5 Kanu, Bouazizi

Semi-finals

07.02.2006

EGYPT - SENEGAL 2-1 (1-0)
Cairo International Stadium
Referee: Divine Evehe (Cameroon), Attendance: 74,100
EGYPT: Essam El-Hadary, Mohamed Barakat, Wael Gomaa, Ibrahim Said, Abdel Zaher El-Saqqa, Mohamed Abdel Wahab, Ahmed Hassan, Mohamed Shawki, Mohamed Aboutraika, Ahmed Hossam 'Mido' (78 Amr Zaki), Emad Abdel Nabi 'Moteab' (90 Hossam Hassan).
SENEGAL: Tony Sylva, Omar Daf (90 Issa Ba), Lamine Diatta, Souleymane Diawara, Pape Malickou Diakhate, Amdy Faye, Pape Bouba Diop, Frederic Mendy (85 Souleymane Camara), Henri Camara (66 El Hadji Diouf), Mamadou Niang, Diomansy Kamara.
Goals: Ahmed Hassan (37 penalty), Amr Zaki (81) / Mamadou Niang (51)

07.02.2006

IVORY COAST - NIGERIA 1-0 (0-0)
Harras al-Hedoud Stadium, Alexandria
Referee: Jerome Damon (South Africa), Attendance: 20,000
IVORY COAST: Jean-Jacques Tizie, Abdoulaye Meite, Arthur Boka, Kolo Toure, Emmanuel Eboue (67 Marc Zoro), Yaya Toure, Didier Zokora, Gilles Yapi Yapo (60 Emerse Fae), Bonaventure Kalou (76 Arouna Koné), Didier Drogba, Romaric N'Dri.
NIGERIA: Vincent Enyeama, Chidi Odiah, Taye Taiwo, Joseph Yobo, Joseph Enakarhire, John Obi Mikel (53 Jay-Jay Okocha), Sani Kaita, Nwankwo Kanu (74 Julius Aghahowa), Obinna Nsofor, Obafemi Martins, Peter Odemwingie (63 Stephen Makinwa).
Goal: Didier Drogba (47)

Third Place Match

09.02.2006

SENEGAL - NIGERIA 0-1 (0-0)
Military Academy stadium, Cairo
Referee: Koman Coulibaly (Mali), Attendance: 11,354
SENEGAL: Pape Mamadou Diouf, Omar Daf, Abdoulaye Diagne-Faye, Guirane N'Daw, Boukary Drame, Pape Malickou Diakhate, Dino Djiba (62 Pape Bouba Diop), Issa Ba, Rahmane Barry (69 Henri Camara), Souleymane Camara (77 Mamadou Niang), Diomansy Kamara.
NIGERIA: Vincent Enyeama, Chidi Odiah, Taye Taiwo, Obinna Nwanneri, Joseph Yobo, Jay-Jay Okocha (67 Wilson Oruma), Garba Lawal, Christian Obodo, John Utaka, Obafemi Martins, Obinna Nsofor (78 Nwankwo Kanu).
Goal: Garba Lawal (79)

Final

10.02.2006

EGYPT - IVORY COAST 0-0, 4-2 on penalties
Cairo International Stadium
Referee: Mourad Daami (Tunisia), Attendance: 74,100
EGYPT: Essam El-Hadary, Mohamed Barakat, Wael Gomaa (22 Ahmed Fathi), Ibrahim Said (114 Abdel Halim Ali), Abdel Zaher El-Saqqa, Mohamed Abdel Wahab, Ahmed Hassan, Mohamed Shawki, Mohamed Aboutraika, Amr Zaki, Emad Abdel Nabi 'Moteab' (82 Hassan Moustafa).
IVORY COAST: Jean-Jacques Tizie, Arthur Boka, Abib Kolo Toure, Didier Zokora, Kanga Akale (61 Bonaventure Kalou), Emerse Fae, Didier Drogba, Blaise Kouassi, Yaya Gnegneri Toure (91 Bakary Koné), Emmanuel Eboue, Arouna Koné.
Penalties: 1-0 Ahmed Hassan, Drogba, 2-0 Abdel Wahab, 2-1 Abib Kolo Toure, Abdel Halim Ali, Bakary Koné, 3-1 Amr Zaki, 3-2 Emanuel Eboue, 4-2 Mojhamed Aboutraika

Twenty-sixth edition - 2008
Qualifying Tournament

The 26th edition of the Africa Cup of Nations saw 49 teams enter the competition though Djibouti then withdrew. The teams were split between 12 qualifying groups with all group winners progressing to the finals, alongside the 3 best runners-up from groups 2 to 11. The finals tournament was held in Ghana and Egypt retained the trophy by narrowly defeating The Indomitable Lions of Cameroon by a single goal.

Group 1

02.09.2006 Gabon – Madagascar 4-0 (1-0)
Goals: Henri Antchouet (38), Daniel Cousin (70 penalty), Chiva Star Nzigou (76, 82)
08.10.2006 Ivory Coast – Gabon 5-0 (3-0)
Goals: Kolo Touré (11), Arouna Koné (22, 55, 70), Aruna Dindane (32)
25.03.2007 Madagascar - Ivory Coast 0-3 (0-2)
Goals: Gohouri Steve (28), Aruna Dindane (35), Diane Amara (81)
03.06.2007 Ivory Coast - Madagascar 5-0
17.06.2007 Madagascar - Gabon 0-2 (0-1)
Goals: Akiremy Owondo Stéphane (25), Meye Roguy (87)
08.09.2007 Gabon - Ivory Coast 0-0

1.	IVORY COAST	4	3	1	0	13	0	10
2.	Gabon	4	2	1	1	6	5	7
3.	Madagascar	4	0	0	4	0	14	0

Djibouti withdrew on 21st August, 2006

Group 2

02.09.2006 Egypt – Burundi 4-1 (3-0)
Goals: Mohammed Zidan (5), Hosni Abd Rabbou (28), Mohammed Abutreika (39), Ahmed Hassan (52 penalty) / Soliman (79 penalty)
02.09.2006 Mauritania – Botswana 4-0 (4-0)
Goals: Saidou M'Bodj (2), Karamoko Moussa (10, 23), Yohan Langlet (31)

07.10.2006 Botswana – Egypt 0-0
08.10.2006 Burundi - Mauritania 3-1 (3-1)
Goals: Yamin Selemani (3, 30), Henry Mbazumutima (44) / Buha Ibrahim (7)
25.03.2007 Egypt - Mauritania 3-0
25.03.2007 Botswana - Burundi 1-0
03.06.2007 Mauritania - Egypt 1-1
03.06.2007 Burundi - Botswana 1-0
16.06.2007 Botswana - Mauritania 2-1
09.09.2007 Burundi - Egypt 0-0
13.10.2009 Egypt - Botswana 1-0
13.10.2009 Mauritania - Burundi 2-1

1.	EGYPT	6	3	3	0	9	2	12
2.	Mauritania	6	2	1	3	9	10	7
3.	Burundi	6	2	1	3	6	8	7
4.	Botswana	6	2	1	3	3	7	7

Group 3

02.09.2006 Uganda – Lesotho 3-0 (2-0)
Goals: Godfrey Massa (28, 40), David Obua (58 penalty)
02.09.2006 Nigeria – Niger 2-0 (1-0)
Goals: Yakubu Aiyegbeni (27), Christian Obodo (60)
08.10.2006 Lesotho – Nigeria 0-1 (0-0)
Goal: Yakubu Aiyegbeni (48)
08.10.2006 Niger – Uganda 0-0
24.03.2007 Nigeria - Uganda 1-0
25.03.2007 Lesotho - Niger 3-1
02.06.2007 Uganda - Nigeria 2-1
03.06.2007 Niger - Lesotho 2-0
17.06.2007 Niger - Nigeria 1-3
19.06.2007 Lesotho - Uganda 0-0
08.09.2007 Nigeria - Lesotho 2-0
08.09.2007 Uganda - Niger 3-1

1.	NIGERIA	6	5	0	1	10	3	15
2.	Uganda	6	3	2	1	8	3	11
3.	Niger	6	1	1	4	5	11	4
4.	Lesotho	6	1	1	4	3	9	4

Group 4

03.09.2006 Sudan – Seychelles 3-0 (1-0)
Goals: Badr Aldeen Galag (20), Haitham Kamal Tambal (77 penalty, 90)
03.09.2006 Mauritius – Tunisia 0-0
07.10.2006 Seychelles – Mauritius 2-1 (1-0)
Goals: Wilnes Brutus (22, 81), Kervin Godon (50)
07.10.2006 Tunisia - Sudan 1-0 (0-0)
Goal: Richard Lado (79 own goal)
24.03.2007 Seychelles – Tunisia 0-3 (0-1)
Goals: Issam Jemaa (13, 76, 80)
25.03.2007 Mauritius - Sudan 1-2
02.06.2007 Sudan - Mauritius 3-0

02.06.2007 Tunisia - Seychelles 4-0
16.06.2007 Seychelles - Sudan 0-2
16.06.2007 Tunisia - Mauritius 2-0 (1-0)
Goals: Issam Jemaa (44), Nafti (50)
09.09.2007 Mauritius - Seychelles 1-1
09.09.2007 Sudan - Tunisia 3-2

1.	SUDAN	6	5	0	1	13	4	15
2.	TUNISIA	6	4	1	1	12	3	13
3.	Seychelles	6	1	1	4	3	14	4
4.	Mauritius	6	0	2	4	3	10	2

Tunisia qualified as the runner-up with the best record.

Group 5

03.09.2006 Rwanda – Cameroon 0-3 (0-0)
Goals: Guy Feutchine (55), Geremi Fotso Njitap (62), Landry Nguemo (84)
03.09.2006 Equatorial Guinea – Liberia 2-1 (1-1)
Goals: Juan Ramon Epitie (24), Rodolfo Bodipo (88) / Zah Kringar (35)
07.10.2006 Cameroon - Equatorial Guinea 3-0 (0-0)
Goals: Mohamadou Idrissou (72, 89), Achille Webo (80)
08.10.2006 Liberia – Rwanda 3-2 (1-0)
Goals: Francis Doe (24), Oliver Makor (68), Dioh Williams (76) / Olivier Karekezi (70), Abedi Mulenda (78)
24.03.2007 Cameroon - Liberia 3-1
25.03.2007 Equatorial Guinea - Rwanda 3-1
02.06.2007 Rwanda - Equatorial Guinea 2-0
03.06.2007 Liberia - Cameroon 1-2
17.06.2007 Cameroon - Rwanda 2-1
17.06.2007 Liberia - Equatorial Guinea 0-0
08.09.2007 Rwanda - Liberia 4-0
09.09.2007 Equatorial Guinea - Cameroon 1-0

1.	CAMEROON	6	5	0	1	13	4	15
2.	Equatorial Guinea	6	3	1	2	6	7	10
3.	Rwanda	6	2	0	4	10	11	6
4.	Liberia	6	1	1	4	6	13	4

Group 6

02.09.2006 Kenya – Eritrea 1-2 (0-0)
Goals: Robert Mambo (64) / Arnold Origi (59 own goal), Yednekachew Shimanugus (67)
03.09.2006 Swaziland – Angola 0-2 (0-1)
Goals: Joao Pereira (21), Manuel Cange (80)
07.10.2006 Eritrea - Swaziland 0-0
08.10.2006 Angola - Kenya 3-1 (1-0)
Goals: Flávio Amado (27, 68), Mateus (60) / Boniface Abani (81)
25.03.2007 Kenya - Swaziland 2-0
25.03.2007 Angola - Eritrea 6-1
02.06.2007 Eritrea - Angola 1-1
03.06.2007 Swaziland - Kenya 0-0
16.06.2007 Eritrea - Kenya 1-0
17.06.2007 Angola - Swaziland 3-0

08.09.2007 Kenya - Angola 2-1
09.09.2007 Swaziland - Eritrea 0-0

1.	ANGOLA	6	4	1	1	16	5	13
2.	Eritrea	6	2	3	1	5	8	9
3.	Kenya	6	2	1	3	6	7	7
4.	Swaziland	6	0	3	3	0	7	3

Group 7

02.09.2006 Tanzania - Burkina Faso 2-1 (1-1)
Goals: Harouna Bamogo (27 own goal), Nizar Halfan (65) / Abdulaye Cissé (37)
02.09.2006 Senegal – Mozambique 2-0 (1-0)
Goals: Moussa Ndiaye (33), Nguirane Ndao (61)
07.10.2006 Burkina Faso - Senegal 1-0 (0-0)
Goal: Narcisse Yameogo (63 penalty)
08.10.2006 Mozambique – Tanzania 0-0
24.03.2007 Senegal - Tanzania 4-0
24.03.2007 Burkina Faso - Mozambique 1-1
02.06.2007 Tanzania - Senegal 1-1
03.06.2007 Mozambique - Burkina Faso 3-0
16.06.2007 Burkina Faso - Tanzania 0-1
17.06.2007 Mozambique - Senegal 0-0
08.09.2007 Senegal - Burkina Faso 5-1
08.09.2007 Tanzania - Mozambique 0-1

1.	SENEGAL	6	3	2	1	12	3	11
2.	Mozambique	6	2	3	1	5	3	9
3.	Tanzania	6	2	2	2	4	7	8
4.	Burkina Faso	6	1	1	4	4	12	4

Group 8

03.09.2006 Guinea - Algeria 0-0
03.09.2006 Gambia - Cape Verde 2-0 (1-0)
Goals: Jatto Ceesay (8 penalty), Assan Jatta (88)
07.10.2006 Algeria – Gambia 1-0 (0-0)
Goal: Karim Ziani (75 penalty)
07.10.2006 Cape Verde - Guinea 1-0 (0-0)
Goal: Lito (52)
24.03.2007 Gambia - Guinea 0-2
24.03.2007 Algeria - Cape Verde 2-0
02.06.2007 Cape Verde - Algeria 2-2
03.06.2007 Guinea - Gambia 2-2
16.06.2007 Algeria - Guinea 0-2
16.06.2007 Cape Verde - Gambia 0-0
09.09.2007 Gambia - Algeria 2-1
09.09.2007 Guinea - Cape Verde 4-0

1.	GUINEA	6	3	2	1	10	3	11
2.	Algeria	6	2	2	2	6	6	8
3.	Gambia	6	2	2	2	6	6	8
4.	Cape Verde	6	1	2	3	3	10	5

Group 9

03.09.2006 Sierra Leone – Mali 0-0
03.09.2006 Togo – Benin 2-1 (1-0)
Goals: Thomas Dossevi (15), Komlan Amewou (75), Abou Maiga (85)
08.10.2006 Mali - Togo 1-0 (0-0)
Goal: Dramane Traoré (90)
08.10.2006 Benin - Sierra Leone 2-0 (1-0)
Goals: Rachad Chitou (22), Mouri Ogoubiyi (77)
24.03.2007 Togo - Sierra Leone 3-1
25.03.2007 Mali - Benin 1-1
03.06.2007 Sierra Leone - Togo 0-1
03.06.2007 Benin - Mali 0-0
17.06.2007 Mali - Sierra Leone 6-0
17.06.2007 Benin - Togo 4-1
12.10.2009 Togo - Mali 0-2
12.10.2009 Sierra Leone - Benin 0-2

1.	MALI	6	3	3	0	10	1	12
2.	BENIN	6	3	2	1	10	4	11
3.	Togo	6	3	0	3	7	9	9
4.	Sierra Leone	6	0	1	5	1	14	1

Benin qualified as joint second best runners-up.

Group 10

03.09.2006 Ethiopia – Libya 1-0 (1-0)
Goal: Dawit Meberahtu (15)
03.09.2006 DR Congo – Namibia 3-2 (1-1)
Goals: Blaise Lelo Mbele (32), Dieudonné Kalulika (62), Fuanda Kinkela (82) / Sydney Plaatjies (37, 60)
07.10.2006 Namibia – Ethiopia 1-0 (1-0)
Goal: Quinton Jacobs (18 penalty)
08.10.2006 Libya - DR Congo 1-1 (0-1)
Goals: Khaled Hussein (57) / Serge Bageta Dikilu (37)
25.03.2007 Libya - Namibia 2-1
29.04.2007 DR Congo - Ethiopia 2-0
01.06.2007 Ethiopia - DR Congo 1-0
02.06.2007 Namibia - Libya 1-0
16.06.2007 Namibia - DR Congo 1-1
17.06.2007 Libya - Ethiopia 3-1
08.09.2007 DR Congo - Libya 1-1
08.09.2007 Ethiopia - Namibia 2-3

1.	NAMIBIA	6	3	1	2	9	8	10
2.	DR Congo	6	2	3	1	8	6	9
3.	Libya	6	2	2	2	7	6	8
4.	Ethiopia	6	2	0	4	5	9	6

Group 11

02.09.2006 South Africa – Congo 0-0
03.09.2006 Chad – Zambia 0-2 (0-0)
Goals: James Chamanga (47), Dube Phiri (69)
08.10.2006 Congo - Chad 3-1 (2-0)
Goals: Abdoulaye Brice (25), Christ Malonga (32), Ondama (46) / Mostonga (89)
08.10.2006 Zambia - South Africa 0-1 (0-1)
Goal: Aaron Mokoena (28)
24.03.2007 Chad - South Africa 0-3 (0-2)
Goals: Surprise Moriri (32), Delron Buckley (45), Sibusiso Zuma (78)
25.03.2007 Congo - Zambia 0-0
02.06.2007 South Africa - Chad 4-0
02.06.2007 Zambia - Congo 3-0
16.06.2007 Zambia - Chad 1-1
Goals: Collins Mbesuma (50) / Hillaire Kedgui (18)
17.06.2007 Congo - South Africa 1-1 (0-0)
Goals: Jean-Vivien Bantimba (65) / Sibusiso Zuma (46)
09.09.2007 Chad - Congo 1-1
09.09.2007 South Africa - Zambia 1-3

1.	ZAMBIA	6	3	2	1	9	3	11
2.	SOUTH AFRICA	6	3	2	1	10	4	11
3.	Congo	6	1	4	1	5	6	7
4.	Chad	6	0	2	4	3	14	2

NB: South Africa qualified as joint second best runners-up.

Group 12

02.09.2006 Morocco – Malawi 2-0 (0-0)
Goals: Marouane Chamakh (53), Mbarek Boussoufa (76)
07.10.2006 Malawi - Zimbabwe 1-0 (0-0)
Goal: Moses Chavula (78)
25.03.2007 Zimbabwe - Morocco 1-1
02.06.2007 Morocco - Zimbabwe 2-0
16.06.2007 Malawi - Morocco 0-1
09.09.2007 Zimbabwe - Malawi 3-1

1.	MOROCCO	4	3	1	0	6	1	10
2.	Zimbabwe	4	1	1	2	4	5	4
3.	Malawi	4	1	0	3	2	6	3

Final Tournament (Ghana)

GROUP A

20.01.2008

GHANA - GUINEA 2-1 (0-0)
Ohene Djan Stadium, Accra
Referee: Eddy Maillet (Seychelles), Attendance: 35,000
GHANA: Richard Kingson, John Mensah, John Paintsil, Eric Addo, Hans Sarpei, Sulley Muntari, Laryea Kingston, Michael Essien, Quincy Owusu-Abeyie (75 Dede Ayew), Asamoah Gyan (79 Baffour Gyan), Junior Agogo.
GUINEA: Kemoko Camara, Dianbobo Balde, Oumar Kalabane, Daouda Jabi, Pascal Feindouno, Kanfory Sylla (90 Mamadou Dioulde Bah), Alseny Camara, Mohamed Sacko, Ismael Bangoura, Victor Correa (61 Naby Soumah), Souleymane Youla (61 Karamoko Cisse).
Goals: Asamoah Gyan (54 penalty), Sulley Muntari (89) / Oumar Kalabane (64)

21.01.2008

NAMIBIA – MOROCCO 1-5 (1-4)
Ohene Djan Stadium, Accra
Referee: Raphael Divine Evehe (Cameroon), Attendance: 1,000
NAMIBIA: Abisai Shiningayamwe, Michael Pienaar, Franklin April (46 Letu Shatimiene), Brian Brendell, Jamunavandu Ngatjizeko, Quinton Jacobs (77 Swartbooi), Oliver Risser, Richard Gariseb, Collin Benjamin, Rudolf Bester (63 Pineas Jacob), Lazarus Kaimbi.
MOROCCO: Khalid Fouhami, Abdeslam Ouaddou, Michael Chretien, El Armine Erbate, Tarik Sektioui (66 Hicham Aboucherouane), Youssef Hadji (70 Moncef Zerka), Badr El Kaddouri, Abderrahmane Kabous, Youssef Safri, Maroune Chamakh, Soufiane Alloudi (61 Youssef Mokhtari).
Goals: Brian Brendell (23) / Soufiane Alloudi (1, 5, 28), Tarik Sektioui (39 penalty), Moncef Zerka (73)

24.01.2008

GUINEA - MOROCCO 3-2 (1-0)
Ohene Djan Stadium, Accra
Referee: Jerome Damon (South Africa), Attendance: 15,000
GUINEA: Kemoko Camara, Dianbobo Balde, Ibrahima Camara (80 Kamil Zayatte), Oumar Kalabane, Daouda Jabi, Pascal Feindouno, Kanfory Sylla, Mohamed Cisse, Fode Mansare (78 Mohamed Sacko), Ismael Bangoura, Souleymane Youla (77 Karamoko Cisse).
MOROCCO: Khalid Fouhami, Abdeslam Ouaddou, Michael Chretien, El Armine Erbate, Tarik Sektioui (63 Maroune Chamakh), Youssef Hadji, Badr El Kaddouri, Houssine Kharja (55 Hicham Aboucherouane), Abdelkrim Kaissi, Moncef Zerka (80 Bouchaib El Moubarki), Youssef Safri.
Sent off: Feindouno (67)
Goals: Pascal Feindouno (11, 62 penalty), Ismael Bangoura (57) / Hicham Aboucherouane (60), Abdeslam Ouaddou (90)

24.01.2008

GHANA - NAMIBIA 1-0 (1-0)
Ohene Djan Stadium, Accra
Referee: Kacem Bennaceur (Tunisia).

GHANA: Richard Kingson, John Mensah, John Paintsil, Eric Addo, Hans Sarpei, Sulley Muntari, Laryea Kingston (65 Andre Ayew), Michael Essien, Quincy Owusu-Abeyie, Asamoah Gyan (65 Baffour Gyan), Junior Agogo.
NAMIBIA: Athiel Mbaha, Michael Pienaar, Hartman Toromba, Brian Brendell (83 Letu Shatimiene), Jamunavandu Ngatjizeko, Sydney Plaatjies (65 Lazarus Kaimbi), Quinton Jacobs, Oliver Risser, Richard Gariseb, Collin Benjamin, Rudolf Bester (69 Pineas Jacob).
Goal: Junior Agogo (41)

28.01.2008

GHANA - MOROCCO 2-0 (2-0)
Ohene Djan Stadium, Accra
Referee: Modou Sowe (Gambia), Attendance: 40,000
GHANA: Richard Kingson, John Mensah, John Paintsil, Eric Addo, Hans Sarpei, Sulley Muntari, Anthony Annan, Michael Essien, Quincy Owusu-Abeyie (88 Haminu Dramani), Asamoah Gyan (87 Baffour Gyan), Junior Agogo (82 Andre Ayew).
MOROCCO: Nadir Lamyaghri, Abdeslam Ouaddou, Michael Chretien, El Armine Erbate, Youssef Hadji, Badr El Kaddouri, Houssine Kharja (46 Tarik Sektioui), Abderrahmane Kabous (89 Abdelkrim Kaissi), Youssef Safri, Maroune Chamakh, Hicham Aboucherouane (55 Moncef Zerka).
Goals: Michael Essien (26), Sulley Muntari (44)

28.01.2008

GUINEA - NAMIBIA 1-1 (0-0)
Sekondi-Takoradi Stadium, Sekondi
Referee: Muhmed Ssegonga (Uganda).
GUINEA: Kemoko Camara, Mamadou Dianbobo Balde, Ibrahima Camara, Oumar Kalabane, Daouda Jabi, Dioulde Bah, Mohamed Sacko, Naby Soumah (69 Kanfory Sylla), Fode Mansare (84 Victor Correa), Ismael Bangoura, Souleymane Youla (75 Karamoko Cisse).
NAMIBIA: Athiel Mbaha, Michael Pienaar, Hartman Toromba, Brian Brendell, Jamunavandu Ngatjizeko, Sydney Plaatjies, Richard Gariseb, Collin Benjamin, Lazarus Kaimbi (64 Pineas Jacob), Muna Katupose (46 Rudolf Bester), Meraai Swartbooi (72 Wycliff Kambonde).
Goals: Souleymane Youla (62) / Brian Brendell (80)

1.	GHANA	3	3	0	0	5	1	9
2.	GUINEA	3	1	1	1	5	5	4
3.	Morocco	3	1	0	2	7	6	3
4.	Namibia	3	0	1	2	2	7	1

GROUP B

21.01.2008

NIGERIA - IVORY COAST 0-1 (0-0)
Sekondi-Takoradi Stadium, Sekondi
Referee: Mohamed Benouza (Algeria), Attendance: 20,088
NIGERIA: Austin Ejide, Taye Taiwo, Onyekachi Apam, Danny Shittu, Joseph Yobo, Seyi Olofinjana, John Obi Mikel, Nwankwo Kanu (56 Onyekachi Okonkwo), Yakubu Aiyegbeni, John Utaka (73 Peter Odemwingie), Obafemi Martins (79 Stephen Makinwa).
IVORY COAST: Boubacar Barry, Abdoulaye Meite, Kolo Toure, Arthur Boka, Emmanuel Eboue, Yaya Toure, Steve Gohouri (46 Abdelkader Keita), Didier Zokora, Didier Drogba (85 Bakary Koné), Salomon Kalou, Aruna Dindane.
Goal: Salomon Kalou (66)

21.01.2008

MALI - BENIN 1-0 (0-0)
Sekondi-Takoradi Stadium, Sekondi
Referee: Jerome Damon (South Africa), Attendance: 11,000
MALI: Mahamadou Sidibe, Cedric Kante, Adama Coulibaly, Souleymane Diamoutene, Amadou Sidibe, Seydou Keita, Mahamadou Diarra, Bassala Toure (71 Drissa Diakite), Souleymane Dembele, Frederic Kanouté, Dramane Traoré (55 Mamady Sidibe, 88 Sammy Traoré).
BENIN: Rachad Chitou, Anicet Adjamossi, Damien Chrystosome, Seidath Tchomogo, Abdul Adenon, Jocelyn Ahoueya (81 Wassiou Oladipupu), Romuald Boco, Jonas Oketola (50 Stephane Sessegnon), Alain Gaspoz, Oumar Tchomogo (69 Abou Maiga), Razak Omotoyossi.
Goal: Frederic Kanouté (49 penalty)

25.01.2008

IVORY COAST - BENIN 4-1 (2-0)
Sekondi-Takoradi Stadium, Sekondi
Referee: Kenias Marange (Zimbabwe), Attendance: 13,000
BENIN: Rachad Chitou, Anicet Adjamossi, Damien Chrystosome (67 Noel Seka), Seidath Tchomogo (58 Abou Maiga), Abdul Adenon, Jocelyn Ahoueya, Romauld Boco, Alain Gaspoz (50 Mouri Ogunbiyi), Stephane Sessegnon, Oumar Tchomogo, Razak Omotoyossi.
IVORY COAST: Boubacar Barry, Abdoulaye Meite, Kolo Toure (44 Steve Gohouri), Arthur Boka, Emmanuel Eboue, Yaya Toure, Didier Zokora, Didier Drogba (68 Boubacar Sanogo), Salomon Kalou, Aruna Dindane, Abdelkader Keita (75 Gervais Yao Kouassi).
Goals: Didier Drogba (40), Yaya Toure (44), Abdelkader Keita (52), Aruna Dindane (63) / Razak Omotoyossi (89)

25.01.2008

NIGERIA - MALI 0-0
Sekondi-Takoradi Stadium, Sekondi
Referee: Abderrahim El Arjoun (Morocco), Attendance: 16,000
NIGERIA: Austin Ejide, Taye Taiwo, Obinna Nwaneri, Danny Shittu, Joseph Yobo, Seyi Olofinjana, John Obi Mikel, Yakubu Aiyegbeni, Obafemi Martins (46 John Utaka), Peter Odemwingie (58 Ike Uche) , Obinna Nsofor (84 Stephen Makinwa).
MALI: Mahamadou Sidibe, Cedric Kante, Adama Coulibaly, Souleymane Diamoutene, Adama Tamboura, Amadou Sidibe (87 Souleymane Dembele), Seydou Keita, Mahamadou Diarra, Mohamed Sissoko (81 Drissa Diakite), Frederic Kanouté, Dramane Traoré (74 Mamadou Diallo).

29.01.2008

NIGERIA - BENIN 2-0 (0-0)
Sekondi-Takoradi Stadium, Sekondi
Referee: Kacem Bennaceur (Tunisia)
NIGERIA: Austin Ejide, Taye Taiwo, Obinna Nwaneri, Danny Shittu, Joseph Yobo, John Obi Mikel, Dickson Etuhu (63 Richard Eromoigbe), Yakubu Aiyegbeni, John Utaka (51 Obinna Nsofor), Peter Odemwingie (87 Rabiu Afolabi) , Ike Uche.
BENIN: Yoann Djidonou, Anicet Adjamossi (46 Mouri Ogunbiyi), Damien Chrystosome, Abdul Adenon, Jocelyn Ahoueya, Romauld Boco, Jonas Oketola (54 Seidath Tchomogo), Alain Gaspoz, Stephane Sessegnon (82 Abou Maiga), Oumar Tchomogo, Razak Omotoyossi.
Goals: John Obi Mikel (52), Yakubu Aiyegbeni (85)

207

29.01.2008

IVORY COAST - MALI 3-0 (1-0)
Ohene Djan Stadium, Accra
Referee: Eddy Maillet (Seychelles), Attendance: 20,000
IVORY COAST: Boubacar Barry, Marc Zoro, Emmanuel Eboue, Siaka Tiene, Emerse Fae, Christian
Koffi N'Dri, Yaya Toure, Didier Zokora, Didier Drogba (75 Boubacar Sanogo), Arouna Koné,
Abdelkader Keita (59 Bakary Koné),.
MALI: Mahamadou Sidibe, Sammy Traoré, Cedric Kante, Adama Coulibaly (46 Mamadou Diallo),
Adama Tamboura, Seydou Keita, Bassala Toure (59 Mahamadou Dissa), Drissa Diakite, Djibril Sidibe,
Frederic Kanouté (46 Mohamed Sissoko), Dramane Traoré.
Goals: Didier Drogba (11), Marc Zoro (55), Boubacar Sanogo (85)

1.	IVORY COAST	3	3	0	0	8	1	9
2.	NIGERIA	3	1	1	1	2	1	4
3.	Mali	3	1	1	1	1	3	4
4.	Benin	3	0	0	3	1	7	0

GROUP C

22.01.2008

EGYPT - CAMEROON 4-2 (3-0)
Baba Yara Stadium, Kumasi
Referee: Modou Sowe (Gambia), Attendance: 42,000
EGYPT: Essam El-Hadary, Ahmed Fathy, Wael Gomaa, Hani Said, Mahmoud Fathalla, Sayed
Meawwad (88 Shadi Mohamed), Hosni Abd Rabbou, Mohamed Shawki, Mohamed Abdullah 'Zidan'
(69 Ahmed El-Mohammadi), Amr Zaky (60 Mohamed Aboutraika), Emad Abdel Nabi 'Moteab'.
CAMEROON: Idriss Carlos Kameni, Rigobert Song, Timothee Atouba, Andre Bikey, Geremi Fotso
Njitap, Jean Makoun (37 Augustin Binya), Stephane Mbia (46 Alexandre Song), Landry Nguemo (46
Achille Emana), Joël Epalle, Samuel Eto'o, Mohamadou Idrissou.
Goals: Hosni Abd Rabbou (14 penalty, 82), Mohamed Abdullah 'Zidan' (17, 45) / Samuel Eto'o (51,
90+2 penalty)

22.01.2008

SUDAN - ZAMBIA 0-3 (0-1)
Baba Yara Stadium, Kumasi
Referee: Badara Diatta (Senegal), Attendance: 35,000
SUDAN: Mahjoub El Moez, Hamouda Bashir (80 Saifeldin Ali Idris), Alaeldin Ahmed Gibril, Rtshard
Justin Lado, Mohamed Ali Khider, Haitham Mostafa, Omar Bakheit, Faisal Agab (57 Alaeldin
Babiker), Badreldin El Doud, Mugahid Mohamed (24 Yousef Alaeldin), Haitham Tambal.
ZAMBIA: Kennedy Mweene, Clive Hachilensa, Joseph Musonda, Kennedy Nketani, Billy Mwanza,
Ian Bakala, Felix Katongo, James Chamanga (82 Clifford Mulenga), Rainford Kalaba, Jacob Mulenga,
Dube Phiri (70 Emmanuel Mayuka),.
Goals: James Chamanga (3), Jacob Mulenga (51), Felix Katongo (59)

208

26.01.2008

CAMEROON - ZAMBIA 5-1 (3-0)
Baba Yara Stadium, Kumasi
Referee: Yuichi Nichimura (Japan), Attendance: 10,000
CAMEROON: Idriss Carlos Kameni, Rigobert Song, Timothee Atouba, Andre Bikey, Augustin Binya (63 Alain Nkong), Geremi Fotso Njitap, Alexandre Song, Modeste Mbami (67 Jean Makoun), Achille Emana (77 Mohamadou Idrissou), Samuel Eto'o, Joseph Désiré Job.
ZAMBIA: Kennedy Mweene, Clive Hachilensa, Joseph Musonda, Kennedy Nketani (38 Himoonde), Billy Mwanza, Ian Bakala (82 William Njovu), Chris Katongo, Isaac Chansa, James Chamanga (64 Felix Nsunzu), Felix Katongo, Jacob Mulenga.
Goals: Geremi (27), Joseph Désiré Job (31, 81), Achille Emana (43), Samuel Eto'o (65 penalty) / Chris Katongo (89)

26.01.2008

EGYPT - SUDAN 3-0 (1-0)
Baba Yara Stadium, Kumasi
Referee: Bonaventure Coffi Codja (Benin), Attendance: 15,000
EGYPT: Essam El-Hadary, Ahmed Fathy, Wael Gomaa, Hani Said, Mahmoud Fathalla (56 Ahmed Hassan), Sayed Meawwad, Hosni Abd Rabbou, Mohamed Shawki, Mohamed Abdullah 'Zidan' (56 Mohamed Aboutraika), Amr Zaky (80 Ahmed El-Mohammadi), Emad Abdel Nabi 'Moteab'.
SUDAN: Mahjoub El Moez, Alaeldin Ahmed Gibril (46 Saifeldin Ali Idris), Rishard Justin Lado, Mohamed Ali Khider, Amir Damar, Musa Al Tayeb, Alaeldin Babiker (81 Faisal Agab), Haitham Mostafa, Yousef Alaeldin, Badreldin El Doud, Haitham Tambal (60 Abdelhamid Amari),.
Goals: Hosni Abd Rabbou (29 penalty), Mohamed Aboutraika (78, 82)

30.01.2008

EGYPT - ZAMBIA 1-1 (1-0)
Baba Yara Stadium, Kumasi
Referee: Koman Coulibaly (Mali).
EGYPT: Essam El-Hadary, Ahmed Fathy, Wael Gomaa, Hani Said, Shadi Mohamed, Sayed Meawwad, Hosni Abd Rabbou, Mohamed Shawki, Ahmed Hassan (60 Mohamed Aboutraika), Amr Zaky (60 Mohamed Abdullah 'Zidan'), Emad Abdel Nabi 'Moteab' (77 Ibrahim Said).
ZAMBIA: Kennedy Mweene, Clive Hachilensa, Joseph Musonda, Billy Mwanza (30 Kampamba Chintu), Ian Bakala, Chris Katongo, Isaac Chansa (77 Rainford Kalaba), James Chamanga, Felix Katongo, Hichani Himonde, Jacob Mulenga (66 Dube Phiri).
Goals: Amr Zaky (15) / Chris Katongo (87)

30.01.2008

CAMEROON - SUDAN 3-0 (2-0)
Tamale Sports Stadium, Tamale
Referee: Kokou Djaoupe (Togo), Attendance: 10,000
CAMEROON: Idriss Carlos Kameni, Rigobert Song, Timothee Atouba (46 Bill Tchato), Andre Bikey, Geremi Fotso Njitap, Alexandre Song, Modeste Mbami, Joël Epalle (76 Paul Essola), Achille Emana (57 Bertin Tomou), Joseph Désiré Job, Samuel Eto'o.
SUDAN: Mahjoub El Moez, Rtshard Justin Lado, Mohamed Ali Khider, Amir Damar, Musa Al Tayeb, Haitham Mostafa, Omar Bakheit (50 Mohamed Tahir), Yousef Alaeldin, Faisal Agab (61 Alaeldin Babiker), Hamouda Bashir, Haitham Tambal (77 Hassan Isaac Korongo).
Goals: Samuel Eto'o (27 penalty, 90), Mohamed Ali Khider (34 own goal)

1.	EGYPT	3	2	1	0	8	3	7
2.	CAMEROON	3	2	0	1	10	5	6
3.	Zambia	3	1	1	1	5	6	4
4.	Sudan	3	0	0	3	0	9	0

GROUP D

23.01.2008

TUNISIA - SENEGAL 2-2 (1-1)
Tamale Sports Stadium, Tamale
Referee: Yuichi Nichimura (Japan), Attendance: 12,000
TUNISIA: Hamdi Kasraoui, Radhi Jaidi, Karim Hagui, Radhouane Felhi, Wissem Bekri, Joahar Mnari, Mejdi Traoui, Chaker Zouaghi (80 Mehdi Ben Dhifallah), Issam Jomaa (85 Yassine Mikari), Yassine Chikhaoui, Francileudo dos Santos (62 Kamel Zaiem).
SENEGAL: Tony Sylva, Habib Beye, Souleymane Diawara, Abdoulaye Faye, Guirane N'daw, Ousmane N'doye (62 Papa Bouba Diop), Moustapha Bayal Sall, El Hadji Diouf, Mamadou Niang (86 Babacar Gueye) , Diomansy Kamara, Frederic Mendy (61 Henri Camara).
Goals: Issam Jomaa (9), Medji Traoui (82) / Moustapaha Bayal Sall (45), Diomansy Kamara (66)

23.01.2008

SOUTH AFRICA - ANGOLA 1-1 (0-1)
Tamale Sports Stadium, Tamale
Referee: Koman Coulibaly (Mali), Attendance: 15,000
SOUTH AFRICA: Moeneeb Josephs, Tsepo Masilela, Bryce Moon, Aaron Mokoena, Nasief Morris, Benson Mhlongo, Siphiwe Tshabalala (46 Lerato Chabangu), Teko Modise, Surprise Moriri (75 Thembinkosi Fanteni), Steven Pienaar (63 Elrio van Heerden), Sibusiso Zuma.
ANGOLA: Lama, Rui Marques, Carlos Manuel Gonçalves Alonso 'Kali', Yamba Asha, Marco Airosa (88 Loco), Andre, Paulo Figueiredo (51 José Nsimba Baptista 'Zé Kalanga'), Sebastião Felisberto Graça Amaral Gilberto, Mendonça (65 Edson), FLÁVIO da Silva Amado, Alberto Mateus Contreir Gonçalves Manucho.
Goals: Elrio van Heerden (87) / Alberto Mateus Contreir Gonçalves Manucho (29)

27.01.2008

SENEGAL - ANGOLA 1-3 (1-0)
Tamale Sports Stadium, Tamale
Referee: Djamel Haimoudi (Algeria), Attendance: 10,000
SENEGAL: Tony Sylva, Habib Beye, Souleymane Diawara, Abdoulaye Faye, Guirane N'daw (83 Papa Modou Sougou), Papa Bouba Diop, Moustapha Bayal Sall, El Hadji Diouf, Mamadou Niang, Diomansy Kamara (70 Henri Camara), Frederic Mendy (63 Babacar Gueye).
ANGOLA: Lama, Maurito (71 Dede), Rui Marques, Carlos Manuel Gonçalves Alonso 'Kali', Yamba Asha, Marco Airosa, Andre Macanga, Sebastião Felisberto Graça Amaral Gilberto (82 Mateus), José Nsimba Baptista 'Zé Kalanga', FLÁVIO da Silva Amado, Alberto Mateus Contreir Gonçalves Manucho (87 Loco).
Goals: Abdoulaye Faye (20) / Alberto Mateus Contreir Gonçalves Manucho (49, 67), FLÁVIO da Silva Amado (77)

27.01.2008

TUNISIA - SOUTH AFRICA 3-1 (3-0)
Tamale Sports Stadium, Tamale
Referee: Kokou Djaoupe (Togo), Attendance: 12,000
TUNISIA: Hamdi Kasraoui, Radhi Jaidi, Karim Hagui, Sabeur Ben Frej, Yassine Mikari, Mehdi Nafti, Joahar Mnari (76 Chaker Zouaghi), Mejdi Traoui, Yassine Chikhaoui (81 Issam Jomaa), Francileudo dos Santos (66 Mehdi Ben Dhifallah), Chaouki Ben Saada.
SOUTH AFRICA: Moeneeb Josephs, Tsepo Masilela (62 Brett Evans), Bryce Moon, Aaron Mokoena, Nasief Morris, Benson Mhlongo, Teko Modise, Steven Pienaar, Thembinkosi Fanteni (59 Katlego Mphela), Lerato Chabangu (46 Elrio van Heerden), Sibusiso Zuma,.
Goals: Francileudo dos Santos (8, 34), Chaouki Ben Saada (32) / Katlego Mphela (86)

31.01.2008

SENEGAL - SOUTH AFRICA 1-1 (1-1)
Baba Yara Stadium, Kumasi
Referee: Alex Kotey (Ghana)
SENEGAL: Bouna Coundoul, Lamine Diatta, Ibrahima Faye, Souleymane Diawara, Abdoulaye Faye, Papa Bouba Diop (46 Babacar Gueye), Pape Malick Ba, Moustapha Bayal Sall, Henri Camara, Mamadou Niang (60 Papa Waigo N'diaye), Diomansy Kamara (82 Papa Modou Sougou).
SOUTH AFRICA: Moeneeb Josephs, Tsepo Masilela, Bryce Moon (80 Lance Davids), Aaron Mokoena, Nasief Morris, Elrio van Heerden, Siphiwe Tshabalala, Kagisho Dikgacoi, Teko Modise, Surprise Moriri (71 Lerato Chabangu), Sibusiso Zuma (90 Thembinkosi Fanteni).
Goal: Henri Camara (36) / Elrio van Heerden (14)

31.01.2008

TUNISIA - ANGOLA 0-0
Tamale Sports Stadium, Tamale
Referee: Bonaventure Coffi Codja (Benin), Attendance: 10,000
TUNISIA: Hamdi Kasraoui, Radhi Jaidi (75 Radhouane Felhi), Karim Hagui, Sabeur Ben Frej, Yassine Mikari, Mehdi Nafti, Joahar Mnari, Chaker Zouaghi, Kamel Zaiem (67 Mehdi Ben Dhifallah), Issam Jomaa (79 Yassine Chikhaoui), Amine Chermiti.
ANGOLA: Lama, Maurito, Rui Marques (59 Mateus), Carlos Manuel Gonçalves Alonso 'Kali', Yamba Asha, Marco Airosa (69 Loco), Andre Macanga, Sebastião Felisberto Graça Amaral Gilberto, José Nsimba Baptista 'Zé Kalanga' (83 Mendonça), FLÁVIO da Silva Amado, Alberto Mateus Contreir Gonçalves Manucho.

1.	TUNISIA	3	1	2	0	5	3	5
2.	ANGOLA	3	1	2	0	4	2	5
3.	Senegal	3	0	2	1	4	6	2
4.	South Africa	3	0	2	1	3	5	2

Quarter-finals

03.02.2008

GHANA - NIGERIA 2-1 (1-1)
Ohene Djan Stadium, Accra
Referee: Mohamed Benouza (Algeria), Attendance: 45,000
GHANA: Richard Kingson, John Mensah, John Paintsil, Eric Addo, Hans Sarpei, Sulley Muntari, Anthony Annan, Michael Essien, Quincy Owusu-Abeyie (74 Haminu Dramani), Asamoah Gyan (62 Laryea Kingston), Junior Agogo.

NIGERIA: Austin Ejide, Taye Taiwo, Obinna Nwaneri, Danny Shittu, Joseph Yobo, Seyi Olofinjana, John Obi Mikel (85 Obinna Nsofor), Dickson Etuhu (71 Richard Eromoigbe), Yakubu Aiyegbeni, Peter Odemwingie, Ike Uche.
Sent off: Mensah (60)
Goals: Michael Essien (45), Junior Agogo (83) / Yakubu Aiyegbeni (35 penalty)

03.02.2008

IVORY COAST - GUINEA 5-0 (1-0)
Sekondi-Takoradi Stadium, Sekondi
Referee: Djamel Haimoudi (Algeria), Attendance: 14,000
IVORY COAST: Boubacar Barry, Abdoulaye Meite, Arthur Boka, Emmanuel Eboue, Christian Koffi N'dri, Yaya Toure, Didier Zokora, Didier Drogba (76 Bakary Koné), Salomon Kalou, Aruna Dindane (70 Arouna Koné), Abdelkader Keita (74 Emerse Fae).
GUINEA: Kemoko Camara, Ibrahima Camara, Kamil Zayatte (88 Oumar Kalabane), Daouda Jabi, Samuel Johnson (67 Naby Soumah), Mamadou Dioulde Bah, Mohamed Sakho, Mohamed Alimou Diallo, Fode Mansare, Ismael Bangoura, Souleymane Youla (60 Karamoko Cisse).
Goals: Abdelkader Keita (25), Didier Drogba (70), Salomon Kalou (72, 81), Bakary Koné (86)

04.02.2008

EGYPT - ANGOLA 2-1 (2-1)
Baba Yara Stadium, Kumasi
Referee: Yuichi Nichimura (Japan), Attendance: 6000
EGYPT: Essam El-Hadary, Ahmed Fathy, Wael Gomaa, Hani Said, Shadi Mohamed, Sayed Meawwad (66 Mahmoud Fathallah), Hosni Abd Rabbou, Mohamed Shawki, Mohamed Aboutraika (90 Ibrahim Said), Amr Zaky (71 Ahmed Hassan), Emad Abdel Nabi 'Moteab'.
ANGOLA: Lama, Maurito (46 Mendonça), Rui Marques, Carlos Manuel Gonçalves Alonso 'Kali', Yamba Asha, Marco Airosa, Andre Macanga, Sebastião Felisberto Graça Amaral Gilberto, José Nsimba Baptista 'Zé Kalanga' (73 Mateus), FLÁVIO da Silva Amado (84 Edson), Alberto Mateus Contreir Gonçalves Manucho.
Goals: Hosni Abd Rabbou (23 penalty), Amr Zaky (38) / Alberto Mateus Contreir Gonçalves Manucho (27)

04.02.2008

TUNISIA - CAMEROON 2-3 (1-2, 2-2)
Tamale Sports Stadium, Tamale
Referee: Koman Coulibaly (Mali), Attendance: 15,000.
TUNISIA: Hamdi Kasraoui, Radhi Jaidi, Karim Hagui (38 Sabeur Ben Frej), Radhouane Felhi, Wissem Bekri, Mehdi Nafti (71 Issam Jomaa), Joahar Mnari, Medji Traoui, Yassine Chikhaoui, Francileudo dos Santos (86 Amine Chermiti), Chaouki Ben Saada.
CAMEROON: Idriss Carlos Kameni, Rigobert Song, Timothee Atouba (109 Bill Tchato), Andre Bikey, Geremi Fotso Njitap, Jean Makoun (65 Augustin Binya), Alexandre Song, Stephane Mbia, Achille Emana (61 Joël Epalle), Samuel Eto'o, Mohamadou Idrissou.
Goals: Chaouki Ben Saada (35), Yassine Chikhaoui (81) / Stephane Mbia (19, 93), Geremi Fotso Njitap (28)

Semi-finals

07.02.2008

GHANA - CAMEROON 0-1 (0-0)
Ohene Djan Stadium, Accra
Referee: Abderrahim El Arjoune (Morocco), Attendance: 45,000
GHANA: Richard Kingson, John Paintsil, Eric Addo, Hans Sarpei, Sulley Muntari, Haminu Dramani, Anthony Annan, Michael Essien, Quincy Owusu-Abeyie (62 Baffour Gyan), Andre Ayew (86 Ahmed Barusso), Junior Agogo.
CAMEROON: Idriss Carlos Kameni, Rigobert Song, Timothee Atouba, Andre Bikey, Geremi Fotso Njitap, Alexandre Song, Stephane Mbia, Achille Emana (77 Augustin Binya), Joseph Désiré Job (62 Alain Nkong), Samuel Eto'o, Mohamadou Idrissou (46 Joël Epalle).
Sent off: Bikey (90)
Goal: Alain Nkong (71)

07.02.2008

IVORY COAST - EGYPT 1-4 (0-1)
Baba Yara Stadium, Kumasi
Referee: Eddy Maillet (Seychelles), Attendance: 30,000
IVORY COAST: Boubacar Barry (39 Stephan Loboue), Abdoulaye Meite, Kolo Toure, Arthur Boka, Emmanuel Eboue, Yaya Toure, Didier Zokora, Didier Drogba, Salomon Kalou (59 Bakary Koné), Aruna Dindane (78 Arouna Koné) , Abdelkader Keita.
EGYPT: Essam El-Hadary, Ahmed Fathy, Wael Gomaa, Hani Said, Shadi Mohamed, Sayed Meawwad (78 Mahmoud Fathallah), Hosni Abd Rabbou, Ahmed Hassan, Mohamed Aboutraika, Emad Abdel Nabi 'Moteab' (68 Mohamed Abdullah 'Zidan'), Amr Zaky (87 Ibrahim Said).
Goals: Abdelkader Keita (64) / Ahmed Fathy (12), Amr Zaky (62, 67), Mohamed Aboutraika (90)

Third Place Match

09.02.2008

GHANA - IVORY COAST 4-2 (1-2)
Baba Yara Stadium, Kumasi
Referee: Jerome Damon (South Africa), Attendance: 40,000
GHANA: Richard Kingson, John Mensah, John Paintsil, Eric Addo (90 Barusso), Hans Sarpei, Sulley Muntari, Haminu Dramani (90 Harrison Afful), Anthony Annan, Michael Essien, Baffour Gyan (20 Quincy Owusu-Abeyie), Junior Agogo.
IVORY COAST: Tiasse Koné, Arthur Boka, Marc Zoro, Siaka Tiene, Emerse Fae (83 Aruna Dindane), Christian Koffi N'Dri, Didier Zokora, Didier Drogba, Salomon Kalou (74 Gervais Yao Kouassi), Boubacar Sanogo, Abdelkader Keita (64 Yaya Toure).
Goals: Sulley Muntari (10), Ouincy Owusu-Abeyie (70), Junior Agogo (80), Haminu Dramani (84) / Boubacar Sanogo (24, 32)

10.02.2008

EGYPT - CAMEROON 1-0 (0-0)
Ohene Djan Stadium, Accra
Referee: Bonaventure Coffi Codja (Benin), Attendance: 35,500
EGYPT: Essam El-Hadary, Ahmed Fathy, Wael Gomaa, Hani Said, Shadi Mohamed, Sayed Meawwad, Hosni Abd Rabbou, Ahmed Hassan, Mohamed Aboutraika (89 Ibrahim Said), Emad Abdel Nabi 'Moteab' (60 Mohamed Abdullah 'Zidan'), Amr Zaky (84 Mohamed Shawki).
CAMEROON: Idriss Carlos Kameni, Bill Tchato, Rigobert Song, Timothee Atouba, Geremi Fotso Njitap, Alexandre Song (16 Augustin Binya), Stephane Mbia, Joël Epalle (65 Modeste Mbami), Achille Emana (55 Mohamadou Idrissou), Alain Nkong, Samuel Eto'o.
Goal: Mohamed Aboutraika (77)

Twenty-seventh edition – 2010
Qualifying Tournament

The qualifying tournament for the 27th edition of the Africa Cup of Nations once again doubled as qualifying tournament for the finals of the FIFA World Cup 2010, so holders Egypt and hosts Angola participated amongst the 53 countries who entered – a record for the competition. The finals tournament itself was overshadowed by a terrorist attack on the team bus of the Togo team as it travelled through a disputed enclave of Angola on the way to the tournament. The death of three people on the bus in this attack and injury to a number of players led to the withdrawal of the team by the Togolese government and they were subsequently disqualified from the competition by the CAF after failing to appear for their first game. This meant that just 15 teams competed in the finals tournament and Egypt duly won the trophy for an unprecedented third consecutive time after defeating Ghana in the final.

Preliminary stage

The ten countries who were lowest in the FIFA World Rankings in July 2007 played off against each other in a preliminary round.
The Central African Republic and Sao Tomé e Príncipe immediately forfeited for financial reasons and the Seychelles and Swaziland therefore qualified automatically for the first stage.

14.10.2007 Madagascar – Comoros 6-2 (2-1)
Goals: Faneva Ima Andriantsima (30, 40, 48 pen, 56), Rija Rakotomandimby (65), Carolus Tsaralaza (79) / Daoud Midtadi (6), Ibor Bakar (53 pen)
17.11.2007 Comoros - Madagascar 0-4 (0-1)
Goals: Lalaina Nomenjanahary (38, 52), Rija Rakotomandimby (62), Hubert Robson (74)
17.10.2007 Sierra Leone – Guinea Bissau 1-0 (1-0)
Goal: Kewullay Conteh (17)
17.11.2007 Guinea Bissau - Sierra Leone 0-0
16.11.2007 Djibouti - Somalia 1-0 (0-0) [played only one leg due civil war in Somalia]
Goal: Hussein Yassin (84)

First stage

The 48 countries were divided into 12 groups to play for qualification to the final stage. Angola, hosts and Egypt, winners of the 2008 edition, together with South Africa, hosts of the 2010 FIFA World Cup all played. The winners of each group and the 8 best runners-up qualified for the final stage.

Group 1

31.05.2008 Tanzania - Mauritius 1-1 (0-1)
Goals: Danny Mrwanda (69) / Wesley Marquette (39)
31.05.2008 Cameroon - Cape Verde 2-0 (1-0)
Goals: Rigobert Song (8), Samuel Eto'o (57 pen)
07.06.2008 Cape Verde - Tanzania 1-0 (0-0)
Goal: Babanco (73)
08.06.2008 Mauritius - Cameroon 0-3 (0-2)
Goals: Andre Bikey (11), Samuel Eto'o (27), Gustave Bebee (87)
14.06.2008 Tanzania - Cameroon 0-0
15.06.2008 Mauritius - Cape Verde 0-1 (0-0)
Goal: Dady (43)
21.06.2008 Cameroon - Tanzania 2-1 (0-0)
Goals: Samuel Eto'o (65, 89) / Danny Mrwanda (72)
22.06.2008 Cape Verde - Mauritius 3-1 (1-0)
Goals: Dady (45, 58), Marco Soares (78) / Andy Sophie (67)
06.09.2008 Mauritius - Tanzania 1-4 (1-4)
Goals: Wesley Marquette (13) / Kigi Makasi (12), Nizzar Khalfan (20), Jerson Tegete (30, 35)
06.09.2008 Cape Verde - Cameroon 1-2 (1-0)
Goals: Lito (38) / Achille Emanie (51), Tchoyi Somen (65)
11.10.2008 Tanzania - Cape Verde 3-1 (2-1)
Goals: Athuman Iddy (6), Jerson Tegete (27), Mrisho Ngasa (75) / Semedo (35)
11.10.2008 Cameroon - Mauritius 5-0 (1-0)
Goals: Samuel Eto'o (26, 46 pen), Albert Meyong (56, 72), Jean Makoun (70)

1.	Cameroon	6	5	1	0	14	2	16
2.	Cape Verde	6	3	0	3	7	8	9
3.	Tanzania	6	2	2	2	9	6	8
4.	Mauritius	6	0	1	5	3	17	1

Group 2

31.05.2008 Namibia - Kenya 2-1 (1-1)
Goals: Wilko Risser (14), Costa Khaseib (89) / Austin Makacha (40)
01.06.2008 Guinea - Zimbabwe 0-0
07.06.2008 Kenya - Guinea 2-0 (1-0)
Goals: Dennis Oliech (3, 50)
08.06.2008 Zimbabwe - Namibia 2-0 (1-0)
Goals: Gilbert Mushangazhike (26, 85)
14.06.2008 Kenya - Zimbabwe 2-0 (1-0)
Goals: Macdonald Mariaga (13), Dennis Oliech (88)
14.06.2008 Namibia - Guinea 1-2 (1-2)
Goals: Rudolf Bester (42) / Ismael Bangoura (22), Pascal Feindouno (45)
22.06.2008 Zimbabwe - Kenya 0-0
22.06.2008 Guinea - Namibia 4-0 (2-0)
Goals: Pascal Feindouno (23), Ismael Bangoura (27, 55, 60)
06.09.2008 Kenya - Namibia 1-0 (1-0)
Goal: Mohammed Jamal (44 pen)
07.09.2008 Zimbabwe - Guinea 0-0
11.10.2008 Namibia - Zimbabwe 4-2 (3-0)
Goals: Wilko Risser (18, 53), Rudolf Bester (30), Paulus Shipanga (43) / Esrom Nyandoro (58), Cuthbert Malajila (85)

12.10.2008 Guinea - Kenya 3-2 (1-0)
Goals: Ismael Bangoura (31), Mamadou Bah (51), Kamil Zayatte (80) / Francis Ouma (70), Dennis Oliech (90)

1.	Guinea	6	3	2	1	9	5	11
2.	Kenya	6	3	1	2	8	5	10
3.	Zimbabwe	6	1	3	2	4	6	6
4.	Namibia	6	2	0	4	7	12	6

Group 3

31.05.2008 Uganda - Niger 1-0 (0-0)
Goal: Ibrahim Sekajja (53)
01.06.2008 Angola - Benin 3-0 (0-0)
Goals: FLÁVIO da Silva Amado (62), Job (81), Mendonça (86)
08.06.2008 Benin - Uganda 4-1 (2-1)
Goals: Razak Omotoyossi (16, 87), Oumar Tchomogo (21), Stephane Sessegnon (70) / Eugene Sepuya (9)
08.06.2008 Niger - Angola 1-2 (1-1)
Goals: Ismael Alassane (3) / FLÁVIO da Silva Amado (30), Yamba Asha (71)
14.06.2008 Uganda - Angola 3-1 (2-0)
Goals: Eugene Sepuya (6), Andrew Mwesigwa (18), Dan Wagaluka (73) / Mantorras (90)
14.06.2008 Niger - Benin 0-2 (0-0)
Goals: Seidath Tchomogo (54), Razak Omotoyossi (70)
22.06.2008 Benin - Niger 2-0 (1-0)
Goals: Jocelyn Ahoueya (45), Karim Oumarou (53 own goal)
23.06.2008 Angola - Uganda 0-0
07.09.2008 Niger - Uganda 3-1 (0-1)
Goals: Issoufou Alhassane (68, 86), Daouda Kamilou (88) / David Obua (33)
07.09.2008 Benin - Angola 3-2 (1-1)
Goals: Khaled Adenom (1), Razak Omotoyossi (52, 65) / FLÁVIO da Silva Amado (12), Loco (84)
12.10.2008 Angola - Niger 3-1 (0-1)
Goals: Kassaly Daouda (53 own goal), Gilberto (66), Zé Kalanga (70) / Moussa Mallam (19)
12.10.2008 Uganda - Benin 2-1 (0-1)
Goals: Geofrey Massa (50, 53) / Razak Omotoyossi (30)

1.	Benin	6	4	0	2	12	8	12
2.	Angola	6	3	1	2	11	8	10
3.	Uganda	6	3	1	2	8	9	10
4.	Niger	6	1	0	5	5	11	3

Group 4

01.06.2008 Equatorial Guinea - Sierra Leone 2-0 (0-0)
Goals: Falcao Carolino (47), Juan Epitie Dyowe (57)
01.06.2008 Nigeria - South Africa 2-0 (2-0)
Goals: Ikechukwu Uche (10), Obinna Nwaneri (44)
07.06.2008 South Africa - Equatorial Guinea 4-1 (2-0)
Goals: Kagisho Dikgacoi (9, 90), Surprise Moriri (33), Thembinkosi Fanteni (62) / Juvenal Edjogo (78 pen)
07.06.2008 Sierra Leone - Nigeria 0-1 (0-0)
Goal: Joseph Yobo (89)

14.06.2008 Sierra Leone - South Africa 1-0 (1-0)
Goal: Mohammed Kallon (21 pen)
15.06.2008 Equatorial Guinea - Nigeria 0-1 (0-1)
Goal: Joseph Yobo (5)
21.06.2008 South Africa - Sierra Leone 0-0
21.06.2008 Nigeria - Equatorial Guinea 2-0 (1-0)
Goals: Aiyegbeni Yakubu (45), Ikechukwu Uche (84)
06.09.2008 Sierra Leone - Equatorial Guinea 2-1 (1-0)
Goals: Kewullay Conteh (30), Sheriff Suma (73) / Rodolfo Bodipo (83 pen)
06.09.2008 South Africa - Nigeria 0-1 (0-0)
Goal: Ikechukwu Uche (69)
11.10.2008 Equatorial Guinea - South Africa 0-1 (0-1)
Goal: Siphiwe Tshabalala (9)
11.10.2008 Nigeria - Sierra Leone 4-1 (3-1)
Goals: Chris Obodo (20), Victor Obinna (34), Peter Odemwingie (45), Chidi Odiah (50) / Joseph Yobo
(31 own goal)

1.	Nigeria	6	6	0	0	11	1	18
2.	South Africa	6	2	1	3	5	5	7
3.	Sierra Leone	6	2	1	3	4	8	7
4.	Equatorial Guinea	6	1	0	5	4	10	3

Group 5

01.06.2008 Ghana - Libya 3-0 (1-0)
Goals: Prince Tagoe (17), Manuel Agogo (54), Laryea Kingston (64)
07.06.2008 Libya - Gabon 1-0 (1-0)
Goal: Moise Brou (5 own goal)
08.06.2008 Lesotho - Ghana 2-3 (0-2)
Goals: Sello Muso (89), Lehlohonolo Seema (90) / Laryea Kingston (15), Manuel Agogo (41, 63)
14.06.2008 Gabon - Ghana 2-0 (1-0)
Goals: Roguy Meye (45), Stephane Nguema (59)
15.06.2008 Lesotho - Libya 0-1 (0-0)
Goal: Ahmed Osman (85)
20.06.2008 Libya - Lesotho 4-0 (1-0)
Goals: Osama Salah (3), Omar Dawood (50), Younues Al Shibani (68), Hesham Shaban (80)
22.06.2008 Ghana - Gabon 2-0 (1-0)
Goals: Prince Tagoe (31), Sulley Muntari (75)
28.06.2008 Gabon - Lesotho 2-0 (1-0)
Goals: Fabrice Do Marcolino (45, 63)
05.09.2008 Libya - Ghana 1-0 (0-0)
Goal: Ahmed Osman (86)
07.09.2008 Lesotho - Gabon 0-3 (0-0)
Goals: Bruno Ecuele (56), Roguy Meye (72), Zita Mbanangoye (90)
11.10.2008 Gabon - Libya 1-0 (0-0)
Goal: Zita Mbanangoye (82)
11.10.2008 Ghana - Lesotho 3-0 (2-0)
Goals: Stephen Appiah (19), Manuel Agogo (24), Matthew Amoah (62)

1.	Ghana	6	4	0	2	11	5	12
2.	Gabon	6	4	0	2	8	3	12
3.	Libya	6	4	0	2	7	4	12
4.	Lesotho	6	0	0	6	2	16	0

Group 6

31.05.2008 Senegal - Algeria 1-0 (0-0)
Goal: Ibrahima Faye (80)
01.06.2008 Liberia - Gambia 1-1 (0-1)
Goals: Oliver Makor (82) / Mustapha Jarjue (17)
06.06.2008 Algeria - Liberia 3-0 (2-0)
Goals: Rafik Djebbour (16), Karim Ziani (20, 47 pen)
08.06.2008 Gambia - Senegal 0-0
14.06.2008 Gambia - Algeria 1-0 (1-0)
Goal: Mustapha Jarjue (19 pen)
15.06.2008 Liberia - Senegal 2-2 (0-0)
Goals: Dioh Williams (74), Oliver Makor (85) / El Hadji Diouf (47), Cheikh Gueye (55)
20.06.2008 Algeria - Gambia 1-0 (1-0)
Goal: Antar Yahia (33)
21.06.2008 Senegal - Liberia 3-1 (2-0)
Goals: Ibrahima Sonko (8), El Hadji Diouf (32), Henri Camara (63) / Dioh Williams (89)
05.09.2008 Algeria - Senegal 3-2 (0-0)
Goals: Cheikh Gueye (60 own goal), Rafik Saifi (66), Antar Yahia (72) / Issiar Dia (53), Modou Sougou (90)
06.09.2008 Gambia - Liberia 3-0 (2-0)
Goals: Njogu Demba (10, 76), Ousman Jallow (26)
11.10.2008 Senegal - Gambia 1-1 (0-0)
Goals: Kader Mangane (65) / Aziz Corr Nyang (85)
11.10.2008 Liberia - Algeria 0-0

1.	Algeria	6	3	1	2	7	4	10
2.	Gambia	6	2	3	1	6	3	9
3.	Senegal	6	2	3	1	9	7	9
4.	Liberia	6	0	3	3	4	12	3

Group 7

31.05.2008 Botswana - Madagascar 0-0
01.06.2008 Ivory Coast - Mozambique 1-0 (0-0)
Goal: Sekou Cisse (75)
08.06.2008 Madagascar - Ivory Coast 0-0
08.06.2008 Mozambique - Botswana 1-2 (0-1)
Goals: Miro (60) / Diphetogo Selolwane (30), Boitumelo Mafoko (82)
14.06.2008 Botswana - Ivory Coast 1-1 (1-0)
Goals: Diphetogo Selolwane (25) / Abdoulaye Meite (65)
15.06.2008 Madagascar - Mozambique 1-1 (0-1)
Goals: Guy Mamihasindrahona (90 pen) / Dario (33)
22.06.2008 Mozambique - Madagascar 3-0 (1-0)
Goals: Manuel José Luis Bucuane 'Tico-Tico' (23), Danito (52), Domingues (64)
22.06.2008 Ivory Coast - Botswana 4-0 (2-0)
Goals: Boubacar Sanogo (16), Didier Zokora (22), Sekou Cisse (46, 70)
07.09.2008 Mozambique - Ivory Coast 1-1 (0-0)
Goals: Miro (56) / Bakary Koné (48)
07.09.2008 Madagascar - Botswana 1-0 (1-0)
Goal: Stephan Rabemananjara (24)
11.10.2008 Ivory Coast - Madagascar 3-0 (1-0)
Goals: Boubacar Sanogo (41, 55), Salomon Kalou (65)
11.10.2008 Botswana - Mozambique 0-1 (0-1)
Goal: Genito (6)

218

1.	Ivory Coast	6	3	3	0	10	2	12
2.	Mozambique	6	2	2	2	7	5	8
3.	Madagascar	6	1	3	2	2	7	6
4.	Botswana	6	1	2	3	3	8	5

Group 8

31.05.2008 Rwanda - Mauritania 3-0 (1-0)
Goals: Olivier Karekezi (15), Abedi Said (67 pen), Labama Bokota (72)
31.05.2008 Morocco - Ethiopia 3-0 (2-0)
Goals: Abdessalem Benjellouni (4), Hicham Aboucherouane (13), Houssine Kharja (85)
07.06.2008 Mauritania - Morocco 1-4 (0-2)
Goals: Ahmed Teguedi (82 pen) / Tarik Sektioui (9), Abdessalam Benjelloun (37), Youssef Safri (58), Houssine Kharja (79)
08.06.2008 Ethiopia - Rwanda 1-2 (1-0)
Goals: Tesfaye Tafese (44) / Abedi Said (59), Olivier Karekezi (82)
13.06.2008 Mauritania - Ethiopia 0-1 (0-0)
Goal: Said Saladin (90)
14.06.2008 Rwanda - Morocco 3-1 (1-0)
Goals: Abedi Said (15), Labama Bokota (68), Olivier Karekezi (90) / Youssef Safri (78)
21.06.2008 Morocco - Rwanda 2-0 (1-0)
Goals: Youssef Safri (12 pen), Nabil El Zhar (49)
22.06.2008 Ethiopia - Mauritania 6-1 (1-1)
Goals: Teferra Fikru (38 pen, 89), Andualem Niguisse (55, 63), Mohamed Mesud (83), Girma Adane (90) / Voulani Ely (44)
06.09.2008 Mauritania - Rwanda 0-1 (0-0)
Goal: Bola Bobo (79)
07.09.2008 Ethiopia - Morocco n/p
11.10.2008 Morocco - Mauritania 4-1 (1-0)
Goals: Youssef Safri (35), Youssef Hadji (55, 60), Merouane Zemmama (65) / Ahmed Teguedi (67)
11.10.2008 Rwanda - Ethiopia n/p

1.	Morocco	4	3	0	1	11	5	9
2.	Rwanda	4	3	0	1	7	3	9
3.	Mauritania	4	0	0	4	2	12	0

Ethiopia was excluded from the qualifying tournament by FIFA on 12th September 2008, following a conflict between the FIFA and the leadership of the Ethiopian FA. All their previous results were annulled.

Group 9

01.06.2008 Burundi - Seychelles 1-0 (0-0)
Goal: Yamin Ndikumana (81)
01.06.2008 Tunisia - Burkina Faso 1-2 (1-0)
Goals: Tijani Belaid (38) / Yssouf Koné (85, 87)
07.06.2008 Seychelles - Tunisia 0-2 (0-2)
Goals: Issam Jomaa (9), Chaouki Ben Saada (43)
07.06.2008 Burkina Faso - Burundi 2-0 (2-0)
Goals: Moumouni Dagano (23 pen, 44 pen)
14.06.2008 Seychelles - Burkina Faso 2-3 (0-1)
Goals: Philip Zialor (47), Don Annacoura (53) / Maoumouni Dagano (25, 57, 78)
15.06.2008 Burundi - Tunisia 0-1 (0-0)
Goal: Radhi Jaidi (70)

21.06.2008 Burkina Faso - Seychelles 4-1 (2-1)
Goals: Charles Kabore (21), Mahamoudou Kere (28), Issouf Ouattara (54), Yssouf Koné (89) / Bernard Stange (44)
21.06.2008 Tunisia - Burundi 2-1 (2-1)
Goals: Chaouki Ben Saada (21 pen), Issam Jomaa (44) / Henry Mbazumutima (45)
06.09.2008 Seychelles - Burundi 1-2 (0-1)
Goals: Philip Zialor (63) / Henry Nbazumutima (28), Claude Nahimana (58)
06.09.2008 Burkina Faso - Tunisia 0-0
11.10.2008 Tunisia - Seychelles 5-0 (4-0)
Goals: Hichem Essifi (5, 68), Yassin Nikari (18), Sabeur Frej (20), Fahid Ben Khalfallah (43)
12.10.2008 Burundi - Burkina Faso 1-3 (1-1)
Goals: Claude Nahimana (43 pen) / Aristide Bance (15), Moumouni Dagano (60, 80)

1.	Burkina Faso	6	5	1	0	14	5	16
2.	Tunisia	6	4	1	1	11	3	13
3.	Burundi	6	2	0	4	5	9	6
4.	Seychelles	6	0	0	6	4	17	0

Group 10

01.06.2008 Mali - Congo 4-2 (3-1)
Goals: Seydou Keita (1, 61), Adama Coulibaly (32), Soumaila Coulibaly (42) / Lys Mouithys (5, 74)
07.06.2008 Chad - Mali 1-2 (1-2)
Goals: Hillaire Kedigui (37) / Frederic Kanouté (4, 22)
08.06.2008 Congo - Sudan 1-0 (0-0)
Goal: Wilfrid Endzanga (70)
14.06.2008 Chad - Congo 2-1 (1-1)
Goals: Hillaire Kedigui (44 pen), Syriakata Hassan (48) / Gervais Batota (42)
14.06.2008 Sudan - Mali 3-2 (1-0)
Goals: Alaeldin Yousif (45), Mohamed Tahir (70), Haytham Kamal (86) / Frederic Kanouté (63, 90)
22.06.2008 Congo - Chad 2-0 (1-0)
Goals: Lys Mouithys (14), Franchel Ibara (64)
22.06.2008 Mali - Sudan 3-0 (1-0)
Goals: Frederic Kanouté (23), Seydou Keita (58, 66)
06.09.2008 Sudan - Chad 1-2 (0-1)
Goals: Haytham Kamal (75) /Marius Mbaiam (29), Syriakata Hassan (81)
07.09.2008 Congo - Mali 1-0 (0-0)
Goal: Wilfrid Endzanga (87)
10.09.2008 Chad - Sudan 1-3 (1-1)
Goals: Leger Djime (34) / Ahmed Adil (4), Faisal Agab (48 pen), Saifeldin Ali (76)
11.10.2008 Sudan - Congo 2-0 (1-0)
Goals: Mohamed Tahir (30), Faisal Agab (73)
11.10.2008 Mali - Chad 2-1 (1-0)
Goals: Sidi Yaya Keita (44, 82) / Betolngar Misdongarde (64)

1.	Mali	6	4	0	2	13	8	12
2.	Sudan	6	3	0	3	9	9	9
3.	Congo	6	3	0	3	7	8	9
4.	Chad	6	2	0	4	7	11	6

Chad were disqualified from the African Cup of Nations 2010 but their matches remained relevant for the FIFA World Cup qualification tournament.

Group 11

31.05.2008 Togo - Zambia 1-0 (1-0)
Goal: Adekanmi Olufade (16)
08.06.2008 Swaziland - Togo 2-1 (0-0)
Goals: Siza Dlamini (55), Collen Salelwako (73) / Adekanmi Olufade (88)
15.06.2008 Swaziland - Zambia 0-0
21.06.2008 Zambia - Swaziland 1-0 (0-0)
Goal: Christopher Katongo (86 pen)
10.09.2008 Zambia - Togo 1-0 (1-0)
Goal: Felix Katongo (31)
11.10.2008 Togo - Swaziland 6-0 (3-0)
Goals: Moustapha Salifou (16), Emmanuel Adebayor (29, 47, 72, 85), Adekanmi Olufade (44)

1.	Zambia	4	2	1	1	2	1	7
2.	Togo	4	2	0	2	8	3	6
3.	Swaziland	4	1	1	2	2	8	4

Eritrea withdrew from the competition.

Group 12

31.05.2008 Malawi - Djibouti 8-1 (2-1)
Goals: Elvis Kafoteka (3), Essau Kanyenda (19, 46, 48), Joseph Kamwendo (66), Moses Chavula (73), Robet Ngambi (78), Noel Mkandawire (83) / Ahmed Hassan Daher (23)
01.06.2008 Egypt - DR Congo 2-1 (0-1)
Goals: Amr Zaki (68). Ahmed Eid (80) / Nkongolo Ilunga (43)
06.06.2008 Djibouti - Egypt 0-4 (0-1)
Goals: Amr Zaki (40), Hosni Abd Rabo (46 pen), Ahmed Hassan (53), Ahmed Eid (64)
08.06.2008 DR Congo - Malawi 1-0 (0-0)
Goal: Zola Matumonia (76)
13.06.2008 Djibouti - DR Congo 0-6 (0-3)
Goals: Dieumerci Mbokani (24, 47), Shabani Nonda (30), Zola Matumonia (39, 51), Mabi Mputu (80)
14.06.2008 Malawi - Egypt 1-0 (0-0)
Goal: Chiukepo Msowoya (90)
22.06.2008 DR Congo - Djibouti 5-1 (2-0)
Goals: Shabani Nonda (10, 45, 52), Tshinyama Tshiolola (60), Dieumerci Mbokani (64) / Moussa Hirir (85)
22.06.2008 Egypt - Malawi 2-0 (1-0)
Goals: Emad Abdel Nabi 'Moteab' (17, 50)
05.09.2008 Djibouti - Malawi 0-3 (0-1)
Goals: Chiukepo Msowoya (30), Moses Chavula (63), Atusaye Nyondo (67)
07.09.2008 DR Congo - Egypt 0-1 (0-1)
Goal: Mohamed Aboutraika (30)
11.10.2008 Malawi - DR Congo 2-1 (0-1)
Goals: Robert Ngambi (56), Chiukepo Msowoya (83) / Tresor Lua Lua (13)
12.10.2008 Egypt - Djibouti 4-0 (1-0)
Goals: Emad Abdel Nabi 'Moteab' (18), Ahmed Hassan (49), Mohamed Aboutraika (65), Said Riyad (90 own goal)

1.	Egypt	6	5	0	1	13	2	15
2.	Malawi	6	4	0	2	14	5	12
3.	DR Congo	6	3	0	3	14	6	9
4.	Djibouti	6	0	0	6	2	30	0

Rwanda, Kenya, Tunisia, Togo, Gabon, Sudan, Malawi and Mozambique all qualified for the final stage along with the 12 group winners. Gambia, Cape Verde and South Africa were eliminated, Angola qualified as hosts.

Final stage

The top three teams in each group qualified for the final tournament and Angola qualified automatically as hosts.

Group A

28.03.2009 Togo - Cameroon 1-0 (1-0)
Goal: Emmanuel Adebayor (11)
28.03.2009 Morocco - Gabon 1-2 (0-2)
Goals: Mounir El Hamdaoui (84) / PierreAubameyang (34), Roguy Meye (45)
06.06.2009 Gabon - Togo 3-0 (1-0)
Goals: Bruno Ecuele (11), Roguy Meye (67), Moise Brou (81)
07.06.2009 Cameroon - Morocco 0-0
20.06.2009 Morocco - Togo 0-0
05.09.2009 Gabon - Cameroon 0-2 (0-0)
Goals: Achille Emana (65), Samuel Eto'o (67)
06.09.2009 Togo - Morocco 1-1 (1-0)
Goals: Moustapha Salifou (3) / Adel Taarabt (90)
09.09.2009 Cameroon - Gabon 2-1 (1-0)
Goals: Jean Makoun (25), Samuel Eto'o (64) / Daniel Cousin (90)
10.10.2009 Cameroon - Togo 3-0
Goals: Geremi Fotso Njitap (29), Jean Makoun (46), Achille Emana (54)
10.10.2009 Gabon - Morocco 3-1 (1-0)
Goals: El-Armine Erbate (43 own goal), Eric Mouloungui (65), Daniel Cousin (70) / Adel Taarabt (88)
14.11.2009 Morocco - Cameroon 0-2 (0-1)
Goals: Achille Webo (19), Samuel Eto'o (52)
14.11.2009 Togo - Gabon 1-0 (0-0)
Goal: Floyd Ayite (71)

1.	CAMEROON	6	4	1	1	9	2	13
2.	GABON	6	3	0	3	9	7	9
3.	TOGO	6	2	2	2	3	7	8
4.	Morocco	6	0	3	3	3	8	3

Group B

28.03.2009 Kenya - Tunisia 1-2 (0-1)
Goals: Dennis Oliech (70) / Ammar Jemal (6), Issam Jomaa (79)
29.03.2009 Mozambique - Nigeria 0-0
06.06.2009 Tunisia - Mozambique 2-0 (1-0)
Goals: Ouissen Ben Yahia (21 pen), Oussama Darragi (89)
07.06.2009 Nigeria - Kenya 3-0 (1-0)
Goals: Ikechukwu Uche (2), Victor Obinna (72 pen, 77)
20.06.2009 Kenya - Mozambique 2-1 (1-0)
Goals: Julius Owino (8), Macdonald Mariaga (72 pen) / Domingues (49)
20.06.2009 Tunisia - Nigeria 0-0
06.09.2009 Mozambique - Kenya 1-0 (0-0)
Goal: Manuel José Luis Bucuane 'Tico-Tico' (66)

222

06.09.2009 Nigeria - Tunisia 2-2 (1-1)
Goals: Peter Odemwingie (23), Michael Eneramo (80) / Sliti Nabil (24), Oussama Darragi (89)
11.10.2009 Nigeria - Mozambique 1-0 (0-0)
Goals: Victor Obinna (90)
11.10.2009 Tunisia - Kenya 1-0 (1-0)
Goal: Issam Jomaa (1)
14.11.2009 Kenya - Nigeria 2-3 (1-0)
Goals: Dennis Oliech (15), Allan Wetende (77) / Obafemi Martins (60, 81), Aiyegbeni Yakubu (64)
14.11.2009 Mozambique - Tunisia 1-0 (0-0)
Goal: Dario (83)

1.	NIGERIA	6	3	3	0	9	4	12
2.	TUNISIA	6	3	2	1	7	4	11
3.	MOZAMBIQUE	6	2	1	3	3	5	7
4.	Kenya	6	1	0	5	5	11	3

Group C

28.03.2009 Rwanda - Algeria 0-0
29.03.2009 Egypt - Zambia 1-1 (1-0)
Goals: Amr Zaki (27) / Francis Kasonde (56)
06.06.2009 Zambia - Rwanda 1-0 (0-0)
Goal: Rainford Kalaba (78)
07.06.2009 Algeria - Egypt 3-1 (0-0)
Goals: Karim Matmour (60), Abdelkader Ghezzal (64), Rafik Djebbour (77) / Mohamed Aboutraika (86)
20.06.2009 Zambia - Algeria 0-2 (0-1)
Goals: Madjid Bougherra (21), Rafik Saifi (66)
05.07.2009 Egypt - Rwanda 3-0 (0-0)
Goals: Mohamed Aboutraika (64, 90), Hosni Abd Rabo (74 pen)
05.09.2009 Rwanda - Egypt 0-1 (0-0)
Goal: Ahmed Hassan (67)
06.09.2009 Algeria - Zambia 1-0 (0-0)
Goal: Rafik Saifi (59)
10.10.2009 Zambia - Egypt 0-1 (0-0)
Goal: Hosni Abd Rabo (69)
11.10.2009 Algeria - Rwanda 3-1 (2-1)
Goals: Abdelkader Ghezzal (22), Nadir Belhadj (45), Karim Ziani (90+5 pen) / Mafisango Mutesa (19)
14.11.2009 Egypt - Algeria 2-0 (1-0)
Goals: Amr Zaki (3), Emad Abdel Nabi 'Moteab' (90+5)
14.11.2009 Rwanda - Zambia 0-0

1.	ALGERIA	6	4	1	1	9	4	13
	EGYPT	6	4	1	1	9	4	13
3.	ZAMBIA	6	1	2	3	2	5	5
4.	Rwanda	6	0	2	4	1	8	2

FIFA World Cup Qualification Play-Off

18.11.2009 Algeria - Egypt 1-0 (1-0)
Goal: Antar Yahia (40)

223

Group D

28.03.2009 Sudan - Mali 1-1 (1-1)
Goals: Mudathir El Tahir (24) / Frederic Kanouté (20)
29.03.2009 Ghana - Benin 1-0 (1-0)
Goal: Prince Tagoe (1)
07.06.2009 Benin - Sudan 1-0 (1-0)
Goal: Razak Omotoyossi (22)
07.06.2009 Mali - Ghana 0-2 (0-0)
Goals: Kwadwo Asamoah (66), Matthew Amoah (78)
20.06.2009 Sudan - Ghana 0-2 (0-1)
Goals: Matthew Amoah (6, 52)
21.06.2009 Mali - Benin 3-1 (1-1)
Goals: Modibo Maiga (29), Mamadou Diallo (76), Frederic Kanouté (84) / Seidath Tchomogo (15)
06.09.2009 Benin - Mali 1-1 (0-0)
Goals: Mohamed Aoudou (87) / Mahamadou Samassa (72)
06.09.2009 Ghana - Sudan 2-0 (1-0)
Goals: Sulley Muntari (14), Michael Essien (52)
11.10.2009 Mali - Sudan 1-0 (0-0)
Goal: Frederic Kanouté (89)
11.10.2009 Benin - Ghana 1-0 (0-0)
Gal: Mohamed Aoudou (89)
14.11.2009 Sudan - Benin 1-2 (1-1)
Goals: Hassan Abakar (45 pen) / Razak Omotoyossi (34 pen), Djiman Koukou (62)
15.11.2009 Ghana - Mali 2-2 (0-1)
Goals: Matthew Amoah (65), Anthony Annan (83) / Lassana Fane (23), Tenema Ndiaye (68)

1.	GHANA	6	4	1	1	9	3	13
2.	BENIN	6	3	1	2	6	6	10
3.	MALI	6	2	3	1	8	7	9
4.	Sudan	6	0	1	5	2	9	1

Group E

28.03.2009 Burkina Faso - Guinea 4-2 (2-0)
Goals: Mahamoudou Kere (23), Alain Traoré (30), Moumouni Dagano (55 penalty, 71) / Pascal
Feindouno (65 penalty), Kamil Zayatte (86)
29.03.2009 Ivory Coast - Malawi 5-0 (3-0)
Goals: Romaric (1), Didier Drogba (6 penalty, 27), Salomon Kalou (59), Bakary Koné (70)
06.06.2009 Malawi - Burkina Faso 0-1 (0-0)
Goal: Moumouni Dagano (68)
07.06.2009 Guinea - Ivory Coast 1-2 (0-1)
Goals: Sambegou Bangoura (65) / Bakary Koné (43), Romaric (70)
20.06.2009 Burkina Faso - Ivory Coast 2-3 (1-1)
Goals: Jonathan Pitroipa (27), Aristide Bance (78) / Yaya Toure (14), Mamadou Tall (54 own goal),
Didier Drogba (70)
21.06.2009 Guinea - Malawi 2-1 (2-0)
Goals: Pascal Feindouno (24, 42) / Chiukepo Msowoya (89)
05.09.2009 Malawi - Guinea 2-1 (0-1)
Goals: Chiukepo Msowoya (46, 59) / Oumar Kalabane (37)
05.09.2009 Ivory Coast - Burkina Faso 5-0 (1-0)
Goals: Saidou Panandetiguiri (9 own goal), Didier Drogba (48, 64), Yaya Toure (54), Kader Keita (68)
10.10.2009 Malawi - Ivory Coast 1-1 (0-0)
Goals: Jacob Ngwira (64) / Didier Drogba (67)

224

11.10.2009 Guinea - Burkina Faso 1-2 (0-1)
Goals: Mamadou Bah (82) / Moumouni Dagano (37), Habib Bamogo (59)
14.11.2009 Burkina Faso - Malawi 1-0 (0-0)
Goal: Moumouni Dagano (47)
14.11.2009 Ivory Coast - Guinea 3-0 (2-0)
Goals: Gervinho (16, 31) Siaka Tiene (67)

1.	IVORY COAST	6	5	1	0	19	4	16
2.	Burkina Faso	6	4	0	2	10	11	12
3.	Malawi	6	1	1	4	4	11	4
4.	Guinea	6	1	0	5	7	14	3

Final tournament (Angola)

GROUP A

10.01.2010

ANGOLA – MALI 4-4 (2-0)
Estádio 11 de Novembro, Luanda
Referee: Essam Abd El Fatah (Egypt), Attendance: 45,000
ANGOLA: Carlos Alberto Fernandes, Rui Marques, Carlos Manuel Gonçalves Alonso 'Kali',
Francisco Zuela, Sebastião Felisberto Graça Amaral Gilberto (81 Paulo Enoque Guilherme), Fernando
Agostinho da Costa 'Xara', Aderito Waldemar Dede (25 DJALMA Braume Manuel Abel Campos),
Rosa Stelvio Cruz, Alberto Jose Mabina, FLÁVIO da Silva Amado (84 Arsenio Cabungula Love),
Alberto Mateus Contreir Gonçalves Manucho. Trainer: Manuel José de Jesus (Portugal)
MALI: Mahamadou Sidibe, Ousmane Berthe, Bakary Soumare, Souleymane Diamoutene, Adama
Tamboura, Bakaye Traoré (57 Lassana Fane), Mahamadou Diarra, Mamadou Bagayoko (74 Moustapha
Yattabare), El Hadj Traoré, Modibo Maïga (34 Seydou Keita), Frederic Kanouté. Trainer: Stephen
Keshi
Goals: FLÁVIO da Silva Amado (36, 42), Sebastião Felisberto Graça Amaral Gilberto (67 penalty),
Alberto Mateus Contreir Gonçalves Manucho (74 penalty) / Seydou Keita (79, 90+3), Frederic Kanouté
(88), Mustapha Yatabare (90+4)

11.01.2010

MALAWI – ALGERIA 3-0 (2-0)
Estádio 11 de Novembro, Luanda
Referee: Badara Diatta (Senegal), Attendance: 1000
MALAWI: Swadick Sanudi, Moses Chavula, James Sangala, Peter Mponda, Russel Mwafulirwa (64
Chiukepo Msowoya), Joseph Kamwendo, Essau Kanyenda, Elvis Kafoteka, Hellings Mwakasungula,
Peter Wadabwa (76 Jimmy Zakazaka), Dave Banda (51 Robert Ngambi). Trainer: Kinnah Phiri
ALGERIA: Faouzi Chaouchi, Madjid Bougherra, Rafik Halliche, Samir Zaoui, Nadir Belhadj, Karim
Matmour (62 Yacine Bezzaz), Hassan Yebda, Yazid Mansouri, Karim Ziani, Abdelkader Ghezzal (79
Hameur Bouazza), Rafik Saifi (63 Abdelmalek Ziaya). Trainer: Rabah Saadane
Goals: Russel Mwafulirwa (17), Elvis Kafoteka (35), Dave Banda (48)

225

14.01.2010

ANGOLA – MALAWI 2-0 (0-0)
Estádio 11 de Novembro, Luanda
Referee: Désiré Doue Normandiez (Côte d'Ivoire), Attendance: 48,500
ANGOLA: Carlos Alberto Fernandes, Carlos Manuel Gonçalves Alonso 'Kali', Fernando Agostinho da Costa 'Xara', Alberto Jose Mabina, Francisco Zuela, Rosa Stélvio Cruz, Sebastião Felisberto Graça Amaral Gilberto (35 Alexandre Jamuana), Rui Marques, DJALMA Braume Manuel Abel Campos (74 David Magalhães), FLÁVIO da Silva Amado (62 Pedro Manuel Torres Mantorras), Alberto Mateus Contreir Gonçalves Manucho.
MALAWI: Swadick Sanudi, Moses Chavula, James Sangala, Peter Mponda, Joseph Kamwendo (75 Robert Ngambi), Essau Kanyenda, Elvis Kafoteka, Hellings Mwakasungula, Victor Nyirenda (48 Chiupeko Msowoya), Peter Wadabwa (54 Jimmy Zakazaka), Dave Banda.
Goals: FLÁVIO da Silva Amado (48), Alberto Mateus Contreir Gonçalves Manucho (54)

14.01.2010

ALGERIA – MALI 1-0 (1-0)
Estádio 11 de Novembro, Luanda
Referee: Muhmed Ssegonga (Uganda), Attendance: 4,000
ALGERIA: Faouzi Chaouchi, Madjid Bougherra, Nadir Belhadj, Rafik Halliche, Yazid Mansouri, Yacine Bezzaz (70 Hameur Bouazza), Hassan Yebda, Abdelkader Ghezzal (80 Rafik Saifi), Karim Matmour (90 Abdelmalek Ziaya), Abdelkader Laifaoui, Karim Ziani.
MALI: Soumaila Diakite, Ousmane Berthe, Adama Tamboura, Mahamadou Diarra, Tenema N'Diaye (60 Frederic Kanouté), Modibo Maiga, Seydou Keita, Bakary Soumare, Mohamed Sissoko (65 Lassana Fane), Mustapha Yatabare (58 Mamadou Diallo), Abdallaye Maiga.
Goal: Rafik Halliche (42).

18.01.2010

ANGOLA – ALGERIA 0-0
Estádio 11 de Novembro, Luanda
Referee: Jerome Damon (South Africa), Attendance: 40,000
ANGOLA: Carlos Alberto Fernandes, Carlos Manuel Gonçalves Alonso 'Kali', Jamuana, Alberto Jose Mabina, Rui Marques, Francisco Zuela (52 Das Caires), Fernando Agostinho da Costa 'Xara', DJALMA Braume Manuel Abel Campos, Sebastião Felisberto Graça Amaral Gilberto, José Nsimba Baptista 'Zé Kalanga' (64 Ricardo Job), Alberto Mateus Contreir Gonçalves Manucho (90 Johnson Pinto Macaba).
ALGERIA: Fawzi Chaouchi, Madjid Bougherra, Rafik Halliche, Abdelkader Laifaoui, Nadir Belhadj, Karim Matmour (88 Djamel Abdoun), Hassan Yebda, Yazid Mansouri, Karim Ziani, Hameur Bouazza (66 Mourad Meghni), Abdelkader Ghezzal

18.01.2010

MALI – MALAWI 3-1 (2-0)
Estádio Nacional do Chiazi, Cabinda
Referee: Rajindraparsad Seechurn {Mauritius}, Attendance: 21,000
MALI: Mahamadou Sidibe, Souleymane Diamoutene, Adama Tamboura, Ousmane Berthe, Abdoulaye Maiga (50 Samba Sow), Seydou Keita, Mohamed Sissoko, Lassana Fane, El Hadj Mahamane Traoré (60 Mamadou Diallo), Mamadou Bagayoko, Frederic Oumar Kanouté (81 Modibo Maiga).
MALAWI: Swadick Sanudi, Moses Chavula, James Sangala, Peter Mponda, Bryson Elvis Kafoteka (53 Chiukepo Msowoya), Hellings Mwakasungula, Joseph Kamwendo, Peter Wadabwa (46 Atusaye Nyondo), Davie Banda, Russell Mwafulirwa, Esau Kanyenda (71 Robert Ngambi).
Goals: Frederic Oumar Kanouté (1), Seydou Keita (3), Mamadou Bagayoko (85) / Russel Mwafulirwa (58)

1.	ANGOLA	3	1	2	0	6	4	5
2.	ALGERIA	3	1	1	1	1	3	4
3.	Mali	3	1	1	1	7	6	4
4.	Malawi	3	1	0	2	4	5	3

GROUP B

Togo were disqualified from the tournament after missing their opening game against Ghana.

11.01.2010

IVORY COAST – BURKINA FASO 0-0
Estádio Nacional do Chiazi, Cabinda
Referee: Kacem Bennaceur (Tunisia), Attendance: 5000
IVORY COAST: Barry Boubacar Copa, Siaka Chico Tiene, Kolo Touré, Gneri Yaya Touré, Emmanuel Eboué, Souleymane Bamba, Didier Zokora, Ismael Cheik Tiote (81 Aruna Dindane), Yao Kouassi Gervinho (73 Salomon Kalou), Bakari Koné (69 Abdulkader Keita), Didier Drogba. Trainer: Vahid Halilhodzić
BURKINA FASO: Daouda Diakité, Bakary Koné, Paul Koulibaly (46 Ibrahim Gnanou), Saidou Panandetiguiri, Mamadou Tall, Charles Kabore, Mahamoudou Kere, Jonathan Pitroipa, Florent Rouamba, Beli Moumouni Dagano (81 Yssouf Koné), Narcisse Yameogo (62 Habib Bamogo). Trainer: Paulo Duarte

15.01.2010

IVORY COAST – GHANA 3-1 (1-0)
Estádio Nacional do Chiazi, Cabinda
Referee: Jerome Damon (South Africa), Attendance: 23,000
IVORY COAST: Barry Boubacar Copa, Gneri Yaya Touré (71 Emerse Fae), Kolo Toure, Emmanuel Eboue, Souleymane Bamba, Siaka Chico Tiene, Didier Zokora, Ismael Cheik Tiote, Didier Drogba, Salomon Kalou (83 Abdulkader Keita), Yao Kouassi Gervinho (60 Guy Demel).
GHANA: Richard Kingson, Eric Addo, Isaac Vorsah, Samuel Inkoom, Andre Ayew (46 Asamoah Gyan), Agyemang Opoku (76 Harrison Afful), Kwadwo Asamoah, Mousse Narry (46 Michael Essien), Matthew Amoah, Emmanuel Badu Agyemang, Rahim Ayew. Trainer: Milovan Rajevac
Sent off: Eboue (55)
Goals: Yao Kouassi Gervinho (23), Siaka Chico Tiene (67), Didier Drogba (87) / Asamoah Gyan (90 penalty)

19.01.2010

BURKINA FASO – GHANA 0-1 (0-1)
Estádio 11 de Novembro, Luanda
Referee: Eddy Maillet (Seychelles), Attendance: 8000
BURKINA FASO: Daouda Diakité, Mamadou Tall, Bakary Koné, Paul Koulibaly (83 Mohamed Koffi), Mahamoudou Kere, Saidou Panandetiguiri, Charles Kabore (59 Wilfried Benjamin Balima), Florent Rouamba, Habib Bamogo (72 Beli Moumouni Dagano), Jonathan Pitroipa, Youssouf Koné.
GHANA: Richard Kingson, Hans Sarpei, Isaac Vorsah, Samuel Inkoom, Lee Addy, Haminu Draman (90 Agyemang Opoku), Andre Ayew, Matthew Amoah (77 Dominic Adiya), Asamoah Gyan (87 Rahim Ayew), Kwadwo Asamoah, Emmanuel Badu Agyemang.
Sent off: Tall (66)
Goal: Andre Ayew (30)

1.	IVORY COAST	2	1	1	0	3	1	4
2.	GHANA	2	1	0	1	2	3	3
3.	Burkina Faso	2	0	1	1	0	1	1

GROUP C

12.01.2010

EGYPT – NIGERIA 3-1 (1-1)
Ombaka National Stadium, Benguela
Referee: Seechum Rajindraparsad {Mauritius}, Attendance: 18,000
EGYPT: Essam El-Hadary, Hani Said, Wael Gomaa, Ahmed Fathi, Mahmoud Fathallah, Sayed Meawwad, Hosni Abd Rabbou (72 Mohamed Nagui 'Geddo'), Hossam Ghaly (56 Ahmed El-Mohammadi), Ahmed Hassan, Mohamed Abdullah 'Zidan' (85 Mohamed Abdel Shafi), Emad Abdel Nabi 'Moteab'. Trainer: Hassan Shehata
NIGERIA: Vincent Enyeama, Taye Ismaila Taiwo, Joseph Yobo, Obinna Nwaneri, Yusuf Mohammed, Ayila Yussuf, John Mikel Obi (79 Nwankwo Kanu), Dickson Etuhu, Kalu Uche (69 Victor Nsofor Obinna), Chinedu Obasi Ogbuke, Aiyegbeni Yakubu. Trainer: Shaibu Amodu
Goals: Emad Emad Abdel Nabi 'Moteab' (34), Ahmed Hassan (54), Mohamed Nagui 'Geddo' (87) / Chinedu Obasi Ogbuke (12)

12.01.2010

MOZAMBIQUE – BENIN 2-2 (1-2)
Ombaka National Stadium, Benguela
Referee: Khaled Abdel Rahman (Sudan), Attendance: 15,000
MOZAMBIQUE: Kampango, Samuel Luis Campira Chapanga, Dário Khan, Edson Sitoe, Martinho Paito, Elías Pelembe, Simão, Almiro Lobo, Eugénio Bila (82 Momed Hadi), Manuel José Luis Bucuane 'Tico-Tico' (90 Carlos Parruque), Carlos Fumo Gonçalves (65 Helder Pelembe). Trainer: Mart Nooij (Holland)
BENIN: Yoann Djidonou, Félicien Singbo (64 Emmanuel Imorou), Damien Chrysostome, Khaled Adenon, Romuald Boco, Stéphane Sessegnon, Seidath Tchomogo, Jocelyn Ahoueya (57 Djiman Koukou), Mickael Pote, Razak Omotoyossi, Mouri Ola Ogunbiyi (84 Nouihoum Kobenan). Trainer: Michel Dussuyer (France)
Goals: Almiro Lobo (29), Carlos Fumo Gonçalves (55) / Razak Omotoyossi (14 penalty), Dario Khan (20 own goal)

16.01.2010

NIGERIA – BENIN 1-0 (1-0)
Ombaka National Stadium, Benguela
Referee: Hélder Martins de Carvalho (Angola), Attendance: 8000
NIGERIA: Vincent Enyema, Joseph Michael Yobo (51 Omyekachi Apam), Daniel Olusola Shittu, Uwa Elderson Echiejile, Chinedu Obasi Ogbuke, Ayegbeni Yakubu (58 Victor Nsofor Obinna), John Mikel Obi, Peter Osaze Odemwingie, Kalu Uche (73 Sani Kaita), Yusuf Mohamed, Dickson Paul Etuhu.
BENIN: Rachad Chitou (72 Yoann Djidonou), Khaled Adenon, Djiman Kouokou, Damien Chrysostome, Romuald Boco, Razak Omotoyossi, Nouihoum Kobenan (82 Arnaud Seka), Mouri Ola Ogunbiyi, Stéphane Sessegnon, Seidath Konabe Tchomogo, Emmanuel Imorou (66 Félicien Singbo).
Goal: Ayegbeni Yakubu (42 penalty)

16.01.2010

EGYPT – MOZAMBIQUE 2-0 (0-0)
Ombaka National Stadium, Benguela
Referee: Kokou Djaoupe (Angola), Attendance: 16,000
EGYPT: Essam El-Hadary, Hani Said (48 Ahmed El-Mohammadi), Wael Gomaa, Mahmoud Fathallah, Sayed Meawwad, Ahmed Fathi, Hosni Abd Rabbou, Ahmed Hassan, Mahmoud Abdel Razek (68 Mohamed Nagui 'Geddo'), Mohamed Abdullah 'Zidan' (57 Ahmed Eid Abdel Malek), Emad Abdel Nabi 'Moteab'.
MOZAMBIQUE: Kapango, Samuel Luis Campira Chapanga, Dário Khan, Edson Sitoe, Martinho Paito, Simão, Almiro Lobo, Dominguês, Eugenio Bila (87 Carlos Parruque), Carlos Gonçalves (52 Josemar), Manuel José Luis Bucuane 'Tico-Tico' (68 Momed Hadi).
Goals: Dario Khan (47 own goal), Mohamed Nagui 'Geddo' (81)

20.01.2010
EGYPT – BENIN 2-0 (2-0)
Ombaka National Stadium, Benguela
Referee: Daniel Bennett (South Africa), Attendance: 12,500
EGYPT: Essam El-Hadary (76 Abdel Wahed El-Sayed), Ahmed El-Mohammadi, Mahmoud Fathallah, El-Moatasem Salem, Abdel Zaher El-Sakka (53 Mohamed Abdullah 'Zidan'), Mohamed Abdel Shafi, Hossam Ghali, Ahmed Hassan, Hosni Abd Rabbou, Emad Abdel Nabi 'Moteab', Ahmed Raouf (67 Mohamed Nagui 'Geddo').
BENIN: Yoann Djidonou, Felicien Singbo, Damien Chrysostome, Khaled Adenon, Seidath Tchomogo, Romuald Boco, Djiman Koukou, Oascal Angan, Muri Ogunbiyi, Razak Omotoyossi, Arnaud Seka.
Goals: Ahmed El-Mohammadi (8), Emad Abdel Nabi 'Moteab' (24)

20.01.2010

NIGERIA – MOZAMBIQUE 3-0 (1-0)
Estadio Nacional da Tundavala, Lubango
Referee: Koman Coulibaly (Mali), Attendance: 10,000
NIGERIA: Vincent Enyema, Daniel Olusola Shittu, Uwa Elderson Echiejile, Omyekachi Apam, Yusuf Mohamed, Sani Kaita, John Mikel Obi, Dickson Paul Etuhu (72 Ayiila Yussuf), Peter Osaze Odemwingie (84 Victor Nsofor Obinna), Ayegbeni Yakubu (68 Obafemi Martins), Chinedu Obasi Ogbuke.
MOZAMBIQUE: Kapango, Martinho Paito, Simão, Dário Khan, Fanuel, Samuel Luis Campira Chapanga, Eugenio Bila (69 Josemar), Dominguês, Almiró Lobo (75 Momed Hadj), Dário Monteiro (83 Carlos Parrugge), Manuel José Luis Bucuane 'Tico-Tico'.
Goals: Peter Osaze Odemwinigle (45, 47), Obafemi Martins (85)

1.	EGYPT	3	3	0	0	7	1	9
2.	NIGERIA	3	2	0	1	5	3	6
3.	Benin	3	0	1	2	2	5	1
4.	Mozambique	3	0	1	2	2	7	1

GROUP D

13.01.2010

CAMEROON – GABON 0-1 (0-1)
Estadio Nacional da Tundavala, Lubango
Referee: Daniel Bennett (South Africa), Attendance: 15,000
CAMEROON: Carlos Kameni, Rigobert Song, Alexandre Song Billong, Henri Bedimo (76 Eyong Enoh), Nicolas N'Koulou, Geremi Fotso Njitap, Jean Makoun, Achille Emana, Landry N'Guemo (46 Somen Tchoyi), Samuel Eto'o, Pierre Webó (64 Mohammadou Idrissou).
GABON: Didier Oyono, Georges Ambourouet, Bruno Ecuele Manga, Rodrigue Moundounga, Erwin N'Guema Obane, Moise Apanga, Zita Mbanangoye (64 Alain Djissikadie), Cedric Moubamba, Paul Kessany, Alexander Ndoumbou (77 Pierre Aubameyang), Daniel Cousin.
Goal: Daniel Cousin (17)

13.01.2010

ZAMBIA – TUNISIA 1-1 (1-1)
Estadio Nacional da Tundavala, Lubango
Referee: Koman Coulibaly (Mali), Attendance: 17,000
ZAMBIA: Kennedy Mweene, Joseph Musonda, Kampamba Chintu, Thomas Nyirenda, Felix Katongo, James Chamanga (84 Emmanuel Mayuka), Emmanuel Mbola, Rainford Kalaba, Christopher Katongo, Jacob Mulenga, Stophira Sunzu. Trainer: Hervé Renard
TUNISIA: Aymen Mathlouthi, Ammar Jemal, Yassin Mikari, Khaled Souissi, Karim Haggui, Khaled Korbi, Hocine Ragued, Youssef Msakni (90 Mohamed Ali Nafkha), Oussama Darragi (62 Issam Jemaa), Souheil Dhaouadi, Amine Chermiti (81 Chaouki Ben Saada). Trainer: Faouzi Benzarti
Goals: Jacob Mulenga (19) / Souheil Dhaouadi (40)

17.01.2010

GABON – TUNISIA 0-0
Estadio Nacional da Tundavala, Lubango
Referee: Bonaventure Coffi Codja (Benin), Attendance: 16,000
GABON: Didier Oyono, Georges Ambourouet, Bruno Ecuele Manga, Rodrigue Moundounga, Moise Apanga, Zita Mbanangoye, Paul Kessany, Stephane N'Guema (65 Alain Djissikadie), Daniel Cousin, Eric Mouloungui (78 Roguy Meye), Pierre Aubameyang.
TUNISIA: Aymen Mathlouthi, Karim Haggui, Yassin Mikari, Ammar Jemal, Souhaiel Ben Radhia, Hocine Ragued, Souheil Dhaouadi (86 Mohamed Ali Nafkha), Khaled Korbi, Issam Jemaa, Amine Chermiti (69 Ahmed Akaichi), Youssef Msakni (62 Chaouki Ben Saada).

17.01.2010

CAMEROON – ZAMBIA 3-2 (0-1)
Estadio Nacional da Tundavala, Lubango
Referee: Khalif Al Ghamdi (Saudi Arabia), Attendance: 15,000
CAMEROON: Carlos Kameni, Rigobert Song, Alexandre Song Billong, Henri Bedimo (46 Augustin Gilles Binya), Nicolas N'Koulou, Geremi Fotso Njitap, Jean Makoun, Achille Emana (76 Aurelien Chedjou Fongang), Stephane M'bia Etoundi (46 Mohammadou Idrissou), Somen Tchoyi, Samuel Eto'o.
ZAMBIA: Kennedy Mweene, Joseph Musonda (76 Emmanuel Mayuka), Emmanuel Mbola, Thomas Nyirenda, Felix Katongo (62 Isaac Chansa), Rainford Kalaba (52 Francis Kasonde), Kampamba Chintu, Stophira Sunzu, Jacob Mulenga, Christopher Katongo, James Chamanga.
Goals: Geremi Fotso Njitap (68), Samuel Eto'o (72), Mohammad Idrissou (86) / Jacob Mulenga (8), Christopher Katongo (82 penalty)

21.01.2010

CAMEROON – TUNISIA 2-2 (0-1)
Estadio Nacional da Tundavala, Lubango
Referee: Désiré Doue Normandiez (Ivory Coast), Attendance: 19,000
CAMEROON: Carlos Kameni, Alexandre Song Billong, Augustin Gilles Binya (69 Rigobert Song),
Nicolas N'Koulou, Jean Makoun (46 Pierre Webó), Landry N'Guemo (89 Andre Bikey), Eyong Enoh,
Aurelien Chedjou Fongang, Georges Mandjeck, Mohammadou Idrissou, Samuel Eto'o.
TUNISIA: Aymen Mathlouthi, Karim Haggui, Yassin Mikari, Ammar Jemal, Khaled Souissi, Hocine
Ragued (84 Haithem Mrabet), Mohamed Ali Nafkha (52 Chouki Ben Saada), Souheil Dhaouadi, Khaled
Korbi, Issam Jemaa, Amine Chermiti (81 Ahmed Mrabet).
Sent off: Jemal (89)
Goals: Samuel Eto'o (46), Landry N'Guemo (64) / Amine Chermiti (1), Aurelien Chedjou Fongang (64
own goal)

21.01.2010

GABON – ZAMBIA 1-2 (0-1)
Ombaka National Stadium, Benguela
Referee: Mohamed Benouza (Algeria), Attendance: 5000
GABON: Didier Oyono, Georges Ambourouet, Bruno Ecuele Manga, Rodrigue Moundounga, Moise
Apanga, Alain Djissikadie (78 Fabrice Do Marcolino), Zita Mbanangoye, Paul Kessany, Daniel Cousin,
Eric Mouloungui, Roguy Meye (61 Pierre Aubameyang).
ZAMBIA: Kennedy Mweene, Joseph Musonda, Emmanuel Mbola, Thomas Nyirenda, Felix Katongo
(85 Hichani Himonde), Rainford Kalaba (63 William Njobyu), Kampamba Chintu, Stophira Sunzu,
Jacob Mulenga (79 Noah Chivuta), Christopher Katongo, James Chamanga.
Goals: Fabrice Do Marcolino (83) / Rainford Kalaba (28), James Chamanga (62)

1.	ZAMBIA	3	1	1	1	5	5	4
2.	CAMEROON	3	1	1	1	5	5	4
3.	Gabon	3	1	1	1	2	2	4
4.	Tunisia	3	0	3	0	3	3	3

Quarter-finals

24.01.2010

ANGOLA – GHANA 0-1 (0-1)
Estádio 11 de Novembro, Luanda
Referee: Mohamed Benouza (Algeria), Attendance: 50,000
ANGOLA: Carlos Alberto Fernandes, Rui Marques, Carlos Manuel Gonçalves Alonso 'Kali',
Francisco Zuela (76 Enoque Guilherme), Sebastião Felisberto Graça Amaral Gilberto (73 José Nsimba
Baptista 'Zé Kalanga'), Fernando Agostinho da Costa 'Xara', Rosa Stelvio Cruz (57 Ricardo Job),
Alberto Jose Mabina, FLÁVIO da Silva Amado, DJALMA Braume Manuel Abel Campos, Alberto
Mateus Contreir Gonçalves Manucho.
GHANA: Richard Kingson, Hans Sarpei, Isaac Vorsah, Samuel Inkoom, Lee Addy, Haminu Draman
(79 Eric Addo), Andre Ayew (90 Rahim Ayew), Asamoah Gyan (62 Mattew Amoah), Kwadwo
Asamoah, Emmanuel Badu Agyemang, Agyemang Opoku.
Goal: Asamoah Gyan (15)

24.10.2010

IVORY COAST – ALGERIA 2-3 (1-1, 2-2)
Estádio Nacional do Chiazi, Cabinda
Referee: Eddy Maillet (Seychelles), Attendance: 10,000
IVORY COAST: Barry Boubacar Copa, Guy Demel, Gneri Yaya Touré, Kolo Touré, Souleymane Bamba, Siaka Chico Tiene, Didier Zokora (96 Aruna Dindane), Ismael Cheik Tiote (72 Emerse Fae), Didier Drogba, Salomon Kalou (83 Abdulkader Keita), Yao Kouassi Gervinho.
ALGERIA: Fawzi Chaouchi, Anthar Yahia (85 Slimane Raho), Nadir Belhadj, Madjid Bougherra, Rafik Halliche, Mourad Meghni (90 Hameur Bouazza), Yazid Mansouri, Karim Ziani (106 Djamel Abdoun), Hassan Yebda, Karim Matmour, Abdelkader Ghezzal
Goals: Salomon Kalou (4), Abdulkader Keita (89) / Karim Matmour (40), Madjid Bougherra (90), Hameur Bouazza (93)

25.01.2010

EGYPT – CAMEROON 3-1 (1-1, 1-1)
Ombaka National Stadium, Benguela
Referee: Jerôme Damon (South Africa)
EGYPT: Essam El-Hadary, Ahmed El-Mohammadi, Mahmoud Fathallah, Hani Said, Wael Gomaa, Ahmed Fathi, Sayed Meawwad, Hosni Abd Rabbou (85 Hossam Ghali), Ahmed Hassan (118 Mohamed Abdel Shafi), Mohamed Abdullah 'Zidan' (67 Mohamed Nagui 'Geddo'), Emad Abdel Nabi 'Moteab'.
CAMEROON: Idriss Carlos Kameni, Henri Bedimo (105 Andre Bikey), Geremi Fotso Njitap (105 Paul Alo'o Efoulou), Nicolas Nkoulou, Aurelien Chedjou, Alexandre Song, Enoh Eyong, Georges Mandjeck, Achille Emana (88 Achille Webo), Samuel Eto'o, Mohamadou Idrissou.
Sent off: Chedjou (111)
Goals: Ahmed Hassan (37, 94), Mohamed Nagui 'Geddo' (91) / Ahmed Hassan (25 own goal)

25.01.2010

ZAMBIA – NIGERIA 0-0, 4-5 on penalties
Estadio Nacional da Tundavala, Lubango
Referee: Esam Abd El Fatah (Egypt), Attendance: 10,000
ZAMBIA: Kennedy Mweene, Joseph Musonda, Stophira Sunzu, Hichani Himonde, Emmanuel Mbola, Christopher Katongo, Thomas Nyirenda, William Njobvu (114 Clifford Mulenga), Felix Katongo (98 Noah Chivuta), James Chamanga (68 Emmanuel Mayuka), Jacob Mulenga
NIGERIA: Vincent Enyeama, Yusuf Mohamed, Dan Shittu, Onyekachi Apam, Uwa Echiejile, Peter Osaze Odemwingie, Sani Kaita, John Mikel Obi, Dickson Etuhu (62 Ayila Yussuf), Chinedu Obasi Ogbuke (91 Victor Nsofor Obinna), Ayegbeni Yakubu (70 Obafemi Martins).
Sent off: Onyekachi (107)
Penalties: 1-0 Noah Chivuta, 1-1 John Mikel Obi, 2-1 Christopher Katongo, 2-2 Obafemi Martins, 3-2 Emmanuel Mayuka, 3-3 Victor Nsofor Obinna, Thomas Nyirenda, 3-4 Peter Osaze Odemwingie, 4-4 Kennedy Mweene, 4-5 Vincent Enyeama.